The Real Worlds of Canadian Politics

The Real Worlds
of Canadian Politics

CASES IN PROCESS AND POLICY

Fourth Edition

Robert M. Campbell, Leslie A. Pal, Michael Howlett

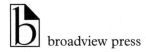

broadview press

National Library of Canada Cataloguing in Publication

Campbell, Robert M. (Robert Malcolm), 1950–
    The real worlds of Canadian politics : cases in process and policy / Robert M. Campbell, Leslie A. Pal, Michael Howlett.—4th ed.

Previous eds. by Robert M. Campbell and Leslie A. Pal.
Includes bibliographical references and index.
ISBN 1-55111-518-2

    1. Political planning—Canada—Case studies.   2. Canada—Politics and government—1993– —Case studies.   I. Pal, Leslie A. (Leslie Alexander), 1954–   II. Howlett, Michael, 1955–   III. Title.

FC635.C337 2004   320.6'0973'09049   C2004-900707-6

Broadview Press, Ltd. is an independent, international publishing house, incorporated in 1985.

North America
Post Office Box 1243,
Peterborough, Ontario,
Canada K9J 7H5
Tel: (705) 743-8990
Fax: (705) 743-8353

3576 California Road,
Orchard Park, New York
USA 14127

UK, Ireland, and Continental Europe
NBN Plymbridge
Estover Road
Plymouth pl6 7py UK
Tel: 44 (0) 1752 202301
Fax: 44 (0) 1752 202331
Fax Order Line:
   44 (0) 1752 202333
Customer Service:
   cservs@nbnplymbridge.com
Orders: orders@nbnplymbridge.com

*Australia and
New Zealand*
UNIREPS
University of
New South Wales
Sydney, NSW, 2052
Tel: + 61 2 96640999
Fax: + 61 2 96645420
info.press@unsw.edu.au

Broadview believes in shared ownership, both with its employees and with the general public; since the year 2000 Broadview shares have traded publicly on the Toronto Venture Exchange under the symbol BDP.

We welcome any comments and suggestions regarding any aspect of our publications—please feel free to contact us at the addresses below, or at broadview@broadviewpress.com / customerservice@broadviewpress.com / www.broadviewpress.com

Broadview Press Ltd. gratefully acknowledges the financial support of the Government of Canada through the Book Publishing Industry Development Program for our publishing activities.

Cover design and typeset by Zack Taylor Design, www.zacktaylor.com

This book is printed on 100% post-consumer recycled, ancient forest friendly paper.

Printed in Canada

Contents

Preface to the Fourth Edition

The first edition of *The Real Worlds of Canadian Politics* was published 15 years ago, in 1989. The case study approach to Canadian politics and public policy was a unique contribution at the time and was successful in reaching a wide and extended classroom audience across the country. The cases were presented in a deliberately dramatic narrative style, emphasizing the passions, personalities, and unpredictability of politics as demonstrated in interesting and compelling contemporary cases. As a companion volume to more traditional textbooks in Canadian politics, the book appeared to fill a niche, illustrating the "real worlds" of Canadian politics while offering an opportunity for discussion and debate in the classroom.

The success of the first edition led to the production of subsequent editions in 1991 and 1994. The popularity of the volumes was substantially related to the contemporary character of the case studies, which offered students immediate access to the politics unfolding in their lives, but also offered a kind of "diary" of the contemporary political scene. By definition, history moves along, so that particular case studies become quickly less compelling and useful in the classroom. Hence, the authors felt enormous pressure to revitalize the book by presenting new or updated case studies. Three editions were produced in a dizzying and intense five-year period, and the rush of research and writing all of these cases inevitably took its toll on their exhausted authors, who also had other commitments and interests to pursue. With the publication of the third edition in 1994, *The Real Worlds of Canadian Politics* took a sabbatical break.

Since that time, the idea of renewing *The Real Worlds of Canadian Politics* has been mooted continuously by the authors and others—but was not pursued with commitment until now. Throughout this interregnum, we have been impressed at the continuous demand for a new edition both by instructors and by the publisher. Notwithstanding this ongoing interest, the hard reality was this: such a text requires an enormous amount of intense research and creative writing to produce compelling case studies very quickly in a volume that is lively and contemporary.

The origins of this present volume lie in a proposal made by Michael Howlett to Robert Campbell and Leslie Pal two years ago. His idea was this. Assign a "Real Worlds" style of case study to each of several bright, energetic, and talented doctoral students. Have an editorial team work with this research team to create a research design, a broad overview, a thematic strategy, and a narrative structure that would fit the "Real Worlds" case study model. Have the editorial team work with the research team to produce lively and captivating case studies that capture the essence of Canadian political life and the policy process. This appeared to be an excellent idea, which was pursued enthusiastically and quickly over the next year. The research team was established at Simon Fraser University and Carleton University, and five cases were chosen: gun control, bank mergers, airline deregulation, the softwood lumber dispute, and Nisga'a land claims. Outlines were written; lists of themes and issues were created; chapters were written and rewritten and rewritten—until the present volume was produced.

This fourth edition of *The Real Worlds of Canadian Politics* reflects some of the predominant trends and key activities of the late Liberal government of Jean Chrétien. The softwood lumber dispute extends the issues raised in the second edition's discussion of the Free Trade Agreement, which was passed during the Mulroney era. The case demonstrates how the Liberal government has struggled with the hard realities and politics that continue not only in the free trade world but in countless other policy areas as well. This volume also reconsiders the political and policy implications of the deregulation of the airlines industry, which had been explored in the third edition, and banking, a new case developed for this volume. Just as in the airlines case, the Liberal government had to react to the banking industry's claim that "bigger was better" in the globalized financial environment as it was presented with a merger *fait accompli* that defied the general political desire for increased competition. The Liberal government also confronted highly charged and emotional issues that defied easy or traditional solutions. Aboriginal issues remained as bedevilling as they were when the first edition explored the Oka Crisis. This edition addresses the real worlds of native land claims as illustrated in one of the most dramatic accomplishments to date—the Nisga'a settlement. Earlier editions looked at moral issues like abortion and pornography. This edition explores the explosive issue of gun control, a new case study policy area that the Liberals addressed in the wake of the Montreal Massacre.

The fourth edition of *The Real Worlds of Canadian Politics* was a genuine collaborative enterprise. The research team comprised Karen Lochead, Andrea Migone, and Russell Williams at Simon Fraser University and Samuel Bottomley at Carleton University. Betsy Struthers provided superb copyediting support. Barbara Conolly and the Broadview production team were good-humoured and accomplished in getting the book to press. Finally, Michael Harrison, vice-president of Broadview Press, provided the persistent and dynamic encouragement that made this fourth edition possible. Indeed, this project would not have been pursued or realized without his support.

Robert M. Campbell, Waterloo
Leslie A. Pal, Ottawa
Michael Howlett, Vancouver

Introduction

ROBERT M. CAMPBELL, LESLIE A. PAL, AND MICHAEL HOWLETT

Most undergraduate courses in Canadian politics and public policy rely on specifically written and specialized texts to cast light on the particular subject at hand: federalism, political leadership, parties, and so on. These courses, for which this book has been designed, have at their disposal many large and learned tomes that embrace virtually every detail of the political process in this country. This is an excellent development, much improved over the situation as little as 20 or 30 years ago when only a very few general texts existed on the subject.

In talking to colleagues and in our own teaching, however, we have noticed that the virtues of large and exhaustive texts can become liabilities. It is difficult, for one thing, to write with passion and style when the purpose of the enterprise is analytical, yet most students take introductory courses in politics because they are excited or agitated about what they perceive to be "real politics": fire and blood, strife and conflict, the quest for peace and the chilling disciplines of power.

Perhaps necessarily, unfortunately, even the best introductory texts on Canadian politics sometimes have the character of an autopsy. The system is stretched out on an unyielding slab; readers are given a catalogue of limbs and organs, skeletal features, sinews and nerves; and even the blemishes and congenital deformations of the subject are clinically described and dissected. As useful as such pathology is, however, no student of medicine would ever concentrate exclusively on cadavers in their quest to learn the techniques and skills required to better human health. Similarly, in the study of politics, while rigorous analysis is required, so too is an understanding of the living processes and practices of political life. This means providing students with some exposure to political and policy processes and to institutions and forces as they combine in complex and marvellous ways to produce odd or exciting results.

While we are all attracted to grand theory, we are acutely aware of the inability of such theory to fully capture the complexity and colour of actual politics and policy processes "on the ground." As teachers, we are constantly reminded that our students initially develop their interest in political science through a fascination with policy issues and political personalities. It struck us that there is a way, through a case study approach, to provide a better balance between the intrinsic interest of the political spectacle and the bloodless analysis of the discipline. Most of the main texts presently being used across the country recognize this, of course, and often try to incorporate illustrative examples or perhaps a single case study to demonstrate the ways in which the various parts of the system combine and clash in real life. This book is nothing more than an extended version of this stratagem; instead of a single, short case study accompanying an extensive analytical apparatus, we provide five extensive cases—without the commentary and overtly guided dissection found in most texts. Thus, this book supplements existing texts, opening a small window to shed some light onto the real world of Canadian politics—not a textbook world of clean charts and straight arrows that tidily delineate the flows of power, but a complex and shifting world of issues, personalities, forces, and institutions that combine to make up the political process. We wanted to write a book that would supplement more traditional texts by blending a journalistic style with analysis. We wanted the chapters of this book to be more than merely readable; we wanted to produce narratives that reflected the drama and the passion of the issues, without losing perspective and judgment.

The use of the plural "Worlds" in our title is deliberate. We want to show that beneath the canopy of a single political system there can be tremendous variety in political processes and public policy. But readers should not be misled by the book's title. We do not presume to have the key to understanding the "real worlds" of Canadian politics. We do hope, however, that our chapters tap aspects of Canadian political reality that demand attention and that they will stimulate students' intellectual curiosity and help them further their thinking about the appropriateness of the models and concepts developed in political science to the understanding of the actual practices of Canadian politics and policy-making.

Of course, it is not possible to write case studies without some sense of which facts are important and which are less so. Like any other endeavour in the social sciences, case preparation involves choices about which stories to tell, how to organize the presentation of materials, what to leave in and what to leave out, and what should be highlighted or backlighted in any policy story. These choices are made in accordance with assumptions the authors have about the nature of political life and the relevance of certain facets of social activity and political behaviour to the determination of policy outcomes. This fourth edition, like the previous three, has been written with several specific assumptions in mind.

First, we think that to take *process* and *policy outcomes* seriously means taking a unique sequence of events and understanding it from the perspective of the actors. Why did they do what they did, what structural constraints did they face, and how did these combine to produce (or not produce) policy? Indeed, most people, when they think of politics, think in terms of "stories" and issues and personalities, of "what happened." It is easy to dismiss this as uninformed and superficial, but it captures something that academic analyses often miss: politics as the engagement of living wills, of real persons with interests and passions, visions and mad dreams. Politics at this level—perhaps the primordial level—demands a narrative voice rather than an exclusively analytical one. That is why, in the cases that follow, we have tried to blend the analysis of larger forces with an appreciation of the situation as seen by political actors themselves. We have tried to tell "the story" of how particular events occurred over time, weaving in as best we can the elements of personality and circumstance, irony and comedy.

Second, we are persuaded that different policy areas, to an extent, generate specific configurations of politics. Interest groups, for example, operate very differently in the contexts of free trade and gun control. Hence, we have tried to build fruitful analyses of the role of groups and the larger configurations of power they express upon the basis of meso or *sectoral* level studies of the state and public policy.

Third, we are also convinced that not all elements or ingredients of the political system carry the same weight in each and every case of policy-making, but that very often *institutions* are key. The fact that Canada is a Westminster-style parliamentary democracy with a federal system of government is very often a critical and determining aspect of policy-making in this country. But exactly how these institutions structure political life is complex. Sometimes federalism is key, sometimes it is not. Sometimes the executive does not dominate the legislature, as one would expect in a Westminster-style parliamentary system. And sometimes the appointed judiciary plays only a bit or supporting part in a political drama, as one would expect in a democracy, while at other times it plays a more much central, leading role.

The sectoral cases chosen for this book grapple with this complexity and help to illustrate not only how the different components of the political system interact, but also why certain features are operative in certain circumstances and not in others. As the cases reveal, the key political institutions and players vary enormously from case to case in the many worlds of Canadian politics. They suggest it is useful to consider politics and policy-making in terms of "issue networks" or sectoral-level "subgovernments": processes, actors, institutions, and even political discourse will vary across these networks. In economic policy areas such as the Canada-US softwood lumber dispute, bank mergers, and airline deregulation, producer groups such as manufacturers, labour unions, and government ministries and agencies are lead players, and the terms of debate are for better or worse set within the limits of modern economic and trade theory. The politics of social issues such as Aboriginal rights and title or gun control are entirely different: the actors change, the issues mutate, and the language shifts. Business organizations, for example, have little to do with gun control, and few of the main players in the land claims treaties policy arena rely on economic concepts in making their claims.

Cases have their limits, of course, chief among which is their limited representativeness. Of course it would have been preferable to develop more of them. However, the choice of these cases is not random and was made by taking into account several matters. First, we are concerned with understanding contemporary Canadian politics and policy-making. Although we firmly believe in the need to examine political processes from an historical perspective, that is, as sequences of events in which earlier events in the sequence influence later ones, we have focused very much on present day situations and issues. All five cases presented here are relatively recent, and all reached their policy crescendo during the first years of the new millennium. While together they cast an interesting light on the federal Liberal government in this period, each case study takes pains to develop the background specific to the issue. The chapter on Aboriginal rights and title, for example, examines the legacy of eighteenth-century British law for Canada's treatment of First Nations. The chapter on the softwood lumber dispute goes back to the origins of this trade conflict in the 1950s and 1960s to show why this sector has been a frequent site of Canadian-American tensions.

Secondly, as mentioned above, in keeping with our theme of "many worlds," we deliberately chose cases that sharpen contrasts and illustrate differences between major areas of government activity, such as social and economic policy. Hence, major economic issues such as trade, transportation, and finance are examined in the economic sphere, while those related to criminal law and public safety and to group rights and collective identities are examined in the social field.

Thirdly, we wanted cases which illustrated the dynamics of some of the major "stages" of the policy process, as issues move from the public stage to the formal agenda of government; as debates occur over the best way to grapple with a policy problem; as governments finally decide on a specific course of action (or inaction); as that decision is implemented on the ground; and as the public and a range of actors, both inside and outside government, evaluate the merits and demerits of what has been done. Each of the chapters involves a discussion of all of these elements, but each also highlights a particular stage and the relevance of certain actors and institutions in it. The role of parliamentary committees and cabinet in decision-making, for example, is highlighted in the case study of the fate of Canadian bank merger proposals, while the role of the courts in establishing the legal basis for native land claims is a highlight of the chapter on Aboriginal politics.

We were also guided by some convictions about the nature of politics in the modern Canadian state. New kinds of political issues have arisen on Canada's agenda in the last decade, as they have for many other industrialized nations. Ideological currents have been swirling, and old-style consensus politics has been undermined if not destroyed. The rise of neo-conservative tendencies has generated new policy approaches to economic problems (e.g., free trade) and morality (e.g., tougher child pornography laws). The triumph of provincialism has elevated regional concerns to matters of critical national importance. The maturation of the Charter of Rights in Canada has further constrained parliamentary sovereignty. Technological change has transformed our perception of economic policy and economic priorities. And all national areas of political life have been affected by the increasing awareness of Canadians to events and activities around the world as the process of enhanced communication and interaction, encapsulated in the term "globalization," has proceeded apace. As a result of these developments, profound changes have created new political issues, which in turn affect Canadian political and policy processes and the capacity of Canadian governments to deal with these issues. Trade disputes such as softwood lumber raise questions about national sovereignty and its role in a globalized world; reforms in banking and airline transportation may transform the nature of critical Canadian financial and transportation systems and, both directly and indirectly, affect the livelihoods and activities of millions of people; regionalism in issues like gun control affects national politics; and an evolving political role for the courts in the context of

Aboriginal rights makes politics far less predictable and questions the very basis of Canadian society and the meaning of Canadian democracy.

Each of the five cases contained in this book, while emphasizing one or two of these key themes, also touches on several others that we consider important to anyone trying to grasp the realities of Canadian politics. The issue of citizen participation in politics, for example, often arises as do concerns about the proper scope of government regulation, which were very much evident in both the Air Canada case as well as in gun control. The cases in this edition, therefore, should be read both for their idiosyncrasies and for the larger canvas of Canadian politics they reveal. We have tried, as in the previous editions, to emphasize the colour, life, and sheer unpredictability of politics by using a deliberately dramatic narrative style, but as before we have also tried to flag key themes and broad forces that underpin each of the cases.

As historical narratives, of course, all case studies inevitably are outstripped by events. This fourth edition of *The Real Worlds of Canadian Politics* addresses this problem with a fresh collection of cases that illustrate key themes and forces in Canadian politics. Like the previous editions, this one includes some chapters found in earlier issues and some new cases specifically prepared for this volume. We revived the case on regulatory policy and the battle between Air Canada and Canadian Airlines; extended the earlier discussion of Aboriginal rights first examined in the case study of the Oka dispute; and broadened our earlier discussion of free trade treaties with an analysis of the Canada-US softwood lumber dispute. New chapters deal with gun control legislation and bank merger proposals.

This book may be used in several ways. It should provide some enjoyment by stimulating discussion in classes and tutorials, and its narrative structure should permit a more vigorous and engaged reading than is typical of texts in the field. We have given each essay, inconspicuously we hope, an analytical framework, so that the reader will be introduced to the necessary background on trade law, Aboriginal treaties, or other relevant subjects, as needed. Although this introduction provides a guide to some of the themes expressed in each of the cases, readers should also take note of other aspects of politics that are revealed, even if only briefly, in the narratives. Finally, the cases should not be treated separately. One of our purposes in writing them was to develop sharp contrasts in the different styles of politics that develop around different types of political issues at different stages of the policy process. Readers should think about how the politics of globalization are reflected in economic policy fields (e.g., airlines and banking) and social ones (e.g., Aboriginal rights). How does capitalism affect policy-making, and how do governments respond to different interests? What is the balance of power between different institutions of Canadian government, such as the legislature, the Senate, the judiciary, and the executive? How do party politics affect this institutional balance?

A key point to bear in mind is that the cases allow the examination of different aspects of the same processes or institutions in different political worlds. Parties, for instance, may be examined from the perspective of the differing policy proposals they put forward (e.g., in the case of the bank mergers), the tensions generated between national and provincial wings (e.g., in the gun control case), or their strategies and tactics on issues such as airline deregulation and privatization. The same might be said of political symbols and political language: these arise in different ways in each chapter but are always present in each chronicle.

If read creatively, both for the contrasts they provide and the generalizations they might stimulate, these cases should help develop an analytical appreciation of the policy process as well as a sharp sense of politics as it is lived and felt in Canada at the start of the new millennium, and hopefully contribute to both the analytical sophistication of students as well as their appreciation for the dynamics of the *Real Worlds of Canadian Politics*.

CHAPTER ONE

Locked and Loaded:
Gun Control Policy in Canada

SAMUEL A. BOTTOMLEY

Almost a decade after the passage of the Firearms Act in 1995, gun control remains a very controversial issue in Canadian politics. Few areas of public policy have provoked such strong emotions for such a sustained period of time. While gun control involves substantive policy elements, such as the goal of increasing public safety and preventing firearms-related crime, it also contains a high degree of symbolism, which, in part, explains the longevity of the issue.

The Firearms Act represented a substantial departure from previously established patterns of firearm regulation and gave Canada some of the toughest gun controls in the democratic world. Whereas the vast majority of firearms owners had been relatively unaffected by previous gun control legislation, the Firearms Act brought all gun owners, estimated at 3 million, under a mandatory licencing regime. In addition, all firearms in Canada, approximately 7 million in total, were required to be registered under the act.[1] In the past, federal law required that only handguns and certain "restricted" weapons be registered with authorities. Prior to the passage of the Firearms Act, ordinary long guns such as rifles and shotguns were not covered by gun control legislation. As these guns were the most widely owned by Canadians, requiring their universal registration ushered in a new era in gun control and sparked one of the most heated public policy debates in recent times.

There is more to the politics of gun control in Canada than the Firearms Act. The registry has been a source of tension between the federal government and a number of provincial governments. The administration of the registry has also been the subject of much criticism. It has been plagued by computer glitches, continually extended deadlines for compliance, and a host of other logistical problems. Of particular concern has been the ballooning cost associated with running the program. It has been estimated that by 2004-05 the registry will have cost Canadian taxpayers more than $1 billion, leading opponents to describe it as a "boondoggle." Until these problems are addressed, gun control will remain a controversial topic in Canadian politics.

December 6 is a day of remembrance for many Canadians. On that day in 1989, a man armed with a Ruger Mini 14 semi-automatic rifle went on a rampage through the campus of L'École Polytechnique in Montreal. By the time the police took control of the situation, 14 people had been murdered and another 13 wounded. The gunman took his own life. The incident, which came to be known as the Montreal Massacre, was the worst firearms-related crime in Canadian history. While the high number of casualties shocked Canadians, the horror was compounded when it was revealed that all 14 fatalities were female and that the killer had deliberately targeted women. The fact that the victims were all studying to enter the male-dominated profession of engineering underscored that the Massacre was a crime against women. This was later confirmed by the gunman's suicide note, which blamed feminists for ruining his life.[2]

While Canada had experienced other tragic shootings in the past, the Montreal Massacre received unprecedented media attention and public reaction. Across the country, the news was received with shock, anger, and disbelief that such an incident could happen on Canadian soil. The Mayor of Montreal, Jean Doré, stated: "December 6, 1989 will remain one of the darkest pages of Montreal's history."[3] The story dominated the news for over a week, and coverage continued well into the new year of 1990. Shortly after the shootings, the National Assembly of Quebec declared a three-day province-wide mourning period, and flags flew at half-mast from coast to coast. In Montreal, 5,000 people held a candle-light vigil for the victims, an act that was repeated throughout Canada and on many university campuses. An even greater number of people attended the victims' funerals.[4]

The Montreal Massacre transformed the politics of gun control in a number of ways, most obviously by substantially raising the profile of the issue. Although a majority of Canadians had supported tougher gun laws since the 1960s, gun control had never been as widely debated as it was in the wake of the Montreal shootings. No longer was gun control a mundane area of public policy discussed and debated by police organizations, criminologists, and bureaucrats who focused primarily on crime statistics, it was now a matter of general interest and debate for Canadian citizens.

After the initial shock of the shootings subsided, many in the media began to question the adequacy of Canada's firearms policy with editorials and letters from prominent individuals and organizations calling for much tougher gun controls. The day after the Massacre, a number of opposition Members of Parliament (MPs) demanded that the government act to toughen Canada's gun laws. Police and medical associations increased their calls for tougher gun laws, as did many academics. A petition supporting a complete ban on the private ownership of semi-automatic weapons, circulated by engineering students at L'École Polytechnique, eventually collected as many as half a million signatures, making it what many believed was the largest petition in Canadian history. Suzanne Laplante Edward, the mother of one of the victims, dedicated herself to the cause of tougher gun laws. In the post-massacre environment, even some gun dealers indicated their support.[5]

The Massacre also increased the number of players in the gun control debate. Prior to 1990, all of the interest groups solely concerned with the issue of firearms policy were gun organizations opposed to tougher gun controls. These groups were considered to be very powerful and were credited with blocking many previous attempts at tougher gun controls. This one-sided nature of lobbying meant that previous governments seeking to implement tougher gun controls had few allies. While some organizations, such as the Canadian Bar Association, had long supported tougher gun controls, it was not the main purpose of the organization and was only a peripheral issue for them.

After the massacre, a poster at the L'École Polytechnique stated: "First Mourn, Then Work For Change."[6] That message was taken to heart by Heidi Rathjen and Wendy Cukier who together established Canada's first gun control movement in direct response to the killings: Canadians for Gun Control (later to become the Coalition for Gun Control). Rathjen, an engineering student at the L'École Polytechnique at the time of the Massacre, and Cukier, a professor at Toronto's Ryerson Polytechnic, worked tirelessly throughout the 1990s advocating for, and defending, tougher gun laws. The gun control movement, which had been conspicuously absent in previous debates over gun control, proved to be a very important ally for the government in its pursuit of tougher gun laws.

Due to the misogynistic motivations of the killer, the Massacre also led to the participation of women's groups at the forefront of the debate. While women's groups had always been passively supportive of tougher gun

I: Wendy Cukier: Canada's Gun Control Crusader

Wendy Cukier's name has become synonymous with the Canadian gun control movement. For more than a decade, she has been the leading champion of tougher gun controls in Canada, tirelessly orchestrating media campaigns and press conferences, circulating petitions, countering the arguments made by gun organizations, and lobbying the government and individual politicians to support, and now defend, tougher gun controls.

Cukier's decisions to get involved in the gun control issue was a direct consequence of her shock in response to the 1989 Montreal Massacre. In a 1992 interview, she noted the impact of the tragedy: "[t]he massacre was a real affront to my sense of Canada being a peaceful place to live. In some ways it was the death of innocence in Canada."[7] Her initial anger about the Massacre increased substantially when she discovered how easy it had been for the killer to acquire semi-automatic weapons. After finding that there were no gun control organizations for her to join in Canada, she decided to take matters into her own hands.

Within months of the Massacre, Cukier, together with Heidi Rathjen, founded the organization that became the Coalition for Gun Control. Since then, she has dedicated her life to the cause of gun control. A single mother and Ryerson University business professor, she has given up much of her time to become unpaid president of the Coalition and to campaign for tougher gun controls.

Perhaps the best evidence of Cukier's effectiveness as a gun control advocate is demonstrated by the amount of negative attention she has received from extremists in the gun-rights movement. She has been the victim of smear campaigns, threatened by angry gun-rights activists, and yelled at during public meetings. Many of these attacks have been highly personal. In 1995, a firearms organization organized a "Bricks for Wendy" campaign in which angry gun owners sent her bricks and manure to protest against her activism for tougher gun laws. Over the years she has been called a liar, a Nazi, and part of a government conspiracy. Some gun organizations even encouraged gun owners to register their guns under Cukier's name to protest the gun registry and confuse the system.

Under Cukier's leadership, the Coalition for Gun Control has grown to include over 350 diverse organizations, from trade unions to medical associations. In addition, it claims 12,000 individual members. Although Canada now has one of the toughest gun control regimes among democracies, the Coalition remains active in defending the gun registry against its critics.

Listed Supporters of the Coalition For Gun Control (2003)[8]

Canadian Association of Chiefs of Police
Federation of Canadian Municipalities
Canadian Bar Association
Canadian Public Health Association
Trauma Association of Canada
Canadian Criminal Justice Association
Canadian Association of Emergency Physicians

Canada Safety Council
Association of Universities and Colleges of Canada
Canadian Auto Workers
Canadian Federation of University Women
Canadian Jewish Congress
Canadian Labour Congress
CAVEAT (Canadians Against Violence Everywhere Advocating its Termination)
Canadian Teacher's Federation
Canadian Union of Public Employees
Church Council on Justice and Corrections
Evangelical Lutheran Church of Canada
Humanist Association of Canada
Jewish Women International of Canada
Mennonite Central Committee
National Union of Public and General Employees
Quaker Committee on Jails and Justice
United Church of Canada
YWCA of Canada

Leading Groups Opposed to the Gun Registry[9]

National Firearms Association
Law-abiding Unregistered Firearms Association
Shooting Federation of Canada
Canadian Institute for Legislative Action
Assembly of First Nations[10]
Federation of Saskatchewan Indians
Coalition of Responsible Firearms Owners (representing groups such as):
    Alberta Fish and Game Association
    Responsible Firearms Coalition of British Columbia
    Responsible Firearms Owners of Alberta
    Responsible Firearms Owners of Ontario
    Sporting Clubs of Niagara
    Alberta Arms and Cartridge Collectors Association
    Alberta Civil Society Association

controls, after 1989 they championed the cause. Because of the Massacre, feminists now saw gun control as an important part of the struggle to end violence against women. This sentiment was expressed by many prominent women's groups; at a candle-light vigil for the victims one feminist stated: "Remember the women who were killed because they were women. Let not their deaths be in vain."[11] This feeling was widely expressed. The participation of women's groups in the gun control debates of the 1990s not only helped facilitate passage of tougher gun controls, but also changed the very language of the debate. It is also interesting to note that outside of the cabinet, almost all the leading proponents of gun control after the Montreal Massacre have been women.

Within the cabinet, Justice Minister Allan Rock became the leading advocate of tougher gun controls. Elected to represent the Toronto riding of Etobicoke-Centre in 1993, Rock became the first cabinet minister to publicly question the need for any Canadian, other than police officers and military personnel, to possess a firearm in Canada. As such, he was widely applauded by those in the gun control movement while he became the target of derision by gun enthusiasts. Prime Minister Jean Chrétien was the second most vocal advocate of gun control within the government. Chrétien's active involvement in the issue was crucial for the successful passage of the Firearms Act, which required the imposition of party discipline to keep many Liberal backbenchers from breaking ranks. The direct participation of the prime minister in the gun control debate was a new phenomenon; although previous prime ministers had indicated that they favoured tougher gun controls, they usually remained in the background to buffer themselves from the criticism of angry gun owners.

Of course there is much more to gun control than just the participation of individuals. The debate was also shaped by institutional factors, including party politics, parliamentary competition, and federalism. Like any policy, gun control can only be fully understood in the context of the larger world of Canadian politics. Clearly, party politics shaped the issue substantially. For example, the election of 1993 drastically altered the partisan composition in Parliament: for the first time in Canadian history, both the government and the official opposition—the Bloc Québécois—favoured tougher gun controls, facilitating the passage of the Firearms Act in the face of stiff resistance from the Reform Party. No political party takes a stand on any issue as contentious as gun control without considering the strategic political consequences of doing so. Thus, the parliamentary debate over gun control was much more than merely a debate about its merits or shortcomings; it was also part of a larger battle between competing parties hoping to make political gains at the expense of their opponents.

Gun control is also a highly symbolic issue, concerned much more about values than about material interests. On the surface, the debate has focused on public safety and crime prevention. However, it also deals with "way of life" considerations. Although the divisions are not as clear as some would suggest, the issue has pitted urban Canada against rural Canada, the residents of the prairies against central Canadians. It also represents a clash of values and ideologies. Today, many people see gun control as a Canadian value that confirms Canada's commitment to non-violence. Many gun enthusiasts, on the other hand, view gun control as an infringement of their rights and their ability to engage in long-standing legitimate activities, such as hunting and sports shooting. Without this symbolic importance, the debate over gun control policy would not have been so heated or lasted so long.

Canada has had legislation dealing with firearms since Confederation, and the chronology at the end of this chapter sketches the evolution of Canadian gun control policy. In the past decade, there have been three main stages to the controversy. The first of these was the debate over the Firearms Act itself. From the first time the government proposed tougher gun laws in early 1994 to the Firearms Act receiving royal assent on 5 December 1995 the issue was vehemently contested. While Parliament was the focus of this debate, groups on both sides of the issue mobilized in support of their policy preferences. The second phase began after the Firearms Act become law, when the battle over gun control became an issue of contention between Ottawa and a number of provincial governments opposed to the gun registry. At the centre were two court cases that disputed the constitutionality of the Firearms Act. When the debate became a federal/provincial dispute, the organizations involved followed it into that arena, with Alberta becoming the champion for those hoping to reverse the Firearms Act. The third phase, which overlapped the second in terms of chronology, concerned the implementation of the Federal Firearms Program, which has been plagued by mismanagement and cost overruns. For those opposed to comprehensive gun controls, the expense of the gun registry has provided more rhetorical fodder. However, the problems associated with the administration of the registry are more about government accountability and fiscal management than public safety and gun control. Nevertheless, even eight years after the Firearms Act was passed, the issue remains highly controversial. By 2003 the federal firearms registry was massively over budget, a number of provincial governments had announced they would not cooperate with the federal government, and there were serious concerns about the large number of guns and gun owners that still had not been entered into the system.

The Symbolic Importance of Guns and Gun Control

On the surface, the issue of gun control appears to be a fairly straightforward debate between those who believe tough gun control will reduce gun crime and those who argue that it is an ineffective crime control policy that places an unnecessary burden on "law-abiding" firearms owners. While Canadian firearms policy is ostensibly about public safety and crime prevention, there are many important and subtle issues that underlie the debate. Gun control speaks as much to competing values and visions of Canada as it does to the regulation of firearms. It is a complex issue that takes place in many of the different "worlds" of Canadian politics.

Until fairly recently, guns were not viewed as something that needed to be "controlled." From the earliest days of European settlement, guns were essential tools in the daily life of many Canadians and were often necessary for their very survival. Ownership of firearms was widespread in colonial Canada and, according to historian Merilyn Simonds, almost "every family had a hunting gun." As Canadian society evolved, becoming increasingly urbanized, and values changed, the perception of guns and their place in Canadian society was altered. As Simonds observes: "[o]nce, there were guns in every cabin and canoe. Today, they occupy a more confined and less comfortable place in our lives."[12]

Many in contemporary Canada, including the Liberal government, view gun control as a Canadian "value."[13] As guns are the symbolic representation of violence for a majority of Canadians who no longer have a practical use for firearms, their regulation represents an affirmation that Canadians are a peaceful people committed to promoting non-violence. From this perspective, guns have little or no place in a modern, urban Canada. Notwithstanding the public safety issue, ownership of guns should, therefore, be restricted because they symbolize violence. On the other side of the debate, guns are often seen as an important part of Canadian cultural heritage. For some firearms enthusiasts, gun control represents the intrusion of the state into their private lives and the regulation of legitimate livelihoods and hobbies as well as imposition of urban values onto the Canadian countryside.

From a practical standpoint, firearms remain an important tool for farmers and other rural residents. Farmers and ranchers need firearms to control animal pests that threaten crops, livestock, and property. Furthermore, in many parts of Canada, hunting is more than just a "sporting" activity. For some Canadians, the meat obtained from hunting provides food that would otherwise be unaffordable. In remote Canada, where there are no grocery stores, hunting is essential to the very survival of those who live off the land. It is often difficult for urban dwellers who have no practical use for firearms to comprehend that guns are still necessary in the day-to-day life of many Canadians living in rural environments.

Not surprisingly, gun control is often seen as a symbolic struggle between rural and urban Canada. In Canadian cities, guns are often more associated with crime, gangs, and random acts of violence than with hunting, pest control, and sport shooting. Most high-profile shooting incidents in Canada have occurred in cities, and support for tougher gun laws has always been much stronger in urban areas. A Toronto pharmacist who circulated a petition after a number of fatal shootings in that city captured the sentiment well when he stated: "[p]eople don't see any reason to have guns in Toronto."[14] Because of the rural/urban divide on firearms policy, it has often been suggested that Canada should have two different gun control laws: one for cities and one for rural areas. In fact, at one time the government even publicly considered banning guns in metropolitan areas, while allowing rural gun owners to continue with their traditional gun use. Throughout the history of gun control in Canada, tougher gun laws have generally been championed by urban MPs, with rural MPs leading the resistance against stringent gun control, further reflecting the rural/urban dynamic of the debate.

The symbolic aspect of the gun control issue should not be underestimated. Tens of thousands of gun owners did not take part in numerous anti-gun control protests, write an untold number of letters, and campaign passionately to fight against the Firearms Act merely because they did not want to suffer the minor inconvenience of registering their guns. Many actively opposing tougher gun controls argued that they were defending a way of life, as well as their personal rights and freedoms. While those in the gun control movement focus on the public safety components of gun control, they too are promoting and defending their own vision of Canada with passion and vigour. Thus, the debate over gun control is much more than a debate over public policy; it is also a heated battle between two competing conceptions of Canada that occupy two different political worlds. That Alberta has been a leading opponent of the federal firearms registry points again to the symbolic importance of gun control. Although Alberta criticized the federal firearms program, questioning both its effectiveness in reducing crime as well as the cost of the program, the federal/provincial dispute over the Firearms Act should properly be seen in the context of an ongoing debate about the very nature of Confederation. For many in the prairie provinces, the Firearms Act is another example in a long line of federal policies that favour the opinions of central Canada over those in the West.

The Canadian gun control controversy has also imported some of the symbolism and rhetoric of the highly charged American debate. Indeed, the very term "gun control" originated in the US where it speaks to the heart of the relationship between state and citizen. In fact, the rights of gun owners are enshrined in the Second Amendment of the US Constitution.[15] The powerful National Rifle Association (NRA) is one of the most influential lobby groups in Washington and has successfully fought the implementation of tougher gun laws in the US. For some Canadian gun organizations opposed to tougher gun controls, the NRA represents a model of pro-gun control activism to be emulated. Indeed, the NRA has provided strategic and logistical assistance to some Canadian organizations fighting tougher gun controls. Canadian gun user groups, such as the National Firearms Association (NFA), have sought to imitate the NRA and have adopted much of the rhetoric of the American gun lobby. The language of the NRA, however, does not resonate to the same extent in Canada as it does south of the border and appears threatening and extremist to many Canadians.

For those on the other side of the movement, the US represents a model to be avoided. Those supporting tougher gun laws attribute the high gun crime rate south of the border to its relatively lax gun laws. In fact, it has often been suggested that the American gun problem would spill over into Canada if not for tougher gun laws. This is a powerful argument, and one that is continuously reinforced by exposure of Canadians to American gun crime through the media. The gun control movement in Canada has also borrowed from its counterparts in the American debate. In fact, the Canadian gun control movement can be seen as part an informal network of international gun control movements, with links around the world.

Targets of Gun Control[16]

There is a myriad of ways to regulate firearms that fall between the extremes of completely banning the private ownership of firearms and a regime that has no gun controls whatsoever. Governments can regulate the people who use guns, control how guns can be used, and regulate firearms and equipment. Gun control legislation can, therefore, target different aspects of firearms to differing degrees. This is similar to other policies, such as tobacco regulations that target users through age restrictions, that mandate non-smoking areas, and that control the product itself by requiring filters, tar content, and similar measures.

A regime with strong gun controls will probably regulate guns on many levels, whereas a weak gun control regime may focus on one area only. Under the Firearms Act, the federal government regulates guns on all three of the levels listed below. Canada now has a comprehensive gun control regime, with very strong controls compared to many other countries, especially the US. Since Confederation in 1867, Canada has gone from having almost no firearms regulation to the Federal Firearms Program, which mandates that all gun owners must be licenced, all guns must be registered, and many guns are restricted or banned outright.

II: Targets of Gun Control

1. Controlling People Who Use Guns

	Weak Gun Control Regime	Strong Gun Control Regime
Age restrictions	· Low age requirements (e.g., 12)	· higher age requirements (e.g., 18)
Licencing	· no licence required	· licences or permits required
Screening	· focuses on criminal record only · no background checks · no psychological screening · references not required	· comprehensive background checks including psychological assessments · references required
Training	· new gun owners not required to take safety training courses	· new gun owners must take safety training courses
Punishments	· few specific firearms offences · crimes involving firearms are dealt with through traditional legislation after the fact (e.g., murder, assault)	· specific punishments for crimes involving firearms on top of other offences · tough penalties for non-compliance of gun control regulations

2. Controlling Gun Use

Storage	· lax storage requirements (e.g., guns may be kept loaded and accessible)	· guns must be locked up, out of sight, and kept separately from ammunition
Transportation	· few transportation restrictions (e.g., gun racks permitted in vehicles)	· strict regulations regarding how guns may be moved from place to place
Discharge	· guns may be legally fired in numerous settings	· gun use is restricted (e.g., only at shooting ranges or during hunting season)
Concealment	· concealment is permitted	· concealment is not permitted
Self-defence	· gun use permitted for self-defence	· gun use for self-defence prohibited

3. Controlling Firearms, Ammunition, and Other Firearms Equipment

Restricted weapons	· few weapons are restricted or prohibited	· Many firearms, such as assault weapons and handguns, restricted or banned outright
Registration	· owners not required to register their guns	· mandatory registration of all privately owned firearms
Accessories	· few restrictions on gun-related equipment (e.g., silencers, laser sights)	· safety devices required · silencers, laser sights, etc. prohibited
Import/ export	· few restriction on the importation or exportation of guns	· dangerous weapons not legal for importation

Gun Control at the Practice Range: Bills C-80 and C-17

With the benefit of hindsight, the heated gun control debates of the early 1990s can be viewed as a practice round for the then unforeseen battle over the Firearms Act during the mid-1990s. At the time, Bills C-80 and C-17 were both considered to be very significant changes to Canadian firearms policy. In comparison to the Firearms Act, however, they were both relatively minor pieces of firearms legislation. Of course, those on either side of the issue had no way of knowing that they would be embroiled in a series of battles over firearms policy that would last throughout the entire decade and into the twenty-first century. The controversy over Bills C-80 and C-17 set the tone and mobilized the participants on both sides for the duration of the debate.

Despite the overwhelming calls for much more stringent gun control legislation in the wake of the Massacre, the Conservative government did not propose or endorse significantly tougher gun laws. In fact, Justice Minister Doug Lewis only promised to proceed with the government's previous gun control proposal, announced in May 1989, which would only prohibit "reconvertible" automatic weapons—guns that were manufactured as automatics, then converted into semi-automatics to make them legal for import into Canada. Once in the country, these firearms could easily be reconverted back into automatics. Lewis resisted calls to ban semi-automatic weapons, such as the one used in the Montreal Massacre, stating that "you can't legislate against insanity... [t]here are many thousands of gun owners who act responsibly. Semi-automatics are used for sporting purposes."[17] No action was taken by the government on gun control until more than six months after the Montreal Massacre.[18] The New Democratic Party (NDP) was most critical of Lewis's announcement and called for a complete ban on semi-automatics. With a caucus divided on the issue, the Liberals were also critical of the government, but did not support the total ban on semi-automatic firearms.[19]

On 26 June 1990, Bill C-80 was introduced by the new Conservative Justice Minister, Kim Campbell, more to meet the much-delayed gun

---

III: Canada's Parliamentary Process

First Reading   For all government bills, the legislative process begins when the responsible cabinet minister introduces a bill into the House of Commons for first reading. The title of the bill, along with a brief explanation of its contents, are "read" by the minister. The bill is also printed at this point.

Second Reading   The bill is debated in principle and a vote taken. If the vote passes, the bill moves to the committee stage.

Committee Stage   At the committee stage, a clause-by-clause examination of the bill takes place. Witnesses may testify before the committee, submit briefs, and request alterations. The committee members make changes to the bill in the form of amendments.

Report Stage   After the committee stage, the bill moves to the report stage. Here, MPs may propose further changes and vote on amendments proposed by the committee.

Third Reading   The bill is debated and voted on by MPs. If the vote passes, the bill clears the House of Commons and moves on to the Senate.

The Senate   Once a government bill passes third reading, it moves to the Senate where it goes through a legislative process similar to that of the House of Commons. The Senate has the power to delay, reject, or amend a Commons bill. Lacking democratic legitimacy, the Senate rarely rejects a government bill.

Royal Assent   Every bill must be signed into law by the governor-general. This is done ceremonially in the Senate, in front of a joint sitting of MPs and senators. The granting of royal assent is a symbolic act and is never refused. Once given royal assent, the bill becomes an act of the Canadian Parliament and the law of the land. If a bill does not receive royal assent before the end of the parliamentary session, it "dies on the order paper." If this occurs, Parliament may pass a motion in the following session to restore the bill to the same place in the legislative process where it was before the session ended. If the bill is not re-introduced in this manner it must go through the entire parliamentary process again if it is to become law. Many bills that "die on the order paper" are simply abandoned by the government.

control commitments of the government than as a direct response to the Massacre. The primary component of the law was that automatic weapons converted to semi-automatics would no longer be legal, as they could be easily reconverted. Changes to the Firearms Acquisition Certificate (FAC) process were also included to help screen out potentially dangerous or unstable gun owners. The FAC program, established by legislation passed in 1977, required that anyone wanting to acquire a firearm must demonstrate an understanding of gun safety by taking a mandatory safety course. Along with Bill C-80, the government also planned to prohibit some specific military and paramilitary weapons with large capacity magazines by an-order-in council made possible by regulations passed back in 1977. Supporters of tougher gun control often pointed out that these changes did not cover the weapon used in the Montreal Massacre.

Despite the popularity of gun controls among the public and substantial pressure from many quarters for even tougher regulations, the government effectively killed C-80 in November 1990 by sending it to a special committee that would not have time to report back by the end of the session. In Parliament, Liberal MP Warren Allmand noted that it was both embarrassing and amusing that "a bill presented by the Conservative government ... has more support from the opposition than it does from the government members."[20] The scuttling of C-80 drew attacks from opposition MPs, police chiefs, doctors, and the students from l'École Polytechnique who had organized the massive petition of half a million signatures calling for tougher gun controls. In response, the government stated that new gun control legislation would be on the books by the end of its mandate. The failure of C-80 was largely attributed to opposition by rural MPs, particularly from the government side of the House. Many in the media saw the defeat of C-80 as the work of the powerful gun lobby.[21] As predicted, Bill C-80 died on the order paper in May 1991. The Conservatives, however, did not abandon gun control after its demise.

On 30 May 1991, Campbell introduced Bill C-17 to replace C-80 and fulfill the government's promise for stricter gun control laws. C-17 did not differ substantially from its predecessor and had similar central provisions, including a ban on (re)convertible automatic weapons, a ban on military-style weapons, and restrictions on clip sizes. As introduced, it also called for tougher punishments for those who misused guns, tougher safe-storage regulations for firearms, a four-week cooling-off period between the application to possess a firearm and the issuing of a permit, and mandatory parental consent for those 16 and 17 years of age to own a gun. While C-17 received much criticism from those on the extreme sides of the issue, it was generally praised by moderates on both sides, at least when first intro-duced.[22]

To ensure the passage of C-17 in the Commons against the concerns of the powerful Conservative rural caucus, Prime Minister Mulroney inter-vened and enforced party discipline.[23] With his support, the bill passed easily in the House of Commons by a margin of 189 to 14.[24] Rural Tory MPs opposed to tougher gun controls protected their interests by insert-ing a rarely used provision that would allow them to veto future regulatory definitions of prohibited weapons and illegal ammunition; if 20 MPs or 15 senators disapproved, the regulations would be required to pass a majority vote in both Houses of Parliament.[25] Concern that the Senate would block the bill was unfounded, as the Senate passed it unanimously and without delay. Bill C-17 received royal assent on 5 December 1991, the eve of the second anniversary of the Montreal Massacre, further indicating that, although the Massacre did not lead directly to significantly tougher gun controls, it still remained a powerful symbol in the gun control debate.

Targeting Gun Control: The Lead up to the Firearms Act

Gun control was not an issue of any significance during the election cam-paign of 1993.[26] It was raised on only one occasion by any of the leaders during the campaign and then only briefly. This occurred when the candi-dates were asked during the televised English-language leadership debate what they would do about violent crime. In his answer, Liberal leader Jean Chrétien vaguely stated that gun control was necessary to counter violent crime: "I don't think that handguns should be available as easily as they are. It is all right to be a hunter, but why let people have handguns in Canada? I don't think we need that type of thing. We have to have much tougher laws there."[27] Lucien Bouchard, the Bloc leader, also indicated during the same debate that stricter gun controls should be put in place, but did not elaborate much on that point.[28] No other leader addressed the issue during the debates or throughout the campaign.

The Liberals, who would ultimately emerge victorious, outlined their party platform in a 112-page document entitled *Creating Opportunity: The Liberal Plan for Canada*.[29] Otherwise known as the "Red Book," this docu-ment covered most policy areas under federal jurisdiction. Only one sen-tence, however, dealt with the issue of gun control under the heading "Safe homes, Safe streets":

> To strengthen gun control, a Liberal government will, among
> other measures, counter the illegal importation of banned and
> restricted firearms into Canada and prohibit anyone convicted
> of an indictable drug-related offence, a stalking offence, or any
> violent offence from owning or possessing a gun.[30]

While the Liberals were heavily criticized later for not keeping many
of their more ambitious campaign promises, such as eliminating the GST,
they far exceeded their stated goals regarding gun control. The Red Book
and the campaign of 1993 gave no indication that, within months of being
elected to a majority government, the Liberals would announce and then
pass into law by far the toughest, most comprehensive, and most controversial gun control legislation in Canadian history. If they had, it would
have undoubtedly become a much larger issue in the campaign. As it was,
the election of 1993 was primarily about economic issues.[31]

Despite the comparatively lax gun controls outlined by the Red Book,
the government claimed throughout the gun control debate that, after winning the election of 1993, they had a mandate to pursue comprehensive
gun controls. In fact, the prime minister, the justice minister, and the Liberal House leader often warned backbench Liberal MPs opposed to the
Firearms Act that voting against the gun registry went against a key party
platform and an important election commitment. This revisionist assessment of the Red Book went largely unchallenged, and the idea that tough
gun controls had been approved by the public during the election of 1993
became an important rhetorical pillar for the government.

The 1993 election was a remarkable event in Canadian history. The
collapse of the Conservatives and the NDP and their replacement by the
Bloc and Reform had a substantial impact on gun control policy. Before
the election, gun control was an issue that divided every parliamentary
caucus along rural/urban lines; after, gun control was more clearly defined
along party lines. Despite the fact that the Reform Party became a staunch
defender of the rights of gun owners, the parliamentary environment was
more receptive to tougher gun controls as, for the first time in Canadian
history, both the government and the official opposition indicated their
strong support. Allied with the Bloc, the Liberals were in a much better
situation than previous governments to face the expected barrage of criticism that has always accompanied gun control proposals.

Although gun control was not a prominent campaign issue in the 1993
election, the new Liberal government in Ottawa moved swiftly to propose
tougher firearms legislation. In the early months of 1994, it was still fac-

ing complaints and criticisms surrounding Bill C-17 and its implementation.[32] However, by March of that year the Liberals began to hint that they favoured much tougher gun control than was outlined in that bill.[33] The government's position on the issue was first revealed on 25 March 1994 by the reaction of newly appointed Justice Minister Allan Rock to a petition sponsored by Concordia University calling for a total ban on handgun ownership in Canada in response to another shooting on that campus. The petition was widely circulated and eventually collected more than 200,000 signatures and was supported by more than 200 organizations. Rock, a newly elected Toronto MP, pledged his conditional support, stating that he would work toward developing "a strategy for achieving more effective gun control," including a possible prohibition of handgun ownership.[34]

By April 1994, Rock openly acknowledged his preference that all private firearms should be banned, a position that goes well beyond "gun control." He admitted that he "came to Ottawa... with the firm belief that the only people in this country who should have guns are police officers and soldiers."[35] By confirming that it was his personal preference that all guns, including long guns, be prohibited from private ownership, Rock not only made the most radically pro-gun control statement by any justice minister in history, but also provided an excellent example of the shifting perception of firearms in Canada. This was the first time that prominent members of the government clearly demonstrated their opposition to the very idea of private gun ownership as part of their vision of Canada. Not surprisingly, Rock's public support of such strong gun control and his announcement that tougher gun control measures were forthcoming ushered in the most contentious debate regarding firearms in Canadian history.

Although Rock's personal convictions were to ban all guns, within days he claimed that he had been persuaded that guns were a necessity of life for those in rural and remote Canada who used them for hunting and pest control.[36] Nevertheless, he vowed to present a number of strict gun control options to his colleagues in the Liberal cabinet and caucus for consideration. As with the previous round of gun control measures in the early 1990s, the Liberal firearms initiatives of the mid-1990s coincided with a number of fatal shootings. In early 1994, a rash of high-profile crimes involving guns took place, including the random drive-by shooting of Nicholas Battersby in Ottawa, the murder of Georgina Leimonis during a botched robbery at the Just Desserts Café in Toronto, and the killing of Joan Heimbecker, a McMaster University student, in Hamilton.[37] Beyond these killings, there were growing concerns among police and the public that there was a proliferation of illegal guns in Canada, many of them smuggled from the US.

There was also an increasing perception that violent crime, particularly gun-related crime, was on the rise.[38] The high-profile media attention that focused on the shootings undoubtedly aided the case for tougher gun control and may have prepared the public to accept the unprecedented level of control proposed by the government. The relatively high number of murders involving firearms also effectively countered many of the arguments by gun enthusiasts who argued that tougher gun laws were not necessary.

Of course, fears of Canada devolving to the level of gun violence experienced in the US also played a role in the gun control debate. In fact, concern that US-style gun violence was being imported became a central component of the government's pro-gun control arguments. For example, Rock stated on more than one occasion that he did not want Canada degrading into the gun "madness" of the US. He indicated that Canada should take measures to avoid "falling into a cycle where people believe they have to acquire a weapon for protection of themselves."[39]

While Rock did not rule any other options out, he assured gun owners that, despite his personal preference that guns should only be in the hands of the police and military, he would not consider a complete ban or confiscate firearms on a large scale.[40] He also suggested that, while there may be a need for firearms in rural Canada, there was no need for private individuals to have any guns in cities. In fact, Rock indicated he was considering the creation of "gun-free" zones in Canadian cities so that hunters who resided in urban areas would be required to store their firearms outside city boundaries. He went on to say that changes to the Criminal Code and the Young Offenders Act relating to guns and gun crimes would also be forthcoming.[41]

Within days of having committed the government to move rapidly toward stricter gun control, Rock faced a barrage of criticism. Among MPs, there was substantial opposition to the idea of a total ban on handguns. The move toward tougher gun control was harshly criticized by many Reform MPs, who claimed the proposed measures were "a knee-jerk reaction" to the numerous fatal shootings that preceded the minister's announcement. Reform MP Jim Scott suggested that "[t]he minister seems to be saying that criminals are not responsible for violent crime, gun owners are. He appears intent on making legitimate firearms owners pay the price for the recent spate of crime."[42]

By this point, the Reform Party had become the leading parliamentary opponent of gun controls. This was a new position for Reform, which did not get involved to any significant extent in the gun control debate in the early 1990s. In fact, as late as October 1994, Reform did not have an official position on the issue. In 1991 the party's policy director, Stephen Harper, attributed the lack of a gun control policy to "such a division of opinion [within the party] that we ended up throwing it out as an issue."[43] However, after gaining the support of, and being pressured by, the "gun lobby," as well as seeing a political opportunity to exploit, Reform began developing an anti-gun control policy late that year.[44] Reform's position, which represented the strongest anti-gun control sentiment ever expressed in Parliament, fundamentally changed how the issue played out, dividing it more closely along partisan lines. Furthermore, after Reform came out firmly against Bill C-68, most gun organizations endorsed it. As a result, Reform became increasingly hard-line on the issue.

While Rock may have anticipated resistance on the gun control front from opposition MPs and the gun lobby, he appeared to be caught off-guard by the number of Liberal MPs who were extremely concerned by this new gun control agenda.[45] A substantial percentage of the large rural Liberal caucus expressed its displeasure with Rock's proposals, many even rejecting them publicly. Backbench Liberal MP Reginald Blair, for example, criticized Rock's gun control position as "emotional and premature ... [t]he context is extremely difficult in rural Canada. Firearms are not a problem. In many cases, they are a way of life. We do not have the same rate of crime because of handguns that we are witnessing in the cities."[46] Another Liberal MP, Bob Speller, stated that "[p]eople are saying we should be looking at toughening penalties for the use of handguns in criminal offences and beefing up border patrols to stop the illegal smuggling of guns instead of going after legitimate gun owners."[47] At this point it became apparent that, much like the experience of Kim Campbell on the issue in the early 1990s, Rock's most challenging opposition would come from within his own caucus.

Unlike previous parliaments, the internal strife that the gun control issue caused in the government caucus was, for the first time, offset by the clear support given to tougher gun controls by the official opposition. The separatist Bloc Québécois indicated that they were in favour of tougher gun controls. In fact, the Bloc stated from the very beginning of the debate that it preferred a much tougher stand on firearms control than was suggested by the Liberals. In May 1994, only six months after the 1993 election, the Bloc's critic on justice policy, Pierrette Venne, called "for a total ban on handguns, mandatory registration of all firearms and a mandatory permit for purchasing ammunition."[48] The Bloc proved to be an important ally for the Liberals in Parliament throughout the coming debate.

Despite the concerns of government MPs, Rock's proposals received overwhelming support at the Liberal Party's national convention on 15 May 1994.[49] The resolution, which was sponsored by the National Women's Liberal convention, called for significantly stronger restrictions on handgun ownership, a ban on assault weapon ownership, tougher controls on the purchase of ammunition, measures to control gun smuggling, and harsher sentences for those who used guns during the commission of a crime. The convention also suggested that the government examine the possible creation of a national registry of all guns held in private hands.[50]

In response to the hearty endorsement of gun control by the Liberal Party membership, the prime minister announced that the government would move quickly to put tougher firearms restrictions in the law books and promised to have a new gun control bill introduced by the fall sitting of Parliament. Stating his own personal preference for gun control, Chrétien argued that "... there shouldn't be any more weapons in our streets or in our playgrounds."[51] Regarding handguns, he took an even stronger position: "I ask why there should be any in our society."[52] This position was supported by an Angus Reid-Southam poll on the subject released two weeks before the Liberal convention which indicated that almost 73 per cent of Canadians supported a total ban on the ownership of handguns by private citizens.[53]

It did not take long for opposition to the Liberal's gun control plan to coalesce, both inside and outside of Parliament. Reform leader Preston Manning argued that the proposals passed by the Liberal convention focused on the "marginal aspects" of gun control. Many suggested that the best way to prevent gun crime was tougher sentences for those that misuse guns rather than focusing on law-abiding gun owners.[54] In addition, only two weeks after the Liberal convention, a rally of 2,500 gun enthusiasts and gun rights advocates in rural Alberta (believed at the time to be the largest gun rally in Canadian history) vowed to fight the government's gun control program. At the rally, Dave Tomlinson, president of the National Firearms Association, called for all gun owners to present a unified front against the forthcoming firearms bill. He asserted that the power of firearms owners had already been clearly demonstrated by the fact that the Conservatives had been reduced to two seats by the electorate because of their gun control policy. Two Reform MPs, Jack Ramsay and Leon Benoit, addressed the rally to endorse the right of Canadians to own firearms for the purpose of self-defence.[55]

By August 1994, the gun control debate had become a hot topic in Canadian politics. During that month a number of well-attended gatherings organized by anti-gun control activists took place across the country. In Olds, Alberta, 1,200 gun enthusiasts protested against the proposed gun law and were joined in their opposition by prominent members of the Reform Party and provincial Conservatives. Fifteen hundred people attended a similar rally in Prince George, British Columbia, and other protests took place in Edmonton, Toronto, and Sydney, Nova Scotia.[56] On the other side of the issue, a number of prominent Toronto doctors held a news conference to support the proposed gun control measures.[57] The Canadian Association of Chiefs of Police also came out to strongly endorse the principle of tougher gun control.[58]

On 22 September 1994, a massive rally to protest gun control, called "Fed Up," drew over 10,000 people to Parliament Hill. It attracted people from around the country who vowed to stop Rock's proposals from becoming law. The justice minister addressed the hostile crowd, promising that he would not confiscate any hunting rifles. Nevertheless, he vowed that a "substantial" gun control package would be introduced to Parliament during the fall session and that he would not cave in to pressure.[59] A number of Liberal MPs also attended the rally to protest the new gun law proposals.[60] Outside of Ottawa, protestors marched on the offices of Liberal MPs in BC in an effort to get the government to back down.[61] The level of criticism of Rock's planned gun controls emanating from Liberal MPs was particularly surprising; the justice minister faced tough questions in the House, not only from the opposition benches (as expected), but also from members of his own caucus during question period. It was not all bad news for Rock, however. To counter the widely publicized anti-gun control rally, the Coalition for Gun Control held a press conference emphasizing the positive relationship between gun control and public safety.[62]

After two non-fatal shooting incidents in Ontario during October 1994, the prime minister gave some shape to the government's vague gun control proposals. Chrétien supported a national registry of all firearms in Canada, telling reporters "I believe that we have to force everybody to register their guns … We register all the cars. What's wrong with registering all the guns?"[63] Despite this announcement, a number of pro-gun control groups, including the Bloc Québécois, began to criticize the Liberals for delaying legislation and suggested that the wait was due primarily to the significant divergence of opinion in the caucus on the issue. Remembering that the Conservative government had taken more than five years to implement a relatively weak gun control bill (C-17), supporters of tougher firearms regulation were not yet convinced of the government's commitment on the issue.

Although many members of the Reform Party had been loud in their opposition to the Liberal's gun control plans since they were announced, it was not until October 1994 that the party took an official stand on the issue. The 1,400 delegates to the Reform Convention in Ottawa passed a resolution with more than 93 per cent supporting "the right of law-abiding citizens to own and use firearms."[64] The party also backed tougher sentences for those who misused firearms. While the resolutions passed easily, a number of delegates, citing recent polls, questioned the political value of championing the cause of gun owner's rights.[65] Nevertheless, the overwhelming sentiment at the convention was that law-abiding gun owners should not be penalized by a gun law that would be ineffective in preventing gun violence.[66]

On 30 November 1994, after much anticipation and speculation, Rock publicly outlined the government's gun control proposals.[67] Beyond the licencing and registration of all firearms in Canada, the proposals included a mandatory four-year sentence for the use of a firearm in the commission of a crime. In addition, the Firearms Acquisition Certificate (FAC) would be changed to a Firearms Possession Certificate (FPC). Another significant change was that handgun owners would have to justify ownership of such weapons every five years.[68] Many handguns and assault rifles would be banned outright. The proposals were as tough as had been promised, would cover all Canadians who owned guns, and were to be phased in slowly over a number of years with various provisions coming into force at different times.

Not surprisingly, reaction to the minister's announcement was very vocal and divided into two clear camps. Two days after Rock's outline for gun controls were announced, the Coalition for Gun Control held a news conference that emphasized the broad support gun control had in Canada. The Coalition supported the government's proposals, but vowed to hold Rock to his commitment and urged gun control supporters to counter opposition from the gun lobby. Coalition President Wendy Cukier stated that the gun control debate was a matter of "...the public interest vs. the interests of a vocal minority."[69] At this point those supporting gun control were obviously concerned that the government would back down under pressure applied by gun enthusiast groups as other governments had in the past.[70] The Coalition also announced an aggressive strategy to discredit statements made by pro-gun activists.[71] Among the other groups praising Rock's gun control proposals were Victims of Violence, the Canadian Advisory Council on the Status of Women, and numerous professional organizations.

On the other side of the issue, firearms enthusiasts promised to kill any plans for tougher gun control. John Periochio, president of the Canadian Firearms Action Council, promised to target selected Liberal MPs in both party nominations and during the next election: "We will select MPs that have particularly offended gun owners and get our people into their party at the local level." Furthermore, if Liberal MPs passed Rock's gun control proposals, his organization would "take them out and make them suffer."[72] The strategy of targeting pro-gun control politicians had long been used with varying degrees of success by the NRA in its campaign against gun control in the US. The use of such a tactic by a Canadian gun group demonstrated the growing influence of US gun politics in Canada at this time. The National Firearms Association (NFA) also committed itself to killing Rock's legislation and predicted that most gun owners would not comply with the registry or participate in the licencing portion of the proposal. The participation of groups like the NFA, who emphasized the rights of gun owners, represented a fundamental change in anti-gun control activism, which was previously dominated by hunting, target shooting, and "outdoors" organizations.

Early in 1995, a number of polls were conducted, all demonstrating strong support for tougher gun control in Canada. From Rock's perspective, the most favourable poll released was commissioned by the province of Alberta and showed that, despite the opposition of the provincial government to gun control and the perception that Alberta was a hotbed of anti-gun control sentiment, a full 64 per cent of Albertans supported the federal gun initiative.[73]

In January 1995, as reports circulated that a substantial number of Liberal MPs, especially those representing rural ridings, would vote against the firearms bill, the prime minister made it clear that those Liberal MPs considering defecting on the issue would be severely punished, with rumours (later denied) that renegades would even be expelled from the caucus and the party. This was a somewhat surprising enforcement of party discipline considering that legislation had yet to be introduced into the Commons. Chrétien's remarks put a number of Liberal MPs under pressure from both sides, as gun-owning constituents also demanded that their MPs represent their interests and fight the proposed bill. The prime minister made it clear that, despite calls for a free vote, there would be no flexibility on the issue; all government MPs would be forced to toe the party line. Nevertheless, many rural Liberal MPs continued to indicate their displeasure at the gun control proposal at a national caucus meeting in early February.[74] One Liberal MP, backbencher Len Hopkins, even went so far as to issue a press release indicating that he would not support Rock's proposal without significant amendments.[75]

Gun Control in Parliament: The Passage of the Firearms Act

After much speculation, the government's long-awaited gun package was introduced into the House of Commons as Bill C-68 on 14 February 1995. In the end, the bill was not a significant deviation from the gun control proposal outlined by the justice minister three months earlier. As tabled in the House, C-68 would forbid the importation of certain weapons, impose mandatory sentences of a minimum of four years for the commission of a serious crime with a gun, create new Criminal Code sentences, and prohibit some assault rifles. While these components of the bill were not overly controversial, the two main provisions—the establishment of a national registry for all privately owned firearms in Canada and the separate licencing of all gun owners, which would impact on every Canadian gun owner—definitely were. The legislation was estimated to affect 3 million Canadians and include 7 million guns.[76] Furthermore, the legislation took the unprecedented step of making non-compliance in the federal firearms program a criminal offence; people who did not register their guns would be given a criminal record on top of any other punishments.

Concern was also raised about the sentences for non-compliance. Under C-68 the maximum penalty for possession of an unregistered firearm was a substantial five years in prison and a $2,000 fine. Canadian gun owners were given five years to register their guns, with various portions of the bill being phased in over time. Concerns were also raised about the potential cost of the bill and how much of the expense of administering it would be borne by individual gun owners. These and other details had not been worked out at the time of the bill's introduction. Rock praised the bill by arguing that it "...will help us preserve the peaceful character of Canadian society and help the police fight crime and violence on the streets and in the home."[77] Most gun control advocates warmly welcomed C-68, with the usual concerns about the government bowing to pressure and weakening as the debate wore on. Predictably, gun-rights activists criticized the bill for being "unjust" and promised to stop it from becoming law.[78] In Parliament, the introduction of C-68 was the subject of substantial debate. It was criticized by the Bloc for not being strong enough and by the Reform Party for its inefficiency regarding cost, its ineffectiveness regarding crime control, and its unfair burden to law-abiding citizens.[79] Being attacked on both sides proved to be beneficial to the government; unlike previous rounds of gun control, parliamentary division on the issue gave the government the favourable position of appearing to occupy a compromise position.

After the introduction of C-68, a number of Liberal backbench MPs became even more vocal in their attacks on the legislation. Some rural Liberal backbenchers went as far as to publicly state that they would vote against the bill, while others indicated that they would put pressure on the prime minister to weaken it. Ontario Liberal MP Bob Nault, for example, was extremely critical of Rock and Chrétien, stating that he and other rural Liberal MPs planned to "start targeting our prime minister and other cabinet ministers because Rock doesn't seem too interested in listening."[80] For a backbencher in a newly elected government, this represented an extremely strong condemnation of the cabinet.

The Liberals, however, were not the only party divided over C-68. The NDP, which had urged tighter gun controls during the debates surrounding C-80 and C-17, would not support C-68 in the Commons. Despite overwhelming support for gun control among the NDP party executive and membership, eight of the nine members in the NDP caucus announced they would fight Rock's gun control package.[81] The opposition of the NDP caucus was not particularly surprising, given that it consisted entirely of Western MPs. Like the Liberals and the NDP, a number of Reform Party MPs also had difficulty in deciding how to vote during the second reading of C-68. Despite a clear party position on the issue, some Reformers felt a tension between the party platform and their own personal opposition to the bill on one hand and the populist ideology of the Reform Party on the other. Reform's populism dictated that the preferences of constituents should determine how an MP votes in Parliament. Given the surprising popularity of gun control in some ridings held by Reform, this tension placed many Reform MPs in a bind. Only Stephen Harper voted in favour of Bill C-68 because a clear majority of his Calgary constituents indicated they supported it through a poll he commissioned on the subject. However, the conflict between representing the party platform and the wishes of constituents continued to be a thorn in the side of the party until after the third reading of C-68.

Much anticipation led up to the second reading of Bill C-68 in the Commons on 5 April 1995. While there was no real danger that the bill would be defeated, it was not clear how many Liberal MPs, if any, would break ranks over the issue. On the morning before the vote, the prime minister warned his caucus that it was "a serious matter" to oppose the government on a vote regarding a significant policy issue.[82] A number of Liberal backbenchers expressed their discontent by absenting themselves. It was estimated that as many as 30 of the 49 Liberal MPs not in the House for the vote were Liberal MPs who had previously indicated their disapproval of Rock's gun control package. In the end, only three Liberal MPs, all from rural Ontario, voted against the bill.[83] Nonetheless, given the size of the Liberal majority, combined with the support of the Bloc Québécois, C-68 passed second reading easily by a margin of 173-53. With the exception of Stephen Harper, all Reform MPs present in the House voted against the Bill, as did Conservative Elsie Wayne (who represented half of the two-member Conservative caucus).

While Harper was praised by his Reform colleagues, including party leader Preston Manning, for breaking party ranks on the gun control issue to reflect the preferences of his constituents, the three maverick Liberal MPs did not escape punishment. The day after the vote all three were removed from their seats on parliamentary committees by Liberal Party whip Don Boudria.[84] Boudria defended his actions with a revisionist assessment of the Liberal Party platform, arguing that "[i]t was felt necessary that as a result of the three voting against a measure which is in the Red Book—a commitment on which we were elected—that we have to have members on the committees who espouse Liberal values"[85] One of the ousted Liberals, Benoît Serré, noted how the prime minister's heavy handedness contrasted with the Red Book promise to loosen party discipline and have more free votes on controversial issues in Parliament.[86] The enforcement of party discipline on this issue was largely seen as a message sent by the prime minister and the justice minister that they were serious about gun control and would not back down on the issue as the previous Conservative administration had done. It also served to remind those other Liberal MPs who were contemplating voting against C-68 at third reading that they would also be punished.

After second reading, the bill was sent to the Common's Committee on Justice and Legal Affairs for hearings and consideration of possible amendments. In a move designed to limit debate and to prevent the gun lobby from gaining momentum, C-68 was placed on the legislative fast-track. Debate had already been limited on the second reading of the bill, and the committee was to meet for only a limited period and report back to the Commons in time for the bill to pass third reading before the summer recess.[87] Some observers suggested that the rush could be attributed to fears by the government that backbench Liberals in rural constituencies would face mounting pressure over the summer to vote against the bill. Much of the existing opposition within the Liberal caucus was attributed to confrontations between angry gun owners and rural MPs over the previous Christmas recess.[88]

By May 1995, the governments of Saskatchewan, Alberta, and the Yukon Territory had formally expressed their desire to opt out of the national gun registry portion of C-68. At the Common's Justice Committee hearings, Saskatchewan and Alberta argued that the registry impinged on provincial jurisdiction over the regulation of property—a position supported by Preston Manning. In fighting C-68, the Reform leader had contacted all provincial premiers urging them to mount pressure on Ottawa to have the bill referred to the Supreme Court to test its constitutional validity.[89] Rock rejected outright any possibility of any opting out, arguing that gun control would not be effective unless it was a national program.[90]

The Justice Committee hearings not only cemented opposition from some provinces, it also brought new criticisms of C-68 to the forefront. Initially, most criticized the bill on the grounds that it would inconvenience gun owners without being an effective deterrent to gun-related crime and that a national gun registry would be extremely expensive to set up and administer. These criticisms were indeed repeated at the committee hearings. However, as the bill became more heavily scrutinized, its expansion of police powers also became a central issue. Sections 99 through 102 outlined new inspection powers given to the police to enforce the government's gun control measures.[91] Under these sections, police were permitted to enter private homes and business establishments at a reasonable time of day without a warrant. They were required only to suspect, with reason, that a firearm or restricted weapon was present in the private residence, even if legally possessed. The provisions went so far as to allow police entry into a private home without a warrant if they suspected it contained ammunition. This meant that the dwelling of every person with a registered firearm, or who was licenced to possess firearms, could be legitimately searched by the police, as could any other private house in which authorities suspected there were weapons present.

The bill would also require that citizens aid the police in conducting inspections. Under Section 101, people were entitled to refuse a search; however, doing so permitted the police to seek a warrant solely on the grounds that entry was refused.[92] Critics of C-68 argued that these sections violated the Charter of Rights, the common law, and the principles of English liberty inherited by Canada.[93] This belief became one of the central pillars of the Reform Party's attack on C-68, as demonstrated by Reform's gun control critic Jack Ramsay who stated "[w]hen this bill passes our freedoms are gone ... Mr. Rock is being absolutely unreasonable and irresponsible when he moves in this fashion to make criminals out of law-abiding citizens." Reform and other pro-gun groups also began asserting that outlawing a large number of firearms under C-68 was tantamount to confiscation or expropriation without compensation.[94]

During the Justice Committee hearings, a number of groups other than those representing gun enthusiasts also emerged to challenge C-68. For example, the Canadian Civil Liberties Association, which favoured gun control in principle, attacked the inspection provisions. The head of the association, Alan Borovoy, announced that "[t]his is another example of creating unnecessary powers and hoping they won't be abused."[95] In a surprising move, prominent members of the medical community, which historically had been strongly in favour of gun control, began to question its value. In its testimony to the committee, the Canadian Medical Association (CMA) argued that C-68 would have little or no impact on murder and suicide rates.[96] Most other health organizations continued to support the bill, and the CMA later reasserted its support as well.

Another long-time supporter of gun control also indicated its disapproval of Bill C-68. The Canadian Bar Association attacked the bill on the grounds that the organization could not support searches of private property without a warrant.[97] Some legal experts argued that the "search and seizure" components of the bill would not survive an inevitable Charter challenge.[98] A substantial number of Aboriginal groups also noted their opposition. However, many of these were concerned with C-68's violation of treaty rights and traditional hunting activity rather than with the issue of gun control in general.[99]

Some groups took a more extreme position on the issue. For example, during its presentation to the Commons Justice Committee, the president of the Saskatchewan Outfitters Association suggested guns were part of the Canadian way of life. However, "[o]ne man, Allan Rock, has stated that he intends to change that culture. Stalin and Adolf Hitler also changed their countries' cultures." He maintained that the ultimate goal of the Liberals in enacting C-68 was to create a society where only police and military personnel have firearms, which "bears strong resemblance to Nazi Germany and Communist Russia, among others."[100] Many other groups used this slippery slope argument: that gun control invariably leads to gun confiscation, which in turn must lead to autocratic government and tyranny.[101] This new variety of extremist rhetoric became more prevalent as the gun control debate became more heated, but generally proved to be a counterproductive strategy that offended more moderate gun owners.

Another conspiracy-minded group, the Montreal-based Friends of Liberty, went so far as to claim that the true purpose of C-68 was to disarm the Québécois population to prevent Quebec nationalists from achieving sovereignty if the Parti Québécois (the PQ) were successful in the impending referendum.[102] An equally interesting argument came from the president of the Responsible Firearms Owners of Alberta, who expressed his concern that the prairies could become plagued with coyotes, gophers, and other vermin if too many gun owners turned in their firearms to avoid paying the licencing and registration fees.[103]

The hearings at the Commons Justice Committee were a focal point for groups involved in the gun control debate. While many interest groups were active throughout the gun control debate of the 1990s, their influence on government policy was limited. This is demonstrated by the fact that the government made only a few changes. Of course, groups on both sides were influential in framing the issue for the media and the public. The Coalition for Gun Control was particularly effective in this regard, helping the government in putting a positive spin on the Firearms Act and countering arguments made by gun enthusiasts.

Despite the criticisms presented at the committee hearings, Rock, who continued to have the support of many groups, vowed to remain firm.[104] However, during his own testimony to the Committee, the justice minister proposed that changes be made in both the sentencing provisions and sections dealing with the inspection powers of police, perhaps responding to the criticisms of the Canadian Bar Association.[105] Under the proposed changes, police would need a warrant to search the premises of an individual who owned less than ten guns. Those that failed to register their gun(s) would still receive a criminal record, but the punishments would be reduced substantially.[106] These proposals were accepted by the Liberal-dominated committee, who amended the penalties to a maximum six-month sentence or a $2,000 fine for failing to register a firearm and who agreed also with the Rock proposal to reduce the new police powers.

While designed to quell criticism of C-68, these changes only angered anti-gun control groups who argued that they did not go nearly far enough. The move also was met with disapproval by pro-gun control groups who opposed any reduction in penalties for non-compliance and feared that the minister was giving in to the gun lobby.[107] Some in the media attributed the weakening of C-68 to increasing pressure on the justice minister from the rural Liberal caucus; immediately prior to Rock's announcement, two more Liberal backbenchers, John O'Reilly and Bernie Collins, indicated they would vote against the bill at final reading. In fact, many rural MPs admitted that they had never faced such anger in their ridings on any other issue.[108]

The prime minister, however, remained committed to gun control, stating that "[i]t's a policy of the government and we won't back down. It's the right policy. We don't check only the polls before we act. But it so happens that in this case the people are with us."[109] Chrétien went on to threaten any MP who was considering voting against the government on the issue and chastised O'Reilly and Collins for publicly airing their disapproval of the bill: "[t]hey had a chance to talk. They have a lot of freedom. They made all the speeches they wanted. They discussed this thing in caucus for a year. Even myself, sometimes, I don't win in the caucus or in the cabinet. I go along with the rest."[110] Chrétien made it clear that the government would not back down from C-68 regardless of the vocal opposition of the gun lobby or the reservations of rural MPs and their constituents. Liberal Whip Don Boudria even suggested that renegade Liberal MPs should try to catch a 24-hour flu on the day of the vote, to avoid punishments.[111] As the final Commons vote approached, a minimum of 29 Liberal MPs had publicly stated their opposition to C-68.[112]

The Reform caucus was also divided on the issue. Three Reform MPs, including party whip Jim Silye, indicated that they would vote in favour of C-68, because polling in their ridings indicated that a majority of their constituents supported the law.[113] All three represented urban ridings in Calgary (Silye), Edmonton (Ian McClelland), and Vancouver (Ted White). These departures from the hard-line anti-gun control position proved to be somewhat embarrassing to the Reform Party and discredited their claim that the Liberals would suffer during the next election for passing C-68.

Reform's policy of polling on the gun control issue also caused Stephen Harper, the lone Reform MP who voted for the law at second reading, to reverse his previous position and vote against it on the strength of a second, more scientific poll conducted in his riding.[114] Reform leader Preston Manning was criticized for not polling his constituents on the issue and thereby avoiding the possible embarrassment of having been one of the most vocal critics of C-68 yet in the end having to vote for it.[115] The NDP also remained divided on the issue, with eight of nine MPs still indicating they would vote against the wishes of the party. Even some rural Bloc MPs began to have reservations regarding the bill.[116]

Adding to the contentiousness of the already heated debate over C-68 was the Liberal decision, supported by the Bloc Québécois, to limit debate on the third reading of both this bill and another hotly contested piece of legislation, Bill C-41, which called for increased sentences for those convicted of hate crimes. With the help of the Bloc, the Liberals managed to reduce the allocated time for the Commons to debate C-68 to only 12 hours. Considering that the Justice Committee had sent back 267 proposed amendments, this was not nearly enough time for adequate debate. Preston Manning called the government's alliance with the Bloc to ram two unpopular laws through Parliament "close to treasonous," and, furious with the shortened debate schedule, he stated that the move was "despicable, anti-democratic and anti-Canadian." He attributed the Bloc's cooperation to their desire to end the parliamentary session to prepare for the upcoming separatist referendum in Quebec.[117]

On 13 June 1995, after only two days of debate, Bill C-68 was approved after third reading by the substantial margin of 192-63. Given the high degree of speculation regarding the outcome, some in the media described the vote as anti-climatic.[118] Only nine of the approximately 30 disgruntled Liberal MPs voted against the bill. The opposition voted as expected with three Reformers voting for it, eight NDPers against (with Svend Robinson voting in favour), and the Bloc unanimously in support. Rock described the passage of C-68 in the Commons as "a great day for Canada." He also tried to assure critics that his gun control bill was a compromise that protected Canadians and still respected gun owners: "I've taken pains at every turn to emphasize that farmers and hunters and ranchers, target shooters and collectors will be able to continue their use of firearms as in the past. I very much believe that in 10 years we'll look back at the registration of all firearms and wonder what the fuss was about."[119]

After C-68 cleared the House, there was much speculation that the Conservative majority in the Senate would attempt to significantly amend the bill and delay it by referring it back to the Commons.[120] Ron Ghitter, Conservative senator and Tory spokesman on the issue, promised that gun control would not be rushed through the Senate. In particular, he argued that C-68 should be put under the thorough scrutiny of the Senate's legal affairs committee, which he recommended should conduct public hearings on the issue. This move was accurately believed to be an obvious plan by Tory senators to kill the bill. By returning the amendments to the Commons, they would force another vote there. Ghitter revealed that one of the amendments would be to decriminalize the penalty for not registering firearms.[121] Since the Liberal government would not accept such a weakening of the bill, C-68 would have to be modified again (back to its original form) by the government. The Senate then would have to reconsider it. By this time the legislative session would end, and the bill would die on the order paper, thus causing C-68 to join the other failed attempts at strong gun control in Canadian history. At any rate, the Senate frustrated Rock by announcing that it would not even begin to consider C-68 until the recall of Parliament after the summer recess.

When C-68 was placed on the Senate's agenda, 51 senators were listed as Conservative, 50 as Liberals, and three as independents. By August 1995, however, it became clear that party divisions would not hold on a Senate vote on gun control. Therefore, despite the vocal criticism of many Senate leaders regarding C-68, it was uncertain what strength the anti-gun control forces actually had. The first sign that the Senate would not give C-68 as rough a treatment as expected came when it was revealed that the Senate Committee would study the bill for only ten days, substantially limiting the time for debate. Despite delaying attempts by some Tory senators, the date for the vote on C-68 was finally scheduled for 22 November, leaving plenty of time to pass it before the end of the session, set for 15 December.[122]

As the vote approached, a number of senators indicated that they were unsure of how they were going to cast their ballot. Many observers predicted that the vote would be very close, with the outcome uncertain.[123] The division on the package of amendments submitted by the Conservatives was indeed as close as predicted, as it was defeated by a vote of 53 to 46. However, the vote on the bill itself was not as close as many suspected it would be. After the failure of the amendment package, Bill C-68 passed the Senate easily by a margin of 64-28 with 11 abstentions. It then received royal assent on 5 December 1995, on the eve of the sixth anniversary of the Montreal Massacre, and was proclaimed into law as the Firearms Act.

Reaction to the passage of the bill was predictable. Allan Rock argued that the Firearms Act was a significant piece of legislation that reflected Canadian values "because it reaffirms our character as a peace-loving, non-violent nation." Like many government officials, including the prime minister, Rock used the passage of the act to contrast Canada's gun control laws with those of the US: "We have decided to follow a different route from the US where citizens are often encouraged to arm themselves for self-defence. We Canadians don't want our children and grandchildren growing up in a society like that."[124] Chrétien himself remarked that Canadian gun control laws gave Canada "a personality of our own" and that the law would be the envy of many liberal US legislators.[125] Not surprisingly, those in favour of gun control, especially the coalition for gun control, celebrated their victory with some disbelief that they had accomplished their goals.[126]

While those fighting for gun control claimed victory with the passage of the Firearms Act into law, those who fought against gun control did not reconcile themselves to defeat. Within days of the bill being passed by the

Senate, those provinces that opposed C-68 threatened to challenge the legality of gun control measures before the Supreme Court.[127] In addition, the various hard-line members of the gun lobby promised to continue fighting the law three ways. First, they vowed to support the provinces in their fight against gun control. Second, some of the more radical elements embarked on a campaign to encourage non-compliance. Third, following C-68's proclamation into law, most gun-rights activist groups opposed to gun control committed themselves to organizing against the Liberals in the next election. By targeting many apparently vulnerable rural Liberal incumbents, it was believed that the balance of power could be shifted and the Liberals defeated and replaced by a (Reform) government, which would rescind the Firearms Act.

Rock tabled the draft regulations to support the Firearms Act on 2 May 1996. These outlined five types of gun licences: (1) permits to acquire and possess firearms; (2) licences for minors to possess firearms; (3) possession-only permits for those individuals that own firearms but will not be acquiring new ones; (4) 60-day permits for non-Canadian residents to use a gun while in Canada; and (5) licences for crossbows.[128] The regulations also stated that the licencing provisions would go into effect in 1997, with gun owners having four years after that to obtain a licence. The timetable for registration of firearms was to be even longer, with owners having until 2003 to register their guns. A week later, however, Rock withdrew the regulations, arguing that more time was needed to study their implementation. Those opposed to gun control suggested Rock reconsidered the regulations after discovering their unpopularity with Canadians.[129]

By this time opposition of a different sort began to emerge. Throughout the gun control debate, many First Nations leaders had expressed their concerns and opposition to gun control, mainly on the grounds that they violated Aboriginal treaty rights. On 3 February 1996, opposition to the application of the Firearms Act to Aboriginal people grew stronger as the Assembly of First Nations (AFN) threatened to take the government to court on the issue. Chief Ovide Mercredi stated that the AFN would fight the law, unless all Aboriginal and Inuit hunters were exempted from all federal firearms legislation.[130] According to the Firearms Act, the fees associated with licencing and registration did not apply to Aboriginal people; however, they were required to get a firearms licence and register their guns. Mercredi was also angry about the application of the regulations regarding storage and transportation to Aboriginal people, stating that "[w]e have treaty rights and Aboriginal rights to hunt. When the treaties were signed there was no discussion about issues like storage or registration."[131]

In response to the concerns of First Nations' groups, the federal government created a separate firearms regulatory regime for Aboriginal peoples in 1998. The Aboriginal Peoples of Canada Adaptations Regulations were designed to include Aboriginal people under the Firearms Act and, at the same time, to recognize the First Nations' treaty rights outlined in the constitution and to "respect the traditional lifestyles of Aboriginal Peoples."[132] The regulations, which were altered after consultations with First Nations' organizations, allowed a role for community Elders in the screening process for those seeking to obtain a firearms licence and permitted Aboriginal people under the age of 12 to obtain a minor's permit to take part in traditional hunts. Among the other regulatory differences was that, in certain circumstances, some Aboriginal people, such as Elders and those living in remote areas, did not need to pass the safety training course; instead, they were only required to demonstrate an understanding of firearms law and gun safety.

Despite these accommodations, many First Nations' organizations continued to resent the application of the Firearms Act to Aboriginal people. From the perspective of First Nations' leaders, the federal government's gun control program was an intrusion on their right to self-government and treaty rights and an imposition on their traditional hunting practices.[133] As a result, many First Nations' groups opposed Aboriginal participation in the federal firearms program and demanded federal recognition of their right to regulate firearms for their own communities. The rejection of the Firearms Act by Aboriginal people was confirmed in July 2003 when it was revealed by the Department of Justice that only a small percentage of Aboriginal gun owners had obtained a licence and registered their guns by the required deadline to do so.[134] Another yet unresolved issue relating to the application of the Firearms Act to Aboriginal people deals with First Nations' gun owners who live off reserve, in particular, those who live in urban areas. In this case, Aboriginal and non-Aboriginal people living in the same city and even in the same neighbourhoods may be subject to different firearms regulations. Notwithstanding these problems, the government has indicated (as of July 2003), that Aboriginal people will not be exempted from the Firearms Act.[135]

The Election of 1997 and the "Invisible" Issue of Gun Control

When the Firearms Act became law in 1995, many observers predicted that gun control would become an important issue in the next election. For gun enthusiasts, the election of 1997 was the first opportunity to mobilize the "gun vote" in an effort to oust the Liberals and to elect a Reform government committed to rescinding the controversial act. Although firearms organizations rented billboard advertising space and distributed signs and bumper-stickers reading "Remember C-68 when you vote," gun control did not become an important issue during the election which ran from 27 April to 2 June 1997.[136] It may have had some impact on a few ridings, but overall its impact was minimal, especially given all the rhetoric of the gun lobby. In terms of media coverage, gun control was a significant issue on only a single day of the national campaign. One reporter even referred to it as an "invisible" issue.[137] After the election, polling data confirmed that it was not important to voters.[138] The main issues of the day were jobs, taxes, and national unity, along with health care and crime issues (of which gun control was only a part).

While Reform promised to repeal C-68 and replace it with significantly tougher penalties for those who misuse guns, gun control did not figure prominently in Reform's campaign strategy. Instead, Reform focused on economic issues, promising to lower taxes to stimulate job creation, and shifting later in the campaign almost exclusively to the issue of national unity.[139] Reform's neglect of gun control during the campaign can probably be best attributed to the fact that it had already solidified the C-68 protest vote, so there was little to be gained by reminding the majority of Canadians, especially those in urban Canada who supported tougher gun control, of its opposition.

Firearms regulation was mentioned in the Liberal campaign document, "Securing Our Future Together" (better known as Red Book II). One page of the 104-page Liberal platform proudly trumpets the accomplishments of the government on gun control. It begins: "[e]ffective gun control is central to the Liberal government's strategy to reduce and prevent violent crime. Canada's new gun control law is one of the toughest in the Western world. It is solidly supported by Canadians, including the police..."[140] Despite this mention, the Liberals used the gun control issue sparingly on the campaign trail, introducing it only towards the end in Montreal where Chrétien was joined by relatives of victims of the Montreal Massacre.[141] Publicizing the Liberal record on gun control in Quebec, where C-68 was very popular, was a direct attack on Jean Charest and the Conservatives who, as part of their new party platform, vowed to repeal C-68. One observer noted the strategic considerations involved with the gun control issue:

> the decision to raise the profile of the gun control issue also
> spoke to the diminished expectations of the Liberals in West-

ern Canada. If they thought themselves competitive in Western seats with sizeable rural populations, they would have been far more reluctant to talk about their controversial legislation. But once those seats weren't going their way anyhow, the strategists felt free to use the issue.[142]

By far the most surprising aspect of the 1997 campaign relating to gun control was the decision of the Conservatives to endorse the repeal of the Firearms Act. This position was part of a deliberate effort to move the party to the right of the political spectrum during the campaign to better compete with Reform. Conservative leader Jean Charest's opposition to gun control did not turn out to be a wise strategy, as those who supported tougher gun control were very critical of the move, and those who were against it generally saw the switch as political opportunism and continued to back Reform.[143] Although the NDP had endorsed gun control with the selection of their new leader, Alexa McDonough, it was not a significant component in their campaign, which almost entirely focused on the issue of jobs.[144] The NDP could hardly become the champion of tougher gun controls when eight of their nine MPs had voted against the Firearms Act. While the Bloc Québécois supported gun control, it was not central to their campaign, except perhaps as part of a package of measures to control motorcycle gangs and organized crime in Quebec.

Ultimately, the Liberals were re-elected with a slim majority of 155 seats out of a total of 301. At this point, one could be forgiven for assuming that the gun control issue had been settled. Although it was not a serious campaign issue, the government that passed C-68 into law had been returned to office, thereby giving democratic legitimacy to a controversial gun control program that had never faced public scrutiny through election. The gun control issue, however, would not die. Some in the gun lobby gave themselves credit for reducing the number of Liberal seats, and a few of the Liberal incumbents targeted by the NFA and other pro-gun groups went down to defeat. While the gun lobby did seem to lose momentum following the election, the hard-liners vowed to continue the fight.

Shortly after the 1997 election, Anne McLellan took over the justice portfolio from Allan Rock. Her appointment was a clever strategic move by the prime minister, as she represented half of the entire Liberal caucus elected from Alberta.[145] By appointing an Albertan as justice minister, Chrétien could better counter opposition to the many federal justice initiatives from the Alberta government, including the constitutional challenge to the Firearms Act which was in the process of taking shape. By using

McLellan as the spokesperson for Ottawa's justice policy, he reduced the characterization of these debates from being disputes between central Canada and the West to disputes between Albertans with differences of opinion. This may have been particularly useful on the gun control issue as it reinforced the point that most Albertans supported C-68. Furthermore, it may have also helped counter some of the rhetoric of the gun lobby, the largest and most extreme of which were headquartered in Alberta. Upon her appointment, however, McLellan did not anticipate dealing with the gun control issue to any great extent, indicating that she felt that "the election has determined issues like … gun control in large measure."[146]

The Provinces Take Aim at the Firearms Act

Following the successful passage of the Firearms Act, a coalition of provinces led by Alberta became the leading opponent of the federal firearms program. In fact, even prior to the passage of the act, Alberta Premier Ralph Klein promised to fight the Liberals on the gun control issue. Although Alberta was the first province to publicly criticize C-68, it was quickly joined by Manitoba, Saskatchewan, Ontario, and, finally, by Nova Scotia and New Brunswick. The governments of the Yukon and Northwest Territories (NWT) had also been consistent adversaries of the federal government on gun control. Like many other issues, the opposition of the provinces to federal policy is more complicated than it appears. While it is undoubtedly the case that Alberta and the other provinces oppose the federal firearms program for its content, there are always political points to be made in attacking the federal government, especially in Alberta where the Firearms Act is often cited as another example in a long litany of policies that demonstrates the bias inherent in Canadian politics. In the eyes of many Albertans and Westerners, the current federal arrangement favours the interests of central Canada (Ontario and Quebec) over Western Canada. In that context, gun control is also seen symbolically as the imposition of the values of Ontario and Quebec on Albertans. The opposition of Ontario and Nova Scotia to the Firearms Act could best be attributed to ideological differences between Conservative provincial governments that generally favoured smaller government and the federal Liberals who see a larger role for government.

Like many federal/provincial disputes, the Firearms Act ended up in court. In June 1997, the government of Alberta filed documents outlining its arguments against the Firearms Act through a reference to the Alberta Court of Appeal (ACA).[147] The proceedings, which began on 8 September 1997, attracted a significant amount of media attention.[148] For those involved, the stakes were high; the proponents of gun control who had worked diligently for years to see the passage of the Firearms Act feared all would be lost if the courts struck down the law. In fact, there were concerns that if Alberta won the case, portions of the federal gun control regime passed in 1991 and 1977 would also be ruled unconstitutional. For the gun lobby, however, the court challenge was seen as one of the last meaningful chances to reverse their previous political defeats.

At the ACA, *Reference re The Firearms Act*[149] was limited to a jurisdictional challenge of Ottawa's authority to licence and register firearms. Alberta did not seek to attack the law on other legal grounds, including a potential Charter challenge. Consequently, Alberta's case rested primarily on the premise that, while Ottawa could justifiably regulate dangerous weapons, the regulation of "ordinary" guns such as shotguns and rifles properly fell entirely under the provincial jurisdiction of "property and civil rights."

The ACA handed down its decision a year later, on 29 September 1998, rejecting Alberta's position by the slim margin of three to two. According to the majority of the court, the Firearms Act fell within the federal criminal law power and was, therefore, constitutional.[150] Having relied on this interpretation, the justices in the majority did not have to address the federal government's second defence of the constitutional validity of the act, which rested on the residual clause of the Constitution Act, 1982. The federal government had argued that even if the Firearms Act did not fall under the jurisdiction of the criminal law power, the legislation could be justified under the federal government's right to make laws for the "peace, order and good government" of the country.

The Supreme Court Challenge: Reference re Firearms Act

In February 2000, Alberta's appeal of the ACA's decision made it to the Supreme Court of Canada.[151] Alberta continued to be supported by the intervening governments of Ontario, Manitoba, Saskatchewan, the Yukon, and the NWT. In addition, Nova Scotia and New Brunswick, who did not participate in the original Firearms Reference, now supported Alberta at Canada's highest court. By this point, the Alberta government had also acquired a number of new, non-governmental allies intervening on its behalf: the Coalition of Responsible Firearms Owners and Sportsmen (CORFOS), the Law-Abiding Unregistered Firearms Association (LUFA), and the Shooting Federation of Canada (SFC). The Federation of Saskatchewan Indian Nations also was involved in challenging the act.

Intervening on behalf of the federal government in support of the Firearms Act were three municipal governments (the cities of Winnipeg, Montreal, and Toronto) and, independently in their own right, the Canadian Association of Chiefs of Police, the Canadian Pediatric Society, the Association pour la santé publique du Québec, the Canadian Association for Adolescent Health, the Alberta Council of Women's Shelters, the Fondation des victimes du 6 décembre contre la violence, Canadians Against Violence Everywhere Advocating its Termination (CAVEAT), and the Coalition for Gun Control.

While more arguments were presented at the Supreme Court than at the ACA, Alberta's position was essentially the same. Once again the case was limited to the question of whether or not Parliament had the constitutional authority to enact the Firearms Act. In a relatively short decision released on 15 June 2000, the court unanimously ruled that the Firearms Act constitutes a valid exercise of Parliament's jurisdiction over criminal law:

> The law in "pith and substance" is directed to enhancing public safety by controlling access to firearms through prohibitions and penalties. This brings it under the federal criminal law power. While the law has regulatory aspects, they are secondary to its primary criminal law purpose. The intrusion of the law into the provincial jurisdiction over property and civil rights is not so excessive as to upset the balance of federalism.

Since all guns are capable of causing harm or death, the court argued that "it follows that all guns pose a threat to public safety. As such, their control falls within the criminal law power."[152]

Despite rejecting the provincial challenges to the Firearms Act, the Supreme Court did open the door to further challenges on two main grounds. The first of these involves Aboriginal Canadians who "argue that it discriminates against them and violates treaty rights."[153] The court also hinted that the legislation may discriminate against the Charter rights of rural or northern Canadians who are disproportionately affected by the legislation. Therefore, the court very much left open the possibility of a treaty or Charter challenge in the future.

The Debate Continues:
Implementing the Billion-Dollar Gun Registry

Many gun owners continued to be skeptical about the impact of the new firearms law on crime, and the gun lobby continued to oppose the act. Concerns were also raised regarding the escalating cost of licencing all gun owners and registering all guns in Canada. Critics were quick to attack the many logistical and computer problems that plagued the Canadian firearms program as the licencing and registration processes progressed. Having lost the political battle, some gun user groups, such as the Law-abiding Unregistered Firearms Association (LUFA), promised to fight the Firearms Act by advocating non-compliance, their hope being that, if enough people failed to register their weapons, the system would be scrapped.

Although opposition to the Firearms Act seemed to diminish after the 1997 election, as the deadline for licencing gun owners and registry approached, gun-user groups renewed their campaign. On 22 September 1998, just one week prior to the start of the licencing and registration provisions, the gun lobby organized its last large-scale protest on Parliament Hill. The rally, called "Fed Up II," drew 9,000 people from across Canada to express their dislike of the federal gun laws.[154]

The registration and licencing provisions were initiated on 1 December 1998 to the cheers of gun control advocates and the chagrin of the gun lobby that had vowed to stop the registry from ever being implemented. Gun owners now had until 1 January 2001 to obtain a licence and January 2003 to register their guns. The hard-line gun lobby now moved to encourage non-compliance and continued to support the provincial governments who had begun to appeal the decision of the Alberta Court of Appeal to the Supreme Court of Canada. The federal amnesty that allowed people to turn in any firearms made illegal or restricted by the act also began on 1 December 1998. On the same date, the Canadian Firearms Centre (CFC) was created to oversee the federal firearms program.

Once again, interest in the issue subsided after the licencing and registration deadlines were reached. Increasingly administrative, logistical, and cost issues surpassed the debate over gun control itself. The registration was hampered by a number of computer breakdowns which prompted Garry Breitkreuz, the Reform critic on the issue, to suggest that it would take 233 years to register all the guns in Canada at the rate the National Firearms Centre was able to process each registration, averaging just 360 per day.[155] The Reform Party also criticized the growing bureaucracy needed to administer the registration. In May 1999, it was discovered that 621 federal civil servants were administering the program, with 184 future hirings already approved and many more slated.[156] By 1999 the government projected that the total cost for the registry to taxpayers would be $120 million with at least an additional $50 million annual operating expenses.

In June 1999, the chief spokesperson for the registry drew criticism for releasing misleading numbers that suggested a much higher participation rate in the gun control program than actually existed. According to the CFC, 1.3 million firearms had been registered and 411,000 people had been licenced by 24 May 1999.[157] However, through an access to information request, the Reform Party discovered that only 66,000 guns had been registered along with only 5,500 licences issued, far short of the Liberal's goal of 1.3 million new guns and half a million owners signed up in the first six months of the program.[158]

Despite the fact that the Firearms Act was now law and had been legitimated by the Supreme Court, a number of hard-line gun activists and organizations such as the National Firearms Association (NFA) still refused to admit defeat on the gun control issue by the time of the general election of 27 November 2000. In fact, the NFA organized an ambitious campaign to provide support for Canadian Alliance (formerly Reform) candidates in every riding by providing local volunteers who would help get the "gun vote" out.[159] They also specifically pinpointed a number of ridings where they thought they could defeat Liberal MPs. One of their biggest targets was Justice Minister Anne McLellan. While the efforts of the NFA may have made the vote close, it failed to unseat her. The gun lobby also failed in its attempt to make the Firearms Act a significant campaign issue outside of a few ridings, despite a fairly extensive effort and wide distribution of signs featuring C-68 with a line through it and the words "the Home Invasion Bill."[160] Except for the most extreme gun-rights hardliners, the re-election of the Liberals in 2000 ended any serious possibility of repealing the Firearms Act.

On 3 December 2002, Auditor-General Sheila Fraser released a scathing report on the registry.[161] She publicized what everyone had long known: that the gun registry and licencing program were massively over budget. From the outset, critics had accused the government of deliberately underestimating the costs to make the registry more politically palatable. In 1995, it was estimated that the program would cost Canadian taxpayers only $2 million ($119 million minus $117 million recovered in fees). The cabinet had known about the ballooning costs as early as 1997, but had not made them public. By 1998, the Justice Department indicated that the program was over budget, but did not provide any figures. Fraser, however, confirmed that, as of 2002, the government had spent $688 million on the program and only recovered $59 million in fees. She estimated the cost of the program would rise to more than $1 billion by 2004-05. Fraser also chastised the Justice Department for keeping Parliament in the dark regarding the rising expenses.[162] She argued that the department had deliberately underestimated the cost to the government by a large margin. In fact, Fraser said that the Firearms Act was so mismanaged that a full audit could not be conducted.

As the 1 January 2003 deadline for gun owners to register their guns approached there were increasing concerns on a number of fronts. Anti-Firearms Act activists were hoping for a high level of non-compliance, which would jeopardize the program. Others attempted to sabotage the registration process by attempting to overload the system's computers by registering many times under false names. The latter tactic may have been successful. It was later revealed in June 2003 that the registry's computers had crashed during the peak registration period, and many people who thought they had registered had not been entered in the system.

On 25 March 2003, the government had to impose strict party discipline to pass an additional $59 million to keep the firearms program running.[163] The program suffered another blow that June, when the provincial governments of Nova Scotia and Ontario joined Alberta, Saskatchewan, and Alberta in stating that they would not prosecute individuals who violated the registry. The impact of this was widely overstated by the media; police would still be able to lay charges based on registry violations in those provinces. However, to express their opposition to the registry, those five provinces would not prosecute registry violations in court, leaving that responsibility (and expense) to federal Crown prosecutors.

As of 1 July 2003, more than 300,000 gun owners had not registered their guns, leading some to question the effectiveness of the registry. In addition, an estimated 1.5 million long guns had not been registered. However, people continued to obtain licences and to register their guns after the deadline, moving the percentage of guns and gun owners closer to the original goals of the government. Despite all the problems associated with the gun registry, it appears to have been accepted gradually by the vast majority of Canadian gun owners, with only the most militant refusing to comply. However, because of the mismanagement and cost overruns associated with the program, it will probably be some time before the controversy over gun control, the Firearms Act, and the gun registry fades away.

Discussion

The ongoing controversy over gun control and the firearms registry demonstrates the complexity involved in politics and policy-making. The real world of Canadian politics takes place on many levels, with many different actors participating at different times and in different political contexts. The interaction of personalities, institutions, and events have all shaped the path the gun control issue has taken and influenced the political outcomes of the debate. Gun control has remained a controversial issue in Canadian politics for almost 15 years. The primary reason it has lasted so long is because of the symbolism connected to the issue. At the heart of the gun control debate are competing visions of Canada that occupy two (or more) distinct "worlds" of Canadian politics.

The passage of the Firearms Act in 1995 was a dramatic event, not only in terms of federal firearms policy, but also for Canadian politics in general. Perhaps the most remarkable aspect of the gun control controversy is the rapidity with which the politics of the issue changed. Only a few years prior to the Firearms Act becoming law, the passage of comprehensive gun controls was considered to be a political impossibility. It was thought that any government pursuing firearms legislation similar to the Firearms Act would face overwhelming opposition and probably suffer significantly at the ballot box. In fact, since the late 1960s, a number of prominent federal cabinet ministers indicated that they, like the majority of Canadians, supported tougher gun control. However, comprehensive gun controls could not be passed in Parliament because of the vehement opposition by gun enthusiasts and many rural MPs. Even as recently as the early 1990s, the gun lobby was considered to wield a substantial amount of power. By the mid-1990s, however, the politics of gun control had changed so drastically and so quickly that the government was able to pass a comprehensive gun control regime despite strong opposition.

So what had changed to allow comprehensive gun controls? With the benefit of hindsight, it can be argued that the "planets were aligned" for proponents of gun control in the mid-1990s. A number of events, some connected and others unrelated, came together to create a favourable political environment for tougher gun controls. In the real worlds of Canadians politics there are many unpredictable events that impact on policy and politics. In policy terms, the Montreal Massacre was a random occurrence that changed the politics of gun control at a number of levels. While the Massacre did not directly influence lawmakers at the time, it changed the language and framed future gun control debates. It raised sensitivities to the gun control issue and led directly to the creation of Canada's first gun control movement and pushed women's organizations to embrace the cause.

Shortly after the massacre, the election of 1993 (the results of which had nothing to do with gun control) created a new parliamentary environment that was uniquely receptive to a policy of tougher gun controls. With the support of the official opposition Bloc Québécois, the Liberal government was in a favourable position to see the Firearms Act through to its passage. In addition, after the election of 1993 gun control became a strategic wedge issue for the Liberals against their new parliamentary opponent in English Canada, the Reform Party. The appointment of Allan Rock, who admitted he saw little need for the private ownership of firearms, as justice minister was also a favourable event for gun control activists, as was the commitment of the prime minister to tougher gun laws.

In understanding why or when any given policy change occurs, it is essential to consider that policy within a broader political framework. While the issue of gun control is ostensibly about public safety and crime reduction, firearms policy must also be understood in the context of party politics and parliamentary competition. There is no doubt that, in passing the Firearms Act, the Liberals had the goal of reducing gun-related crimes and promoting the Canadian value of non-violence. However, no policy change as controversial or drastic as the Firearms Act is ever made without considering the political ramifications of embarking on it.

Only Jean Chrétien, Allan Rock, and the inner circle of Liberal advisors and strategists know with certainty what were the political motivations for the government to push through tougher gun laws despite the inevitability that they would face extremely vocal opposition from angry gun owners and rural MPs. Nevertheless, it seems likely that, after the election of 1993, there were for the first time political gains to be made for the government to pursue tougher gun control. That election was a disaster for the governing Conservatives who were reduced to only two seats. The NDP also failed to retain official party status. The replacement of the Tories and the NDP by two new parties, the Block and Reform, changed the way gun control policy played out in Parliament.

For a number of reasons, the new parliamentary dynamic established by the 1993 election made gun control a more attractive policy for the Liberals. For example, by pursuing a policy of tougher gun control, the Liberals would cement their electoral strength in Quebec where gun controls were the most popular. At the same time, it was clear that the loudest opposition to C-68 would come from areas, such as the prairies, where the Liberals had traditionally not done very well electorally so they did not have much to lose by angering gun owners in places like Alberta. In fact, it was probably also the case that most angry gun owners were not Liberal voters anyway. As a result, there was more to be gained politically in pursuing tougher gun control than there was at risk for the Liberals.

The opposition ranks in 1993, particularly in the Reform Party, were full of parliamentary newcomers; moreover, both the Bloc and Reform were newly formed political parties that had not yet cut their teeth in federal politics. The Liberals could capitalize on this particularly weak opposition to push through a very controversial policy such as gun control. In addition, because the opposition was now split between two regional parties (the Bloc Québécois and Reform) for the first time in Canadian history there was no obvious government-in-waiting or national opposition party. The official opposition Bloc, which only ran candidates in Quebec, was inherently incapable of winning enough seats to form the government. Reform was also regionally contained in the West and was unlikely to be able to form the next government, especially considering it had no realistic chance of winning any seats in Quebec. It was also apparent that it would take a number of years, at least more than one election, for the Conservatives to recover from their resounding electoral defeat in 1993. The NDP, which had also been substantially reduced in the Commons and also did not retain official party status, did not present a serious threat either. Therefore, the Liberals could be much more courageous on controversial matters such as gun control, knowing that they faced a divided opposition comprised of four parties, none of which appeared able to win the next election.

Undoubtedly, the Liberals could anticipate difficulty pushing through comprehensive gun controls. In fact, they faced a serious split on the issue within their own caucus. They could also predict tough resistance from the opposition benches and vocal outrage from many gun owners. However, they would not be the only party to have difficulty with the issue. The traditional opposition parties' line on gun control was that, although they were in favour of tougher gun laws, they could not support the government's wrongheaded proposal that would be an unjust imposition on honest, law-abiding gun owners and which would not be effective in reducing gun crime. The NDP had occasionally favoured tougher gun laws, but, like every other federal caucus, was divided on the issue, with many of its rural MPs opposed to stricter firearms control. Eventually, eight of the nine member NDP caucus voted against the Firearms Act. By opposing comprehensive gun controls, Reform was cornered into a policy position supported by a minority of the public. In addition, it is not inconceivable that Liberal strategists viewed gun control as a wedge issue that would help reinforce the image of Reform as a western, rural, right-wing movement. It is not too much of a stretch to assume that Liberal Party strategists used the gun control issue in the hopes that it would help limit any potential Reform gains in vote-rich urban Canada, particularly in southern Ontario. In addition, the political risks, such as a minor backbench revolt among the Liberals (which did occur), were mitigated by the Bloc's obvious support of tougher gun controls. With the Bloc's support and the imposition of strict party discipline, there was little doubt that the Firearms Act would become law.

Not only could the Liberals claim the middle ground between the Reform Party's strong opposition to and the Bloc's support for tougher gun laws, but, for the first time, the government also had allies outside of the Commons. As we have seen, the Montreal Massacre had inspired a collection of groups and individuals to work for more stringent gun controls, including the Coalition for Gun Control, victims groups, and various women's organizations and professional associations.

Although the election of 1993 may have facilitated the passage of comprehensive gun controls in Parliament, there remained a substantial amount of opposition to the Firearms Act throughout the 1990s and into the twenty-first century. This opposition followed the Firearms Act through a number of different stages and in many different institutional arenas. While the federal government remained the leading advocate for comprehensive gun controls throughout the debate, those opposed to tougher gun controls and the gun registry included gun rights groups, the Reform Party, Conservative senators, the governments of Alberta and other provinces, civil libertarians, and fiscal conservatives.

Immediately after Allan Rock announced that the government was moving towards comprehensive gun controls, gun enthusiasts began working to pressure the government to back down. They lobbied government MPs, pressured the cabinet, engaged in grassroots activism, and attacked the proposal in the media. However, due to the highly centralized nature of Canada's parliamentary system, the prime minister dominates the agenda of the government. Therefore, lobbying MPs, writing letters to cabinet members, and other similar forms of political activism are ineffective unless they also manage to sway the prime minister. The strength of party discipline in the Canadian Parliament often ensures that backbench MPs are shut out of the policy-making process, especially on an issue as controversial as gun control. In the case of the Firearms Act, gun enthusiasts faced a prime minister who was committed to bringing in comprehensive gun control in the face of strong opposition. Furthermore, polling data undoubtedly demonstrated to him that gun control was very popular among the "silent" majority of Canadians and that implementing tougher gun laws would not hurt the Liberals in the next election.

When the grassroots pressure tactics employed by firearms enthusiasts proved unsuccessful, and C-68 was introduced in Parliament, the Reform Party became the leading critic of the government's gun control proposals. Because the government had a firm majority in Parliament and was supported by the Bloc Québécois, it was able to force C-68 through the House of Commons relatively quickly. The institutional focus of opposition to the Firearms Act then moved to the Senate, where it appeared that C-68 might be defeated. It was not. In fact, given all the controversy surrounding Bill C-68, the large number of government backbenchers and senators who publicly opposed the bill, and all speculation regarding how the vote would go, the Firearms Act passed through the legislative process with remarkable ease.

Once a policy becomes law there are a number of ways by which it can be reversed or overturned. First, the government can be defeated in the next election by a new administration which may revisit the issue. Second, the constitutionality of the law can be challenged in court. Third, the implementation of the policy can be prevented. Those opposed to gun control embarked on all these strategies.

Gun organizations such as the NFA worked hard to make gun control a central issue in the 1997 election and urged gun owners to "remember C-68 when you vote." They employed the time-tested strategy used by the NRA in the US of targeting certain ridings where gun control might be particularly unpopular and attempting to defeat government candidates. However, their efforts were largely unsuccessful in both the elections of 1997 and 2000. For the second strategy of challenging the constitutionality of the Firearms Act, the provinces took the lead. This is a common practice in Canadian politics whereby the provincial level of government is often the most effective opposition for a federal government with a majority in the House of Commons. It also demonstrates that a provincial government can be the most powerful and assertive advocate of regional interests. The Firearms Act was much less popular in the prairies than it was elsewhere, which explains to a significant extent the participation of Alberta, Saskatchewan, and Manitoba in the constitutional challenge. To those against gun control, the court challenge was perhaps the last remaining legitimate chance to overturn the act. The third strategy employed by hard-line gun groups was the attempt to block the implementation of the act through non-compliance, which would force the government to rewrite the legislation and scrap the gun registry.

For those opposed to the Liberal's gun control law, the administrative problems with the gun registry bring hope that the Firearms Act will be repealed or reduced in impact. The implementation of the firearms program, which should have been a largely administrative matter, has been an ongoing embarrassment for the government and has taken on a political life of its own. The solicitor-general has taken steps to improve the operation of the Firearms Program, including the establishment in June 2003 of an advisory group of experts external to government which has the goal of improving the administration of the program.

Despite all the problems associated with the federal firearms program, given that the Firearms Act is law and its provisions are in force, it will be very difficult to remove. It is unlikely that any government in the foreseeable future will reopen the issue of gun control to any significant extent. Many individuals, organizations, and politicians will vigorously oppose any liberalization of the act, and there would be much more to be lost than gained for any government, of any political stripe, contemplating substantial changes to it. Barring a successful Charter challenge, a substantial shift in public opinion, or a significant institutional realignment, the Firearms Act and comprehensive gun control will remain on the books. Nevertheless, until the federal firearms program is fully implemented with stable funding, controversy will continue.

Chronology

1867: First federal firearms legislation passed, entitled An Act to Prevent the Unlawful Training of Persons in the Use of Arms.

1892: Firearms regulations are included in the first Criminal Code.

FEBRUARY 1976: Bill C-83 is introduced in Parliament. The bill would have been Canada's first comprehensive gun control law. However, it was withdrawn by the government after facing intense opposition and replaced by the much less stringent Bill C-51.

6 DECEMBER 1989: Fourteen female students at L'École Polytechnique are murdered by a man with a legally obtained semi-automatic firearm. This incident, known as the Montreal Massacre, has a profound and lasting impact on the politics of gun control.

1990

JANUARY: In response to the Massacre, Wendy Cukier and Heidi Rathjen begin working together to establish Canada's first gun control movement. Soon after the Massacre, the two women create Canadians for Gun Control, later to become the Coalition for Gun Control. Since then, the Coalition has been the leading champion of tougher gun controls.

26 JUNE: Bill C-80 introduced.

12 MAY: Bill C-80 dies on the order paper. The bill had been abandoned by the government months earlier.

1991

30 MAY: Bill C-17 introduced.

7 NOVEMBER: Bill C-17 passed in the House of Commons by a vote of 189-14.

5 DECEMBER: Bill C-17 receives royal assent on the eve of the second anniversary of the Montreal Massacre.

1993

25 OCTOBER: The election of 1993. Reduced to only two parliamentary seats, the Conservative government suffers the worst electoral defeat in Canadian history. The Liberals become the government. Among their campaign promises is a very vague commitment to gun control. Two new parties, the Bloc Québécois and the Reform Party, become important parliamentary entities. The Reform Party will become a vocal opponent of gun control, while the Bloc will strongly support the government's tougher gun laws.

1994

24 MARCH: Justice Minister Allan Rock announces that he favours much tougher gun laws, including a possible ban on handguns.

15 MAY: At its national convention, the Liberal Party overwhelmingly endorses the justice minister's calls for tougher gun control proposals.

22 SEPTEMBER: More than 10,000 angry gun owners march on Parliament to protest against plans for tougher gun control in a rally called "Fed Up."

30 NOVEMBER: Justice Minister Allan Rock formally announces the government's gun control proposals.

1995

14 FEBRUARY: Bill C-68, which would later become the Firearms Act, introduced in the House of Commons.

5 APRIL: Bill C-68 passes second reading in the House of Commons by a margin of 173-53.

13 JUNE: Bill C-68 passes third reading in the House by a margin of 192-63.

22 NOVEMBER: A significant amendment package to Bill C-68 (which would have effectively killed it) is narrowly defeated in the Senate with 53 senators voting against the amendments and 46 voting in favour. Immediately after that vote Bill C-68 passes in the Senate by a margin of 64 to 28 with 11 abstentions.

23 NOVEMBER: The Province of Alberta announces that it will challenge the constitutionality of Bill C-68. It is supported by Saskatchewan, Manitoba, Ontario, the Yukon, and the NWT.

5 DECEMBER: Bill C-68 receives royal assent on the eve of the sixth anniversary of the Montreal Massacre and becomes law as the Firearms Act.

1997

3 FEBRUARY: The Assembly of First Nations threatens to challenge the constitutional validity of the *Firearms Act* on the grounds that it violates Aboriginal treaty rights.

2 JUNE: The election of 1997 returns the Liberals to power with a slim majority government. The issue of gun control was not an important election issue despite the controversy over the Firearms Act and the effort of many gun organizations to make gun control a prominent issue. During the campaign they wanted Canadians to "Remember C-68 when you vote." As part of their platforms, both the Conservatives and Reform endorse the repeal of the Firearms Act.

8 SEPTEMBER: The Alberta Court of Appeal begins hearing Alberta's challenge of the gun registry. *Reference re the Firearms Act* centres entirely on Alberta's contention that the *Act* violates provincial jurisdiction.

1998

22 SEPTEMBER: Nine thousand angry gun owners protest the gun registry in an event called "Fed Up II." Protestors are instructed to behave politely to help rehabilitate the image of gun owners.

29 SEPTEMBER: The Alberta Court of Appeal rejects Alberta's claim by a margin of 3-2. Shortly after, Alberta indicates that it will appeal its case to the Supreme Court.

1 OCTOBER: The Firearms Act was due to begin its process of gradual implementation on this date. However, due to logistical difficulties, the date is moved to 1 December. This is the first of many deadlines that the government is unable to meet regarding the implementation of the Firearms Act.

1 DECEMBER: The implementation of the Firearms Act begins. The Canadian Firearms Centre begins operating. The agency is responsible to Parliament through the Justice Department.

2000

15 JUNE: The Supreme Court upholds the constitutionality of the Firearms Act, unanimously ruling that it does indeed fall under federal jurisdiction according to the Constitution.

27 NOVEMBER: The federal election of 2000. Gun organizations target a number of MPs during the campaign because of their stand on gun control. Justice Minister Anne McLellan barely retains her Edmonton riding. Gun control is not an issue of significance during the national election campaign

1 JANUARY 2001: The deadline passes for gun owners to obtain a firearms licence.

2002

9 OCTOBER: Bill C-10, An Act to Amend the Criminal Code (cruelty to animals and firearms), passes third reading in the House. The bill is designed to address the many logistical and administrative issues associated with the implementation of the Firearms Act.

28 NOVEMBER: Using a rare procedure, the Senate splits Bill C-10 into two parts: C-10a dealing with firearms and C-10b dealing with cruelty to animals. Although the Senate does not amend the bill, the mere fact that it is altered means that it must be sent back to the Commons for approval.

3 DECEMBER: Federal Auditor-General Sheila Fraser chastises the government for its mismanagement of the firearms registry. She confirms what has been long suspected: that the registry is more than $1 billion over budget. Fraser is also extremely critical of the mismanagement of the registry and the degree to which Parliament has been misled on the issue.

2003

1 JANUARY: The "final" deadline to register firearms. Due to technical problems and logistical difficulties, it is later announced that gun owners can register their firearms by 1 July 2003 without being prosecuted.

18 MARCH: Four Liberal MPs and two Liberal senators publicly denounce the rising costs associated with the administration of the *Firearms Act.*

25 MARCH: The firearms registry survives a crucial vote in the House regarding the funding of the program. Without an infusion of an additional $59 million the registry would not have enough money to make it to the end of the fiscal year. With the support of the Bloc and the imposition of strict party discipline, the vote passes by a margin of 173-75.

1 APRIL: Responsibility for the firearms program is moved from the Justice portfolio to the Solicitor-General's office.

13 MAY: Bill C-10a receives royal assent.

3 JUNE: Ontario and Nova Scotia join Alberta, Saskatchewan, and Manitoba as provinces that refuse to prosecute offences relating to the firearms registry.

4 JUNE: The Solicitor-General announces that the firearms registry has been plagued by massive computer problems. As a result many people who registered before the January 1 deadline were not entered in the system.

18 JUNE: The Solicitor-General confirms that anyone registering their guns or seeking to obtain a licence will not be prosecuted for missing earlier deadlines, despite the fact that gun owners had been required to obtain a licence by 2001.

1 JULY: The "grace period" ends for those who have not yet registered their guns. More than 300,000 licenced gun owners still have not registered their guns.

Notes

1. Canada, "Background Information on Firearms Control" (Ottawa: Department of Justice, 1994) 20.

2. Heidi Rathjen and Charles Montpetit, *December 6: From the Montreal Massacre to Gun Control: The Inside Story* (Toronto: McClelland and Stewart, 1999) 30.

3. Rathjen and Montpetit 3.

4. Patricia Boyer and Barrie McKenna, "Quebec mourns slaying of women at university," *Globe and Mail* 8 December 1989: A1. See also, Stevie Cameron, "Hun-

dreds in Toronto mourn killing of 14 women," *Globe and Mail* 8 December 1989: A13; Canadian Press, "Thousands of mourners wait in silence to pay final respects to slain women," *Globe and Mail* 11 December 1989: A1.

5. Most Canadian dailies ran editorials supporting tougher gun laws. See, for example, "Time for really tough gun control," *Montreal Gazette* 15 January 1990: B2; "Wanted: the will for real gun reform," *Montreal Gazette* 15 January 1990: B3. See also, Geoffrey Stevens, "Here's a gun law to dream about," *Toronto Star* 7 January 1990: B3; and Christopher Young, "Talking about guns won't stop horror," *Calgary Herald* 21 December 1989: A4; Richard Cleroux and Craig McInnes, "Opposition MPs demand long-promised gun control amendments," *Globe and Mail* 8 December 1989: A13; Paul Wlecek, "Authorities seek right to check gun buyers' mental history," *Winnipeg Free Press* 10 December 1989: A1; Canadian Press, "Gun Controls need tightening, criminologist warns," *Montreal Gazette* 7 December 1989: A4; Paul Wlecek, "Officials united in calls for stricter gun controls," *Winnipeg Free Press* 19 January 1990: A1; David Johnson, "Half-million demand a tougher law," *Montreal Gazette* 10 April 1990: A1; Wlecek, "Officials united."

6. Rathjen and Montpetit 29.

7. David Vienneau, "Gun law crusade inspired by tragedy," *Toronto Star* 30 July 1992: A1.

8. Taken from the Coalition's website at www.guncontrol.ca, 10 June 2003. While the Coalition claims to have more than 350 organizations that support it, they only list these groups to prevent the others from being the target of potential harassment by militant gun organizations.

9. This is not an exhaustive list. Many provincial, regional, and individual hunting and sports shooting organizations also voiced their opposition to the registry. Unlike the pro-gun control side which was united under the umbrella of the Coalition for Gun Control, those groups actively opposing the Firearms Act were not as well-coordinated and ran the spectrum of opinion on the subject. In fact, during the heat of the gun control debate, dozens of small radical anti-gun control groups emerged. These groups were not influential in the debate, and their participation may have actually been counter-productive as their extremism frightened many Canadians and may have underscored the very need for gun controls. In addition, only firearms-related groups are listed here. Groups such as the Canadian Civil Liberties Association (CCLA) opposed the registry for the powers it granted to police to enforce the Firearms Act. The CCLA was, however, in favour of gun control in principle. Other groups also fell between the two sides, advocating for tougher gun controls, but not supportive of the gun control regime set out by the Firearms Act. Therefore, presenting a simple dichotomy of groups for and against the gun registry can be misleading.

10. Aboriginal groups were (and continue to be) primarily concerned with the impact of the gun registry on their treaty rights, rather than with the issue of gun control itself. The primary concern of groups such as the AFN has been to get Aboriginal people exempted from the registry; in general, they have not opposed the principle of gun control or the application of the act to other Canadians.

11. Cameron A13.

12. Merilyn Simonds, "Code of Arms," *Canadian Geographic* March/April 1996: 48 and 45.

13. See, for example, The Liberal Party of Canada, *Creating Opportunity: The Liberal Plan for Canada* (Ottawa: Liberal Party of Canada, 1993). The Liberals argue that "[f]or most Canadians, the non-violent character of Canada is one of the distinguishing features of Canadian identity" (84).

14. Tom Fennell, "Taking aim on guns," *MacLean's* 15 April 1994: 10.

15. The Second Amendment of the US Constitution reads as follows: "A well regulated Militia, being necessary to the security of a free State, the right of the people to keep and bear Arms, shall not be infringed." There has been a long-standing debate in the US regarding the interpretation of the Second Amendment. See for example, Robert J. Spitzer, *The Politics of Gun Control* (New York: Seven Bridges Press, 1998), chapter 2. For an interesting perspective on the American gun control debate, and the American "gun culture," see Michael Moore's controversial documentary film, *Bowling for Columbine* (2002) Alliance Atlantis.

16. Adapted by the author from a similar chart by Leslie A. Pal in "Gun Control," *The Government Taketh Away: The Politics of Pain in the United States and Canada*, ed. Leslie A. Pal and R. Kent Weaver (Washington DC: Georgetown University Press, 2003) 239.

17. Canadian Press, "Lewis promises to renew gun control in light of shooting," *Halifax Chronicle-Herald* 8 December 1989.

18. This differs from the experience of gun control in the United Kingdom and Australia where large-scale massacres were quickly followed by government promises of much stricter gun control, which were quickly put into law.

19. Canadian Press, "Lewis promises..." A4.

20. House of Commons, *Debates* 22 November 1990: 15615.

21. Mary Lamey, "Students at Lepine's school angry gun-control law delayed," *Montreal Gazette* 29 November 1990; Peggy Curran, "I'll see gun law passed, Campbell insists," *Montreal Gazette* 7 December 1990: B1; Peggy Curran, "Rural gun lobby triumphs as government shelves bill," *The Montreal Gazette* 24 November 1990: A14; Christopher Young, "Gun Lobby moves convince minister to delay new bill," *The Vancouver Sun* 26 November 1990: A14 and A7.

22. Daphne Bramham, "Both sides praise new gun control," *Globe and Mail* 31 May 1991: A1. As time went on, both sides became increasingly critical of the bill.

23. Canadian Press, "Mulroney intervenes in Tory fight on gun control," *Globe and Mail* 2 October 1991: A5.

24. Only one Conservative MP (Bob Speller) voted against the bill. Bob Cox, "House passes gun bill," *Winnipeg Free Press* 8 November 1991: C34.

25. Geoffrey York, "Gun-control bill leaves room for challenge," *Globe and Mail* 31 May 1991: A6.

26. For a good overview of the 1993 election, see Alan Frizell et al., eds., *The Canadian General Election of 1993* (Ottawa: Carleton University Press, 1994).

27. David Vienneau, "Rock, PM in agreement on need for gun controls," *Toronto Star* 19 April 1994: A10.

28. Vienneau, "Rock, PM in agreement" A10.

29. Liberal Party of Canada, *Creating Opportunity: The Liberal Plan for Canada* (Ottawa: The Liberal Party of Canada, 1993).

30. Liberal Party of Canada, *Creating Opportunity* 84.

31. According the Frizzell at al., "[t]he single most important factor in the election, without doubt, was the state of the economy" (2). Other issues included the Constitution and the legacy of the Mulroney Conservatives.

32. See, for example, Bob Cox, "Gun-permit questions invade our privacy firearms activist says," *Montreal Gazette* 12 January 1994: B1.

33. Terrance Wills, "Justice minister backs stronger gun control," *Montreal Gazette* 25 March 1994: A1. The petition was also inspired in part by the 1992 killing of four employees of Concordia University, all shot with handguns.

34. Wills, "Justice minister backs stronger gun control."

35. David Vienneau, "Handgun ban being studied," *Toronto Star* 12 April 1994: A1.

36. Stephen Bindman, "Minister considers ban on handguns in Canada," *Calgary Herald* 12 April 1994: A3.

37. David Vienneau, "PM vows to get tough on guns," *Toronto Star* 16 May 1994: A1.

38. See for example, Joseph Hall, "Illicit guns good as gold," *Toronto Star* 13 April 1994: A6; Tom Fennell, "Taking aim on guns," *Maclean's* 25 April 1994: 10-12; Wendy Cukier, "A gun to Parliament's head," *Toronto Star* 15 April 1994: A27

39. Vienneau, "Handgun ban."

40. Bindman, "Minister considers ban."

41. Vienneau, "Handgun ban."

42. David Vienneau, "MPs, gun buffs loading up for protest," *Calgary Herald* 18 April 1994: A2.

43. Lynda Hurst, "Meet the Canadian gun lobby," *Toronto Star* 28 April 1991: B7.

44. Michelle Lalonde, "Firearms lobby urges members to sign up with Reform Party," *Montreal Gazette* 10 August 1991: B1. Despite Reform's lack of a gun control policy, a number of groups opposed to C-80 and C-17 urged their members to join the Reform Party.

45. David Vienneau, "Rural Liberals fight gun control," *Montreal Gazette* 18 April 1994: A7.

46. David Vienneau, "Rural Liberal MPs join fight against banning handguns," *Vancouver Sun* 19 April 1994: A8.

47. Vienneau, "Rural Liberals fight gun control"; Vienneau, "PM vows to get tough on guns."

48. Manon Cornellier, *The Bloc* (Toronto: James Lorimer and Company, 1995) 124.

49. Vienneau, "PM vows to get tough on guns."

50. Terrance Wills, "Tougher gun control promised," *Montreal Gazette* 16 May 1994: A1.

51. Bob Cox, "Call for tougher gun control closes Grit policy convention," *Halifax Daily News* 16 May 1994: 8.

52. Wills, "Tougher gun control promised."

53. Ian Austen, "Get rid of handguns most say; 73% support ban for civilians," *Montreal Gazette* 2 May 1994: A2.

54. Sheldon Alberts and Allyson Jeffs, "Manning blasts Grits on gun control," *Calgary Herald* 17 May 1994: A1; Sheldon Alberts and Allyson Jeffs, "Law-abiding gun owners 'to be victims,'" *Vancouver Sun* 17 May 1994: A4.

55. Gordon Jaremko, "Gun owners targeting plan to ban handguns," *Calgary Herald* 29 May 1994: A1.

56. Canadian Press, "Prince George rally draws biggest crowd in gun-curb protest," *Vancouver Sun* 30 August 1994: A6.

57. Rebecca Bragg, "Gun control public health issue, MDs say," *Toronto Star* 25 August 1994: A1.

58. Campbell Clark, "I'll toughen gun control—minister," *Montreal Gazette* 26 August 1994: A1.

59. Tim Harper, "Gun owners take aim at bid to tighten rules; 10,000 rally on Parliament Hill," *Toronto Star* 23 September 1994: A1; Monte Stewart, "New gun laws promised 'this fall,'" *Vancouver Sun* 23 September 1994: A4.

60. Tim Harper, "Guns debate grows emotional," *Toronto Star* 21 September 1994: A12. Liberal MP Paul Steckle vowed to attend the rally, stating that "I'm not going to embarrass my government, but I've got to listen to my constituents. There's a substantial portion of our caucus which believe these law-abiding gun owners must be listened to."

61. Vancouver Sun Staff, "Wildlife group protests controls," *Vancouver Sun* 23 September 1994: B8

62. Harper, "Guns debate grows emotional."

63. Joan Bryden, "PM favors mandatory gun registration," *Montreal Gazette* 22 October 1994: A9.

64. Sheldon Alberts, "Reformers toughen stand against crime; Delegates back rights to gun ownership," *Ottawa Citizen* 16 October 1994: A6.

65. Norm Ovenden, "Legitimate gun owners made welcome here," *Edmonton Journal* 16 October 1994: A3. One Reform delegate stated: "We risk being totally offside on this issue.... There must be restrictions on the use of firearms for everyone, including law-abiding citizens. That's a practical matter."

66. Some delegates even suggested the Liberal gun law would actually be counter-productive; a delegate from Saskatoon stated: "[f]urther rock-headed weapons legislation will only increase the violence in our society." Ovenden.

67. For a good overview of Rock's proposal and the controversy surrounding it, see Anthony Wilson Smith, "Allan Rock's war on guns," *Maclean's* 12 December 1994: 22-23.

68. Derek Ferguson, "7 million guns would require registration," *Toronto Star* 1 December 1994: A13.

69. Paul Wells, "Gun control: advocates, opponents draw up battle lines," *Montreal Gazette* 2 December 1994: B1. Cukier also stated that gun control "is an investment in our future. We are calling on that silent majority, which says in the polls they support gun control but doesn't do anything about it, to act" in David Vienneau, "Advocates of gun control urge supporters to rally," *Toronto Star*, 2 December 1994: A16.

70. Vienneau, "Advocates of gun control."

71. Doug Fischer, "Supporters of gun control taking careful aim at firearms advocates," *Vancouver Sun* 2 December 1994: A6.

72. Wells, "Gun control: advocates, opponents draw up battle lines"; Fischer, "Supporters of gun control..."

73. Anthony Johnson, "Most Albertans support gun control," *Calgary Herald* 31 January 1995: A1.

74. Canadian Press, "PM puts MPs under the gun," *Calgary Herald* 30 January 1995: A2.

75. David Vienneau, "Gun law gets opening shot in Commons," *Toronto Star* 13 February 1995: A9.

76. David Vienneau, "Ottawa sticks to its guns with law," *Toronto Star* 15 February 1995: A1.

77. Doug Fischer, "Firearms legislation 'as tough as Rock,'" *Vancouver Sun* 15 February 1995: A4.

78. Jim Bronskill, "Rock solid on gun control," *Halifax Chronicle-Herald* 15 February 1995: A1.

79. Fischer, "Firearms legislation 'as tough as Rock.'"

80. Jim Bronskill, "MPs ready to fight gun bill," *The Montreal Gazette* 15 February 1995: B1.

81. Peter O'Neil, "NDP's opposition to gun law 'outrageous'," *Vancouver Sun* 8 March 1995: A4.; David Vienneau, "NDP stunned as 8 MPs aim to oppose gun law," *Toronto Star* 14 March 1995: A9.

82. Doug Fischer, "Rock's gun-control bill approved in principle," *Montreal Gazette* 6 April 1995: A14.

83. Tim Harper, "3 Liberals from rural Ontario buck party on gun bill," *Toronto Star* 6 April 1995: A2. The dissenting Liberal MPs were Rex Crawford, Benoît Serré, and Paul Steckle. See, also, Tim Harper, "3 MPs pay price for gun bill revolt" *Toronto Star* 7 April 1995: A10

84. Jim Bronskill, "PM takes tough stand on Liberals who break ranks on gun control," *Halifax Chronicle-Herald* 17 April 1995: C16.

85. Harper, "3 MPs pay price."

86. Susan Delacourt, "MPs' ouster raises question of tolerance," *Globe and Mail* 7 April 1995: A4. Preston Manning accused the Liberals of ramming C-68 through second reading.

87. Harper, "3 Liberals from rural Ontario."

88. Tu Thanh Ha, "Rush order placed on gun-control bill, "*Globe and Mail* 4 April 1995: A1.

89. Tu Thanh Ha, "Exemption from gun bill sought by 3 governments," *Globe and Mail* 10 May 1995: A1. Saskatchewan's opposition came from the "all party delegation of the Legislative Assembly of Saskatchewan," rather than from the government itself.

90. Canadian Press, "No opting out, Rock says," *Winnipeg Free Press* 26 April 1995: A6.

91. Canada, House of Commons, "Bill C-68: An Act respecting firearms and other weapons," 1st session, 35th Parliament (1994-95) 41-44.

92. Canada, House of Commons, "Bill C-68" 43.

93. For a good expression of opposition to C-68 on the grounds that it impinges on long-established Canadian civil liberties, see Shafer Parker, "Much more than mere gun control: Rock's firearms bill tramples century old freedoms for everyone, not just gun owners," *Western Report* 24 April 1995: 26-29. In this article, Allan Rock is compared to Oliver Cromwell for their mutual disrespect for civil liberties. Throughout the gun-control debate of the mid and late 1990s, *Western Report* (and its affiliates) remained steadfastly opposed to C-68, representing a unique position on the subject in the Canadian media.

94. Parker 28.

95. Tracey Tyler, "Gun control bill attacked," *Toronto Star* 13 May 1995: A12.

96. Canadian Press, "Doctors unsure of legislation," *Calgary Herald* 12 May 1995: A8.

97. David Vienneau, "Under siege, Rock likely to amend gun control bill: Bar association worries about sweeping search powers," *Toronto Star* 13 May 1995: E4.

98. Canadian Press, "Parts of gun bill might be unconstitutional," *Montreal Gazette* 9 May 1995: A7.

99. See for example, Stevens Wild, "Bands urged to defy law," *Winnipeg Free Press* 5 May 1995.

100. Canadian Press, "Gun controls resemble Nazi Germany," *Vancouver Sun* 2 May 1995: A6.

101. This is a common theme in the literature of groups such as the Law-Abiding Unregistered Firearms Association (LUFA).

102. Jim Bronskill, "Keeping Quebecers docile is true aim of gun-control bill, rights group hints," *Winnipeg Free Press* 7 May 1995: A3.

103. Vienneau, "Under siege, Rock likely to amend gun control bill."

104. Doug Fischer, "Gun registration proving to be Rock's Achilles heel," *Montreal Gazette* 15 May 1995: A10.

105. Doug Fischer, "Rock offers to soften gun penalties," *Montreal Gazette* 20 May 1995: A1.

106. David Vienneau, "Measures to soften gun bill proposed," *Toronto Star* 20 May 1995: A3.

107. Mary Nemeth, "Fighting Back: Farmers, hunters and firearms enthusiasts are turning the gun control debate into trench warfare," *MacLean's* 5 June 1995: 14-15.

108. Larry Johnsrude, "Rock may bow to gun revolt: Two more Grits come out against bill," *Winnipeg Free Press* 19 May 1995: A3.

109. David Vienneau, "Chrétien threatens gun bill rebels," *Toronto Star* 22 May 1995: A1.

110. Vienneau, "Chrétien threatens gun bill rebels."

111. David Vienneau, "Torn MPs face high noon on gun law, *Toronto Star* 13 June 1995: A21.

112. Nemeth 14.

113. Kim Lunman, "Silye voting for gun controls," *Calgary Herald* 13 June 1995: A3.

114. Lunman, "Silye voting for gun controls." According to Harper, the first poll showed 64 per cent of his constituents were in favour of C-68. However, a later more "scientific" poll indicated that approximately 60 per cent of his constituents opposed the bill.

115. Norm Ovenden, "Manning won't consult voters," *Calgary Herald* 18 May 1995: A20.

116. Vienneau, "Torn MPs face high noon on gun law."

117. Tu Thanh Ha, "Liberals, BQ combine to limit debate," *Globe and Mail* 9 June 1995: A4.

118. See, for example, Doug Fischer, "Gun-control fight goes to Senate; Nine Liberal MPs break party ranks to vote against law," *Montreal Gazette* 14 June 1995: A1.

119. Kim Lunman, "Gun control on hair trigger," *Calgary Herald* 14 June 1995: A1.

120. David Vienneau, "Battle for gun control may not be finished," *Toronto Star* 17 June 1995: B1.

121. Doug Fischer, "Tory senators plotting new strategy to kill controversial gun-control bill," *Vancouver Sun* 13 September 1995: A4.

122. David Vienneau, "Senators set to vote on gun legislation; controversial Bill C-68 will be dealt with Nov. 22," *Toronto Star* 19 October 1995: A17.

123. Pat Carney, "Senator Carney doesn't know how she'll vote on gun-control legislation—for the women of Montreal or of BC," *Vancouver Sun* 21 November 1995: A15. Jim Bronskill, "Key gun control vote too close to call," *Winnipeg Free Press* 22 November 1995: B6.

124. David Vienneau, "Tough gun law gets royal assent today," *Toronto Star* 5 December 1995: A2.

125. Sheldon Alberts, "Senate backs control of guns," *Calgary Herald* 23 November 1995: A1.

126. Canadian Press, "Two win after long, hard fight," *Calgary Herald* 7 December 1995: A16.

127. Marta Gold, "Alberta ponders court challenge," *Calgary Herald* 24 November 1995: A3; Canadian Press, "Romanow threatens to challenge gun-control law," *Vancouver Sun* 19 December 1995: A3.

128. Canadian Press, "Rock tables gun-control regulations," *Winnipeg Free Press* 3 May 1996: B2.

129. Monte Stewart, "Rock scraps regulations," *Calgary Herald* 9 May 1996: A1.

130. Jim Morris, "Leave us out of gun law, aboriginals tell Rock," *Montreal Gazette* 4 February 1997: A8.

131. Jim Morris, "Mercredi warns Grits of gun-law court challenge," *Calgary Herald* 4 February 1997: A11.

132. An outline of the *Aboriginal Peoples of Canada Adaptation Regulations (Firearms)* is available at the Canadian Firearms Centre website at www.cfc-ccaf.gc.ca.

133. For a thorough examination of the politics of Aboriginal treaty rights, see chapter 5.

134. For example, only 1 per cent of gun owners in the Mohawk community of Akwesasne had complied with the Firearms Act despite the firearms-related problems observed there. In Northern Manitoba, only 847 gun licence applications were received from 12 First Nations communities with a population of 17,129. Other Aboriginal communities had similarly low compliance rates. Tim Naumetz, "Gun registration rejected by a majority of Aboriginals," *Edmonton Journal* 23 July 2003: A6.

135. Federal Solicitor-General Wayne Easter committed the government to enforce the Firearms Act as it relates to Aboriginal peoples: "Whether you are Aboriginal, whether you are French, whether you are English, whether you are Scottish, or any culture or nationality, on this law [the Firearms Act] we believe the same rules should apply to all people." Naumetz A6.

136. Edward Greenspon, "Following the Campaign Trail '97," *The Canadian General Election of 1997*, ed. Alan Frizzell and Jon H. Pammett (Toronto: Dundurn Press, 1997) 21-38; Dale Eisler, "Gunning for the Grits," *MacLean's* 26 May 1997: 17.

137. Canadian Press and Southam Newspapers, "Gun control comes out of party holsters as day's issue," *Vancouver Sun* 22 May 1997: A3.

138. For an overview of voting behaviour in the 1997 election see, Jon H. Pammett, "The Voters Decide," Frizzell and Pammett 225-48. Not only was there little interest in gun control, the election itself did not attract much interest. Pammett notes that "[t]he lack of public interest in the 1997 election campaign is not only illustrated by the drop in the voting turnout rate... [i]t can [also] be seen... in the category of people who, when asked about the most important issue to them in the election said they did not know or that there was none." (236).

139. Greenspon 21-38.

140. *Securing Our Future Together: Preparing Canada for the 21st Century* (Ottawa: Liberal Party of Canada, 1997) 89.

141. Canadian Press and Southam Newspapers, "Gun control comes out of party holsters."

142. Greenspon 33.

143. Susan Delacourt, "Charest supports appeal to right," *Globe and Mail* 5 May 1997: A8; Murray Campbell, "Gun control triggers emotions," *Globe and Mail* 23 May 1997: A6.

144. Greenspon 34.

145. The Liberals only managed to elect two MPs out of a possible 26 in Alberta. The Reform Party captured the remaining 24 seats.

146. Sheldon Alberts, "McLellan sticks to guns," *Calgary Herald* 12 June 1997: A3.

147. Alberta was supported by the governments of the provinces of Ontario, Saskatchewan, Manitoba, the Yukon, and NWT. Alberta was also aided by two non-governmental interveners, the Shooting Federation of Canada and the Alberta Fish and Game

Association. On the other side, supporting the federal government as interveners, was the Coalition for Gun Control, the Canadian Association of Chiefs of Police, and the Alberta Council of Women's Shelters.

148. See, for example, Chris Cobb, "Provinces take legal shot at federal *Firearms Act*," *Vancouver Sun* 8 September 1997: A3; Eoin Kenny, "Gun control said lost if ruling is negative," *Globe and Mail* 12 September 1997: A4; Brian Laghi, "Existing gun laws at risk, court told," *Globe and Mail* 11 September 1997; Don Martin, "Alberta's challenge doomed," *Calgary Herald* 10 September 1997: A19.

149. 164 *Dominion Law Review* (4th), 1998: 513.

150. Chief Justice Fraser, who supported the constitutionality of the Act, summarized the majority opinion: "I regard the pith and substance of the licencing and registration provisions as being to protect public safety from the misuse of ordinary firearms, whether in crime or otherwise. In fact, it seems to me that effective gun control is doomed to failure without some proactive, preventative means of licencing and registering *all* firearms. Only upon knowing who has what guns will it be possible to reduce the likelihood that guns will be misused, whether criminally or otherwise... [Therefore,] this legislation [is] squarely within Parliament's criminal law power."164 DLR: 598-601; emphasis in original.

151. *Reference re Firearms Act* (Can.) [2000] 1 SCR: 783.

152. *Reference re Firearms Act* 791, 810.

153. *Reference re Firearms Act* 815.

154. Chris Cobb, "Don't go off half-cocked, gun lobbyists warned: Organizers expect 20,000 at tomorrow's Parliament Hill rally," *Montreal Gazette* 21 September 1998: A7. In an attempt to rehabilitate the image of those opposed to the Firearms Act, participants were given explicit instructions not to drink or take drugs prior to the rally, to dress respectfully (no military camouflage or hunter's orange), and to be polite to reporters and tolerant of those who addressed the crowd in a language other than English.

155. George Koch, "Gun registration could take 233 years, Reform MP claims," *National Post* 7 April 1999: A4.

156. Jonathon Gatehouse, "Bureaucracy multiplies at gun registry," *National Post* 20 May 1999: A7. This number did not include firearms bureaucrats in Québec, as that province had chosen to administer the registry provincially, rather than let the federal government run the program.

157. Lorne Gunter, "Fiddling gun-registry figures," *Montreal Gazette* 25 June 1999: B3.

158. Gunter. Concern about low participation in the program had led the CFC to include all previously registered handguns (which were required to be registered starting in 1934); a total of 1.2 million handguns had already been registered well in advance of the Firearms Act. To further push ownership licence numbers up, the CFC also included all those who had a valid FAC under the old system despite the fact that they were required to re-licence themselves under the new act. These statistical shenanigans were very detrimental to the registry process and increased suspicions and mistrust among many already cynical gun owners.

159. Norm Ovenden, "Gun groups aiming at killing arms laws," *Edmonton Journal* 7 September 2000: A6.

160. Ovenden, "Gun groups aiming at killing arms laws."

161. The December 2002 report of the Auditor-General is available on-line at www. oag-bvg.gc.ca.

162. In her report, Fraser stated that "[t]he Department of Justice Canada did not provide Parliament with sufficient information to allow it to effectively scrutinize the Canadian Firearms Program and ensure accountability. It provided little financial information and insufficient explanations for the dramatic increase in the cost of the Program." The Report of the Auditor-General, December 2002, is available at www. oag-bvg.gc.ca.

163. Tim Naumetz, "Liberal MPs tow [sic] line, give $59 million to gun registry," *Ottawa Citizen* 26 March 2003.

CHAPTER TWO

Air Farce: Airline Policy in a Deregulatory Environment

ROBERT M. CAMPBELL, LESLIE A. PAL, AND ANDREA MIGONE

If people want to throw insults at me, cream pies at me, whatever they
want to throw at me, they can throw them at me because I believe in
what we are doing and I am committed to what we are doing.
Air Canada CEO, Robert Milton[1]

My exposure to motor racing makes me aware that no
race is won in the first four laps, but many are lost.
Canadian Airlines CEO, Kevin Benson[2]

Airline policy presents an opportunity to analyze a quintessentially Canadian issue. It offers a view of regional politics by opposing, as it does, western and eastern Canadian interests, by showcasing the Canadian need to carefully balance them all in a seemingly endless juggling game. It provides an analysis of federal policy-making within the context of deregulation and, therefore, an opportunity to gauge Ottawa's commitment to carry on with unpopular reforms. At the same time as it tackles domestic industrial and labour issues (many of which reflect provincial interests and concerns), it also deals with global trends and international agreements. Finally, it showcases a host of type-A personalities, a common sight in Canadian policy-making, as they deal with the highly symbolic issue of what to do with national airlines.

The analysis of Canadian airline policy over the past two decades yields the image of federal authorities consistently sticking to a regime of deregulation, mitigated by some key expectations regarding competition, safety, and consumer protection. These are goals that the airlines, now individuated as the primary actors in the sector, must achieve on their own because Ottawa refuses to intervene directly in all but the most extreme situations. Policy direction replaced policy intervention. Deregulation and privatization became the decisive influences in the sector, but the result was price wars and cutthroat competition between the two major national airlines: Air Canada, headquartered in Montreal, and Canadian Airlines, which was based in Calgary.

Nested within this conflict are a variety of issues: the split between eastern and western interests; the awkward, at times almost schizophrenic, policies that attempt to manage simultaneously national concerns and global economic pressure towards free-market solutions and deregulation; the limited role played by the provinces in a sector whose economic impact is disproportionately provincial; and the periodic appearance of courts and regulatory bodies, which achieve little more than to slow down and depoliticize the process.

These issues unfolded over many years, and a select chronology is offered at the end of this chapter, but, in the end, the result was the predictable collapse of Canadian Airlines. This pyrrhic victory left Air Canada so weakened that it had to file for bankruptcy on 1 April 2003. The company's future is unclear as management and personnel still fight courageously to get back on their feet, but the cycle seems poised to repeat itself as new low-fare options, like WestJet, begin to seriously challenge some of Air Canada's market segments. One wonders if absolute domination of the national market is a viable strategy not only for Air Canada, but also for consumers and workers, and what if anything the federal government will do if another round of bitter price competition begins. Ottawa appears unfazed by the vicissitudes of the airline industry over the past 15 years and is unlikely to abandon its commitment to market solutions, which have proven stronger even than the long-standing preference for a two-airlines policy.

In this chapter we explore the struggle that, over the past 20 years, has been the major factor in airline policy development in Canada. Beginning in the mid-1980s, the policies and assumptions that had dictated airline legislation and practices began to change dramatically all over the world. Deregulation, privatization, globalization, sector alliances and mergers, the emergence of new markets, the two wars in Iraq, and the events of September 11, 2001 all impacted on the way airlines conduct their business and on the very viability of strong regulation in the industry.

The always-burdensome demands imposed on entrepreneurship and political direction by airline policy everywhere in the world was magnified in the Canadian context by national issues. Not only was the nature and scope of the sector being redesigned, first by the privatization of Air Canada in 1988 and then by the progressive deregulation of the following decade, and not only was the industry subject to the vagaries of an ever more interconnected world, but Canada also faced specific challenges of its own. The Canadian market is, by comparison to most national airline markets in the industrial world, relatively small, and it suffers from obvious regional rivalries as traffic clusters around two major regional hubs—Toronto-Montreal-Ottawa and Vancouver-Edmonton-Calgary. This has fostered a regional rivalry epitomized in the long-drawn, bloody battle between Air Canada and Canadian Airlines.

While the economic spillovers of increased business or corporate failure impacted most dramatically on the provinces, regulative and legislative power are entrenched in, and firmly held by, the federal level. All along, Ottawa's strategy has been to ensure that deregulation and a market approach were implemented along with some core elements of competition and consumer protection. Direct intervention in the sector, as noted above, was replaced with policy direction: ultimate policy goals were stated, but the choice regarding the means to achieve them was left to the industry.

In a nutshell, this chapter deals with the adaptive abilities of the airline industry to face rapidly changing economic and regulative environments. The great bulk of the story revolves around the struggle between Air Canada and Canadian Airlines. These two dominated the Canadian market but could not have been further apart from one another. Canadian Airlines symbolized western pride and business values; Air Canada was still commonly associated with government monopoly and the Ontario-Quebec region. Both companies believed that, in the new deregulated market, only one of them could achieve a dominant position, the only position that could assure them of continued viability and profits; because of this, they ultimately designed their strategies to dispose of their competition.

The means to this end were simple: increasing capacity and cutting fares. This was an extension of the policies that all airlines had followed in the 1980s. The obvious issue with such a strategy is that it puts enormous stress on whoever applies it. Federal authorities were faced with just as complicated a task: keeping to their policy plan for deregulation and market approach while balancing western and eastern Canadian concerns; assuring continued employment without overtly subsidizing either company; protecting competition by having, for as long as possible, two major airlines in the country; and keeping it all under a more-or-less coherent-looking policy framework.

By the early 1990s both companies were already in financial trouble with Canadian Airlines bleeding more profusely and faster than its Montreal rival. Ottawa refused to bail either out and stuck to its market approach. It would have preferred to see the two airlines share the Canadian market, so as to keep competition going, but if the situation kept deteriorating, it was ready to consider a merger between the two. Air Canada's President, Hollis Harris, had proposed this option all along, but Canadian Airlines was looking for an injection of cash from American Airlines to keep afloat. The two companies kept skirmishing over options, and the Conservative government in Ottawa kept to the sidelines, always repeating its market approach mantra. As Canadian's economic situation approached the brink of disaster, Ottawa's stance appeared to be favouring Air Canada. What some critics could generally describe as lack of political direction from the nation's capital, others could as easily label as a deliberate effort to crush Air Canada's western competitor.

Early in the summer of 1992 Canadian Airlines' management turned down a heavy-handed attempt at merger from Air Canada; however, its own attempt at reaching an agreement with American Airlines failed too, and it was forced back to the table to negotiate a possible merger with its Canadian rival. It was not to be. Ottawa, from whence strong pressure had been exerted to solve the financial crisis of the two companies through a merger, was faced with mounting critiques, continued resistance from Canadian's management and personnel (the latter had even come up with a workable financial rescue plan for their company), and a new offer from American Airlines. In the end, the federal government relaxed its stance, and Canadian got back on its feet. This brief summary of those early years is deceptive in its simplicity. Throughout this period, there were continuous court battles, acrimonious statements from federal and provincial politicians, and consistent finger pointing. In the end, the courts had little real impact on the process, except for progressively depoliticizing the issue and slowing down attempts at solution.

One can understand perhaps the predicament in which Ottawa found itself, but not excuse it. Yes, this was a Catch-22 situation; yes, it was impossible to please everyone involved; yes, some of the reactions from the main actors were overblown, and both companies should have been held accountable for their business decisions. Nevertheless, the Conservative policy was, in that particular situation, half-hearted at best.

This double dilemma in which the Mulroney government found itself—East versus West, competitiveness versus nationalism—was Ottawa's responsibility alone, as it "enjoyed" exclusive jurisdiction in this area.[3] The dilemma was neatly captured in a statement by Alan Redway, a colleague of Transportation Minister Jean Corbeil:

> Pity the poor Minister of Transport. If he lets American Airlines buy an investment in Canadian Airlines International, he will be accused of allowing foreigners to get control of our skies … and putting Air Canada in jeopardy.
>
> On the other hand, if he does not let American buy an interest in Canadian, and encourages a merger of Canadian and Air Canada, he will be accused of creating job losses at Canadian and eliminating competition. Then, if either Air Canada or Canadian should ask for financial help, he will be accused of subsidizing business and encouraging inefficiency.[4]

This was a policy case that demanded adroit political leadership and assertive action. But in letting market forces determine the outcome, the Conservative government appeared to be behaving in an irresponsible way, concerned more about political and electoral considerations than about the health of the industry. It tried to do and say as little as possible, lest it alienate the considerable and passionate forces on either side and upset the delicate electoral balance it had forged between western Canada and Quebec in the 1984 and 1988 elections. To media and industry experts, Air Canada, Canadian, and the opposition parties, this seemed to be a case of policy procrastination and ostrich-like behaviour.

In 1993 a Liberal government took over from Brian Mulroney's Progressive Conservative party. The airline policy framework did not change: Ottawa was still committed to deregulation, competition, and a market approach. At the same time, both Air Canada and Canadian Airlines were moving to gain new markets through which they hoped to stem the losses accruing from the competition in which they were locked. For both companies this meant looking at expanding their presence in Europe, Asia, and the US. The 24 February 1995 Open Skies agreement signed with the US and open access to Japan and Hong Kong all played into this strategy; at the same time, new discount carriers like WestJet were undermining the position of the two larger airlines. On balance, though, the price war was crushing Canadian Airlines, which had "shallower pockets" and was, perhaps, not as well managed as its rival. In 1996, the Calgary company went through a massive management restructuring as Kevin Benson, its former Chief Financial Officer (CFO), became president, and key American Airline personnel were transferred to Alberta to try and salvage the situation. The short-term effects were positive, but they could not change the reality of Canadian's position, and, when management asked for more sacrifices from its employees, the Canadian Autoworkers Union (CAW) mounted a bitter struggle against further firings, wage cuts, and increased workloads. Ottawa, through Transport Minister David Anderson, refused to be dragged into what it called a business situation. Little financial help was forthcoming from the federal government and what was offered generally carried very heavy conditions. Whatever rescue could be mustered came from the provinces of Alberta and British Columbia (BC) where most of the negative impact of lost jobs and business would be felt.

Eventually, the CAW had to go back to the negotiating table and agree, in an eleventh-hour meeting, to large concessions; the airline had to make do with whatever cash it could get, but its planes, for a time, kept on flying. The federal government stuck to its hands-off approach and let the airlines sort out their issues as long as a reasonable degree of competition was assured and no monstrous loss of jobs could be directly attributed to Ottawa's policy. By 1999, Canadian's situation was desperate again, and, sensing that this time the company would not recover, both Gerry Schwartz's ONEX Corporation and Air Canada began to probe the ground to take over the beleaguered airline. The ONEX bid appeared strong for a while but then got bogged down in political and economic issues, opening the way for Air Canada's merger offer. On 6 July 2000, Canadian Airlines became a fully owned subsidiary of its former rival. After over ten years of fierce struggle, intense price and route wars, failed international and domestic mergers and alliances, interventions by provincial and federal authorities and by the courts, Air Canada finally managed to impose its dominance on the Canadian airline sector.

Things seemed to be looking up: with its main competitor gone, profits on the rebound, and a reasonably buoyant US economy, the future of the company appeared to be positive. In April 2003, however, Air Canada filed for bankruptcy protection, proceeded to further reduce its workforce, and announced that it could not and would not honour the labour contracts it had negotiated barely 12 months earlier. The brutally aggressive policies of the 1990s, economic and political factors, high costs, and a good dose of sheer bad luck came together to cripple the airline. At the same time, the federal commitment to let the private sector solve its own problems seems to have, if not fostered, at least tacitly allowed a protracted slugging match between the two airlines that left both exhausted and vulnerable to the events of the turn of the century like the attacks of 9/11, and the SARS crisis.

Over the past two decades the federal government has been following an air transportation policy based on four pillars: (1) the careful liberalization of the domestic and international market to maximize the benefits of competition in terms of prices, service quality, and company competitiveness; (2) a commitment to the survival of at least one, but possibly two, major national carriers; (3) a shift away from direct policy intervention in the sector to policy direction; and (4) an attempt at maintaining some degree of balance and stability as far as regional and labour issues were concerned.

This approach might appear as almost schizophrenic to an outside observer: it created a mix of strong statements as to what type of intervention Ottawa would engage in if the airlines would not adhere to these principles voluntarily and of comments emphasizing the fact that the market, and not government, should be trusted to take care of business issues.

The end result was not at all a policy vacuum, but rather a set of general statements of principle and of specific concrete interventions that appear to have reshaped the policy style of the sector away from heavy government policy intervention and towards policy direction. However, the new "deregulatory" world of Canadian politics remained a world of politics, as the airlines case amply demonstrates. In this world moved not only the large players like Air Canada, but also a host of autonomous agencies, holding quasi-judicial powers and tasked with pursuing the public interest, like the National Transportation Agency and the Competition Tribunal, as well, of course, as the courts where Air Canada and Canadian launched a series of billion-dollar lawsuits against each other. It also failed to automatically create a competitive market, ultimately dooming Canadian's efforts to failure.

Our discussion opens with a brief historical review of the Canadian airline industry, an examination of its deregulation in the mid-1980s, and a summing up of post-deregulation developments. A presentation of the current state of the industry will set the stage for our analysis of the politics of airlines policy in Canada.

Background

To penetrate the dense world of airlines policy one needs to examine four contributing factors:

1. the historical background to the Canadian airline industry;

2. the deregulation of the airline industry in the mid-1980s;
3. the merger mania that ensued in the 1990s; and
4. the impact of recession, globalization, and the September 11 attacks on the industry.

1. Historical Background

Discussion of transportation policy is typically informed by Mackenzie King's wonderful aphorism, "If some countries have too much history, we have too much geography." Indeed, as Garth Stevenson writes, "The history of Canada is essentially the history of the conquest of distance and barriers by successively more effective and sophisticated forms of transportation."[5]

Canadian governments have traditionally played an active and considerable role in the world of transportation, and transportation policy has been structured in a traditional process. A minister heads the Department of Transportation, which was created in 1935 and first headed by the legendary C.D. Howe. It sets broad policy guidelines, implemented by a quasi-independent regulatory agency, originally the Canadian Transportation Commission (CTC) and, since 1988, the National Transportation Agency. Generally headed by powerful personalities, these agencies have had close relations with governments, and their chairs have enjoyed enormous authority.

Liberal electoral domination for the pre- and post-World War II era extended to domination of transportation policy. In the railroad era, politics was bifurcated by Liberal support of the state-run Canadian National Railway (CNR) while the Conservatives favoured the Canadian Pacific Railway (CPR). When airplane policy had to be developed (to link Canada's regions without relying on the US), C.D. Howe created a Crown corporation—Trans-Canada Airlines, the forerunner of Air Canada—because the Liberals distrusted the largest air company at the time, Canadian Pacific Airlines, in which the CPR had a financial interest. The Trans-Canada legislation stipulated that its shares were to be owned by CNR, although 49.8 per cent could be sold to the private sector. Instead of purchasing these shares (to form a CNR-CPR airline), CPR extended its investment to gain control of Canadian Pacific Airlines. Developments in the airline industry have subsequently been informed by partisan political and ideological differences. The Liberals favoured a state-led policy of airline regulation with Trans-Canada and then Air Canada, centred in Montreal, at the core. The Conservatives were partisans of the more entrepreneurially driven Canadian Pacific, headquartered in Vancouver and later Calgary.

For five decades, cabinet made the key strategic decisions that affected the airline industry. The situation in Canada was no different from that in most industrial countries. Governments, either directly, or indirectly through regulatory bodies, established a regulatory framework for the operation of the airline industry. Governments made basic policy decisions, including setting air fares, approving routes, and determining which airlines would be allowed to fly which routes. This regulatory approach was informed by a variety of policy goals, from concern for safety to protection of the domestic airline industry, from ensuring the existence of flights to remote areas to protecting against destabilizing booms and busts in an industry characterized by large investment needs. Most countries followed a policy of creating and protecting a national carrier or "champion," for reasons of security and national pride as well as to ensure their country's participation in an advanced industrial sector of the economy. Thus, governments set rigorous safety, financial, and national standards for entry into the market; protected much of the domestic market for their champions; and set prices fairly high even within very active and competitive markets to allow "cross-subsidization" of routes to remote areas. Perhaps the most critical area was the determination of which airline would fly which air routes, how often, and at what price. If Canadian Pacific wanted to schedule an inexpensive flight between Vancouver and Toronto, it first needed government approval for that flight at the proposed price. This was designed, ostensibly, to ensure that there would be a stable supply of air routes to all parts of the country and not an over-supply in dense urban markets.

This process favoured Trans-Canada, as cabinet assigned it the principal and most lucrative domestic routes. Government decisions established a pattern in the airline industry by the 1950s. Canadian Pacific became basically an international carrier with a strong domestic presence in the West; Trans-Canada dominated the domestic market in all corners with a strong European connection. However, increasing traffic, changing technology, rising incomes, and a public taste for competitive market choice saw Trans-Canada's (and later Air Canada's) privileged status weakened, even under Liberal political regimes. The decision to allow Canadian Pacific to fly from Vancouver to Montreal daily (and then twice daily), the "division of the world" policy (which assigned Canadian Pacific the Asian, Pacific, Latin American, and Southern and Eastern European markets), and the 25 per cent policy (which allowed Canadian Pacific to increase its capacity until it reached 25 per cent of the transcontinental total) elevated Canadian Pacific to near-equal status with Air Canada by the late 1970s. However, by this time, the airlines' boom years had ended and the energy crisis had hit. Airline expansion and profitability were less likely than in the past. Air Canada remained the larger and more profitable company in a relatively stagnant market.

2. Deregulation

A consumer price revolt against regulation of air fares and routes, as well as broad populist criticism of the state, set the stage for the "revolution" in airline policy in the late 1970s and early 1980s, particularly in the US. This revolution preceded the election of Ronald Reagan in 1980. The left-liberal Democratic administration of Jimmy Carter passed the Airline Deregulation Act in 1978, ending the practice whereby fares and the determination of services were determined by the regulatory arm of government. The Civil Aeronautics Board was disbanded, and by 1983 the American airline industry had been deregulated, leaving decisions on fares and routes to the market.

Deregulation of the Canadian airline industry soon followed, initiated by a left-Liberal government and completed by Mulroney's Conservatives. Re-evaluation of airlines policy culminated, in 1984, in the release of Transport Minister Lloyd Axworthy's position paper, "New Canadian Airline Policy." The paper contrasted Canada's regulatory past unfavourably with the ostensibly beneficial results of America's airline deregulation. The Liberals proposed to encourage any carrier to apply to fly on any route and to allow airlines to set their own fares. As Axworthy sparred with the CTC over implementing this policy, the Liberals lost the 1984 election. But the policy die had been cast.

The Liberals' deregulatory initiative fit comfortably with the Conservatives' agenda to cut back the state's role in the economy and increase private initiative and the role of the market in order to stimulate innovation, competitiveness, and growth. Over and above privatization of Crown corporations, tax reform, and deficit and spending cuts, the Conservative government planned to deregulate the economy and identified national transportation as one of its first targets for deregulation.[6] Transport Canada released a white paper entitled *Freedom to Move* that argued that the existing National Transportation Act (1967) had been designed to protect transportation industries to allow them to grow; now that the sector was mature, it was time to release it from regulation, which inhibited innovation and competitiveness.[7]

Bill C-18 was introduced in 1986. After extensive hearings (which attracted little public attention), the National Transportation Act was

I: The Legislative Context For Canadian Transportation Policy

1961: The MacPherson Commission report made the principle of competition between modes a central tenet of the National Transportation Act of 1967.

1967: National Transportation Act 1967.

1987: National Transportation Act 1987. First major revision of the sector's legislation. The principle of competition is now applied so as to require competition within modes and not just among different modes of transportation as in the 1967 legislation. Airline regulation was noticeably simplified with this act.

1993: Statutory review of the National Transportation Act by the National Transportation Act Review Commission. Particular attention was paid to legislative restrictions that impaired the ability of carriers to rationalize operations.

1996. Canada Transportation Act 1996. Introduced changes to the National Transportation Act 1987 and to the Railway Act. Changes again went in the direction of more deregulation and commercialization. Air travellers now had new consumer protections including the prohibition for airlines to sell tickets before obtaining licencing and a requirement that new carriers meet a minimal financial fitness test, while the 1987 licensing requirements for airlines operating in the far North were streamlined.

1999: Standing Committee on Transport. House of Commons produces *Restructuring Canada's Airline Industry: Fostering Competition and Protecting the Public Interest.*

2000: Amendments to the Canada Transportation Act 1996 (Bill C-26). These were spurred by the Air Canada/Canadian merger and addressed fare levels, market exit, and terms and conditions of carriage. The act now established the power to review airline acquisitions and mergers and instituted the office of the Travel Complaints Commissioner within the National Transportation Agency.

2002: Final Report of the Transportation Act Review Panel.

2002 APRIL: Publication of *Airline Restructuring in Canada: Third Interim Report.*

passed in August 1987 and came into effect in 1988. In his summary statement, Minister of Transportation John Crosbie pointed to two central features of the new transportation regime. First, it was to serve the needs of the customer, not those of the industry. Second, "competition and market forces [are to be] the prime agents in providing for or spurring on viable and effective transportation systems," not regulation or government.[8] The legislation provided for complete freedom for airlines to enter or exit any domestic market and to set fares at levels of their choosing. Previously, airlines had to demonstrate "public convenience and necessity" to the CTC when proposing to establish a new route, which criterion had been used to limit entry and restrict competition. Airlines would now have to demonstrate only that they were "fit, willing, and able" to provide the service.

There would be no conditions on offering service; no route, destination, or flight schedule conditions; no regulation of fares or direction to use particular equipment. Discontinuing a route would simply require 100 days' notice and no explanation.

Bill C-18 replaced the CTC with the National Transportation Agency (NTA) as the government's "referee" of Canadian transportation. It was to be more flexible, market-oriented, and "passive," reflecting the government's philosophy of "smarter," market-sensitive regulation. The NTA was directed to take action only when cases were brought to it, such as mergers and acquisitions. It was to be guided by the central principle that the transportation system was to be shaped and driven by market and competitive forces.

Crosbie maintained that these measures were more responsible than the previous regulatory regime. The government would set transportation policy and be held accountable for it: "We will not slough off responsibility to someone else."[9] The government hoped that deregulation of transportation would result in more market players, competition, innovation, lower costs, and better services. Under political pressure, though, the government amended the legislation to include regional economic development as a formal goal of transportation policy.

Bill C-18 had intended and unintended consequences; these cannot be analyzed in any detail here but, as determined by the legislation, a National Transportation Act Review Commission was established and gave its report in early 1993.[10] It reported that flights were more frequent, prices were lower, and that the quality of service had increased.

3. Merger Mania

In these years, perhaps the most dramatic result of deregulation was the reduction in the number of airlines. The major carriers responded to the new competitive environment by buying out small and regional carriers and their competitors. This led to the emergence of Pacific Western Airlines (PWA) as the rival of Air Canada. Founded by a bush pilot in northern BC in 1946, Calgary-based PWA had, by the mid-1960s, become Canada's third-largest carrier. The Alberta government bought it in 1974 as part of its "province-building" battles with Ottawa and eastern business, but sold it to the public in 1983. It swallowed up CP Air (and its $600 million debt) in December 1986 for $300 million and bought out the bankrupt Wardair in early 1989. By the early 1990s Canada had two airline families: Air Canada and Canadian Airlines International, the latter owned by PWA.

II: Merger Mania 1986-1993

Air Canada

1987: Acquires 85 per cent of AirBB and merges with Austin Airways and Air Ontario to establish 75-per-cent-owned Air Ontario.

1988: Fills gap in its connector network by taking a 75 per cent stake in the newly created Air Alliance and by acquiring 90 per cent of NWT Air, and also by negotiating a commercial and code-sharing agreement with Air Toronto.

1989: Buys remaining 10 per cent of NWT Air.

1991: Purchases the remaining 51 per cent of Air Nova and creates Air Canada Regional Airline Holdings to manage its regional airline investments.

1992: Announces commercial alliances with United Airlines and Air France and boosts its stake in Continental Airlines.

Canadian Airlines

1986: PWA buys CP Air.

1987: PWA purchases 49 per cent of Ontario Express, 45 per cent stakes in Air Atlantic and Cam Air, 35 per cent of Inter-Canadien, and increases its holdings in Time Air to 46 per cent.

1990: PWA buys Wardair and later amalgamates it with Canadian; Inter-Canadien leaves PWA to form the independent carrier Intair; Frontier Air is purchased by Ontario Express.

1991: Frontier Air starts operating as a Canadian partner. PWA creates Canadian regional Airlines Ltd. to consolidate management of its affiliates and purchases the remaining shares of Time Air and Ontario Express; Canadian Regional purchases 70 per cent of Intair's turbo-prop operations and re-establishes Inter-Canadien as a Quebec affiliate; Ontario Court of Appeal approves the sale of Air Toronto to Ontario Express.

1992: Strikes alliance with American Airlines.

Source: National Transportation Agency, Annual Review, 1991, 1992

Their intense rivalry reflected both competitive realities and their different corporate cultures and backgrounds.

Despite the emergence of this industrial concentration, in 1993 the National Transportation Act Review Commission concluded that

> We are unable to find situations in which the country, overall, may been better with the previous regulatory framework ... the regulatory reforms have been successful in achieving their established objectives.

> The withdrawal of government from direct management of the transportation section, and from the business of balancing economic interests through regulation, is a timely and appropriate policy.[11]

Whatever the appropriateness of the broad policy regime, the Canadian airline industry threatened to bleed to death by the early 1990s. In 1992, Air Canada and Canadian were jointly losing over $1.5 million *a day*. Their combined losses in 1991 and 1992 were around $1.5 billion, and mergers and acquisitions had saddled them with enormous long-term debt.[12] Political opponents blamed deregulation and destructive competition, while deregulation supporters like the National Transportation Act Review Commission blamed the airlines themselves: "We do conclude that their difficulties were largely a product of the carriers' decisions and not unique to a market which had recently been deregulated."[13] The fact was that the entire global airline sector was experiencing intense difficulties and undergoing wide-ranging changes.[14]

4. The Impact of Recession, Globalization, and the September 11 Attacks

The industry was enormous, its 800 carriers employing more than 3 million people, flying 9,000 jets and thousands more turboprops from 14,000 airports, carrying 125 billion people and 22 million tons of freight. Its most recent troubles started with the Gulf War, when passenger travel dropped by one-third. Next, the early 1990s recession arrived, and, as a cyclically sensitive industry, airline activity dropped. Airlines lost $4.8 billion on their international services alone in 1992 (the US carriers lost $5 billion on their domestic services). Never very profitable to begin with, the sector saw the first three years of the 1990s wipe out all of its 1980s profits. Airlines cut prices to increase the number of passengers and to get in position for the economic recovery. But this move drained cash at an alarming rate and pushed them to the financial wall. This situation was exacerbated by their megadebt—a function of their airplane purchases in the boom 1980s. A new Boeing 747 cost around $150 million, and airlines bought planes by the basket during that decade: jet-airline orders totalled $330 billion between 1985 and 1990. Since there were no passengers to fill these planes, many of them were parked in the desert. Interest charges bankrupted legendary companies like Eastern Airlines and Pan Am.

Excess capacity still haunts the industry, but increasing international competition is an equal concern. As in other sectors of the economy, it has become impossible for a national airline to survive unless it is internationally competitive and has a strong international presence. Over and above competitive price and service considerations, domestic airlines must be capable of providing integrated travel connections from continent to continent. In Canada the 1990s hailed the "Open Skies" agreement with the US, which allowed the carriers of the two nations to fly directly into each other's cities, and a number of bilateral agreements with other nations were also concluded. These steps were all aimed at increasing the degree of liberalization of the domestic market.

As the air industry becomes increasingly deregulated, airlines can conceivably establish a presence in each domestic market, but this would be very expensive. So national airlines look to partners in other countries to provide these connections in the most price-competitive way. This has pushed airline companies into elaborate international partnerships to gain economies of scale as well as for fear of being left behind. A typical industrial scenario was Scandinavian Airlines teaming up with KLM (with its share in Northwest), Swissair (and its share in Delta and Singapore Air), and Austrian to compete against megacarriers like British Airways, which has deals with smaller, lively airlines like Deutsche BA, Qantas, France's TAT, and US Air. The top 20 airlines' share of passenger miles was 47 per cent in 1981 and rose to 60 per cent in 1992. In 2001 the share of the four largest airline alliances (Star Alliance, Oneworld, Sky Team, and KLM/Northwest)[15] was 60 per cent; the top ten airlines held 73 per cent. Competition, rising costs, and changing consumer patterns also saw airlines search for new sources of equity investment, thereby encouraging a further internationalization of the industry.

Summary

To sum up, four major factors shaped airlines policy in Canada in the 1990s:

1. The Canadian airline industry had basically been a competitive and antagonistic duopoly, with one carrier (Air Canada) situated in eastern Canada and supported by the Liberals and the other (PWA) situated in western Canada and favoured by the Conservatives. Neither enjoyed a particular healthy financial position.

2. After deregulation, the airline industry was marked by intense market competition, and the government adhered to a hands-off policy, refraining from direct policy intervention but still voicing the principles it considered necessary for the healthy development of the sector.

3. Merger mania in the 1980s led both to the reduction in the number of airlines and a spiraling increase in costs as smaller companies were acquired by larger ones.

4. The airline industry has been influenced by globalization pressures and has endured intense financial difficulty and rapid internationalization or conglomeration.

Airline Policy in the 1990s

In 1991 Canadian Airlines and Air Canada had such a dismal year that airline policy was thrust back on to the political agenda. Their combined losses totaled $400 million, and they eliminated 2,200 jobs. Transport Minister Corbeil commented that this was "not pleasant," but he attributed job loss to "the difficulty that exists in the airline industry around the world." As the two airlines teetered on the brink of oblivion, Corbeil sketched out the two basic policy scenarios that played out—back and forth and again—over the next two years: "It is preferable for the consumers to have two airlines, but if the survival of the two requires a merger, we are ready to discuss it."[16] Thus, the government's opening policy position was "competition if possible, but not necessarily competition; a merger if necessary, but not necessarily a merger." This did not change in the next two years, during which time the government did not take an interventionist or activist role. It let the airlines themselves take policy initiatives in the deregulated market-oriented world.

The first option, the merger option, predominated in early 1992. Air Canada's new president—Hollis Harris, a top gun recruited from Delta and Continental Airlines—unleashed a barrage of tough measures to deal with Air Canada's deficit: the *enRoute* credit card system was sold to Citibank; the airline's fleet of five DC-8 freighters was put up for sale; and 10 per cent of management and 5 per cent of its administration, for a total of 9 per cent of its work force, were cut (accounting for the loss of 1,800 jobs).[17] Moreover, Air Canada took dead aim on the conquest of Canadian. It first increased its own capacity by 10 per cent to force Canadian to match its challenge and cut prices; it then aggressively marketed the idea of a "Made in Canada" solution, one that did not require American involvement and so implied a merger between Air Canada and Canadian.

It hired super-lobbyist William Neville, former head of Prime Minister Joe Clark's staff and the front man for various lobbies, including the tobacco industry. "I believe that the problems of the airlines should be solved within Canada," declared Neville as Air Canada released a Decima poll indicating that 85 per cent of Canadians favoured a merger rather than an American takeover. "Few countries have more than one airline," observed Air Canada's Chair, Claude Taylor; "With one larger airline Canada would have a stronger presence globally."[18] The day after he became president, Harris asserted that there was room for only one airline in Canada. Air Canada made two offers to purchase Canadian, both rejected in mid-March. In one Air Canada offered to buy Canadian's international routes, including the Japanese route that Air Canada desperately wanted for an Asian initiative (this offer would have left Canadian a domestic carrier). In the other, Air Canada proposed a merger, with it in the dominant position.[19]

Canadian slammed Air Canada's efforts to lobby Ottawa to halt its attempts to find an international investor, and it accused Air Canada of "dirty tricks" and predatory pricing in an effort to bankrupt Canadian. Characterizing the fare war as "economic insanity" and "economic irresponsibility," PWA president Rhys Eyton asserted that "it's either an effort to try to push us to the wall or to grab more market share," and "the market's not there." He accused Harris of being "an old gunslinger out of the American West."[20]

PWA pursued the second option instead—an injection of foreign equity into the domestic industry. In March 1992 PWA called off Air Canada merger talks and signed an agreement to enter into exclusive negotiations with American Airlines, a deal it had cultivated for a while. This brought an immediate negative reaction from Air Canada. Harris, just as his company was itself negotiating an alliance with US Air, insisted that a Canadian/American deal "could force both national carriers eventually to integrate with the existing United States system." Air Canada declared that it would object to any deal in front of the NTA, insisting that even a 25 per cent investment by American—the legal limit on foreign ownership—would shift control of the company south of the border.[21]

These preliminary skirmishes revealed a number of realities surrounding airlines policy. First, both airlines were in trouble and the status quo was not a viable policy option. Second, the two companies simply did not like each other and it appeared that a policy "consensus" between them would be difficult to engineer. Third, the politics of the situation comprised simple but powerful symbolic themes that the players were in a position to exploit in any number of directions. In a rare debate over the government's alleged abandoning of Canada's transportation system, talk about a merger rang a monopoly alarm bell while talk of foreign equity rang the Americanization one.[22] Lastly, it became clear that the government was not going to intervene in what was, in narrow terms at least, a private-sector matter. While the opposition charged political neglect and policy irresponsibility, the government tolerated Air Canada's hyper-aggressive and potentially destructive initiatives on capacity and fares. The choice between the merger and foreign investment option brought an apparently indifferent response from Corbeil: "We will look at any proposal that will ensure that we maintain a viable, efficient and secure airline industry in Canada."[23]

1992: From Merger to Merger

Political posturing and debates moved from the hypothetical to the actual in the spring of 1992 when PWA announced that a 25 per cent American investment deal in Canadian was near completion.[24] The opposition pounced quickly, asserting that American's presence would totally transform the Canadian industry. It accused the government of burying its head in the sand and demanded political leadership in decisions concerning airlines industry development: "This government and its members play their fiddle while vital Canadian interests are at risk." But Transport Minister Corbeil was unmoved and continued to play a market tune: "The people who are the most concerned about the survival of the airline industry are the airline companies themselves. They certainly know what is best for them in the future, and if they have any plans to ask for changes in the present laws they will apply to us." The government maintained that the Canadian/American initiative was none of its business; it was a market matter, for the market to sort out.

As Minister of State (Transport) Shirley Martin put it, "The airlines are private companies ... they are making private decisions. We as a government will work with them as best we can to make sure we have a healthy industry."[25] As the House of Commons was about to break for its summer recess, hundreds of Air Canada workers marched on Parliament protesting the impending job losses they alleged would result if the American/Canadian deal was allowed to proceed.[26] Despite criticism from Air Canada and nationalists, momentum built for the "international option." In a global environment that seemed to propel airlines into international alliances, both Air Canada and Canadian were seeking international partners.[27] Air Canada itself had tried to join forces with US Air but had been beaten to the punch by British Airways in July and so switched its attention towards

III: Gemini

A computer reservation system (CRS) has three distinct components:

- the internal reservation system, which lists a seat inventory, seats sold and available, prices, and other passenger information. An airline has its reservation system "hosted" in a CRS and can run continuous data checks to adjust prices on seats according to supply and demand;
- the distribution system, consisting of a network of telecommunications equipment and computer terminals, linking the CRS and travel agents;
- the computer software and switching systems, required to receive travel agents' requests, interface with various databases, assemble information, provide alternatives, and register bookings. They also access railway and bus schedules, hotel availability, and car rental.

The CRS system receives basic fees for hosting an airline schedule and a transaction fee from all the bookers. Terminals are leased to travel agents, who are given discounts geared to the amount of business they generate. The CRS is extremely lucrative; revenues in Europe and North American amount to billions of dollars.

A CRS is extremely expensive to develop, requiring huge front-end costs, which limits systems use to big market players alone. Systems have been consolidated to cut costs and exploit economies of scale. There are presently five megasystems: Galileo (which actually combines Gemini and the Covia system), Sabre, Worldspan, Amadeus, and SystemONE.

Daunted by the costs of updating their obsolete systems, Canadian and Air Canada joined forces with United Airlines to form Gemini. This CRS has access to 200 airlines through its links to Apollo and the European Galileo system. It provides hosting service for VIA Rail. Gemini is the largest CRS in the world; in Canada, it provides a national telecommunications network with its hub in Winnipeg.

a bid for the bankrupt Continental Airlines, the fifth-largest carrier in the US. But this deal was by no means certain, and Air Canada faced the prospect of competing with a stronger Canadian Airlines.[28]

On 25 July PWA's deal with American also fell through, and the Calgary airline announced that it would begin merger talks with the hated Air Canada. In both these developments it appeared that the federal government played an active role.

The deal with American had been all but concluded by early July and a signing date of 30 July had been tentatively set.[29] This had been put off for a fortnight in the face of American's final negotiating demands, including requests that Canadian's bank loans be renegotiated, that its unions accept a wage freeze, and that Canadian withdraw from its computer reservation system (Gemini) and join American's system (Sabre). The most pressing problem at the time was that American asked PWA to come up with an extra $195 million in bridging finance. PWA had little cash reserves, carried a colossal debt load, and was perilously close to bankruptcy.

In mid-July, a number of PWA board members went, quite literally, knocking on Finance Minister Mazankowski's door, asking for financial help in closing the American deal. They met at his hometown of Vegreville, Alberta, placing a symbolic "western" spin on the issue. An alarmed Mazankowski phoned Prime Minister Mulroney the next morning to report how bad PWA's situation appeared to be. A well-attended summit was held in Calgary a few days later, on 21 July. On the federal side Mazankowski's Deputy Minister, Fred Gorbet, and Corbeil's deputy, Huguette Labelle, came from Ottawa. Three provincial governments sent representatives: BC (Finance Minister Glen Clark; his deputy, Michael Costello; and Wilson Parasiuk, head of the BC Trade Development Corporation), Alberta (Treasurer Dick Johnston and his deputy, Alistair MacPherson), and Ontario (the deputy ministers of the Treasury and Industry Departments, Eleanor Clitheroe and Tim Armstrong). Finally PWA was represented by Rhys Eyton, Canadian Pacific chair William Stinson, and board member Ron Southern.

Southern categorized PWA's financial situation in the direst possible terms and concluded that bankruptcy could be expected within months, if not weeks. The governments were asked to put together a financial aid package comprising $150 million in loan guarantees (to have cash available to close the American deal) and $195 million in government guarantees for a proposed share issue.

The next day, Mazankowski presented Prime Minister Mulroney with two scenarios: PWA bankruptcy or a merger with Air Canada. Ottawa decided to turn down the PWA overture and pursue the merger. The matter was handed over to Glen Shortcliffe, the new clerk of the Privy Council Office and one of the most feared bureaucrats in Ottawa (he had been nicknamed "The Enforcer" and "The Prince of Darkness"). Shortcliffe phoned Eyton with Ottawa's counterproposal: the government would provide a cash injection by purchasing three surplus A310 planes. But this purchase appeared to require that PWA break off talks with American and begin merger talks with Air Canada. Air Canada chair Claude Taylor sat in the room with Shortcliffe during the call, and Eyton was asked if he wanted to begin then and there. A stunned and livid Eyton declined the offer.

Why did the government choose not to support PWA financially in its efforts to merge with American? After all, there were a substantial number of jobs at stake (a merger with Air Canada would involve an estimated 1,000 job cuts), PWA was a central presence in the western economy, and its continued viability would ensure domestic airline competition. Ottawa's decision was a complex matrix of factors. The first was its continuing commitment to stay out of the market process. As Mazankowski put it, "These are two private organizations and we had expected that the negotiations that Canadian was having with [American] would have been on a straight commercial basis."[30] Once this deal required public support, Ottawa backed off. Second, a split in the PWA board between optimists like Rhys Eyton and pessimists like Ron Southern who looked for a quick, simple solution in a merger with Air Canada, confused federal officials and forced Ottawa to make its own assessment of what was best for PWA.[31] Third, the British Airways and US Air alliance made Ottawa concerned that the Montreal-based Air Canada would be left isolated and exposed, which raised the Quebec issue. The Minister of National Defence, Marcel Masse, a strong Quebec nationalist, argued that his department's purchase of the three A310s should be made contingent on PWA's allying with Air Canada and not with American. A Transport Department official noted that "as soon as the future looked hazier for Air Canada, the word went out to deny Canadian. This was dictated by political forces, not commercial realities."[32]

Generally, the provincial reaction was that, since Ottawa had created the airlines mess, it should provide the solution.[33] The Alberta government had been embarrassed by a number of spectacular fiascos in public enterprise and support of high-tech initiatives. Premier Don Getty declared, "The thought of just going in on some kind of blanket situation, I couldn't find acceptable."[34] Also, despite the fact that PWA was headquartered in Calgary, there were far more Canadian jobs in BC, where Canadian provided 6,000 direct jobs, than in Alberta (a fact pointed out by Getty).[35]

Without the backing of Ottawa and the provinces, PWA really had no choice but to abandon the talks with American: it had insufficient cash and equity to close the deal. Its board met on 25 July and made the inevitable decision, over the wishes of its chair, Eyton, and its president, Kevin Jenkins.[36] The decision was announced on 27 July: merger talks would begin with Air Canada.

The government was quietly noncommittal in reacting to Canadian's cancellation of its American talks and the reopening of merger talks with Air Canada. Corbeil continued to declare that the government would stay out of the talks and hoped for a private-sector solution to the problems of the airline industry.[37] But it was not Corbeil, the sixth Conservative transport minister in eight years, who emerged as the key government player in the airlines area. It was Finance Minister Don Mazankowski. His was the most significant pronouncement when the Canadian/American talks were called off; he offered that "the only other option is a merger" with Air Canada.[38]

Mazankowski was a westerner with a record of looking after western interests. Canadian had deep roots in western Canada, where it had become a symbol of the "New West." Its image was more entrepreneurial and anti-establishment than that of Air Canada (which was perceived as a tool of central Canadian government) and had, by the 1990s, acquired a substantial presence in, and was well connected to, the western business establishment. Its board comprised the elite of western Canadian business, including former Alberta Premier Peter Lougheed; Ron Southern, Chief Executive Officer (CEO) of Atco Ltd.; William Stinson, chair and CEO of Canadian Pacific; Herbert Pinder Jr., a director of Royal Bank and John Labatt Co.; and Roderick McDaniel, long-time friend of Lougheed and top Tory fundraiser. The PWA board felt that they had a natural ally in Mazankowski.[39] But politics in Canada comprises a small world: although Mazankowski was a westerner, he also had strong ties with Air Canada. He was a close personal friend of its chair, Claude Taylor, with whom he shared deep Baptist religious convictions. He was also a tennis partner of Hugh Riopelle, Air Canada's Ottawa-based lobbyist.

Both sides hired high-powered consultants whose job it was to ensure that the lobbying impact of their client was maximized.[40]

PWA officials reacted bitterly when the government and Mazankowski seemed to favour Air Canada and the merger option, with all of this option's employment, economic, and psychological consequences for western Canada. They grumbled publicly that the Air Canada merger had been forced on them against their wishes, that cabinet had forced a pro-Quebec and anti-West solution.[41] Many westerners also felt that the airline deal was being used as a chip in constitutional bargaining. Jobs loomed large, with a disproportionate number of Canadian and Air Canada jobs—and the headquarters and offices of each—situated in western Canada and Quebec, respectively. The Alberta government, which had earlier declined to help PWA financially, waded in and declared that it might block the merger; Treasurer Dick Johnston claimed that the provincial legislation under which PWA functioned disallowed anyone from owning over 10 per cent of its shares.[42] The Alberta caucus intervened to denounce the merger as being bad for western Canada. "This is the most volatile issue that members have dealt with in a long time," stated caucus chair Ken Hughes; "it goes to the heart of western Canadian pride and aspirations." To quell a potential backbench revolt, Mazankowski and equally high-powered western ministers Harvie Andre and Joe Clark attended a caucus meeting, attempting to dispel the impression that the government and the bureaucracy had forced the Air Canada merger and insisting that the government was committed to a private-sector solution.[43]

These PWA-led grumblings generated a rare policy intervention from the prime minister, who feared political alienation in the West. "We got involved with the PWA thing at the request of PWA," Mulroney insisted, "and now in Alberta we've got people suggesting that we intervened to help Air Canada. I'm waiting for some of the directors of PWA to stand up in Alberta and indicate exactly what happened," to clear up the "falsehoods" about the government's role. The government did not favour any particular outcome, as long as it was a private-sector solution. "This was an outrage, a bloody outrage," Mulroney continued on a second day of complaints, "when [PWA] came knocking at our door asking for help rather than let the market decide. We were told that they were going under. The loss for PWA and Alberta would have been tremendous. We stepped in only to help." (It remained unclear what exactly this help involved.) "To have people in Alberta encouraged to believe that we would take an action to favour Quebec as opposed to Alberta in this thing is damaging in the extreme. It's false and it's damaging in the extreme. And it's cheap as hell." Despite the prime minister's entreaties, PWA officials did not speak out to clear the air.[44]

Thus, the policy pendulum had swung from the international (American Airlines) option to the domestic (merger) option. Opposition concerns then moved quickly from the Americanization theme to the monopolization theme, emphasizing its negative impact on consumer interests. Unions and the provinces feared job losses.[45] Pressured by its members—particularly from the West—the Standing Committee on Consumer and Corporate Affairs held two days of hearings.[46] These were perfunctory, uneventful, and without impact. The unions were predictably concerned about job losses and demanded regulation. Experts and interest groups were divided on whether an American takeover or a monopoly was worse.[47]

The merger talks unfolded uneventfully. Ottawa encouraged a fast process to settle uncertainty, and Air Canada made a quick offer by fax on 28 July, in which Air Canada would have 60-65 per cent of the shares in the new company. The PWA board, unhappy about the prospect of minority status, unanimously rejected this first offer. But in asking Air Canada for a second offer, PWA risked running out of cash and time. It appeared that it might have no option but to accept any offer (by this time PWA was losing

$800,000 a day, and Air Canada was losing $1.5 million a day). A deal surfaced in mid-August, but obstacles appeared. The Standing Committee on Consumer and Corporate Affairs insisted on a full-scale set of hearings. An ad hoc committee of business people led by Calgary mayor Al Duerr was pressuring provincial Tories in Edmonton and the Alberta federal caucus to help PWA (at the same time, federal officials were discussing the merger with Quebec transportation officials). Finally, an employee-based group against the Air Canada merger—the Council of Canadian Airlines Employees—attempted to devise ways to find the bridging finance required to fuel the American deal. Founded in August by ex-PWA executive Sidney Fattedad, the council comprised all of the unions and employee groups (save for the CAW), representing 80 per cent of Canadian employees. It proposed to raise $150 to $200 million in new capital by applying 10 per cent of gross salaries over the next three years to buy shares in the company.[48] The PWA board met on 14 August to review two proposals: a second Air Canada offer and the Fattedad plan. Air Canada continued to give itself 60 per cent control of the merged company, but allowed for a higher price for shares (above market value), promised equal board representation, committed the merged company to maintaining employment in the West, and proposed a mutually developed financial and operating plan. The board also heard a presentation from Art Smith, a former Calgary MP who reported that the BC and Alberta governments would likely back the Fattedad plan.[49] The employee groundswell and proposal gave PWA pause.

The Air Canada merger plan was rejected because the share price was considered to be too low (i.e., lower than American's offer), because Air Canada would have 60 per cent control of the merged company, because there would likely be 10,000 jobs lost, and because Air Canada insisted that Canadian negotiate exclusively with it over the remainder of the merger discussions.[50] PWA returned instead to talks with American.

Fall 1993: Back to the International Solution

Critics had insisted that Ottawa was to blame for the scuttling of the Canadian/American deal and that the government had forced PWA to negotiate a merger with Air Canada. But in quick order, first the domestic option of an Air Canada merger collapsed, and then the international option was resurrected. The key factor was the Council of Canadian Airlines Employees' plan. Air Canada maintained that PWA had been able to reject its offer because the council had poisoned public opinion against the merger option.[51] This was a new development in Canadian politics: corporate employees themselves organizing to affect public policy in order to save their jobs—whether through lobbying MPs and cabinet ministers, marching on Parliament, placing media ads, or talking to boards of trade and on talk shows. "Their efforts have been very strong," reported NDP transportation critic Iain Angus; "They meet with us in our offices and they corner us on planes and pull us up to the cockpit for a chat."[52]

As Canadian positioned itself for its American alliance, Air Canada pursued an international option as well. It announced an alliance with United Airlines and joined with a Texas partner in bidding for Continental Airlines.[53] (Later in September it entered into an alliance with Air France.)[54] These moves seemed to make the American/Canadian alliance more palatable politically.

The international strategy required PWA to acquire a sufficiently large aid package to tide it over and allow it to meet American's financial conditions. It headed to four sources: the provincial capitals, Ottawa, its employees, and the courts. BC declared its willingness to guarantee $50 million, but only if Ottawa became involved in the financial aid package.[55] Ottawa signalled "approval" of the latest variant of a "market" solution when the Department of National Defence purchased three of Canadian's unused Airbus Industries A310 jets for $150 million.[56] The employee-based package began to firm up, with the pilots being the first in a series of groups to endorse the council plan by committing themselves to invest as much as 15 per cent of their pay over four years.[57] Finally, PWA itself made a key move when it attempted to disassociate itself from its Gemini reservation system to meet American's requirement that it hook into American's Sabre system.

It was too little, too late. Canadian faced tremendous cash pressures and government financial support was not forthcoming substantially or quickly enough. Provincial governments were caught between conflicting interests (archetypical here was the case of Manitoba which had to choose between the loss of hundreds of jobs from the demise of Gemini and a continued western presence in the airline industry) or put forward presumptuous demands like Alberta's request that the merged airline be headquartered in Alberta. As the financial aid package and employee-based proposal unravelled, all the provinces criticized Ottawa's lack of leadership and involvement.[58]

Thus, the international option went off the rails again. Throughout the process, Ottawa maintained its hands-off position and anticipated a market solution. Indeed, there was a further market twist: Air Canada made yet another offer to merge with Canadian.

In early September Air Canada made three bizarre modifications to its previous offer, which showed every sign of panic and expediency. First, the so-called exclusivity clause was dropped. This would allow PWA to negotiate with other suitors while the merger process was unfolding. Second, a "holding company" model was proposed, whereby neither company would continue to exist and retain its identity. Third, there would be corporate headquarters in both Montreal and Calgary.[59] This was a ridiculous proposal, reflecting a strategic political and public relations logic but little financial or business sense. The offer demanded an immediate response, as it would expire at midnight on 9 September. Over the weekend, the Council of Canadian Airlines Employees repackaged its proposal, by now comprising $100-150 million cuts in gross pay and contract extensions until 1995. Their motto had become "Better Dead than Red" (Air Canada's corporate colour). The CAW continued to remain outside of the employee plan.[60]

PWA reluctantly accepted Air Canada's offer on 9 September. "We've been let down by the provincial governments and let down by one union," claimed Canadian's President Eyton.[61] It appeared that the "Made in Canada" solution had won and that Canada would now have one big airline. The government continued to remain on the market sidelines and watch the airline solution unfold. It gave no indication of whether it favoured or wanted to encourage this development.

In the days before Parliament adjourned for the constitutional referendum, the airline industry commanded some parliamentary attention in question period, hardly the format for an informed public debate on a complex matter. The opposition focused on two themes—loss of jobs and the evils of monopolization—and asked whether the government favoured one or two domestic airlines, a merged Air Canada/Canadian, or an American presence in the airlines. The government gave its standard response: these are private matters involving private companies and not the government's responsibility, and there are agencies independent of the government—the Competition Tribunal and the NTA—that will eventually comment on the appropriateness of any particular development. The opposition accused the government of hiding behind these processes and not taking a firm stand. It played the western card as well. "The loss [of jobs] will be disproportionate in the West," claimed Lloyd Axworthy. "Another vital institution to western Canadians is being gutted with the complicity of this government," concluded David Kilgour. The opposition also claimed that the airlines' financial difficulty was the government's responsibility, as deregulation had generated overcompetition and predatory pricing. Corbeil rejected calls for re-regulation, which, as Mazankowski declared, would be "going against the grain of everything that is occurring internationally."[62]

While the politicians went through the motions of this pseudo-debate, a joint PWA/Air Canada merger committee proceeded with the difficult task of merging two corporations with different histories, corporate philosophies, traditions, and needs. Air Canada extended PWA a $100 million line of credit to tide it over financially during the course of the talks. A pre-merger agreement was signed in early October, but this did not sort out the really tough issues. On 18 October the merger committee managed to produce a plan, only to see it rejected by both boards on 29 October. The key stumbling block was whether there would be one or two operating units. The merger committee was sent back to work. But Air Canada pulled the plug on 3 November, claiming that the pre-merger agreement was unworkable.[63]

The domestic solution would not fly, and PWA started talking with American again.

The International Solution Again: PWA and American Make a Deal

The airlines industry was by now in a tense and uncertain state of emergency; a major initiative was required to stabilize the situation. Air Canada took back its $100 million line of credit, and PWA planned to seek court protection against its creditors. The two airlines were now losing $2 million a day. Canadian's days seemed numbered.[64] But the prospect of going to the gallows clears the mind considerably. Canadian's impending bankruptcy focused the attention of some of the key players.

First, the Council of Canadian Airlines Employees' plan was resurrected when the CAW announced on 10 November that it would participate in the employee investment scheme. This was a major development, for the CAW had been backing the domestic option of a merger with Air Canada. All the unions now supported the American/Canadian deal, both morally and financially.[65]

Second, Howard Wetston, director of investigation and research of the Bureau of Competition Policy, petitioned the Competition Tribunal to amend the 1989 consent order that had legitimated the Gemini CRS monopoly. Wetston argued that unless released from Gemini, Canadian would not be able to make its alliance with American. And if this alliance did not proceed, PWA would likely go bankrupt or be forced to merge with Air Canada, which would diminish airline competition. Either development would eliminate competition in the industry. Air Canada was livid and claimed that Wetston had no authority to intervene in a private, market matter—to, in effect, bankrupt Gemini.[66] A week later, Gemini sued PWA for $1.5 billion in an Ontario court, claiming that PWA had breached its fiduciary responsibilities as a member of Gemini by trying to get out of the partnership. (PWA had filed in an Alberta court to dissolve Gemini, a petition rejected because Alberta was not the province in which to file such a suit.) Covia—United Airlines—also sued PWA and American for $1.2 billion for unlawful interference with Gemini's business activities.[67] PWA in turn sued Air Canada for $1 billion in the Alberta Court of Queen's Bench, alleging predatory pricing practices from January through April 1992 when, it claimed, Air Canada was flooding the market with excess capacity in order to bankrupt PWA.[68] These tit-for-tat lawsuits muddied the policy process. Each side tried to wear down its opponents. Moreover, each party was trying to impress the public and politicians in order to improve its position in advance of what was considered to be an inevitable political resolution of this mess. A political decision now seemed imperative, for it would take the airlines years to extricate themselves from this tangled legal and regulatory web, by which time the industry might have collapsed. It was in Air Canada's interest to wait out the legal and regulatory processes, for it had the deeper pockets to ensure its survival until Canadian went bankrupt. Political inaction, then, seemed to be a deliberate policy favouring Air Canada.

Both airlines started knocking on government doors again, particularly Ottawa's. In a 10 November meeting with Transport Minister Corbeil, PWA president Rhys Eyton reported that unless his company was also provided with loan guarantees, it would have to file for bankruptcy protection. PWA proposed to revive the employee-backed plan to link it and American through a 25 per cent purchase of the former by the latter. This required three-year loan guarantees of $90 million from Ottawa and $100 million from the provinces, as well as $100 million in bridge financing from Ottawa. A subcommittee examined the plan.[69]

Ottawa once again found itself forced to choose between regional and policy considerations, between a rock and a hard place. On the one hand, there were intense western pressures to devise a financial salvation package for PWA. Calgary MP Bobbie Sparrow insisted that "the feds just have to come into the package; there's too many jobs at stake in Calgary and Vancouver."[70] Quebec, too, played a regional card with all levels of government taking a clear pro-Air Canada stance, claiming that, if financial help was forthcoming, it would be unthinkable to subsidize only one airline.[71] PWA president Eyton replied to this: "Maybe you have to examine the help that's been given to [Air Canada] over the years too—the loans they've been given, the assets, lines of credit they've had.... I think they've had their share of help in the past."[72]

For Ottawa though, offering financial assistance to Canadian would hardly be consistent with the government's deregulated, market approach. Moreover, providing PWA with a financial salvation package might unleash equity arguments to offer equal assistance to the other airline. Indeed, Air Canada threatened to sue the government if it intervened to help Canadian, characterized the government's action as interference in private-sector market decisions, accused the government of Americanizing the airlines industry, and demanded financial subsidies equal to any assistance Ottawa might extend to Canadian.

The government's first response was to listen to what Canadian had to say, so Corbeil and Mazankowski agreed to a meeting with Canadian leaders, the employee buyout group, and American officials. Days earlier Air Canada had successfully gained a stake in Continental Airlines with Air Partners PL, a Texas group (for US $450 million, they each received a 27.5 per cent stake in the company).[73] The government made no promises to Canadian, with Mazankowski insisting that they were simply "exploring the initiative ... to see whether or not we can participate in a solution that will be in the national interest."[74]

But should Ottawa participate financially at all? Not according to the Royal Commission on National Passenger Transportation, whose 19 members' report called for the government to get out of transportation altogether and end its $5 billion a year in subsidies. Already held back because of the constitutional debate and referendum, the report was released at a bad time for the government.

The Commission took the clear position that a market solution should be found to the airline situation. Corbeil responded that the report "is a framework for future planning. We have to grapple with a problem that exists now."[75] As discussions with Canadian continued, the government was slammed for its "do-nothing" policy, its lack of plan, and its playing "mental ping-pong" in alternating between domestic and international approaches to the issue. Corbeil insisted that the government was "looking for ways ... to reconcile fiscal constraints with its desire to support Canadian."[76]

On 24 November, Corbeil made a statement in the House of Commons that seemed to settle the airlines matter. He argued that the Canadian industry needed to be rationalized, as there was substantial overcapacity; he defended deregulation and reaffirmed the government's commitment to a market-and-competition-driven transportation industry; and he outlined nine considerations that informed the government's response to the Canadian/American deal.[77] He concluded by announcing that the government would provide up to $50 million in financial assistance to the PWA/Employee Council/American Airlines deal.[78] On one level, it appeared that the government had emerged from the sidelines to support the international option over the "Made in Canada" option. However, the policy announcement was criticized for being as equivocal and delaying as earlier government pronouncements had been. One political columnist called the announcement "a travesty of a policy declaration. It reads like something a couple of undergraduates taking their first course in transportation economics might have penned over a few beers." The Liberals accused the government of providing a $50 million band-aid "while giving no indication of what outcome the government really hopes to achieve."[79]

Ottawa's financial support was modest and far less than PWA had asked for, but it was better than nothing or the strict approach. Corbeil insisted that was it: "There will be no more than $50 million from the federal government." He maintained that there were too many uncertainties in the plan, that $190 million was too large a request, and that the remainder should be made up by employees and the provinces. Nonetheless, PWA president Eyton put a brave face on the situation: "I wouldn't say only $50 million.... That's a very large degree of support."[80]

Ottawa's $50 million appeared to be conditional on a number of factors, including its demand that the airlines cut capacity.[81] If this was not forthcoming, the government threatened to "recalibrate" the industry, a euphemism for the politically incorrect word "regulate." Corbeil's parliamentary secretary, Lee Richardson, exhorted: "Guys, get it together. Resolve it between yourselves or we're going to take any action that is necessary to stop the fare wars." Canadian appeared to be willing, but there was no guarantee that Air Canada would play along, particularly as it was not in its interests to cut capacity. There was nothing in the government's announcement to induce Air Canada to behave in this way. The NDP's Iain Angus declared that "$50 million with no strings attached, no return to regulation, and no forced ending to crazy competition is clearly outrageous."[82]

Corbeil's announcement did not clarify a number of policy issues. What exactly would be the future of the Canadian airline industry and Air Canada and Canadian's respective roles in it? The Gemini situation remained unresolved, though it was as great a stumbling block to a Canadian/American deal as was the financial dimension. Would the market sort out the airlines' future, or would the government provide counterbalancing assistance

---

IV: The American Deal With PWA/Canadian

American Airlines was prepared to invest $246 million to be taken in voting and nonvoting convertible and preferred shares, at the closing of the deal with PWA/Canadian, if certain conditions were met:

- American would have a 25 per cent voting interest and a one-third equity interest in Canadian.
- The Gemini computer reservation system must release PWA from its contract for hosting services so that a variety of administrative, marketing, and data management processing services could be provided to Canadian through the Sabre system.
- PWA/Canadian's balance sheet had to be strengthened, by raising $125 million in equity from the public and by employees contributing $120-150 million in salary reductions over three years in exchange for equity.
- American Airlines would appoint two members to the eight-member board of directors. These two members would have veto rights over a number of management decisions, including appointment of the chief executive officer; annual business, capital, and financial plans; capital expenditures over a threshold amount; and mergers and acquisitions over a certain amount.
- American Airlines would provide processing services for Canadian mainly through its Sabre system, including operations planning, pricing and yield management, food and beverage support services, international base operations, and technical services and accounting.
- All current foreign route authorities of PWA/Canadian would be in full force and effect as of closing.

Source: House of Commons Debates, 24 November 1992: 13901

---

to Air Canada (and Quebec) on the ground that, as Nic Leblanc, MP from Longueil, complained, "in helping Canadian Airlines we will just hurt Air Canada"?[83] Nor did the decision clarify the issue of foreign involvement in the Canadian airline industry. For the first time, details of American's offer were made public, and it appeared that American would have a substantial amount of control in Canadian for its 25 per cent stake (see Inset IV). Finally, would the government intervene to give some direction to the airline industry or would it allow the Byzantine world of courts and regulatory processes to drag out this process interminably?

Airlines Policy Enters the Legal and Regulatory Maze

Once governments were on side, PWA sought to resolve the other conditions of the American deal. It stopped payments on its bank loans and leases to conserve cash as a first step in restructuring its debt. Creditors would be asked to participate in PWA salvation, along with its employees and various governments. This was essentially a declaration of bankruptcy, with Canadian betting that its creditors would not push it into receivership. PWA asked them to swap $900 million in debt for common shares (in the process increasing the number of shares from 48 million to 1.85 billion). American signed a conditional investment agreement with Canadian in late December to give PWA a bargaining chip in these negotiations. It also attempted to get union approval for a four-year wage give-back and a three-year wage freeze.[84]

The PWA "debt-for-equity" survival plan won approval from its shareholders in late August, although not without enduring a few scares.[85] But this challenge was trivial in light of all the market, legal, and regulatory obstacles the company had to face. First, it continued to function in an unregulated, duopolistic market in which it was the weaker player. It cut 15 per cent of its capacity in response to Ottawa's demand, but Air Canada cut its capacity by only 3 per cent. It thus felt forced to revive its cancelled flights for competitive reasons. Transport Minister Corbeil deplored this action and threatened again to "recalibrate" the industry, but this remained an empty threat. When asked by critics and by PWA president Eyton to do something to deal with industry overcapacity ("a nudge or a bang on the head," requested Eyton), Corbeil replied, "Why does the company not do it? They have the liberty to do it themselves. They do not have to ask the Minister of Transport to do what they can do without any interference from the minister." Corbeil accused the companies of lacking the "self-discipline to bring down capacity." The government continued to maintain a hands-off, market-oriented policy. In response to criticisms that it lacked any airline policy, former transportation minister Crosbie declared:

> The policy is a policy of deregulation .... [The present situation] is a problem that the airlines have to solve. They are in the private sector and they have to do their best to solve their own problems. If there is overcapacity in the Canadian airlines industry, [it] was not created by the Government of Canada. We did not put a gun to anyone's head in the airline industry telling them to go out and purchase more aircraft. [86]

Furthermore, the government was also committed to not intervene in the Competition Tribunal's deliberations on Gemini and to wait for the NTA's judgment on whether the American investment in Canadian met the test of the public interest. This led Lucien Bouchard to complain that "everyone is responsible except the minister in charge."[87]

Meanwhile, the heated issue of the Gemini arrangements went before the Competition Tribunal on 1 February and continued until 4 March.[88] In a 2-1 verdict, the tribunal ruled in late April that it did not have the jurisdiction to release PWA from its Gemini commitments. This was a tremendously disappointing result, not only for PWA but for the airline policy process itself, for it had consumed three crucial months of time without advancing the resolution of the case. What was particularly irksome was that the tribunal concluded that, if it had had jurisdiction, it would have ruled in Canadian's favour. Its view was that not being allowed to withdraw from Gemini would kill Canadian and lessen competition, that a merger with Air Canada also would lessen competition, and that Gemini would not die if Canadian were released.

With these arguments the tribunal essentially invited PWA to appeal its decision to the Federal Court.[89] This symbolic victory for PWA suggested to many the *reductio ad absurdum* of allowing a legal/regulatory process to determine airline policy. The case dragged on and on and seemed to call for government priority-setting, vision, and leadership. But this would have required a messy intervention in the market and awkward compromises to keep the various regions and players happy.

Paralleling the tribunal hearings were the lawsuits and counter lawsuits filed by the airlines, by now consolidated into one megacase in Ontario's general division court.[90] PWA received a second body blow in April when the Ontario court dismissed its appeal to have Gemini dissolved on the grounds that it was insolvent. In arguments that disagreed with the Competition Tribunal's analysis, the court ruled that Gemini seemed to be at the point of making a profit: "It would neither be just nor equitable to permit a disgruntled minority or one partner acting in its own self-interest to be able to dismantle the business and to frustrate the substantial investment of the other partner." Indeed, the court accused the PWA directors on the Gemini board of breaching their fiduciary duty by not declaring their conflict of interest when PWA was negotiating with American to join the Sabre system.[91]

PWA appeals of this ruling to the Ontario Court of Appeal[92] and to the Supreme Court[93] both went nowhere. The consequences of these decisions could be far-reaching and costly, as Gemini's original lawsuit was for $1 billion.[94]

In July, PWA went before the Federal Court of Appeal to appeal the Competition Tribunal's April decision that that tribunal did not have jurisdiction to release PWA from its Gemini commitments. In a split decision the Court ruled that the Competition Tribunal did indeed have the authority to free PWA from Gemini. It argued that the Gemini arrangement existed in substantially changed circumstances, as one of the parties to the original deal was now facing imminent failure. The Gemini partners could be asked to reach an agreement, and if this was not successful, the tribunal could then dissolve Gemini.[95]

This decision simply returned the process to where it had been months before. Air Canada appealed the court decision all the way up to the Supreme Court, which refused to hear its appeal in October. Air Canada also filed motion to expand the terms of reference of the Competition Tribunal's hearing. The tribunal had indicated that it did not want to hear any new information, but Air Canada insisted that it listen to that airline's $1 billion offer to buy Canadian's international routes.[96] This would muddy the waters, as it presented a third option, which did not seem to require the elimination of competition (viz., a merger or Canadian's demise). Even if the Competition Tribunal eventually ruled in PWA's favour, this decision could be appealed to the Federal Court and then to the Supreme Court.[97] By early August, the Competition Tribunal had not yet taken up the Gemini case, and a panicky PWA, defeated in the Ontario court and running out of time and money, pleaded with the federal government to step in and force a negotiated settlement between PWA and the other Gemini partners. PWA had offered its one-third stake and $21.5 million to its Gemini partners to be released from the system. However, Air Canada was not interested; it is "our understanding that Mr. Eyton's willingness to talk is restricted to ... how we wind up Gemini. On these grounds we don't think that's appropriate."[98] Ottawa refused to be drawn in and thus allowed the convoluted legal processes to unfold endlessly, letting PWA and airline policy twist in the regulatory winds.

Meanwhile, on the other regulatory track, the National Transportation Agency was to determine whether the American/Canadian deal was in the "public interest."[99] The NTA began its hearings with eight days in Calgary beginning 22 March and concluded hearings on 21 April after 11 days in Hull, Quebec. During this process, 174 participants appeared before the agency. Provinces, mayors, boards of trade, transportation authorities, interest groups, unions, experts, and interested parties rehearsed the familiar arguments for and against American's investment in Canadian: job losses, competition, regional economic health, national control, high technology. Its deliberations focused on two critical areas: competitiveness and Canadian ownership. With respect to the latter, the NTA concluded that

American's 25 per cent investment would not give it control of Canadian. Concerning competitiveness,

> The Agency concludes that Canadian has every right to take such action as it deems necessary to survive and to return to profitability.... This is the nature of a competitive market place and Air Canada has the same right. Under this scenario, competition and market forces will determine the future of the Canadian aviation industry. This is in keeping with the objectives of the national transportation policy specified in section 8 of the National Transportation Act, 1987.

The NTA declined to comment on whether Canada could support two airlines: "These matters must be resolved by market forces coupled with existing and future government policies and not under the narrow proceedings" of a hearing. With this, the agency unanimously declared that American's investment in Canadian was not counter to the public interest.[100]

Air Canada appealed the NTA decision to cabinet, arguing that "without this intervention by the federal cabinet, Canada's airlines will be relegated to playing a subsidiary role" as feeders to the major American airlines.[101] On 23 June, Transport Minister Corbeil quietly announced in a press release that the cabinet had upheld the NTA decision: "After careful analysis, the government has concluded, consistent with our policy of fostering a strong, viable and competitive airline industry that, on balance, it should not overturn the NTA decision."[102] Parliament then recessed for the summer, and the Mulroney era ended with an airline policy ostensibly in place.

But had an airline policy actually been determined? And was the uncertainty surrounding the airline industry actually settled? Apparently not, for the case rolled on and on. In a gesture of supreme insight and cynicism, Air Canada dusted off its old offer of $1 billion in cash and debt concessions to buy Canadian's international routes just days before PWA's critical meeting with its creditors to discuss the debt-for-equity survival plan. As it was structured, the deal offered $200 million for PWA's international routes and the rest was the assumption of the $800 million dollars of debt carried by the company.

PWA had announced second-quarter losses of $130.6 million, bringing its 1993 losses to $238 million and its losses since 1991 to over $1 billion. The company was slowly bleeding to death. Air Canada was aware of this and knew that Canadian management would reject the offer, for if it accepted the deal, a domestic-only PWA operation would embark on a steady decline towards industrial marginalization and oblivion.

But the offer was not really aimed at PWA management; rather, it was directed to Canadian's creditors, political actors, and the Competition Tribunal. Creditors might be tempted to choose to take the cash rather than the Canadian stock-for-debt offer, and the offer presented the government and other political actors with an alternative policy option to the American deal or PWA bankruptcy. This alternative could keep them and the airline issue on the sidelines as the federal election approached. Canadian denounced the offer as "a cynical exercise," "a public relations strategy," and a "diabolical plot," and rejected it as having no merit.[103]

But what of the government? Its quiet resolve to uphold the NTA decision appeared to settle matters, to signal policy approval of one of the two ways of solving the airline industry's problems. Instead, the issue dragged on and on because, in an extreme case of the tail wagging the dog, the Gemini issue had been left to linger in the courts. This prevented a final choice between the international and domestic strategies, as all parties, before making their final moves, waited for the Competition Tribunal to render a final judgment on the CRS. PWA's Eyton asked Prime Minister Kim Campbell to intervene to resolve the issue, but she declined: "I think that there are some issues now that are in front of the courts and other tribunals that have to be resolved .... I believe this is a question the companies should be resolving themselves."[104]

As the country was poised to move from the Mulroney era to the Campbell or Chrétien era, the airline case threatened to become an election issue. Indeed, the airlines dragged themselves into the next, electoral round of this winner-take-all policy fight. With their resources and stamina dwindling, they initiated a pre-election media blitz, placing ads that supported their respective positions.[105]

These ads were aimed at making an impact on government officials who, in a case like the airlines stalemate, were traditionally tasked with brokering solutions that neither pleased nor alienated any one group. The airlines and their allies used the media as well as employee marches on Parliament Hill, employer-interest group lobbying, and expensive, well-connected consultancy firms to influence these officials.

But to what effect? The government had deregulated transportation in 1987 and got out of the airline transportation business by privatizing Air Canada. By introducing legislation to establish two regimes to oversee the transportation scene, the Competition Bureau and the NTA, and by endowing them with broad policy goals, it had committed itself to a

policy of non-intervention. Governments in the past, though, had traditionally bailed corporations out of their jams, and PWA and Air Canada
proceeded on the assumption that this government would eventually step
in to resolve the case. The trick for the government, then, was to convince
the airlines that it would not intervene, regardless of whatever market scenario unfolded.

That was the official line, as the government insisted over and over again
that it favoured a market solution by the "private" players. It expressed
no particular enthusiasm for either the Air Canada merger or the Ameri-
can/Canadian alliance. The airlines continued to pressure the government,
even though it stated continuously that it did not intend to intervene. This
case was fuelled by one of the most powerful and explosive ingredients of
the real worlds of Canadian politics: regional passions and rivalries. Canadian Airlines symbolized westerners' deeply held hopes and aspirations
for the West's economic future and its capacity for economic self-reliance.
In Air Canada, they saw a bloated, bureaucratic behemoth, fed by eastern
Canadian and central government favouritism and a lust for monopoly.
For Quebecers, Air Canada remained a central and towering figure representing its high-tech, international aspirations in the aerospace industry
and a test case of Canada's willingness to allow Quebec's economic garden
to bloom. Canadian played the competitiveness and efficiency cards, while
Air Canada played the nationalist, anti-American card. In practical terms,
the case became a zero-sum game with Gemini as the wild card that would
determine who took the pot. This was not a case that lent itself to brokerage, although that might have been possible had the government acted
quickly in 1990 or 1991.

But the government did not intervene; it let the market, regulatory, and
legal processes unfold. By sticking to its deregulatory principles and offering the $50 million loan guarantee to the American/Canadian deal, Ottawa
made a show of not abandoning PWA, but such a modest initiative could
not (and did not) ignite a violent reaction from Quebec. This looked a bit
like brokerage politics as it pleased neither side, but it failed to resolve the
issue.

It must be recalled that the Mulroney government stuck its neck out
outrageously on similarly divisive and explosive issues, like the GST, free
trade, and privatization. It was capable of making a divisive policy decision
and had done so in the past. But not in the airlines' case. Indeed, the manner in which this case dragged on revealed another dimension of Canadian
politics. When governments distance themselves from direct regulation or
management of the economy, they separate "traditional" political institu-

tions and processes from the policy dynamic. Indeed, in the airline case, once the deregulatory legislation was in place, Parliament played a diminished role. There was then little to no public debate on airlines policy, for the government deflected public criticism and debate away from Parliament to the courts and regulatory bodies. But this did not imply that politics and policy simply went away.

By the end of 1993 the process had not provided many encouraging results. On the one hand, the endless back and forth had done little to clarify the position of the two airlines as they moved ever closer to what looked like financial meltdown. On the other, the results contained little apparent rationality. In an effort to bring labour costs down, employees signed a deal that brought them down by 17 per cent over the following three years; they also managed to purchase an equity stake in their company worth about $200 million.

A Thorny Inheritance: Liberal Airline Policy After Mulroney

The new Liberal government (elected in October 1993) inherited this difficult situation and set out to try some kind of mediation between the two airlines in the Gemini case. Prime Minister Jean Chrétien appointed former prime ministerial aide Stanley Hartt to try to cool heads before any further escalation. The Liberals resorted to a good dose of old-fashioned brokerage, and the Gemini case was resolved not by the Competition Tribunal but by the fact that Air Canada dropped its appeal on 27 January 1994. Rumours had it that Air Canada would be compensated for allowing Canadian out of the Gemini deal with the rights to fly into some airports in the Far East that had been previously under Canadian's monopoly. It received the rights to fly into Osaka the day after it dropped the appeal.[106]

By the end of March Canadian was ready to move to the SABRE reservation system. PWA President Rhys Eyton was deeply disappointed by the treatment received by his company and had been unable to stop the slow but consistent drift of Canadian Airlines into ever worse financial waters. Both companies had closed 1993 with losses (Air Canada was in the red for $326 million; Canadian had lost $291.8 million), but the impact was felt much more intensely by the western carrier.

In 1994, both airlines focused on expanding their options by acquiring new markets. For Air Canada this meant gaining access to the extremely profitable East Asian markets (Hong Kong, Japan, South Korea) and the business travellers that originated and arrived there, along with keeping an eye on important European airports like Heathrow to which it gained access early in the year.[107] This required lobbying hard for the opportunity, and this is exactly what the Montreal-based company started to do. Canadian, instead, had to defend its Asian markets and planned to exploit to the best of its capacities the close relationship it had developed with American Airlines. This strategy began to bear fruits when, in April 1994, Canadian signed a deal with AMR Corporation (American's parent company) designed to help the Calgary carrier to get back on its feet using feeder traffic from American. At the same time it was cutting jobs to control costs,[108] and reinforced its Asian sector by initiating service to China.[109]

The difficulties of the project and the structural pitfalls of the aviation industry, though, were never very far from executives' minds. Drew Fitch, Senior Vice-President of Finance at Canadian, commented that "this is just an industry that's labour intensive, dependent on government for [air service treaties], subject to taxation like no other industry, leads into a recession and lags out of a recession … before I say any more I'll get all depressed but there is no question the industry is going to survive."[110] Beginning in November, Canadian was allowed to fly directly into Washington, DC, three times a day. The decision, argued Air Canada's spokesperson Kim Robertson, was "clearly a tactical move to prevent Air Canada from taking advantage of the route."[111]

Canadian Airlines' monopoly in Japan came to an end when Air Canada was allowed to fly into Osaka. Harris was understandably overjoyed: "we're pulling out all of the stops to make this a success. Air Canada people have been working for years to finally see the Maple Leaf fly to Japan."[112] Harris himself and a group of Air Canada executives were on the inaugural flight to Osaka.

On 24 February 1995 the US and Canada signed the "Open Skies" pact that allowed for immediate access for Canadian airlines to US destinations, while phasing in access for American companies to Canada's major airports. This was an important opportunity for both carriers, and they increased their cross-border flights by a factor of four.[113] Air Canada came out on top from the early stages of this competition, having increased its US market share to 30 per cent from its original 25 per cent. Having ended the previous year with a substantial amount of cash in reserve ($775 million) Air Canada also continued to increase its capacity by buying more aircraft and in December finally managed to break the monopoly that Canadian had held in Hong Kong.

The federal government implemented new rules regarding second carriers being allowed into a destination already served by a primary Canadian airline. The new policy basically allowed for a degree of competition if the primary carrier handled over 300,000 passengers per year at any specific airport. So, while not being allowed a daily service to Hong Kong, Air Canada had that route added to its own. It was perhaps a move consistent with the notion of fostering competition, but it further heightened the business competition between two airlines already dangerously overextended financially.

In Canada, most of the effort from both carriers was concentrated in the regional market. In particular, Canadian tried to gain a foothold in the Toronto-Ottawa-Montreal area, which had been traditionally the domain of Air Canada's Rapidair. The strategy that inspired this move was premised on the ability of Canadian to retain the business frequent flyers that used its regional shuttle service. If that happened, these business travellers could be sold international tickets too. This was a desperate move with very little hope of succeeding, and, to make things worse, it came at a time when Canadian was being challenged in its stronghold: the Calgary-Edmonton-Vancouver market. Smaller companies, like WestJet and Greyhound Air, were slowly succeeding in taking Canadian business away by marketing a discount service. Canadian had also been busy for months negotiating with its unions to reduce its wage burden, which was now becoming very heavy, finally securing important concessions from its pilots and other workers.[114] This was necessary because, even in an industry that always relied on labour, Canadian Airlines employed an average of 165 persons per plane, while Air Canada needed "only" 120; the industry average, however, was 100.

In June, Canadian was projecting an end-of-year profit of $50 million based on the synergies that were beginning to show from their agreement with American Airlines. Canadian CEO Kevin Jenkins went on the record forecasting that his company would be back on track by the end of the year. It was not to be. First, the projected surplus turned into a loss of $35 million dollars, and then, just before Christmas, the adjusted financial figures for the carrier came out. In one day the stock value dropped 10 per cent from $5.00 to $4.50. Most of the problems had been brought about by a change in the accounting department where the new CFO, Kevin Benson, had changed the manner in which costs were accounted and the time period in which they were posted. It was not that the previous system was illegal or even wrong, but it cut Canadian operations considerably more slack. The revised 1995 balance sheet looked bad, and the previous accounting department looked sloppy. Along with a notable slice of Canadian Airlines' financial credibility also went many senior level managers, including the vice-president for marketing and sales, Terry Francis. Over time they were replaced, notably by three American Airlines managers: Richard Haddock, George Muller, and Barbara Amster. There were also calls for Jenkins's resignation. Dave Park, President of the Canadian Airlines section of the International Association of Machinists and Aerospace Workers (IAM&AW), was particularly direct: "Look at other airlines," he said, "other airlines are making money. Why isn't Canadian? It has to be the senior management of this airline is incapable of running the airline."[115]

Among the new arrivals Barbara Amster was certainly the star. She was given the difficult job of turning Canadian around. Amster, the former vice-president of yield management and distribution at Fort Worth noted that Canadian "was a company in shock … I did find something of the battered child syndrome. People were just trying to hang on."[116]

Her first order of business was to make Canadian profitable again by ruthlessly cutting those routes that may have been prestigious but had only brought financial woes. She was undaunted by the difficulty of the situation and had a clear plan of action. It was a difficult plan for sure, but not complicated: "I knew right away that Canadian lacked enough winning segments that were profitable twelve months of the year. We quickly began talking, in a philosophical way, about major change. It was when I saw the [draft] winter schedule [for 1996-97] that I said 'This has got all the same stuff in it. Paris is still in and Frankfurt is still in. You guys won't make it through another winter.'"[117] The most sensible option (many at the time would have said the only option) was to go with Asia, all the way. Amster was realistic about this strategy too: "The problem was that the Canada-Asia market isn't big enough and is seasonal. Sixty-five percent of Canada-Japan traffic moves in June, July, August and early September."[118] The second part of this strategy was to use American traffic to the US to prop up Canadian for the rest of the year. Now, at last, the Calgary airline had something looking like a viable plan. It remained to be seen if it would work.

Management within the company was adamant that changes were coming; in a communiqué to its employees, the company noted that the airline cannot afford to continue with our current cash flow and survive.[119] One way to ensure survival was also to take the lead in marketing, and Canadian immediately began offering fare cuts, a move that was met with skepticism from Air Canada. Hollis Harris's comments were just one of many; he noted: "I don't know what their inside cash position is, but I do know that they have been making very bad business decisions on discount airline fares.… If they weren't hurting for cash, why would they do that?"[120] Barbara Amster had already defended this decision. "For the past four or five years," she said, "Canadian has not led any initiative. We're starting to come out and lead now."[121]

While the two companies were trying to expand their revenue base, Ottawa did not change its airline policy. Policy direction still ruled the day. Any potential changes, like allowing multiple airlines to fly out of the same airport (as was the case in Hong Kong) or from the same country, did not fit in with the federal government's ongoing focus on competition.

As mentioned above, in the new year things within Canadian were going from bad to worse: the bad rap earned the previous December prompted Canadian employees (who had sunk a sizeable share of their wages into the company) to come out and critique Jenkins harshly for his conduct. Unions were upset by the concomitant loss of jobs and what they saw as poor economic performance and asked that he be replaced. The board of directors rejected this request, and Jenkins stayed on. The situation looked grim indeed: the problems for Canadian had begun with the 1989 purchase of Wardair, at the time the third airline in Canada. The heavy debt with which the company saddled itself had continued to affect operations and had contributed to consolidated losses of C$1.4 billion between 1990 and 1996.

Air Canada's situation, in contrast, was so good that it even refused grants from an Ottawa-Quebec offer to upgrade its Dorval maintenance base. In February it announced a $129 million profit; soon after its CEO, Hollis Harris, decided that he had completed his mandate to bring new financial stability to the company and resigned. He was replaced by Lamar Durrett, whose plan of action was to check Canadian's possible recovery by going after its shared operations with American Airlines. He began by asking the US Department of Transport to investigate the Canadian Airlines/American Airlines deal and to express an opinion with regard to possible violation of the Sherman Act. While the Department of Transport replied in May by granting anti-trust immunity to the operation, this bode well for Air Canada's own possible partnership with United Airlines.

Shake-up: Canadian Changes Management

On 29 May 1996 the new Canadian Transportation Act received royal assent. Among the changes it implemented was the creation of the Canadian Transportation Agency and a shift in policy that effectively allowed Canadian airlines licences to operate in full freedom with regards to routes, types of aircraft, airports, and so forth.

This was exactly the kind of development that Canadian Airlines had been demanding for a long time. It came too late. Embattled in a bitter fight with its unions and seemingly unable to stop his company's financial nosedive, CEO and Chairman Kevin Jenkins resigned on 28 June. Former CFO Kevin Benson replaced him. Jenkins came from a deeply religious background, and before leaving he assembled his senior staff and read from Philippians: "Whatever is true, whatever is noble, whatever is right, pure and lovely, admirable, if anything is excellent or praiseworthy, think about such things." Amen. Jenkins apparently wanted to stop thinking about airlines. He moved to Westain Corporation, where the closest thing to airlines was the aerospace material production portfolio.

The new CEO, Kevin Benson, was a South African with no experience in running an airline, even if he held a pilot's licence. On the other hand, he had experience in restructuring companies, having turned around Trizec Corporation, a Calgary-based property company, earlier that decade. The situation there was supposed to have been so draining that Benson allegedly promised to himself to never get involved in anything like it again. He loved challenges and fast-paced environments, though; his true passion was auto racing. When Canadian Airlines came looking for him in 1995 and offered him the CFO position, he accepted right away. His all-out, no half-measures style was well-suited for the Calgary-based company: he had a vision and labour liked him better than they liked Jenkins.[122]

Things appeared to look up in the short term: management got rid of some prestigious but unprofitable routes like Paris and Frankfurt, sold its Canadian Holidays business, disposed of some equipment and property, and generally reduced costs so that its cash-in-hand figures began to rise. In July, Canadian even hired some more staff in its Vancouver hub.

Things were not going quite as well from a structural point of view, though. While making money on its international routes, especially to Asia, PWA was dropping fast in its domestic business where it averaged 64 per cent capacity.[123] This meant that over one-third of seats on every plane flying within Canada were empty. In November 1996, Canadian Airlines was once again strapped for cash. Furthermore, Air Canada was lobbying furiously to be allowed to fly into Hong Kong. This drew sharp critiques from Canadian's management who accused the Montreal-based competitor of trying to put an end to the "two airlines policy," which had been a tenet of Canadian airline policy in the past. This notion was hinted at by Transport Minister David Anderson himself in the Commons at the beginning of October 1996. Air Canada President and CEO Lamar Durrett denied this allegation: Air Canada just wanted open and equal access to a booming market.[124] In a bid to forestall disaster, Benson proposed a restructuring plan premised on three points:

1. reducing domestic capacity and focusing instead on international flights;

2. reducing overhead and service costs due to both American Airlines and provincial and federal governments in Canada; and

3. reducing costs by asking for a 10 per cent cut in wages from its employees.

Benson argued that these measures would save about $200 million in costs and would not involve more than 250 lay-offs. He needed two years, he said, to bring PWA around, but to do so he needed the help of all six of the unions representing Canadian's employees. However, his options were shrinking rapidly. Not only did he need to bring his employees on board, he also needed deferrals on the 1992 loan payments due to Ottawa and to the BC and Alberta governments. Furthermore, American Airlines was not necessarily bound to make a deal with PWA now that Air Canada too had routes into Asia, or with anyone else for that matter, since the new Boeing 777 could fly directly from New York into Asia.

As the remote possibility of a federal bailout disappeared, the whole board of directors of Canadian Airlines resigned on 15 November to prevent personal consequences from the impending bankruptcy.[125] The situation appeared desperate. Then during the month of December, the IAM&AW, Canadian Union of Public Employees (CUPE), CAW, and the Canadian Airline Pilots Association all agreed to wage cuts; American Airlines agreed to reduce its fees over the next few years; and the federal government and the provinces of Alberta and BC agreed to shoulder some costs. Ottawa came up with $20 million in fuel tax rebates but only in exchange for Canadian agreeing to forgo the write-off of future business losses in a 1-20 ratio. For every dollar received now, Canadian would agree to not claim $20 of its future business tax write-offs for operating losses.

Benson might have been desperate but he was not going to add insult to injury and turned the offer down.[126] He instead proposed a debt-restructuring package that would allow his company time to get through the losses of the next two quarters and to put Canadian's regional airlines up for sale, although he found no buyers. This was, in fact, a blessing in disguise because these companies did feed a consistent stream of passengers into Canadian's business and would begin recovering financially during 1997. The stumbling block of the plan was to be the latest demand that employees agree to further wage cuts to which the CAW was adamantly opposed.

Among the governments that acted promptly was the NDP in BC. Concerned because of the many jobs located in Vancouver, Premier Glen Clark went to Dallas in early December 1996 to talk with American Airlines executives to extract some kind of assurance that American was still going to support Canadian Airlines and that Vancouver would remain the hub for their flights to Asia.[127] A few days before, Clark and Benson had held a joint conference during which the BC government had pledged $12.4 million for lower paid Canadian employees (later both BC and Alberta would join Ottawa in offering fuel-tax relief), and the premier cautiously noted that "I am not arguing for re-regulation or an end to Open Skies, but some policy environment that allows carriers to compete."[128] This was not the first time the federal government was being prodded towards taking some kind of active measure to solve an increasingly scary-looking mess. Earlier during the week the BC Employment and Investment Minister Dan Miller had met in Vancouver with Transport Minister David Anderson (himself elected in BC) and at the end of the meeting summarized the provincial positions: "We think they [Ottawa] should take a leadership position ... any positive signal from the federal government would be most helpful."[129] Premier Clark was even more direct at a BC Federation of Labour meeting: "I want to tell you right here and right now that I will not stand idly by and allow Ottawa's malign neglect to lead to the destruction of those jobs [Canadian's 16,400] ... It is beyond belief that a national government with a significant number of BC members of Parliament, including the Transportation Minister, could allow such a critical industry to deteriorate to this point."[130]

So there was a general sense that the situation was urgent and that consequences could be dire, but there was a big difference between this and actually reaching an agreement. Bringing all concerned parties around was to take immense amounts of effort, including the 15 November mass resignation of Canadian's board of directors. It did not help that rumours abounded about the alleged disengagement of both Canadian Airlines' own top brass and of American Airlines' interests in the company. It fell to American's spokesperson Al Becker to dispel these rumours and rally support.

The federal government selected a stance which can be summarized in the position it had with regard to the problems Canadian was having negotiating pay cuts with CAW. Transport Minister Anderson noted that Ottawa was ready to help, but that it "would not get involved in mediating between the company and its unions. If there is no movement, no coming together between the unions and Canadian Airlines, there's no point in meeting because there's nothing government can do that would be a substitute for restructuring that the company and the unions are now discussing" and that "government involvement now with money will not solve the chronic restructuring problem."[131]

This was not necessarily seen as positive policy, especially by the unions. CAW leader Buzz Hargrove was particularly outspoken in his critique of Anderson's position, which he, perhaps correctly, framed as an indirect help to Canadian to go ahead and force through the large pay cuts embedded in Benson's restructuring. Here's what Hargrove had to say about it: "It's a major disappointment. It really is an insult to our members. It's condescending to our people. He [Anderson] hasn't told us anything. He's still playing silly-bugger with people's lives."[132]

American Airlines also offered to cut the fees it received from Canadian by $48 million per year for four years (a total of $192 million) if CAW agreed to the wage cuts included in Benson's restructuring plan. This seemed to be a gesture of great openness from American, and Transport Minister David Anderson used it to put pressure on Buzz Hargrove and the CAW: "There are ten of us together and one on the outside. I would like to see Mr. Hargrove and his union come onside for the benefit of 16,400 workers and their families."[133] This was essential to the deal being successful because, as Benson had stated sometime before: "If employees won't step up to the plate, American won't either."[134]

Both Al Becker's activity (he went on a veritable tour de force of meetings) and the understanding that Benson's statement of 9 November ("There is no Plan B") reflected reality and was not just a stunt brought negotiations back on track. Still, CAW was skeptical of the demands put forward by Benson for further monetary sacrifices to be shouldered by employees when more policy initiative was needed from Ottawa. Hargrove jadedly remarked that union workers had "been there, done that" and that the federal government was simply going to stand and look at thousands of jobs disappear. He quipped that "everybody recognizes the problem ... the government must step in to find a solution to stop it"; his suggestion was that Ottawa should go back to allocating routes to the two airlines as it used to do before 1984.[135] He was even more direct on the issue of federal funding: "It just infuriates me that General Motors, the most profitable and powerful company in the world, in Quebec gets $200 million from this government to support 3,000 jobs and we are offered a lousy $20 million to support 16,000 workers and their families."[136]

Transport Minister David Anderson flatly rejected any re-regulation, leaving the door open for the creation of a committee that would include a range of actors from the airline industry, the unions, the consumers, and the communities most affected. Anderson stated that "there is no question of re-regulation," but he remained open to "additional actions that could be taken by industry and government to help foster a competitive and stable business environment that benefits consumers as well as the industry and its employees."[137]

In the mounting bedlam Geoffrey Elliot, Air Canada's Vice-President of Governmental Affairs, stated that his company would support the removal of foreign investment restrictions in the industry, pointing at the high level of integration within the industry itself. Canadian quickly picked up the same point.[138] Air Canada could well afford to be generous: its third quarter looked bright, having posted a $181 million earning, and the company was still optimistic about increasing its share of the Asian market, so much so that in August it had put in a new order for more Airbus planes[139] with which it intended to increase pressure on its rival.

Ottawa had put forward a great set of goals with which everyone could, as usual, agree, but it was short of details on how to get there. An analyst who wished to remain anonymous noted that CAW's proposal for more direct governmental action included some old-fashioned common sense: "Really what CAW is saying is the government should get in there and tell them [the airlines] to behave more rationally, since they have been unable to do it themselves."[140] At the same time, though, CAW was not allowing a general members' vote within Canadian to take place, concerned that the workers, made skittish by the Cassandra-like scenarios that circulated, would simply go ahead and take the pay cut. This drew heavy critiques from all levels.

The two sides appeared to be moving steadily away from each other, their positions irreconcilable. On 4 December an unusually gloomy Kevin Benson addressed his employees: "I can only apologize to all of you for letting you down … I'm ill-prepared personally to accept the conclusion that's now in front of us, but absent Hargrove changing his mind in the next twenty-four hours, I'm afraid I'm out of options."[141] In the end though, everyone was forced to accept that the sole solution was to bite the bullet and trudge on. On 20 December CAW and IAM&AW voted to accept the pay cuts.[142]

In all this Air Canada had not remained quiet. As we saw, it had intended to go after Canadian right where its competition would feel it the most: in Asia. This had been a long-term strategy, since even in 1996 Air Canada had been pressing hard to get more flights into Hong Kong. Anita Leung, Air Canada representative in the Territory noted that "in fairness, the Canadian government should give us daily flights, I just don't think [Ottawa] is looking at the question with any attention."[143]

The Ministry of Transport replied that, while the minister was "prepared to consider" the issue, this remained a matter of cooperation between the Canadian government and the Territory's administration. This sounded, to Air Canada personnel, as if there still were some policy holdouts in Ottawa. Ms. Leung was convinced that "privatization and deregulation are not working in the full meaning of the words" for Air Canada.[144] The strategy had been successful, and its fruit would show in the future.

Better Days? Recovery in the Late 1990s

In 1997 Canadian embraced a leaner business model, focusing more on cost reductions. It had cut its money-losing routes and had been able to rally support from its unions, its American partners, and from both levels of government. The first two quarters showed some moderate economic improvement. In February the BC government made good on its promise and sent a total of $11.1 million in fuel tax rebates,[145] and Canadian continued to pursue its dual strategy of building up its Vancouver hub and increasing its cross-border traffic into the US with the help of American Airlines.[146] A successful step in this strategy came when Canadian received approval from the Taiwanese government to put American's codes onto its flights from Vancouver to Taipei.[147] Even as the federal government refused to intervene in the market process, the Calgary-based company and its employees had bought some time for themselves.

The work ahead would be difficult and particularly hard; none held any illusions about this, least of all management. The deep-seated problem remained the same: how to wrest enough market share from Air Canada and at the same time post consistent profits, pay off at least some of the crushing debt burden with which Canadian was saddled, and cut operating costs? In practice this would mean convincing more people to fly Canadian, especially in North America; obtaining further labour concessions from a host of already overly skeptical employees; and improving general management yields. The initial results were mixed: while profits showed a degree of improvement, analysts noted a shift in traffic during the year. Jacques Kavofian, with Research Capital Corporation, noted that "it's a market share shift from Canadian to Air Canada," while James David with HSBC James Capel Canada noted that Canadian had been putting too many of its eggs in a single basket: "The Asian routes are the only real source of income for this airline, they cannot stand any deviation from their plans."[148] The shift appeared to be confirmed as the months progressed, and disappointment mounted with the small gain affected by

Canadian, especially when compared with the excellent year Air Canada was having.[149]

Still, in October Canadian was looking good compared to previous years. This prompted Benson to note, at an Empire Club of Canada luncheon where he was the keynote speaker, that his company "was no longer fighting a survival battle."[150] Perhaps just to be on the safe side, the luncheon had been opened by a clergyman who led with a prayer including an intercession for the airline. In the short term it seemed to help: in October the company's stock went (and stayed) above $4; Canadian was now profitable in the Toronto-Ottawa-Montreal triangle, which in the past had been a major source of financial woe; London and the Asian markets were yielding very well; and costs were being contained. Benson could even say that "cash is not a problem ... we are very comfortable."[151]

In the end, though, Air Canada kept increasing pressure on its competitor and forcing it into ever-mounting debt while posting better traffic results.[152] A key element in this approach was the continuous push for extended access to Asia; this required a policy change because, as Durrett put it, "the [current] policy did not envision all these global alliances and Transport is well aware of that and [is] addressing the issue."[153] A second pillar in Air Canada's strategy was to ensure consistent profitability from the company. Over two years it added 38 routes, shifting its revenue base so that 52 per cent of its profits came from international flights; it also tried to control costs more effectively and to reshape its regional carriers.[154] This was not a completely painless process as demonstrated by a pilots' strike between January and March 1997 that cost the airline almost $57 million, but it was done nonetheless.

Canadians' wage cuts, restructuring, and the brave fight put up by its employees and directors had changed the nature of the large gap between the two carriers, a gap that could not be closed under the current circumstances and that we can now say was leading towards the extinction of Canadian Airlines. Deregulation in the sector had not automatically created a better, more competitive market; rather, it had sparked a brutal competition that was now crushing one (if not both) airlines. Although faced with the now probable loss of competition, Ottawa refused to intervene directly to resolve the situation. Its consistent trend towards allowing more competition in all markets, especially in Asia, was hurting Canadian.

Things looked different on the ground: after finally posting a decent quarter, Canadian's management was still keeping a calm approach. CEO Kevin Benson noted that "there is no big celebrations going on anywhere in the company at these results, they are as targeted, no more, no less."[155]

Along with finally showing profits Canadian could brag about having increased by 65 per cent its transborder flights to the US thanks to the affiliation it had established with American Airlines.

At the same time, the federal government seemed marginally better disposed towards Canadian. Finance Minister Paul Martin took a more conciliatory stance with regard to the tax break for fuel tax that Transport Minister David Anderson had negotiated in 1996. The Finance Department agreed to 10-1 ratio ($800 million tax losses to give up in exchange for an $80 million fuel tax rebate), lowering the ratio from the 20-1 offered originally and further sweetening the deal by proposing that the tax write-off could be reinstated if Canadian paid back its fuel tax rebate at some future time.[156]

In April the situation finally appeared to be on track. Canadian even paid back, three years ahead of time, a $12 million loan it had negotiated with Alberta. Alberta Treasurer Stockwell Day quipped, perhaps with little foresight: "I am always thrilled when we take another step towards getting completely out of the business of business.... Canadian's continuing success is another signal that our economy is moving forward." To be fair, at the time it was hard to be pessimistic: Canadian had posted a $5.4 million profit for 1997 and had cut its operating costs by $212 million. It had even signed a deal with Chile's LanChile Airlines to serve that country's market.[157]

This was a good time for the airline industry: even in the midst of the so-called Asian Crisis business picked up, people kept on flying. As further evidence Air Canada posted a $427 million net profit for 1997, its best showing in 60 years. In December concerns over the one-sided source of profits from Canadian's operations, triggered by the crisis in confidence over the Asian economic meltdown resurfaced among airline analysts. Even when David Bell, vice-president and treasurer for Canadian announced that the company had not "felt anything from this recent activity in the last couple of months.... [o]ur results have not been affected negatively at all,"[158] analysts still remained convinced that some much-needed room to manoeuvre had evaporated.

Canadian Airlines worked hard all through 1998, expanding its Vancouver hub and its Asian business[159] and posting a profit. It was looking to generate some $150 million in new cash through a stock issue. Its strategy demanded that capacity be increased to take advantage of new business in Asia and of the full effects of the Open Skies policy so, in 16 months, it increased its fleet from 99 to 161 planes and began hiring again. In September it joined the OneWorld Alliance, and a 1996 profit-sharing agreement, according to which its employees would split 20 per cent of pre-tax earning, kicked in.

In May, Air Canada pilots began a strike which cut deeply into the company's revenues. In contrast to that labour strife, Canadian's CEO, Kevin Benson, noted that Canadian's "employees are far more realistic. They value their jobs more because they've seen them threatened more often.... Do they want to be paid comparably with others? Of course they do. So do I. So do we all. But you've got to be successful, and then you can share the spoils."[160] And this is exactly what Canadian could not do, especially as Air Canada lobbied more aggressively for more and more Asian slots, at the same time hinting that massive economic losses would result from continuing the current policy. This seemed to strike a chord with the Liberal government. Benson tried to appeal to Ottawa by underscoring the problems with allowing more competition in Asia: "Air Canada is advocating a dumping of existing policy in their favour. Their plea is for open skies, but that's not what they mean. Our understanding of open skies is that everybody gets a chance to go at it."[161]

Once again Canadian's pleas seemed to have little effect in Ottawa.

Endgame: The ONEX Bid To Restructure the Airline Industry

The economic situation at Canadian Airlines continued to worsen, and it had become obvious that the airline industry in its present configuration was not viable. The market in Canada had not been able to support both airlines; infusions of foreign capital may have helped in the short-term, but, in the long run, they could not change the structural elements of the situation. In the second part of 1999, Air Canada and ONEX Corporation both made their move towards acquiring control of Canadian. The federal government now faced the very real possibility not only that Canadian's 16,000 employees would be laid off if and when the company folded, but that the West would perceive the federal hands-off policy as tacit support for Air Canada. Ottawa had certainly reduced the visibility and intensity of its intervention in the airline industry during the 1990s, but, if it had not provided detailed policies to the sector, it still had given it policy direction. In particular it had followed two recurring themes: allowing the market to play a larger role while retaining a sound and stable air transportation system.

These goals involved disparate but overlapping elements. More reliance on market mechanisms meant that the federal authorities allowed more competition among airlines and were less concerned with spelling out the details of that competition and less pro-active in seeking specific results. On the other hand, the peculiar geographical configuration of Canada and the relative maturity of its air-travellers' market[162] meant that there were important political issues—especially that of the West (Canadian Airlines) versus the East (Air Canada)—to be addressed. One solution was the "dual designation policy," which allowed the two airlines to compete directly in those markets that were deemed large enough to sustain them both; another was the signing of a variety of bilateral agreements with individual nations that liberalized airline markets.[163] In the end, though, this choice damaged Canadian because it cut deeply into the international profits on which it depended so heavily for its own survival.

The relevance of the two airlines as political symbols for different regions of the country, and their sheer weight as employers, meant that some kind of intervention and some degree of compromise was required. Hints of conflicting policy goals can be found in Ottawa's careful approach to the dual designation policy and in the fact that transport ministers in the 1990s consistently tried to portray themselves more as spectators than as active interveners in the sector even as they provided strong policy direction.

However, by now, Canadian was under serious threat. Despite appealing to market forces to run its course—Transport Minister Colenette was quoted on 25 August 1999 as stating that "We [the federal government] are a bystander at this stage"[164]—Ottawa was now taking concrete steps to find a solution. It had become clear that only a merger was going to save the thousands of jobs that were on the line and retain a decent level of air transportation service across the country. This did not necessarily mean that Air Canada would or should be allowed to gobble up its rival and become the sole master of the Canadian skies. Competition was still a priority, and Ottawa was determined to maintain as competitive an airline sector as possible.

So, in early August, the federal government suspended the Competition Act so that the two airlines could legally begin talks about a merger and then formally stepped back. On August 13, Air Canada proposed to purchase Canadian's international routes, while preserving domestic competition and retaining Canadian employees, along with the assurance that the Calgary headquarters would not be disbanded. This was not very different from previous offers.

Not to be outdone, ONEX CEO Gerry Schwartz, supported by American Airlines, also launched a bid for restructuring the airline industry in Canada. Schwartz noted that the two airlines had been locked in a damaging struggle that had left both badly in need of cash and burdened by overcapacity and massive debt as a result of their previous acquisitions.

In an effort to out-compete each other, they had targeted much the same routes and areas, creating a wasteful set of overlaps. Under the control of ONEX, a merged national airline could increase profitability and rationalize its operations, while keeping almost the entire combined workforce of both airlines.

Schwartz appeared to have a solid shot at making the deal work. His background as a business leader was certainly impressive, as was his record of supporting the Liberal Party. His plan for the takeover called for 54 per cent of the merged airline to be allocated to diffused ownership, 31.1 per cent to be held by ONEX, while the remaining 14.9 per cent would go to American Airlines.[165] ONEX would set up a shell company (AirCo), which would first purchase all of Air Canada shares, either by paying $8.25 cash or by exchanging shares of the two companies on a par basis. If the Air Canada takeover were successful, AirCo would then proceed to offer a merger option to Canadian's stockholders. The latter could exchange their shares for either $2.00 or .24 shares of AirCo.

From a financial and strategic point of view, the success of this operation would have been a masterful coup for ONEX. Although the total acquisition tab ran to about $5.7 billion, the actual new capital would amount to only $1 billion. American Airlines was going to provide half of this money ($250 million directly and $250 million as a loan to ONEX), while ONEX was going to put up $250 million of its own cash and borrow the rest from the Toronto Dominion Bank. Furthermore, most of the total cost was represented by the assumption of debts previously incurred by the two airlines, almost $4 billion.[166] If everything went smoothly, the result would be a company with an equity base of $2 billion and with shares forecast to trade at the $10 level, substantially higher than the $6 paid in mid-August 1999 for Air Canada and sevenfold the $1.50 for Canadian. The plan also called for a reduction of 12.5 per cent of the combined workforce of the two airlines—roughly 5,000 people—on a 50/50 basis (therefore impacting the much smaller Canadian Air workforce disproportionately).

Schwartz's strategy ran into a series of obstacles. First, it had to contend with the ever-present issue of foreign ownership. Many felt that the proposed allocation of shares gave too much control to American Airlines, even though this was not strictly true. If Canadian filed for bankruptcy, American would lose the $246 million it had invested in the company in the early 1990s. Under this deal, American would gain some important new feeder traffic, but its actual share in the new company would be lower than the one it held in Canadian to begin with. Secondly, some were concerned that this deal would mean reduced competition and higher prices.

To complicate matters, Air Canada had no intention of allowing ONEX to not only snap up its rival but to be gobbled itself and announced that it would treat Schwartz's proposal as a hostile bid. On 24 August an Air Canada press release reiterated the fact that Schwartz's proposal was nothing more than a transfer of value from Air Canada to American and that the whole project seemed contrary to the Air Canada Public Participation Act, which fixed foreign ownership at 10 per cent.[167]

Nevertheless, the Liberal government announced that it would allow the deal to proceed. Perhaps they saw the Onex bid as an opportunity to let things roll along the market path and did not implicitly dislike a solution that not only would infuse some new capital into the airline industry as it rationalized the sector but, most importantly, would save a large portion of airline jobs in Canada. Interestingly enough, the government seemed unconcerned at the notion of a merger that would concentrate 80 per cent of national capacity in the hands of a single company, while it had been much tougher on bank mergers just a few months before (see Chapter 3 for a discussion of this issue).

In the end the ONEX bid went nowhere. It was bogged down by the resistance put up by Air Canada, was never fully endorsed by Canadian public opinion, and was gravely damaged when a Quebec judge deemed it to be illegal as it did, in fact, break the 10 per cent foreign ownership limit. Schwartz had no choice but to back away from the deal. For a little while, some talk still lingered that ONEX might go ahead and buy Canadian but this option was not a realistic one, and the ONEX-American Airlines option melted away.

Air Canada Moves In: The End of Canadian

PWA had no energy left to fight a losing battle. Air Canada made an offer to buy all issued and outstanding common shares and non-voting shares of Canadian Airlines Corporation for $2.00 per share. On 5 December 1999, Canadian's board of directors recommended that the offer be approved.[168] A sufficient number of shares were tendered, and early in January 2000 the deal was final. It took a few months to bring all loose ends together but on 6 July 2000 Canadian Airlines became a wholly-owned subsidiary of Air Canada.

This was the end of Ottawa's "Two Airlines Policy." The notion that travellers should be able to choose between two major national air carriers was unique and perhaps even a bit perverse given the size of the market in Canada, but this had been one of the federal government's leading policy principles. As Canadian's financial situation crumbled, Ottawa was forced to back down. Too many jobs were at stake at a time when it was obvious that two major airlines could not compete against one another in Canada and survive. Clearly, moreover, deregulation had not proved to be a panacea for increased competition and better markets, especially when the initial playing field was as uneven as that between Air Canada and Canadian.

In July 2000, the Air Travel Complaints Commission was formed. Between then and the end of the year it received over 1,200 complaints, 82 per cent of which were directed at Air Canada and its affiliates.[169] These complaints, focused mainly on the quality of the service offered by the airlines, were used to support the theory that a monopolistic Air Canada had no incentive to treat passengers well.

Although almost reluctant to intervene directly in the business arena, the federal government had imposed specific limits and demands once Canadian Airlines ceased to exist. Air Canada had to sell Canadian's regional branch, delay the start-up of its own discount carrier, and relinquish some of the slots it owned in Toronto. In addition, Transport Minister Colenette demanded a commitment from the now-dominant airline that it would respect competition in Canada. This type of policy direction, which mixed strong commitment to the principles of open markets, competition, and protection of jobs and consumers, produced seemingly paradoxical results. Air Canada had become a virtual monopolist in the domestic market, but had to maintain competitive practices. It had acquired 80 per cent of national capacity, but had to respect its smaller competitors. Consequences could be dire if Air Canada did not comply: "If we have to let the Americans in, if that's the only way that we can get competition, then we'll let the Americans in," Colenette warned.[170]

The company spent the rest of the year 2000 in restructuring and reorganizing. The federal government seemed content with the steps taken to conform to its policy direction and with the fact that as many jobs as possible had been saved with the merger. It is one thing to allow market forces to shape most of the decisions in the airline sector, it is quite another to find competition suddenly trounced and a monopoly of the sector a possible reality. In order to address these risks, the government amended the Transportation Act in 2000 by introducing Bill C-26. Three broad areas came under its scope: it was geared towards the protection of consumers from monopoly pricing and anti-competitive behaviour; it was aimed at assuring a level playing field for the remaining air companies, which were all small compared to Air Canada; and it was designed to ensure continued service to small and isolated communities.

What the bill could not address completely were the problems arising from the peculiar circumstances of the airline industry in a country whose population centres are as far-flung and widespread as Canada. Plagued by razor-thin profit margins, the industry has to contend with contrasting demands. It must satisfy exacting security and safety standards and must provide services to small and remote communities. However, it cannot cross-subsidize these marginal routes with higher prices on more common ones without attracting criticism from the public and the government. It is an industry that naturally tends towards monopoly or oligopoly, because of its high overhead costs and the difficulties of market entry that require enormous amounts of capital. But it is often regulated by intensely competitive tools, because governments are politically sensitive to consumers' demands for low transportation prices. For these reasons, it is a highly volatile industry but requires massive, long-term capital investment.[171]

Regulation can only go so far in such a setting. Governments can legislate all they want, but it is ultimately high-yield business travellers who make or break an airline; if they do not fly, the company is doomed. Often enough, the reasons for choosing to fly are not necessarily under the control of any government (or private) actor. In any case, Bill C-26 was an interesting attempt at restating the ground rules that Ottawa intended to impose on the airlines: competition, consumer protection, and security of service within the framework of free markets and a modicum of policy direction.

Nonetheless, Air Canada began 2001 with relatively good prospects. Having consolidated its hold on the Canadian airline industry, it could now finally look forward to progressively getting rid of the debt incurred to eliminate its competition. Part of this project was a restructuring of its workforce to lower the high overhead created by the merger. The 2001 forecast of operations announced that 3,500 jobs would be eliminated during the year, primarily through attrition and voluntary separation packages. Moreover, the company would cut its least profitable routes and most expensive planes from its operations, in the hope of seeing profits in the third quarter. These were further painful cuts, but ones that Ottawa could accept.

The terrorist attacks of September 11, however, threw the whole industry into confusion. The US government closed its airspace to commercial flights for a remarkably long period of time, choking the major source of revenue for most large airlines and impacting dramatically on Air Canada's operation. The industry lost billions per day. Even after skies were reopened to traffic, the world was in shock, and many people were not interested in flying, perhaps fearing that more terrorists would use passenger jets to bomb buildings in any Western country. Bookings fell; both economy class passengers (who contribute little to airlines' bottom lines) and business and first class travellers (who are the main source of revenue in the passenger business) showed unwillingness to travel either domestically or internationally. Business people shifted to video-conferencing from red-eye flights; tourists drove to nearby locations rather than flying to other continents. Although recovery could be predicted for the long run, the immediate effect was devastating for an industry that needs a consistent cash flow to maintain and run its airplanes and facilities and that clears a small return, not often above 5 per cent.

After the attacks, Air Canada's new CEO Robert Milton gave an interview to *Maclean's* magazine in which he voiced his concerns over the deep crisis in which the airline industry found itself. In particular, he reiterated the need for the federal government to contribute between $3 billion and $4 billion to shore up his company's operations. A mix of loan guarantees, tax deferrals, and straight cash injections, this money was deemed necessary in the face of a steep liquidity crisis and probable drops in future investment in the sector. Ottawa would not play this game; the government promised that some money would be forthcoming but not nearly as much as Milton had hoped for.

Air Canada absorbed its losses as best as it could by further cutting its workforce, negotiating new financing, and removing many of its narrow-body airplanes from its regional and mainline fleets. Losses for 2001 were staggering: $731 million operating losses and a $1.25 billion net loss. Passenger revenues for the year dropped by over $1 billion, a 12 per cent equivalent.[172] And yet, Air Canada did not fare so poorly among its peers: later in the year it was taken off Moody's *Creditwatch*, and its third and fourth quarter revenues were stronger than expected. Many jobs were chopped, some of the impact was reduced through attrition, job-sharing, and voluntary departures. The demise of the charter airline Canada 3000 helped boost domestic revenues even as Air Canada reduced its domestic capacity. The process of restructuring that had begun in 2000 and had been consolidated during the hi-tech meltdown of 2001 certainly served as an important blueprint for the post 9/11 situation and may have had something to do with the airline's rebound. These were drastic measures for extraordinary times. Although they went against the conditions of the plan negotiated with the federal authorities at the time of the merger, there was very little that Ottawa could do, especially as it refused to be as generous with financial support as the US administration had been to its airlines.

On October 22, Air Canada announced that it had secured over half a billion dollars of new aircraft financing. With about C$1 billion in available cash and credit it was now in a much safer financial position.[173] The fact that it could negotiate these deals itself spoke to the confidence that financial and business institutions had in its stability.

For smaller airlines the September 11 attacks had mixed effects. West-Jet immediately claimed that it did not need any handout from any level of government, let alone a salvage package. This bold statement was true, given the specific operation that WestJet was running: a domestic discount flyer, run superbly but on a small scale that allowed it to absorb the post-September 11 shocks much better than other carriers. Canada 3000 fared much worse; its operation, much more reliant on international and intercontinental routes than WestJet and its pockets much less deep than Air Canada, closed down on 9 November 2001 leaving thousands of passengers stranded and thousands of employees jobless.[174]

Airline companies around the world were in similar straits. Most national governments entered the fray with hefty financial packages to support their national companies (the most striking exceptions being the cases of SwissAir and Sabena in Belgium, which have gone out of business). The aftermath of September 11 provided a massive jolt to airlines everywhere, forcing them to review their policies and to reconsider their approaches to competition. The general trend in the aviation industry towards integration of large and medium airlines into "families" like the StarAlliance—or partnerships like KLM and Air France—has proved to be of some help in this period and will probably continue in the future. Smaller, discount operations like WestJet and the Irish airline Ryan Air have also been quite successful in spite of much economic turbulence and are probably here to stay, even if their ability to truly challenge large companies is doubtful.

The problems Air Canada faced continued to increase as rising costs and increased external and internal pressures mounted. In February 2003 the company announced that it would post a $428 million loss for the previous year with $364 million concentrated in the fourth quarter.[175] The main reason for such results was, according to Air Canada executives, due to increased competition on the domestic front.

Milton sought to muddle through his airline's problems in the usual manner. He asked his employees for $650 million in labour costs concessions, which would result in a smaller workforce and smaller pay cheques for many; this would reduce Air Canada's labour costs by 22 per cent. Management also looked into selling more of its few remaining assets by trying, unsuccessfully, to find a buyer for its regional airline, Jazz, which lost $90 million in 2002. They also explored the option of converting Air Canada Cargo and its ground-handling services to independent subsidiaries and of selling 49 per cent of Air Canada Technical Services. Only a few weeks before this announcement was made, Onex Corporation purchased 35 per cent of the lucrative affinity credit card business Aeroplan (which administered frequent-flyer points for Air Canada).

Within two months, the outbreak of the pulmonary infection SARS (especially in Toronto and Vancouver), the effects of economic slowdown in the US, and reduced bookings due to the military intervention against Iraq led Air Canada to file for bankruptcy protection. Saddled with $13 billion in debt, endemically losing money in its attempt to undercut regional budget airlines like WestJet and Labrador Air, the company reached the breaking point. Air Canada lost $4 million per day during the first quarter of 2003; after the SARS scare began, these losses mounted to $5 million per day.

Using the 2003 court order related to bankruptcy protection, CEO Milton began to trim jobs, firing 200 flight attendants between Vancouver and Edmonton, and refusing to pay the salary hikes negotiated the previous year. The traditional airlines business model, he announced at the beginning of April 2003, was broken, and if Air Canada was to survive it must be fixed quickly and radically. Supported by a US$700 million loan from GE Capital Corporation, he was able to refuse a short-term $300 million loan that the federal government had offered. This refusal was an attempt, on Milton's side, to retain as much latitude as possible in the struggle against WestJet, its major domestic rival. Milton was concerned that, by accepting Ottawa's money, his company would be forced to tone down its price war with WestJet despite Transportation Minister Collenette's protestations to the contrary. Although Ottawa might be concerned about a new fare war during a less than buoyant period, it was issuing only policy directions, not regulations.

Still, the problems for Air Canada might just be beginning. The company was now in the midst of restructuring; aside from curbing its unions, it looked at offloading more assets and finding some degree of cooperation from its many creditors. The first issue was to reduce massive labour costs; after announcing that the top 25 executives in the company would take a 15 per cent cut in their salaries, the company approached its unions. Its aim was to achieve $770 million in reduced labour costs, equivalent to about one-third of its yearly labour cost. Negotiations were undertaken at a pace set by the Ontario Superior Court. The pieces started to fall into place. On 26 May, the airline and CAW reached an agreement that would leave wages more or less unchanged while preserving employee pensions, but would also eliminate a minimum of 827 ticket-agent and call-centre jobs;[176] the final cut might go as high as 1,700 jobs. Of the four unions representing Air Canada's workforce, CUPE, representing flight attendants, accepted up to 2,000 new job cuts in addition to the 400 positions already lost; the IAM&AW also accepted substantial job reductions—up to 1,400 layoffs—and also took a 1.5 per cent wage cut per year for three years.[177] The only union left without an agreement at the end of May was the Air Canada Pilots Association (ACPA). While representing only 3,400 workers, this group had to be brought on board for the reorganization of the company to be viable. On top of a 15 per cent pay-cut, the pilots were asked to accept a variety of productivity concessions and rollbacks, which amounted to a further decrease in pay. Pressure was put on the pilots to accept the deal and keep Air Canada flying, but the ACPA chafed not only because of the lower remuneration but also because it perceived the fast pace of negotiations set by the court as a breach of due process.[178]

Nonetheless, little choice was left to the pilots: they had to negotiate or face the very real possibility that the courts would order Air Canada to cease operations. The ultimate deadline, imposed by Justice James Farley of the Ontario Superior Court of Justice, was midnight Saturday, 31 May. In a nail-biting negotiation, pilots and management hammered out a deal at 3:00 am on Sunday morning, thereby staving off the worst. Even though full details were not released, significant concessions were made by the ACPA.[179] Along with the deal reached with its Jazz regional subsidiary, Air Canada had managed to cut costs by a total of over $1.1 billion. Specifically, reductions of labour costs at Air Canada itself accounted for $766 million, while another $110 million in reduced labour costs came from the deal negotiated with Jazz. Non-unionized and management employees contributed $120 million, and $110 million was saved by redesigning the airline network to be smaller.

These were only the first steps. Once labour costs had been cut—a euphemism for firing people and cutting their wages—employees at Air Canada expected the same kind of dedication from management. It would take some time for all the pieces to fall into place. The restructuring of the largest Canadian airline included significant changes in its services such as moving towards the low-cost model, selling off its larger planes, focusing on a more homogeneous fleet, and transforming Jazz into the equivalent of WestJet. It remained to be seen how the public would react to these changes.

Discussion

The recent history of airlines in Canada is a tale of bitter struggle and burning disappointment. It began with the colossal efforts of the late 1980s and early 1990s and has ended with the dramatically altered landscape after September 11, 2001 and the filing for bankruptcy protection by Air Canada in April 2003. Air Canada carries $13 billion in debt, all accumulated in about 15 years since it was privatized, a chilling situation by any standard, and yet it enjoys some important advantages. It has a firm grip on the Canadian domestic market and, if service standards improve, it is likely to be wholeheartedly supported by Canadians. The key will be to find a way out of the financial chasm in which it is being swallowed. This will likely take political as well as financial muscle.

The industry in Canada has undergone significant restructuring, and new policies have been slowly formulated by the actors. This involved, above all, the practical transition towards a monopoly held by Air Canada. The notion of competition (or lack thereof) is now more than ever central in a market cornered by one single airline that accounts for well over 80 per cent of capacity in the country and is challenged only by a small group of rivals that, while dynamic and, in same cases like WestJet more profitable, still lack the critical mass to provide a real alternative service.

More important still is the fact that, after securing its hegemony in the regular market, Air Canada has recently begun an attempt at putting additional pressure on the discount market by starting mirror operations with its Zip, Jazz, and Tango brands. This seems likely to have repercussions on at least those of its discount competitors who are not able to draw on as many financial resources and match the political clout of Air Canada. However, this tactic has only bled more financial resources from that company, bringing it to the brink of failure.

The ultimate success of Air Canada's 1990s strategy—the elimination of its most dangerous rival—may have been a pyrrhic victory, costing both sides dearly and limiting consumers' choices. To Canadian Airlines, the final decade of the twentieth century brought increasing frustration as it slowly but undeniably lost ground to Air Canada, due to the cutthroat competition to which the two airlines had committed themselves and to the financial pressures derived from the never fully absorbed spate of mergers undergone between 1986 and 1991. Canadian found remarkably little support in Ottawa, from either the Conservative or the Liberal governments. Because both governments' policy was to let market forces run their course, the end result was Air Canada's triumph. The Montreal-based airline had deeper pockets, better routes, and better connections; finally,

Canadian was forced into bankruptcy. Its attempt at propping up its faltering operation through a partnership with American Airlines was never allowed to proceed, as it was perceived as a threat to Canadian control of the domestic skies.

Ironically, the final report of the Transportation Act Review Panel, in October 2002, incorporated, among its many recommendations, suggestions for highly increased competition in a North American Common Aviation Area and proposals for the review of legislation hindering the establishment of foreign-owned domestic carriers. This was exactly the position that had been held by Canadian and, to an extent, by ONEX Corporation.

What was the role of governments throughout the whole process? As noted above Ottawa always embraced the concept that the airlines' business was a market issue, thereby distancing itself from the labour unrest symbolized by airline employees' protest marches and avoiding what generally looked like a lose-lose proposition for any government intervention. There definitely was a shift in the policy style followed in this sector: Ottawa relied less and less on policy intervention and more and more on policy direction. Mixing strong commitment to a specific set of principles deemed necessary for the development of a healthy airlines' industry with aimed intervention, federal authorities managed to retain an offhand approach while imposing some degree of direction on the whole process. Provincial governments, especially in the West, did what they could in the early and mid-1990s but ultimately their contribution was too small to make any long-lasting contribution.

From a cynical point of view one could say that Ottawa sided with Air Canada, given its refusal to help Canadian while opening up foreign markets, especially those in Asia, to Air Canada in the name of competition. As noted above, there might be more than a kernel of truth to this speculation. It must also be said that the situation was particularly complicated and that not very many avenues were open to government intervention. Ottawa could have propped up Canadian through a mix of loan guarantees and an infusion of cash, but how could such an intervention be explained at a time when government was disengaging from intervention in the sector and when the competition between the two rivals was so tight? Could Ottawa seriously be expected to support one company and not the other?

Moreover, the federal government's philosophy resisted changing the policy framework of the industry. Ottawa was not keen on relaxing the rules that dealt with foreign ownership of domestic carriers; even today, despite the recommendations of the Transportation Act Review Panel, there is no real guarantee that a new policy will be formulated. What certainly changed was the attitude towards monopoly control of the airline industry. By allowing Canadian Airlines to become part of Air Canada, Ottawa implicitly accepted the notion of quasi-monopolistic control of commercial air service by the latter. It is enough to note here that the Mulroney government had been extremely clear in stressing the importance of allowing competition to develop in the airline industry so that consumers could reap the benefits of better, more efficient companies who could offer fares at a lower price. It was thought that deregulation would provide competition, as if by the stroke of a magic wand. It was not to be. Deregulation generated a brutal conflict and a quasi-monopoly.

In the end federal authorities allowed the situation to progress along very specific tracks. They may not have intervened with detailed regulation to direct the development of airline policy in Canada, but they were very firm on issues like foreign ownership. This meant that Air Canada secured a predominant position in the industry, and that American Airlines was shut out of its deal with Canadian. In an inherently dynamic sector, this approach allowed Ottawa to maintain a buffer zone between its decisions and public opinion, to keep some continuity in the policies it implemented, and to claim that its pledge to a market approach was being respected.

What does the future hold for the airline industry in general? There is no doubt that since September 2001, tourist and business air travel has decreased enormously, but airlines had weathered similar storms before. Small profit margins, enormous overhead costs, and competition from alternative communication systems had already resulted in the need for restructuring. The terrorist attacks worked as a catalyst, denying the industry any residual adjustment space. The future struggle is going to be between increasingly large global carriers and smaller national companies. After filing for bankruptcy protection on 1 April 2003 Air Canada was ultimately successful not only in renegotiating its labour costs structure, thereby cutting $1.1 billion from its costs, but also in asserting its position that the old organizational model "was broken" and deep changes were needed. These changes were achieved at breakneck speed within two months under enormous pressure from court-established deadlines and, once again, with little apparent policy intervention from federal or provincial authorities.

The future is hazy for Air Canada and not just because of the economic situation in which it is embroiled. The policy field is clear only in the sense that the federal government is committed to an arms-length approach, where goals and principles are detailed, but the choice of the means to achieve them is left to the private sector. It will take an enormous effort from all sides to restructure Air Canada, and it may well be that, before this is achieved, Ottawa will need to take things in hand, even if it may dislike doing so.[180]

Chronology

1 SEPTEMBER 1937: The first flight by Trans-Canada Airlines, a Crown corporation, between Vancouver and Seattle.

1964: Trans-Canada Airlines becomes Air Canada.

1978: Deregulation of the American airline industry begins; Air Canada is placed on business footing.

1981: President Reagan completes air deregulation.

1983: Liberal Transport Minister Axworthy introduces government position paper "New Canadian Airline Policy."

1985: Conservative government releases *Freedom to Move*, a discussion paper on transportation reform.

1987: Conservatives amend National Transportation Act (Bill C-18) to deregulate the industry; National Transportation Agency replaces Canadian Transport Committee; PWA buys CP Air for $300 million; Air Canada and Canadian agree to merge their reservation systems.

1988: Ottawa privatizes Air Canada.

1991: The Gulf War and recession spell a horrible year for airlines.

1992

31 JANUARY: National Transportation Act Review Commission appointed.

20 FEBRUARY: Hollis Harris becomes president of Air Canada; declares that Canada can support only one airline.

19 MARCH: PWA announces talks with American Airlines after calling off talks with Air Canada.

30 MARCH: Air Canada declares that it will object to any PWA/American deal before the National Transportation Agency.

APRIL-JULY: Air Canada cuts management staff by 10 per cent, sells its cargo jets, and slashes 1,800 jobs.

18 JULY: PWA board member Ron Southern meets Deputy Prime Minister Mazankowski in Alberta.

23 JULY: The federal government makes it clear that any help for Canadian is conditional on a merger with Air Canada.

25 JULY: Canadian decides to renew talks with Air Canada.

6 AUGUST: PWA rejects the first merger offer from Air Canada.

15 AUGUST: Second merger offer rejected.

18 AUGUST: Air Canada and United Airlines announce their commercial alliance.

1 SEPTEMBER: PWA tables motion to dissolve Gemini and launches court action to get out of Gemini; Gemini counters with its own court challenge.

2 SEPTEMBER: Air Canada proposes a new merger option.

9 SEPTEMBER: PWA accepts Air Canada's revised offer.

8 OCTOBER: PWA and Air Canada enter pre-merger agreement.

27 OCTOBER: Both companies' boards of directors reject the plan but keep talking.

NOVEMBER: The merger option dies. PWA begins to look for new options and funding from federal and provincial governments and from its employees.

20 NOVEMBER: Royal Commission on Transportation recommends market-oriented transportation policy and user-pay travel.

29 DECEMBER: Canadian and American strike an alliance.

1993

FEBRUARY: 1992 losses announced: Air Canada $454 million and PWA $543 million.

27 MAY: National Transportation Agency unanimously approves American investment in Canadian Airlines.

18 AUGUST: Air Canada offers $1 billion to buy Canadian's international routes.

15 DECEMBER: Breakdown of Air Canada-Canadian talks.

1994

26 JANUARY: Air Canada drops the Gemini case.

27 JANUARY: Liberal government designates Air Canada as second carrier to serve Japan.

MARCH: Canadian moves its reservation system to SABRE.

APRIL: Canadian signs a deal with AMR Corporation for traffic-sharing.

NOVEMBER: Canadian Airlines is allowed to begin flying directly into Washington, DC.

DECEMBER: Air Canada is allowed to fly into Hong Kong.

1995

24 FEBRUARY: The US and Canada sign the Open Skies pact.

JUNE: New CFO Kevin Benson revises Canadian Airlines balance sheet; it now shows heavy losses as opposed to the predicted gains.

JUNE-DECEMBER: Employees at PWA progressively begin to question the capacity of management to keep the airline profitable; Air Canada continues to put pressure on Canadian to drive it into further debt.

1996

29 FEBRUARY: Westjet founded.

29 MAY: The new Canadian Transportation Act receives royal assent. It creates the Canadian Transportation Agency and shifts policy so that companies are allowed to operate in full freedom with regards to routes, types of aircraft, and airports.

28 JUNE: Kevin Benson replaces Kevin Jenkins as CEO of Canadian Airlines; a major shake-up ensues and interconnections with American Airlines increase.

NOVEMBER: Canadian Airlines is once again strapped for cash; management asks for large wage reductions and cost control measures from employees; CAW resists these demands. Federal Transport Minister David Anderson rejects calls for re-regulation.

15 NOVEMBER: Mass resignation of Canadian's board of directors.

4 DECEMBER: Canadian's CEO Benson announces that if CAW does not come on board the airline will fold.

20 DECEMBER: CAW and IAM&W vote to accept pay cuts.

DECEMBER: BC comes through for Canadian with political and financial assistance.

1997

JANUARY-MARCH: Pilots' strike at Air Canada; losses are estimated at about $57 million. Nonetheless, the two airlines both begin to show signs of economic vitality during this year, with Air Canada looking much more solid than its rival. In particular Air Canada focuses on reducing costs and increasing its presence in Asia.

FEBRUARY: BC sends $11.1 million in fuel tax rebates to Canadian.

OCTOBER: Canadian's CEO Benson announces that his company is no longer fighting for economic survival.

JANUARY 1998: Both airlines post profits for 1997, with Air Canada posting a $427 million profit, the best showing in 60 years. Throughout the year, both airlines increase capacity dramatically to undercut their rival.

1999

AUGUST: The federal government suspends the Competition Act for 90 days to permit the airlines to talk about restructuring the industry. During the year, the airline market begins to contract; the high operating costs and debt with which Canadian is saddled begin to tell heavily on its bottom line.

20 AUGUST 1999: Air Canada offer to buy Canadian's international routes is rejected.

24 AUGUST: Onex Corporation offers to buy and merge Air Canada and Canadian Airlines.

28 SEPTEMBER: Transport Minister David Collenette announces that any airline merger in Canada will have to meet five principles, among which are serving small communities and fair pricing.

19 OCTOBER: Air Canada rejects the Onex bid and counters with an offer of its own, which includes acquiring Canadian.

5 NOVEMBER: A Quebec court judges Onex's bid illegal as it would give Onex more then 10 per cent of Air Canada.

5 DECEMBER: Canadian Airlines recommends shareholders accept Air Canada's offer to buy the airline.

2 DECEMBER: Ottawa approves Air Canada's takeover of Canadian.

3 JANUARY 2000: Canadian Airlines International officially becomes a subsidiary of its former rival.

2001

11 SEPTEMBER: Al Quaeda terrorists hijack four commercial jet airliners; two are flown directly into the twin towers of the World Trade Center in New York, which subsequently collapse killing thousands of people; one is flown into the Pentagon in Washington, DC; and the fourth crashes in rural Pennsylvania. All the passengers and hijackers are killed.

NOVEMBER: Canada 2000 terminates its operation.

NOVEMBER: Air Canada launches its domestic discount airline, called Tango.

2002

7 FEBRUARY: Air Canada files a $1.25-billion loss for 2001.

APRIL: Air Canada launches Calgary-based, low-fare carrier, Zip.

21 AUGUST: Air Canada says it will cut another 1,300 jobs as demand drops.

2003

6 FEBRUARY: Air Canada floats the ideas of selling its Jazz airline and asks for $650 million in labour-cost concessions as it announces a $428-million loss for 2002.

1 APRIL: Air Canada files for court protection from creditors.

Notes

1. *Vancouver Sun* 5 September 2000.
2. *The Province* (Vancouver) 8 May 1997.
3. The Judicial Committee of the Privy Council Office determined in 1932 that aeronautics was an exclusive federal jurisdiction under the British North America Act section 132 (to allow Parliament to fulfil Canada's obligations under treaties between the British Empire and foreign countries). This jurisdiction was confirmed by the Supreme Court 20 years later under the peace, order, and good government clause. See Garth Stevenson, *The Politics of Canada's Airlines from Diefenbaker to Mulroney* (Toronto: University of Toronto, 1987) 9-10.
4. House of Commons, *Debates* 5 May 1993: 18934-35.
5. Stevenson 4. Much of the historical analysis that follows is taken from this excellent source.
6. On the deregulation strategy, see Eric Nielson's presentation of the government's position, House of Commons, *Debates*, 13 February 1986: 10783-84. Ten guiding

principles were presented, based on a pragmatic strategy of smarter regulation, which were to achieve greater efficiency, greater accountability, and greater sensitivity to those affected by federal regulation.

7. *Freedom to Move: A Framework for Transportation Reform* (Ottawa: Supply Services, 15 July 1985).

8. House of Commons, *Debates* 17 June 1987: 7271ff.

9. House of Commons, *Debates* 19 December 1986: 2318ff.

10. National Transportation Act (NTA) Review Commission, *Competition in Transportation Policy and Legislation in Review* (Ottawa: Supply and Services, 1993).

11. NTA Review Commission 18.

12. See National Transportation Agency (NTA), *Annual Review* (Ottawa: Supply and Services, 1991, 1992).

13. NTA *Annual Review*, 73. The Brookings Institution concluded that deregulation had saved American consumers $100 billion in its first ten years and led to the doubling of the number of passengers. See "Losing Their Way: Special Survey," *Economist* 12 June 1993: 1-22.

14. The following discussion is substantially based on the *Economist*'s special report on the airline industry, "Losing Their Way."

15. International Air Transport Association, various years, *World Air Transport Statistics* (Montreal).

16. *Globe and Mail* 12 September 1991.

17. *Globe and Mail* 27 March, 1 May, 17 June, 11 July 1992.

18. *Globe and Mail* 6 February 1992.

19. *Globe and Mail* 22 February, 31 March, 8 April 1992.

20. *Globe and Mail* 7, 28 February 1992.

21. *Globe and Mail* 20, 31 March 1992.

22. House of Commons, *Debates* 6 February 1992; *Globe and Mail* 20 March 1992. The debate over the private member's motion was on 27 March and 2 April 1992: 8972ff, 9219-47, 9264-90.

23. House of Commons, *Debates* 6 February 1992; *Globe and Mail* 12 September 1991, 20 March 1992.

24. *Globe and Mail* 15 April, 6 May 1992.

25. House of Commons, *Debates* 4 May 1992: 10043; 3 June: 11298-99.

26. House of Commons, *Debates* 18 June 1992, 12352.

27. *Globe and Mail* 22 July 1992.

28. *Globe and Mail* 1 August 1992.

29. Much of the following is derived from a number of *Globe and Mail* feature articles published 30 July; 1, 11, 13, 24, 26 August; 5 September 1992.

30. *Globe and Mail* 24 August 1992.

31. *Globe and Mail* 5 September 1992. This group was also concerned that they would be held personally liable for PWA's financial obligations if the company failed, in the wake of a number of cases where shareholders in bankrupt companies sued company directors.

32. *Globe and Mail* 1 August 1992.

33. *Globe and Mail* 5 September 1992.

34. *Globe and Mail* 13 August 1992; "Royal Canadian Air Wave," *Maclean's* 10 August 1992: 26-27.

35. *Globe and Mail* 1 August 1993.

36. *Globe and Mail* 28 July 1992.

37. *Globe and Mail* 4 August 1992.

38. *Globe and Mail* 29 July, 24 August 1992.

39. *Globe and Mail* 15 August 1992.

40. *Maclean's* 10 August 1992. Air Canada was closely tied to the Liberal elite of Quebec, but it had Senator David Angus on its board, an important Tory fundraiser from Montreal. The Gemini Group was represented by Patrick Howe, a former aide to Joe Clark.

41. *Globe and Mail* 28 July 1992.

42. *Globe and Mail* 7, 10 August 1992.

43. *Globe and Mail* 14 August 1992.

44. *Globe and Mail* 13, 14 August 1992.

45. *Globe and Mail* 28, 29 July 1992.

46. *Globe and Mail* 11, 13, 14 August 1992.

47. House of Commons, Standing Committee on Consumer and Corporate Affairs, *Proceedings* 48 and 49, 19, 20 August 1992. The witnesses were: David Frank, managing director, Horizon Pacific Ventures Ltd.; Gord Currie, airline analyst for Loewen, Ondaatje, and MacCutcheon; CUPE, Airline Division; International Association of Machinists and Aerospace Workers; Canadian Airlines' Employees Council; Transport Institute at the University of Manitoba; Consumers' Association of Canada; and Transport 2000.

48. *Globe and Mail* 1, 6, 8, 11, 24 August 1992.

49. *Globe and Mail* 17, 24 August 1992.

50. *Globe and Mail* 15, 17, 19 August 1992.

51. *Globe and Mail* 24 August 1992.

52. "Air Turbulence," *Maclean's* 14 June 1993: 24-25.

53. *Globe and Mail* 19, 28 August 1992.

54. *Globe and Mail* 24 September 1992.

55. *Globe and Mail* 18 August 1992.

56. *Globe and Mail* 26 August 1992. Air Canada, predictably, protested that it had eight unused Lockheed L1011 widebodies for sale, but the Department of National Defence insisted that the A310s were the planes it wanted and that it had bought them for a good price. Ironically, these planes had been part of the Wardair fleet that Canadian had inherited in PWA's purchase of the bankrupt company. The planes had already been sold to Lavalin, which in turn went bankrupt! Ironically, as well, while Canadian bid on the conversion of the A310, the contract was awarded to Canadair of Montreal, a fact that was not announced at the time for fear of alienating Alberta voters in the referendum campaign. *Globe and Mail* 18 September 1992.

57. *Globe and Mail* 27 August 1992.

58. *Globe and Mail* 2 September 1992.

59. *Globe and Mail* 20 August 1992.

60. *Globe and Mail* 11 September 1992; "United They Fly," *Maclean's* 21 September 1992: 30-31.

61. *Globe and Mail* 3 September 1992.

62. *Globe and Mail* 10 September 1992.

63. Transport Canada, information statement 169/92, by the Minister of Transport Jean Corbeil, on the decision by the board of directors of PWA corporation to enter into a merger with Air Canada, 9 September 1992

64. House of Commons, *Debates* 8 September 1992: 12720; 9 September: 12765-66; 10 September: 12964-67; 14 September: 13068-69; 16 September: 13195-96, 13288-89; 17 September: 13296; *Globe and Mail* 11 September 1992.

65. *Globe and Mail* 11 September; 9, 10, 30 October; 3, 4 November 1992.

66. *Globe and Mail* 6 November 1992.

67. *Globe and Mail* 11, 13 November 1992.

68. *Globe and Mail* 6, 7 November 1992.

69. *Globe and Mail* 13 November 1992.

70. *Globe and Mail* 18 November 1992.

71. *Globe and Mail* 11 November 1992.

72. *Globe and Mail* 12 November 1992.

73. *Globe and Mail* 13 November 1992; House of Commons, *Debates* 17 November 1992: 13495; 18 November 1992: 13533.

74. *Globe and Mail* 14 November 1992. It must be admitted that Air Canada had had a head start in the deregulated environment, particularly as it—not the government—had pocketed the hundreds of millions of dollars raised in the sale that privatized it.

75. *Montreal Gazette* 10 November 1992.

76. *Globe and Mail* 13, 14, 17 November 1992.

77. The industry's financial difficulties, the large number of jobs at stake, the dedication of Canadian's employees, Ottawa's own financial constraints, the need to limit taxpayer risk, the airline assistance already provided, the complications of court and regulatory processes, the goal of airline financial stability, and the requirement that PWA be controlled by Canadians.

78. *Globe and Mail* 20 November 1992; House of Commons, *Debates* 19 November 1992: 13648.

79. House of Commons, *Debates* 16 November 1992: 13401-3; 17 November 1992: 13493; 20 November: 13707-8; 23 November: 13800ff.

80. Jeffrey Simpson in *Globe and Mail* 25 November 1992; Liberal critic John Manley in House of Commons, *Debates* 24 November 1992: 13903.

81. While there had been some intraparty squabbling over the issue, the Canadian employees' loyalty fit Premier Ralph Klein's self-image as a "people person." The American deal also promised to generate fewer job losses: 1,300 versus the rumoured 10,000 in an Air Canada merger. "The Airline Deal," *Alberta Report* 11 January 1993: 12.

82. *Globe and Mail* 25 November 1992.

83. Ottawa directed that capacity to be cut by 15 per cent. Canadian responded by parking two of its Boeing 737s, cancelling 34 flights, and using fewer but bigger planes. Other conditions were that the financial aid was to be used for operations only, that none of it could be used until Canadian had drawn down completely its line of credit from the Royal Bank, that Ottawa would have a veto over security of assets and sale of any equipment or assets, that Canadian would send a representative to board meetings, and that Canadian would have a say on amalgamation or merger talks with a non-partner. *Globe and Mail* 1, 15 December 1992; House of Commons, *Debates* 2 December 1992: 14406-7; 10 December 1992: 15047.

84. *Globe and Mail* 25 November 1992; House of Commons, *Debates* 24 November 1992: 13903.

85. House of Commons, *Debates* 24 November 1992: 13905.

86. *Globe and Mail* 30 November, 1; 30 December 1992.

87. *Globe and Mail* 28 August 1993. Shareholders received an extra share for every one currently held. Debenture holders gave up any debt claims in exchange for common shares and warrants.

88. House of Commons, *Debates* 19 February 1993: 16197; 22 February 1993: 16270; 24 February 1993: 16391; 9 March 1993: 16273. Canadian cut its capacity again

in late August by 10 per cent, at which time it sold a B767-300ER for a net gain of $15.5 million.

89. House of Commons, *Debates* 22 April 1992: 18317.

90. *Globe and Mail* 2, 27 February: 5 March 1993

91. *Globe and Mail* 23 April 1992.

92. *Globe and Mail* 27 February 1993.

93. *Globe and Mail* 3 April 1993.

94. *Globe and Mail* 12 August 1993.

95. *Globe and Mail* 15 October 1993.

96. Gemini and PWA made an out-of-court settlement on 10 December. No details were revealed, but the size of the settlement did not scuttle the deal with American. *Globe and Mail* 11 December 1993.

97. Federal Court of Appeal, Toronto, Ontario. Hugessen, Heald and MacGregar, J.J. Heard, 12, 13, 14, 15, 16 July 1993. Judgment 30 July 1993. Indexed as *Canada (Director of Investigation and Research, Competition Act) vs. 1 Canada*. See also *Globe and Mail* 31 July 1993.

98. *Globe and Mail* 8 October; 1 November 1993.

99. *Globe and Mail* 31 July 1993.

100. *Globe and Mail* 18 June; 6, 12 August 1993.

101. This event was prefaced by the release of the report of the National Transportation Agency Review Commission, which had been mandated to review the impact of the NTA (1987) after its first five years. The Commission backed the deregulation process fully, characterizing its short-term results as painful but necessary. Among other recommendations, it suggested that the 25 per cent limit on foreign ownership of a Canadian airline be increased to 49 per cent. NTA Review Commission, *Competition in Transportation* (Ottawa: Supply and Services, 1993); *Globe and Mail* 31 July 1993.

102. NTA, Decision No. 297-A-1993. See also *Globe and Mail* 28 May 1993.

103. *Globe and Mail* 3 June 1993.

104. Transport Canada, news release 141/93, "Government Upholds National Transportation Agency Decision," Ottawa, 23 June 1993.

105. Air Canada sweetened its offer in mid-December, promising $250 million in cash for Canadian's overseas lines. It pledged $118 million for parts and equipment associated with these operations, as well as guaranteed jobs for the 1,000 employees working on the overseas lines. It also proposed to pick up the $800 million debt associated with the overseas aircraft and offered a new arrangement for frequent flier points and a discount on providing information management services. The offer was rejected. *Globe and Mail* 19, 20, 23, 25 August, 17; 22 December 1993; *The Toronto Star* 21 August 1993. Liberal leader Jean Chrétien argued that Ottawa should appoint a facilitator to help Air Canada and PWA work things out: "Insults exchanged via the national news by airline presidents won't save valuable jobs. If the parties are going to talk, someone is going to have to bring them together—and that is the role of the government." *Globe and Mail* 25 August 1993. Once elected, the Liberals continued the Conservatives' policy orientation, with Minister of Transport Douglas Young insisting that the new government would not get involved while matters were before the courts. *Globe and Mail* 10 November 1993.

106. *Vancouver Sun* 23 March 1994.

107. *Vancouver Sun* 23 March 1994.

108. *Vancouver Sun* 2 April 1994.

109. *The Province* (Vancouver) 3 May 1994.

110. *Globe and Mail* 26 April 1994.

111. *Globe and Mail* 31 August 1994.
112. *Vancouver Sun,* 24 September 1994.
113. Air Canada and Canadian had 102 flights to the US between them before the Open Skies policy and moved to 460 with its implementation. Peter Pigott, *Wingwalkers: A History Of Canadian Airlines International* (Madeira Park, BC: Harbour Publishing, 1998) 327.
114. *Globe and Mail* 24 October 1995; *Financial Post* 21 July, 25 July 1995; *The Province* (Vancouver) 26 May 1995; *The Province* (Vancouver) 27 June 1995.
115. *Vancouver Sun* 23 December 1995.
116. Quoted in Pigott 330.
117. *The Province* (Vancouver) 18 May 1997.
118. *The Province* (Vancouver) 18 May 1997.
119. *The Financial Post* 31 May 1995.
120. *Vancouver Sun* 17 January 1996.
121. *Vancouver Sun* 22 August 1995.
122. Pigott.
123. Pigott 336.
124. *Vancouver Sun* 9 October 1996.
125. *Globe and Mail* 16 November 1996
126. *Globe and Mail,* 9 December 1996.
127. *Vancouver Sun* 2 December 1996.
128. *Globe and Mail* 30 November 1996.
129. *Globe and Mail* 27 November 1996.
130. *Globe and Mail* 27 November 1996.
131. *Vancouver Sun* 21 November 1996.
132. *The Province* (Vancouver) 29 November 1996.
133. *Vancouver Sun* 4 December 1996.
134. *Globe and Mail* 12 November 1996.
135. *Globe and Mail* 7 December 1996.
136. *The Province* (Vancouver) 2 December 1996.
137. *Vancouver Sun* 7 December 1996.
138. *Globe and Mail* 7 December 1997.
139. *The Province* (Vancouver) 2 November 1997.
140. *Globe and Mail* 7 December 1996.
141. *Financial Post* 21 December 1996.
142. *Vancouver Sun,* 21 December 1996.
143. *Vancouver Sun,* 21 August 1996.
144. *Vancouver Sun* 21 August 1996.
145. *The Province* (Vancouver) 9 February 1997.
146. *Vancouver Sun* 14 January 1997.
147. *Vancouver Sun* 31 July 1997.
148. *Financial Post* 16 July 1997.
149. *Financial Post* 18 September 1997.
150. *Financial Post* 29 October 1997.
151. *Globe and Mail* 16 October 1997.
152. *Vancouver Sun* 21 December 1996.
153. *Financial Post* 24 September 1997.
154. *Financial Post* 6 June 1997.
155. *Financial Post* 26 February 1998.
156. *Vancouver Sun* 6 March 1997.

157. *Globe and Mail* 28 January 1998.

158. *Financial Post* 10 December 1997.

159. *The Province* (Vancouver) 22 October 1998; *Vancouver Sun* 20 February 1998.

160. *Vancouver Sun* 24 September 1998.

161. *Vancouver Sun* 7 May 1998.

162. Michel Archambault and Jacques Roy, "The Canadian Air Transport Industry: In Crisis Or In Transition," *Journal Of Vacation Marketing* 9/1 (2002): 5-16.

163. J.A. Clougherty, et al., "An Empirical Analysis Of Canadian International Air Policy: Effects Of Dual Carrier Designation And Partial Liberalization," *Transport Policy* 8 (2002): 219-30.

164. *Globe and Mail* 26 August 1999.

165. *Globe and Mail,* various issues August-September 1999.

166. *Globe and Mail,* various issues August-September 1999.

167. Air Canada, Press Release 24 August 1999.

168. *Globe and Mail* 6 December 1999.

169. Colby Cosh, "Watcher of the Skies," *Report / Newsmagazine (National Edition)* 28/9 (30 March 2001,): 33.

170. *Montreal Gazette* 18 February 2000.

171. Debra Ward, *Airline Restructuring In Canada: Third Interim Report* (Ottawa: Debra Ward, Independent Transition Observer On Airline Restructuring, 2002).

172. Air Canada, *Annual Report* 2001.

173. Air Canada, Press Release, 22 October 2001.

174. *Vancouver Sun* 10 November 2001.

175. Air Canada, *Quarterly Report* 2003.

176. *Vancouver Sun* 27 May 2003.

177. *Vancouver Sun* 29 May 2003; *Globe and Mail* 29 May 2003.

178. *Vancouver Sun* 29 May 2003.

179. *Globe and Mail* 1 June 2003.

180. As this book was going to press, a deal was confirmed on 22 December 2003 that saw Victor Li, a Hong Kong-based Canadian citizen, purchase 31% of Air Canada. This deal will give his company (Trinity Time Investments Ltd.) substantial control of Air Canada, which will likely now emerge from bankruptcy protection.

CHAPTER THREE

Mergers if Necessary, but not Necessarily Mergers: Competition and Consolidation at Canada's "Big Banks"

RUSSELL ALAN WILLIAMS

On 23 January 1998, the Royal Bank and the Bank of Montreal shocked the federal government by announcing a proposed merger that would rewrite Canada's banking map by creating a new "super-bank." There had not been a merger or takeover among Canada's chartered banks in 40 years. Three months later, Toronto Dominion and the Canadian Imperial Bank of Commerce announced a similar move. The banks had good reason to expect government approval for their mergers. Domestic deregulation of the Canadian banking industry, increased competition from foreign and non-traditional financial service providers, and massive technological change in the financial services sector had all paved the way for conglomeration in financial services. Since these changes were in part the product of government decisions to deregulate the industry since 1987 and since government regulators had shown a permissive attitude towards bank acquisitions of other financial service providers, it might have been reasonable to expect approval.

However, Finance Minister Paul Martin rejected the mergers, suggesting that such weighty decisions on the future of Canada's financial services industry would have to await a comprehensive package of sectoral regulatory reforms. Indeed, within two years the government not only passed new legislation that created a specific process for banks when pursuing mergers, but also approved the largest financial services merger in Canada to date—the Toronto Dominion/Canada Trust merger. Despite the rejection of the 1998 merger proposals, by the summer of 2003, the government announced an informal time-line, in which it invited the banks to prepare another round of merger proposals for 2004.

Why did this happen? How is it that the richest and most powerful corporations in Canada could not get their way? Why did the government reject the merger proposal and only two years later create legislation to make such a merger possible?

Introduction

The announcement on 23 January 1998 of a proposed merger between the Royal Bank and the Bank of Montreal shocked the federal government. Aware that their merger would require the approval of federal regulators, the banks did not waste any time in launching their campaign. They argued, as supporters of the merger would throughout the following year, that in the face of massive technological change, globalization, and increased competition from non-traditional financial service providers "size mattered." The merger would result in an increased economy of scale, allowing the banks to make much-needed investments in new technology.[1] Furthermore, the efficiencies achieved would provide better value for customers, placing the banks in a stronger position to challenge their global competitors. For the banks, the merger proposals were the logical, or necessary, consequence of the government's previous decisions to open the market up to competition, particularly competition from foreign and non-traditional financial services companies.

While many among the business press assumed that the merger would ultimately receive federal approval, for Finance Minister Paul Martin, the person ultimately responsible for approving or rejecting the proposals, the situation was not nearly so straightforward. Indeed, the proposed merger posed a number of conundrums for the government.

The first problem was the timing of the merger announcement. In response to already significant changes made to the Bank Act in 1987 and 1992, and the rapid pace of technological change, the government appointed the MacKay Task Force to comprehensively evaluate the future of the Canadian financial services sector. The final report of the task force was due in the fall of 1998, after which both Senate and Commons standing committees would respond to it. New legislation could not be expected for more than a year. By pursuing their merger when they did, the banks were effectively "jumping the queue," demanding that the government make crucial decisions regarding the future of the sector prior to the completion of the task force investigation. The merger proposal, for which the government had received no prior warning, threatened to throw the entire policy process off the rails.

In addition to the problems the proposal created for managing the public policy process, it also posed direct public policy questions. Quite simply, while the thrust of policy reform since 1987 had been to encourage competition in the sector, the mergers threatened to undermine it. Any "super-banks"—newly allowed to provide a full range of financial services—threatened the very competitiveness the government was seeking to support. Thus, the merger posed a basic question: competition or conglomeration? For the government, approving the merger prior to the completion of the policy review process would amount to a "leap in the dark" on core questions regarding the future of financial services in Canada.

A third problem for the government was that the proposed merger was politically unpopular from the outset. While the banks and their supporters might successfully convince the MacKay Task Force and parliamentary standing committees that globalization required that Canada have bigger banks, the public was not so easy to convince. Coming in the midst of years of record-breaking profits for the banks and the proliferation of new banking service fees, an angered public was skeptical of the claims of impending doom for the industry in the absence of mergers. Indeed, the array of organizations that worked to stop the mergers throughout 1998 testified to the unpopularity of the banks' proposal. Citizens groups, unions, and left-of-centre think tanks were joined by small business organizations, provincial governments, a large number of federal government backbenchers, and even some prominent members of the financial services industry itself in calling for the rejection of the merger. The banks' proposals pitted "Bay Street" against "Main Street."

These challenges to a speedy approval of the proposed merger intensified when, less than three months later, the Canadian Imperial Bank of Commerce (CIBC) and Toronto Dominion, in part prompted by the earlier announcement, informed the government of their own merger proposal. If the mergers were approved, Canada would go from six to four chartered banks, two of which would dwarf the entire Canadian financial services industry.

Through an examination of the events leading up to and following the bank merger proposals, this chapter illustrates the complex interaction of policy considerations the government encountered in reforming Canada's financial services sector. The government decision on bank mergers posed questions of public policy that the government had not had time to fully investigate and threatened to undermine an ongoing comprehensive review of the policy sector. Moreover, it risked unpopularity among both the public and Parliament, despite the legitimacy of such mergers within the financial services community. As the discussion below will chronicle, these factors ultimately led the government to reject the mergers in 1998, while accepting the principle that the banks could pursue mergers in the future.

The Changing Climate of Financial Services in Canada

Understanding the broader context in which Finance Minister Paul Martin made his decision regarding the proposed mergers requires some sense of the tensions that had been building within the financial services policy sector over the previous decade. Three themes emerge. First, the government sought to enhance efficiency in the provision of financial services by increasing the number of market participants. However, individual companies inevitably responded to this competitive pressure through a "bigger is better" strategy of business conglomeration in which large firms acquired smaller firms to take advantage of economies of scale. Secondly, government policy-making in the sector often occurred in two somewhat separated streams. Decisions regarding domestic industry deregulation and concentration were dealt with through the normal policy review process of the Bank Act (the legislation governing the industry; see Inset I, p. 162) while policies regulating foreign entry were influenced by Canada's participation in international trade agreements. During the negotiation of the Canada/US Free Trade Agreement (CUSFTA), the North American Free Trade Agreement (NAFTA), and the World Trade Organization's (WTO's) General Agreement on Trade in Services (GATS) Accord on Financial Services, Canadian trade officials gradually committed the Canadian government to remove barriers to foreign banks and non-traditional financial services companies seeking to do business in Canada. These policy changes often occurred simultaneously with complex decisions within Canada governing the future of the sector. Thirdly, since the 1998 merger proposals were dealt with in an "ad hoc" way, a major struggle emerged between the banks and the government over how the role of Parliament in the merger review process should be clarified for future merger proposals.

1. Market Competition and Industry Concentration

By the end of the 1980s federal government regulators had redefined their basic assumptions about how the industry should be managed. In the past the government had attempted through the system of "pillarization" (see Inset I) to limit competition in financial services to support stability and the security of depositors' savings. In the 1980s, the government had come to believe that more competition and more market participants would enhance the efficiency and competitiveness of the sector and perhaps expand the sources of investment capital available to emerging businesses in Canada. However, as is often the case when governments attempt to deregulate markets, simply removing barriers to competition did not necessarily ensure that a competitive market emerged. Rather, large industry participants used their superior resources to squeeze out smaller competitors and behaved in a monopolistic fashion. Since then, while the government seemed to have been committed to increasing the level of competition within the sector, financial services companies, particularly Canada's "big banks," have pursued strategies that promote industry concentration. Thus, a basic tension has emerged between the government's goal and that of major industry participants.

2. Domestic versus International Policy-making

At the same time that the Bank Act was being revised to allow major Canadian financial services companies the latitude to reorganize themselves, barriers to foreign entry into the industry were comprehensively rewritten. In 1989, under the terms of the CUSFTA, size restrictions on US-based foreign banks were removed, potentially allowing US banks easier access to the Canadian financial services market. In 1994, under the terms of NAFTA, the same consideration was extended to Mexican banks. At a broader level, in 1994, in the wake of the establishment of GATS, member states began sectoral negotiations designed to eliminate "trade" barriers which prevented financial service companies in one WTO country from providing financial services in another. As a participant in these negotiations the Canadian government, parallel to its own policy reviews of the domestic regulation of the sector, also consulted widely with the industry as to what Canada's position should be. While these consultations were kept separate from other policy review processes in the sector, the important point is that, from 1994 onwards, it was widely recognized that increased foreign competition was coming to Canada.

While there is no direct legislative link between international agreements removing barriers to foreign entry and changes in the domestic regulation of the Canadian banking industry, the fact that such moves were occurring provided an important political backdrop for how merger proponents came to support the need for mergers. Indeed, for the banks the threat of increased foreign competition created by global services trade liberalization was one of the single most important motivating factors for their rush towards conglomeration. They felt that they would be in a poor position to compete with the size and economies of scale of larger banks in the US, without a massive program of conglomeration within Canada before the full onslaught of foreign competition arrived.

Thus, despite the government's growing support for a deregulated and competitive financial services sector, a consensus emerged among the banks that increased competition, particularly from larger foreign companies, would inevitably require domestic consolidation to ensure efficiency through economies of scale. In the 1990s industry experts increasingly argued that "bigger was better" in financial services.[2] As a result, the government, through the periodic reviews and revision of the Bank Act, and under pressure from the industry itself, also allowed chartered banks to pursue conglomeration aggressively as a key business strategy.

Overall, previous government decisions to allow industry deregulation to increase domestic competition and international agreements binding the Canadian government to allow increased foreign entry created political pressure within the sector for greater conglomeration and industry concentration. This was the context in which the banks and the government engaged over the merger proposals. The banks felt that their "super-mergers" were the logical culmination of over a decade of policy reform, while opponents of the mergers saw them as potentially a turning point which would serve to undermine the drive to increased competition in the sector. Indeed, the bank mergers' most cynical critics throughout 1998 argued simply that the banks, taking advantage of their privileged position in the market, were seeking to head off any competition that might reduce their record-breaking profits and force them to be more responsive to consumer and business needs.

3. The "Ad Hoc" Process of Evaluating Merger Proposals: What Role for Parliament?

Since, by 1998, there was no established policy process for evaluating such a merger proposal as that between two of Canada's largest banks, ultimately the proposal was evaluated in an "ad hoc" way. Indeed, this ad hoc nature stands in stark contrast to the formalized and ongoing policy review process that the government initiated in the late 1990s. Neither the banks, the government, nor the public had any foreknowledge of how events in relation to the mergers would unfold. The mergers obviously required some sort of review by the Competition Bureau and the Office of the Superintendent of Financial Institutions (OSFI). But it was unclear how the government and the finance minister in particular would handle the ultimate political approval or rejection of the mergers, especially in relation to the MacKay Task Force Report and the inevitable responses by parliamentary standing committees. In the end, the timing of the various reports of these investigations, and the contents of the reports themselves, played a crucial role in setting the stage for how the mergers were evaluated by the government.

In recent years, one persistent political context for the merger question has been the struggle between the banks and the government over defining just how the political process of evaluating such mergers should unfold. The banks, embittered by their encounter with the House of Commons in 1998, have sought to minimize the direct role of Parliament in evaluating their mergers. The government, on the other hand, has created legislation that, in theory, expands the role of parliamentary committees in evaluating the public's interest in any mergers between big banks. The outcome of this struggle is still in question; however, it remains a crucial factor in explaining events in the sector.

Background 1988-1998:
A Decade of Change in Canada's Banking Industry

The decade following 1987 was a period of rapid change in the regulation of banking and financial services in Canada. Traditionally, the various functions of banks and other financial services companies were kept separate, divided into "four pillars" or specialized sectors within the industry. Some companies could not offer a full range of services to customers, but had to specialize and compete only within their subsector of the financial services community. Banks could offer basic banking services to individuals and corporate clients, but they could not manage trusts, manage their clients' stock portfolios, or sell them life insurance. Also, until the 1980s, federal regulations reduced competition within these subsectors by limiting the potential for new market participants to emerge. In short, the Canadian financial services industry was tightly regulated to prevent open competition, in large part to avoid extreme industry concentration. Prior to the 1980s, the government was primarily concerned with preventing the emergence of only a few "super-banks" with monopoly-like control over the entire financial industry.

I: The Regulation of the Banking "Pillar" in Canadian Financial Services

Unlike the regulation of many economic sectors in Canada, including aspects of financial services like credit unions and securities dealers in which the jurisdiction is shared with the provincial governments, the regulation of banks in Canada is a purely federal responsibility, conducted principally by the Bank Act. Before 1987, the Bank Act was subject to review and revision every ten years. Then, as the pace of industry reform accelerated due to globalization and technological change, the act was changed to require review and revision every five years. Under the Bank Act, two federal institutions play a role in regulating the industry:

1. The Office of the Superintendent of Financial Institutions (OSFI) is the main regulatory agency, monitoring all federally regulated institutions to safeguard bank depositors from undue loss.

2. The Canadian Deposit Insurance Corporation (CDIC) provides insurance to depositors in federally regulated institutions.

Prior to the policy overhaul initiated by the MacKay Task Force, the Bank Act divided banks into two categories for regulatory purposes:

1. Schedule I banks make up the "first tier" of the banking industry. These banks must be "widely held," meaning that no individual shareholder can control more than 10 per cent of shares. All six of Canada's "big banks" (as they are commonly referred to) are Schedule I banks. Because of the small number of Schedule I banks, an informal "big shall not buy big" rule had emerged that barred mergers between the Schedule I banks.

2. Schedule II banks may be "closely held" by eligible Canadian financial institutions or eligible foreign institutions. Schedule II banks do not enjoy all of the privileges of Schedule I banks and are limited from offering a full array of services. Although there are far more Schedule II banks in Canada, most are small subsidiaries of foreign banks offering limited services to commercial clients.

The rules governing the business activities of Schedule I and II banks and the competition between the two categories of banks have been crucial to government investigations since the MacKay Task Force. In general, the government sought to reduce the restrictions on the activities of Schedule II banks as a way of increasing competition. This became increasingly important as the government confronted the possibility of mergers between Canada's small number of Schedule I banks.

For more information on Canada's banking regulations and the activities of Canadian banks see: http://www.fin.gc.ca.

This carefully designed regulatory environment changed markedly as the divisions between the different types of financial services companies were gradually lifted and as provisions that limited competition from new market participants were steadily abandoned by the government. Under the provisions of the Bank Act, the legislation governing the financial services sector, the government was required to review and revise the act itself every ten years. This periodic review was shortened to every five years after 1987 (see Inset I). Thus, the 1987 Bank Act Review ushered in an era of sustained reform in the sector. This accelerated pace of reform was the government's response to the rapidly changing technology of the financial services sector and to growing industry demands for deregulation and freer markets.[3]

The 1987 changes to the Bank Act allowed banks in all parts of the country to enter the securities trading business (banks in Quebec already had permission to own securities firms). Previously, there had been tight restrictions on banks' rights to offer investment advice or to own and operate subsidiaries that provided these services.[4] Although these changes permitted banks to purchase a securities firm, they were still limited from offering investment advice to their in-house bank clientele via the bank itself. They had to keep their investment-dealing subsidiaries at "arm's length" to ensure that, armed with extensive private information about their basic-banking clients, they would not quickly squeeze out non-bank competitors in securities dealing.

While this deregulation promised to be a boon for the banks' goal of diversifying the range of financial services they could offer their clients, what the government gave with one hand, it could take away with the other. Ominously, less than a year after passage of the 1987 changes, the government lifted size restrictions for US banks' commercial operations in Canada, citing the provisions of CUSFTA for doing so. While this move fit within the broader government goal of increasing competition within the Canadian financial services sector, it was the starting point for a decade of moves that would potentially expand the presence and market shares of foreign banks in Canada. Previously, the Canadian banking sector was virtually closed to foreign competition, as Canadian banks were sheltered from having to compete with larger US banks for Canadian customers. Understandably, the spectre of a post-FTA influx of huge US banks was a concern for Canadian financial services companies.

Fortunately for the banks, in 1992 the Bank Act was amended again. These substantial amendments continued the process of dissolving the traditional pillars of federal banking policy. They erased many of the limitations on the right of financial services companies to offer services outside of their domain, either through the purchase of subsidiaries already active in other sectors or in some cases directly through new "in-house" powers.[5] Also, these changes involved a major updating of the regulation of "near-bank" financial services companies, such as credit unions and trust companies, which had not been addressed in 1987.

The 1992 changes offered the banks two key new powers. For the first time, banks were now allowed to own and operate insurance companies. At the same time, they were given government approval to offer securities services (portfolio management and investment advice) directly as the "arms-length" restriction of 1987 was lifted. Indeed, the 1992 changes allowed all financial service providers to "network" services offered by affiliates active in other pillars of the sector. This allowed companies active in one sector to cluster the type of financial instruments they could provide clients through the acquisition of affiliates in another. Essentially, banks could now offer an almost full range of financial services to their clients, albeit through a web of affiliated companies rather then entirely "in-branch." This was a major deregulation of the financial services sector, which promised to expand the hold of Canada's big banks over the domestic financial services market. The banks, armed with huge existing customer bases (through their basic banking services), were in a privileged position to go after the clients of other financial services companies, offering them insurance and investment portfolio advice.

The government, again interested in promoting increased competition, also altered the Bank Act in such a way as to make it easier for new Canadian competitors to emerge for the big banks. "Widely-held" non-bank financial service providers (such as trust companies, insurance companies, and credit unions with diversified ownership structures) were allowed after 1992 to own and operate second-tier Schedule II banks without many of the restrictions that had previously existed. Indeed, these new banks now had the same ability to network services that Canada's Schedule I banks were given. For example, these changes paved the way for VanCity, a regional Vancouver-based credit union, to establish the Citizens Bank of Canada, a new market participant for basic banking services. Furthermore, the government allowed trust, loan, and life insurance companies to have the full consumer and commercial lending powers that previously had been restricted to the banks.

Overall, the 1992 amendments represented a changing set of assumptions as to how best to promote competitiveness and efficiency—through a self-regulating market rather then through regulatory limits on cartelization.[6] All policy changes were designed to increase competition across all four pillars by allowing for participants of one pillar to move into another, for new participants to emerge, and for foreign competition to enter into the sector.

As in the case of all the changes in federal banking policy over this period, the dominant explanation for these changes was that they were necessary due to the complex interaction of new technology, globalization, and new market participants or new market behaviour. According to some, banks had been losing a great deal of business as their commercial clients increasingly financed their debts through market borrowing instead of bank lending. Additionally it was argued that securities dealers could not provide enough of this valuable pool of capital to finance the increased competition engendered by globalization. This required that big banks be allowed to provide a wider range of services without which they could no longer be profitable.[7]

Be that as it may, the changes ushered in a wave of mergers and acquisitions, principally by the large chartered banks. For instance, the Royal Bank paid $1.6 billion dollars to acquire Royal Trustco: " ... the trust company gave Royal access to wealth management, which is another way of saying getting your hands on all of a customer's assets, including RRSPs. This [was] hugely attractive to banks because profit margins are much higher than for traditional services."[8] Sparked by the attraction of lucrative profits to be made in other sectors, a competitive race between the banks to acquire subsidiaries before their major competitors could peaked in the year prior to the proposed super-mergers of 1998.

In 1997, the Royal Bank purchased Richardson Greenshields Limited (a Canadian investment dealer) for $480 million. It also acquired all remaining minority shares of its recently purchased subsidiary, RBC Dominion Securities Limited. Royal Trust purchased the institutional and pension custody business of Montreal Trust and the Bank of Nova Scotia, garnering $120 billion in client assets under administration. The CIBC not only bought all the outstanding shares of Oppenheimer Holdings Inc. (a US securities firm) for $493 million, but also purchased Eyres Reed, an Australian brokerage firm, as well as the pension and institutional trust and custody business of Canada Trust. The Bank of Nova Scotia acquired 95 per cent of the common shares of National Trust for $1.205 billion. Toronto-Dominion Bank (TD) acquired Waterhouse Investor Services Inc. (a discount brokerage in the US) for $726 million.

Each year the banks' overseas holdings grew. More importantly, the number of players in the domestic financial services industry rapidly declined. Perhaps not surprising given the kind of efficiencies this generated for the banks, the profitability of new product lines, and the generally rosy economic climate of the period, the waves of mergers produced several years of record-breaking bank profits. Profits peaked in 1997, when the net income of Canada's five largest banks was $7 billion, a very high rate of return by industry standards.[9] Thus, mainly through the acquisition of subsidiary institutions in other sectors, the banks emerged from deregulation larger, and more successful, than ever (see Inset II).[10]

II: Deposit-Taking Financial Service Corporations, by Asset Size ($ Millions)

While there are a large number of banks in Canada, the size of those banks varies widely. Canada's six largest banks, the "big banks," dwarf all other competitors and control the vast majority of banking business.

Bank	1997
Royal Bank (RBC)	$244,744
Canadian Imperial Bank of Commerce (CIBC)	$237,989
Bank of Montreal (BMO)	$207,838
Bank of Nova Scotia	$195,153
Toronto-Dominion Bank (TD)	$163,852
National Bank	$66,235
Hong Kong Bank of Canada	$23,910
Laurentian Bank of Canada	$13,422
Deutsche Bank (Canada)	$8,727
Citibank (Canada)	$7,180
Bank of America (Canada)	$4,990
Société Générale (Canada)	$4,542
ABN AMRO Bank of Canada	$3,935
BT Bank of Canada	$3,763
Bank of Tokyo-Mitsubishi (Canada)	$3,102
Crédit Lyonnais Canada	$2,712
Banque Nationale de Paris (Canada)	$2,606
Union Bank of Switzerland (Canada)	$2,582
Credit Suisse First Boston Canada	$2,565
Canadian Western Bank	$2,023
Banca Commerciale Italiana of Canada	$1,971
J.P. Morgan Canada	$1,558
Chase Manhattan Bank of Canada	$1,323
Republic National Bank of New York (Canada)	$1,229
Fuji Bank Canada	$1,041
First Chicago NBD Bank, Canada	$1,040
Sanwa Bank of Canada	$955
Swiss Bank Corporation (Canada)	$930

Credit Unions	1998
Vancouver City Savings Credit Union	$5,019
Surrey Metro Savings Credit Union	$2,162
Richmond Savings Credit Union	$1,788
Pacific Coast Savings Credit Union	$1,367
Capital City Savings and Credit Union Ltd.	$1,013
Niagara Credit Union Ltd.	$919
Civil Service Cooperative Credit Society Ltd.	$912
Westminster Savings Credit Union	$882
First Heritage Savings Credit Union	$875
HEPCOE Credit Union Ltd.	$841

Source: Price Waterhouse 37; Department of Finance Canada, *Canada's Credit Unions and Caisses Populaires* http://www.fin.gc.ca/toce/2000/ccu_e.html (downloaded 18 July 2002).

The Origins of the Merger Proposals

1997 was a big year in the Canadian financial services sector. While the banks were engaged in a wave of mergers and acquisitions and reaped record-breaking profits, the government intensified the pace of regulatory reform. The Bank Act was again amended to "fine tune" the changes made in 1992.[11] For the first time, these changes included provisions to protect consumers (in particular, consumer privacy). More importantly, consistent with Canada's international obligations, foreign banks, which had been required to establish separately capitalized subsidiaries to operate in Canada, were now allowed to establish branches directly with only minor restrictions on their operations. Furthermore, under the terms of the WTO/Uruguay Round Agreements, size restrictions on foreign bank operations in Canada were abolished.

More important still, the government established a Task Force on the Future of the Canadian Financial Services Sector as part of a policy review process undertaken in advance of the 1997 changes. The Task Force, after some initial personnel changes, was ultimately chaired by Harold MacKay (and, thus, popularly referred to as the MacKay Task Force). MacKay was given a broad mandate to evaluate the financial services sector as a whole, but the government asked him to focus on a number of issues, including:

- enlarging the contribution of the financial services sector to job creation, economic growth, and the new knowledge-based economy;
- enhancing competition, efficiency, and innovation within the sector;

- increasing the international competitiveness of the sector in light of globalization;
- developing the ability of the sector to take advantage of changing technology; and
- improving the sector's contribution to the best interest of Canada's consumers.

On 13 June 1997 the task force released a discussion paper that asked for responding submissions from members of the financial services community. It received over 220 responses. Most interesting among these was that from the Canadian Bankers Association (CBA) on 29 October. As the "peak" organizational lobby for the big banks, the CBA argued that there were global trends towards conglomeration, that Canadian banks had been facing a surge in competition from new sources in the past two years, and that the combination of these trends promised increased competition for Canadian banks:

> In the past 18 to 24 months alone, the following banks have received or applied for approval to commence business operations in Canada: ING Bank of Canada (The Netherlands), Citizens Bank (Canada), Wells Fargo Bank (US), Rabobank Canada (The Netherlands), First Nations Bank (Canada), Valley National Bank (US), MBNA Canada Bank (US) and Comerica Bank (US).[12]

The CBA criticized the Department of Finance's September 1997 proposal to allow widely held foreign banks to enter the Canadian wholesale banking business directly, rather than through the operation of Schedule II banks. This would "result in increased competition in the wholesale market, because foreign bank branches will rely on the capital base of their considerably capitalized parent rather than on the relatively small capital base of their Canadian subsidiary."[13]

Facing these threats, the CBA recommended that the MacKay Task Force should abolish the "murky" policy that "big shall not buy big," which continued to apply to Schedule I banks. That is, the government should drop the general "rule of thumb" that Canada's five biggest banks should not be allowed to merge with one another. Furthermore, it argued that the system for approving mergers should be amended so that bank mergers could be judged by the general legislation governing corporate mergers; in other words, they would be reviewed only by the Competition Bureau so that OSFI and subsequent "ministerial reviews" would result automatically in approval.[14] Perhaps anticipating that the greatest opponents to such mergers would be ordinary members of Parliament (MPs) who, ever sensitive to the concerns of their constituents, would block any attempt to further reduce competition in the sector, the CBA had already begun plotting the removal of Parliament from the review process.

Both the CBA and the banks themselves also recommended to the task force that the government should further erode remaining restrictions on the array of services they could offer. They proposed that financial service companies should have the flexibility to pursue their own business strategies, offering whatever services made the most sense to them. Rather than continuing to be regulated by the remnants of pillarization, they argued that regulation should be functional: financial services companies should be regulated based not on what sector they were originally in, but rather on the range of activities in which they were involved. If a bank offered auto leasing, for example, it should be regulated as a bank and subject to whatever functional regulations govern automobile leasing. This would provide the industry with flexibility to adopt a range of business strategies.[15]

In their submissions, smaller financial institutions, credit unions, and trust companies frequently rejected this logic, as they worried that it would pave the way for increased conglomeration, with the big banks squeezing out smaller market participants. Indeed, the Trust Companies Association of Canada (TCAC) argued that "the ideal policy and regulatory framework must be one in which a viable second tier group of non-bank institutions in Canada can survive and thrive as a source of competition and innovation in the marketplace." Non-bank financial service firms and their industry associations told the task force that the banks had "become too big and threaten[ed] competition." There was a widespread sense that the process of de-pillarization had consistently favoured the banks. The Independent Investment Dealers Association argued that "[t]he result has been the creation of a single super-pillar. This, independent dealers believe, has led to a lessening of competition, innovation and efficiency within the financial services sector and higher prices for Canadian consumers, with no discernible benefit for the Canadian economy." Even extremely wealthy companies like Power Financial Corporation, which owned Investors Group, the largest mutual fund company in Canada, along with several insurance companies, argued that the banks' domination of financial services was rapidly increasing. They argued that the banks accounted for a staggering 64 per cent of profits by TSE 300 companies between 1992 and 1996.[16]

Underlying the concerns of non-bank financial services companies was the common complaint that the real problem was that government policy was allowing the banks into all facets of financial services while maintaining "privileges" that insulated them from competition in their core business activities. The insurance industry complained that the wide ownership rules for Schedule I banks (that a bank could not be closely held) acted to prevent new entrants into their industry. The Canadian Deposit Insurance Corporation (a Crown corporation that essentially provides bank customers with consumer protection) was another sore spot. Insurance companies and other financial services providers had to fund their own private consumer-insurance plans, while the banks had privileged access to government support. The insurance industry, which was already facing heightened competition from foreign firms expanding into Canada, argued that the banks, armed with their customers' personal account information and in their privileged position, might be able to engage in "tied selling" to lure away their customers' insurance business.[17] Tied selling means that the banks could demand that their customers buy insurance from them as a condition of receiving a personal loan or a mortgage and thus was anathema to smaller, single-pillar firms.

While various participants of the industry contested these ideas regarding the overall regulation of the sector at the task force hearings, few imagined that, within a few months, the banks would propose mergers that dwarfed all previous announcements. However, on closer examination, the writing should have been seen on the wall. In July, the Secretary of State for International Financial Institutions requested and received a "preliminary" statement from the MacKay Task Force on reforming the regulations governing mergers and acquisitions. The major recommendation was that a "big shall not buy big" policy "... should not have general application and that any such proposed transactions be reviewed for approval on their merits." A few months later, on 26 September, Finance Canada released "Foreign Bank Entry Policy," a consultation paper "... in which it suggested eased access for foreign bank activity in Canada, including allowing foreign bank branching."[18] Draft legislation on this issue was due in April 1998. More ominously for the banks, on 12 December, the final negotiations on the GATS Agreement on Financial Services were concluded. It promised reduced barriers to foreign banks wishing to expand operations in Canada.

The Mergers

Convinced that the MacKay Task Force would ultimately endorse the idea that mergers between big banks should be approved in principle and motivated by the looming threat of foreign competition, the Royal Bank (RBC)/Bank of Montreal Group of Companies (BMO) merger was conceived only one week after the wrap-up of the GATS negotiations, on 19 December 1997. At 5:00 p.m., after examining internal company simulations that suggested that the BMO would be the best partner for his RBC, its president, John Cleghorn, met with BMO chairman Mathew Barrett to propose that the two banks should "build a globally competitive financial institution on a merger of equals."[19]

Despite the economic simulations, the two chairmen made an odd combination; they were as different as "chalk and cheese" according to industry insiders.[20] Cleghorn, a former college football star at McGill University, had a reputation for being quietly personable, an erudite devotee of Austrian economist Joseph Schumpeter, and a politically shrewd, "team player." He was also notable for his budget consciousness as a bank CEO. Upon taking over RBC, he sold the corporate jet, closed the executive dining room, and got rid of the company's limousines. Flying business class, he travelled to work on Bay Street by subway, despite making millions from the bank. Cleghorn viewed these moves as a way to signal an end to the RBC's stodgy days as a "high-cost" operator.[21] His "no frills" economy drive was part of a larger effort to make the bank a more aggressive, risk-taking player in the global financial services industry. For Cleghorn, the merger proposal was simply a continuation of this larger strategy.

BMO head Mathew Barrett cut a somewhat different figure on Bay Street. Having risen from the position of branch teller to the top office, he was Canada's most well-known banker. With an eye for publicity, he could be relied upon for good quotes as the unofficial "captain" of the Canadian banking industry. Flamboyant and charming, he led a much less budget-conscious lifestyle than Cleghorn. Indeed, Barrett's personal life often generated headlines—reporters covering the merger issue could never seem to avoid mentioning his second marriage to a former model. If Cleghorn exemplified the quiet power of Canada's banks, Barrett personified their wealth and privilege—there was no subway for Mathew Barrett. He was also known to be the most aggressive of the banker heads. Under his watch the BMO tried to lure clients away from other banks through direct advertising attacks on how they treated their customers. Moves like that were not standard business practice in a sector where market shares among the big banks barely moved from year to year.

Despite these inherent differences, the two chairmen were able to work out a deal quite quickly. Later, Cleghorn told reporters that he believed that the "planets had lined up" in December 1997 and that the government would back his merger proposal.[22] Presented with such an unprecedented opportunity to combine forces, Barrett was unable to refuse a deal. The irony was that, despite their personalities, it was Cleghorn who would have emerged as the man in charge, not Barrett.

Events unfolded quickly from the early meetings between the chairmen. On 23 January 1998, a scant five weeks after their first evening meeting, Cleghorn and Barrett announced their "merger of equals." In a carefully scripted joint press conference, the two bank chairmen framed the central arguments they would put forward over the next year.

Cleghorn, who spoke first, argued that Canadian banks had to respond to the global trend towards conglomeration. Noting that in the three previous years mergers in the US had totalled $1 trillion, he suggested that "size mattered" in banking circles. Their merger, which would create the tenth largest bank in North America, would make it possible for them to compete with their large US competitors and would also make it possible for them to invest in new technologies that would provide their customers with better service and better value.[23]

Barrett made the banks' second key argument in his remarks. He noted quite simply that the Canadian financial services market was attractive to foreign competitors. As a result of Canada's previous liberalizations and its recent accession to the WTO agreement on financial services, the banks were facing a "swelling tide of new entrants." Through expansion into the Canadian market, the new global super-banks identified by Cleghorn threatened the banks' dominance in key sectors. Carefully noting that they accepted this new competition, Barrett argued for the need for a strong, world-class "Canadian choice." His argument for the merger was simple and provocative: "What we don't plan to be is the corner hardware store, waiting for Home Depot to put us out of business. What we do plan is to give the financial equivalents of Home Depot or Wal-Mart the stiffest competition that we can." Barrett, like Cleghorn, emphasized that the merger was not simply about entrenching the banks' dominance in the Canadian market. Rather, he argued that the new, larger bank would be able to expand its operations internationally, ensuring a strong international presence for Canadian banks: "Like Alcan, Bombardier or Nortel, the new bank will be a Canadian champion abroad. It will have the resources to lead any financial deal large or small."[24]

Cleghorn's comments that day were measured; however, he turned later to the more provocative arguments that Barrett provided. In fact, as opponents to the merger lined up, his rhetoric became far blunter. When referring to the threat of increased competition from the US and using imagery drawn from warfare (as the bankers were fond of doing), he told reporters that "We've got to get them in the water before they land on our beach."[25] Both bankers' arguments were defensive—they claimed to be protecting the Canadian market from global competition.

Understandably, given the fact that the industry had not witnessed a merger between two of Canada's big banks in anyone's living memory, the merger was big news. The public was shocked, and the government seemed to be caught off-guard. The news even surprised Toronto's Bay Street, the home of Canada's financial services industry. While many industry experts and participants had been expecting the merger, none thought it would happen so soon. Analysts were surprised not by the banks' intention to merge, but, rather, by their announced intention to do so prior to the government's approval of the plan.[26] Many assumed that there would have to be a lengthy dialogue with the government about how a proposed merger would be "handled" prior to any formal announcement.

This seems to have been the prevalent attitude in Ottawa in the hours after Cleghorn and Barrett's press conference. One official said the news had come "like a bolt from the clear blue sky." Canada's long-serving Finance Minister, Paul Martin, called a press conference for later that day (3:30 p.m.). He was, according to many sources, furious that the government had not been given more of a "heads-up" on what the banks were doing; "more importantly he was miffed that the two banks in question jumped the queue on the orderly process of his task-force review." Martin may also have been upset because the mergers challenged his own plans to be Canada's next prime minister. Eager to lure "progressive liberals" to his leadership campaign, he was trying to shake his image as a fiscally conservative supporter of corporate Canada. Given how Canadians felt about their banks, Martin's acceptance of the merger proposal would only emphasize his big business connections.[27]

At the time of the announced merger, RBC was the most profitable company in Canada: in 1997 it posted a $1.68 billion profit and its return on shareholder equity was 19.5 per cent. Not far behind, the BMO had made $1.31 billion that same year.[28] The public, angered by the proliferation of new service fees and believing that those fees were the basis of the banks' recent success, was skeptical that the banks faced impending doom unless they were allowed to merge. So, at his press conference, Martin announced that any approval of the merger would have to await a full investigation by the Competition Bureau and the OSFI as well as the final report of the MacKay Task Force, thereby setting the stage for a year-long struggle.

The unpopularity of the RBC/BMO merger intensified a few months later when, on 13 April, Toronto Dominion (TD Bank) and CIBC announced similar merger plans. The proposed new bank would have assets worth $460 billion, which would make it the ninth largest bank in North America and twenty-first in the world, just slightly larger than the RBC/BMO merged entity. As well, this new bank would become the world's second largest discount brokerage through the merger of TD's Green Line Investor Services and CIBC's Investor's Edge. This second merger proposal only intensified the struggle over the first one. Considered together—as Martin insisted—they would reduce the number of big banks from six to four, with two super-banks dominating the industry.

Interpreting the Mergers and the Public Interest

Industry insiders expected that, despite the initial unpopularity of the mergers, they would receive government approval. Cleghorn publicly suggested his complete confidence throughout the review process. In a lengthy interview in the April issue of *Report on Business Magazine*, he suggested that the merger was expected to "win government and regulatory approval." He was optimistic that the banks' case for mergers was compelling: "We're regarded as arrogant and standoffish and not in touch with what Canadians want. If we can get our day in court, we can convince Canadians it's in their interest in the long run. If we can't, we don't deserve it."[29]

Cleghorn had good reason to be optimistic. The mergers did seem to jibe with the general deregulatory trajectory of government policy. Various investigations into the industry endorsed the banks' argument that the increased cost of new technologies would be offset by the efficiencies gained by economies of scale, thus putting them in a better position to compete globally. Furthermore, the banks had a great deal of political influence. Aside from being the dominant players in a crucial economic sector and, therefore, a constituency that any government would be reluctant to ignore, they were among Canada's largest and richest companies, donating generously to all political parties, particularly the governing Liberals (see Inset III).

Despite the grounds for optimism, however, the banks faced a serious challenge from the outset. The mergers clearly threatened to upset the

III: Financial Service Company Donations to the Liberal Party (1997)

While opponents of the proposed bank mergers suggested that approval would be aided by the close relationship between the banks and the finance minister, one thing was certain: the banks were (and are) major contributors to federal political parties. According to Elections Canada's disclosure of political party contributions for 1997, the major banks account for a significant portion of campaign finance. Jean Chrétien and Paul Martin's Liberal Party received abnormally large donations from major financial service companies. The banks and their leading subsidiaries donated, respectively:

Bank Of Nova Scotia and Scotia McLeod	$231,672.45
Bank of Montreal and Nesbitt Burns Inc.	$221,342.22
CIBC and CIBC Wood Gundy Securities	$198,580.84
Royal Bank and RBC Dominion Securities	$194,869.58
Toronto-Dominion Bank and TD Securities	$186,207.71
Banque Nationale du Canada	$82,102.62
Canadian Bankers Association	$8,854.81
Canadian Western Bank	$2,000.00

Other important financial service companies donated, respectively:

BCE Inc.	$79,006.78
Midland Walwyn	$78,605.68
Merrill Lynch Canada Inc.	$54,813.96
First Marathon Securities Limited	$34,073.03
Montréal Trust	$34,039.68
Canadian Automobile Dealers Association	$32,173.13
Power Corporation of Canada	$31,000.00
Great West Life Assurance Co.	$29,621.40
Manufacturers Life Insurance Company	$22,606.30
London Life Insurance Company	$20,116.58
Sun Life Assurance Company of Canada	$20,000.00
Canada Trustco Mortgage Company	$12,239.44
Canada Life Assurance Company	$10,693.58
Crown Life Insurance Company	$10,000.00
Dominion of Canada General Insurance Co.	$9,356.30
Credit Union Central of BC	$3,416.90
Credit Union Central of Canada	$550.00

Dwarfed by the large donations made by Canadian banks, foreign financial service providers donated, respectively:

Amex Canada Inc	$3,785.40
Hong Kong Bank of Canada	$300.00
Bank of America Canada	$103.54

Source: Elections Canada, "Registered Political Parties' Fiscal Period Returns for 1997," http://www.elections.ca

policy overhaul of the sector, as well, perhaps, as Martin's hope to become prime minister. They also posed serious questions of public policy for the government concerning how the industry should be regulated in the future. Furthermore, the government had to consider these issues amid considerable public controversy. From the outset, a large number of organizations and competing firms—from small business groups and left-of-centre organizations, to trust companies, competing securities dealers, credit unions, other banks, and large and influential financial services companies such as Power Corporation—began to exert pressure on the government to reject the mergers. The banks also had powerful opponents.

From April onwards, the arduous process of evaluating the mergers began behind closed doors in Ottawa. Both the Competition Bureau and the OSFI launched detailed investigations. However, in the press and before the various committees and task forces examining the issue, opponents and supporters slogged it out over whether or not the mergers were in the "public interest."

For example, as early as 30 April, Murray Dobbin, spokesperson for the Canadian Centre for Policy Alternatives (CCPA), a prominent labour-funded think tank, released his analysis of the problems posed by the merger proposals. Noting how the banks suggested that the mergers were essential to their international competitiveness, he said,

> Canadians are being told to support these mergers so that "our" banks can be competitive with the big global players, as if they were a Canadian Olympic team. But Canada is a country, not a cheerleader for megabanks, and as such it is made up of many diverse interests. And on balance, most of these interests will be damaged by the mergers.[30]

Expressing the fears of a host of social welfare interests, Dobbin argued firms would integrate their operations for greater efficiency. The resulting branch closures would see thousands of jobs lost, thousands of rural communities losing competition for their financial services, and millions of Canadians left with fewer options for borrowing. Given the widespread dissatisfaction with increased service charges and record profits for the banks, the CCPA's arguments represented a general feeling that the mergers would really only further privilege the banks, at the expense of almost everyone else. However, perhaps striking the chord that resonated most clearly with the Canadian public, Dobbin also argued,

But beyond these economic and financial consequences, the merger controversy reveals the enormous political arrogance of these behemoths. So confident that their political power is greater than the democratic authority of the Canadian government, they simply pronounce the new reality in the midst of a parliamentary review of banking regulations. This is a deliberate attempt to pre-determine government policy.[31]

The fact that the banks were "jumping the queue" and effectively dictating the agenda of regulatory reform was perceived as manifestly unfair.

The Canadian Community Reinvestment Coalition (CCRC), an "anti-big-bank" non-governmental organization (NGO) with considerable expertise on the nature of modern banking, reached similar conclusions. It noted that the two super-banks would control over 70 per cent of banking assets, a level of concentration higher than in any other G-7 country. Indeed, "Each bank would be twice as large as the next largest bank in Canada." More importantly, the CCRC challenged the banks' central claim that the intrusion of foreign banks into the Canadian market necessitated mergers. Aside from the continued restrictions that limited entry of foreign banks into Canada (even after the GATS agreement), the cost of opening new branches was still prohibitive; in fact, the number of foreign banks doing business in Canada had actually declined since 1987.[32]

While groups like the CCPA and CCRC might be expected to oppose bank mergers, opposition also came from business groups like the Canadian Federation of Independent Business (CFIB), led by Catherine Swift. Swift emerged as a major thorn in the banks' side during the review process. She questioned the degree to which mergers would reduce the access of small businesses to a competitive market for financial services, particularly in smaller centres, and suggested that it was "imperative" for the interests of small business that parliamentarians block the merger proposals.[33] Because they represented the small business people who often formed the backbone of local riding organizations, political constituencies like the CFIB were hard for Liberal Party MPs to ignore. Swift's tireless opposition to the mergers in 1998 undoubtedly placed pressure on many government MPs to query the merger proposals.

As opponents' arguments were seen by supporters of the merger proposals as little more than unfair "bank bashing," this raised serious questions of public policy for the government. The anti-competitive impact of the mergers in terms of events such as branch closings were important considerations that would be addressed in the Competition Bureau's review of the proposals. Moreover, some experts on banking argued that the merger proposals potentially created conditions for reckless bank behaviour. Bob Jenness, a senior research associate at Informetrica Ltd., and former senior research director at the Economic Council of Canada argued this in a *Monthly Economic Review* article. Bank profits, he declared, are closely tied to macroeconomic policy. For example, low interest rates (provided inflation is also low) produce higher bank profits. Thus, the merged banks, exercising increased political power, might force the government to adopt inappropriate macroeconomic policies in order to shield themselves from the implications of the "aggressive" overseas lending that globalization engenders. Rather than being prudent, the banks, secure in their ability to pressure the government to change policies, might themselves pursue inappropriate business opportunities.[34]

However, the merger proposals received the endorsement of a number of groups. For example, in the middle of July, the Fraser Institute, a Vancouver-based, right-of-centre think tank, released the results of its survey of senior investment managers' attitudes towards financial sector consolidation, which showed that market participants favoured accelerated deregulation and the approval of the bank mergers. Moreover, fully 88 per cent of the people in the financial services sector who favoured the approval of the mergers also rated the finance minister as doing a good job in his portfolio.[35] Of course, this was the crux of the problem for Paul Martin. His most carefully cultivated constituency, the Canadian business community, particularly financial market heavyweights, wanted the mergers to go ahead, but the public did not.

One of the most important figures in the public debates about the mergers was Scotiabank Chairman Peter Godsoe. As the head of the only major bank not to have a merger partner, Godsoe had strong reasons to oppose the proposed mergers; however, the fact that he was the head of a bank also lent his analysis a great deal of credibility. Although many felt that the mergers could spell a "death blow" to Scotiabank, which was perceived as a technologically challenged weak player among the big five banks, Godsoe emerged as a communications nightmare for the mergers. Constantly speaking against government approval of the mergers, he used what the other banks considered to be deliberately loaded, provocative language to raise public opposition. He spoke of the potential "super-banks" as "awesome centres of power," which would make the financial services market "completely anticompetitive," and claimed that the mergers were "absolutely dynamiting our banking system."[36]

More problematic for its competitors was Scotiabank's challenge to the logic used by the pro-merger banks. Although smaller than the others, it had the most international orientation of the big six with 20,000 employees outside of Canada. Mathew Barrett of BMO, speaking before committee hearings evaluating the mergers, argued that Godsoe was concerned only that the post-merger banks would be more competitive than Scotiabank, therefore threatening its business.[37] The problem for Barrett and his allies was that this spoke precisely to the concerns of many merger opponents: that the result of the mergers would be a reduction of competition in the marketplace.

Industry insiders believed that Godsoe's strategy was a play for time so that Scotiabank would be better prepared for the post-merger environment—that anything he did to slow the approval process bought Scotiabank time to prepare strategies to lure newly disaffected customers of the super-banks. In reality, he was actually lending a great deal of credibility to "bank bashing" populists and, ultimately, undermining the case for mergers. By September, in the face of such public opposition, some members of Canada's financial community began to believe that the government would nix the mergers and propose instead a lengthy policy sector overhaul.

Public Policy Evaluation of the Mergers

While the public controversy and debate about the mergers continued into the fall of 1998, in early September the results of the MacKay Task Force Report, the ensuing parliamentary hearings, and the reports of the Competition Bureau and the OSFI began to appear.

On 14 September, the MacKay Task Force released its report. It made a host of complex recommendations regarding the future of the industry in Canada. Its most important short-term contribution was its endorsement of the CBA's recommendation that the "big should not buy big" rule should be abandoned—that, in theory, the big banks should be allowed to merge. This fit well within the broader thrust of the report, which embraced more rapid deregulation of the industry. It embraced the CBA's long-standing idea that financial services companies should be allowed to offer a full range of services, even going so far as to suggest that the banks should be allowed to provide automobile leasing, one lucrative sector from which they were still excluded.[38] The report was a major victory for the banks.

TD Bank Financial Group Chairman and CEO, A. Charles Baillie, applauded the conclusions of the MacKay Task Force:

In particular, we applaud their recommendation that the "big shall not buy big" policy be dropped, allowing for mergers among large institutions. The recommendation on mergers is one in which all Canadians can have confidence as the Task Force membership represents constituencies as diverse as Canada itself.[39]

Arguing that it would take as long as three years for TD and CIBC to fully integrate their operations, Baillie emphasized that the report, by highlighting the speed of change occurring in the sector, supported the need for a quick approval of the merger proposals. He also thanked the task force for supporting the banks' argument that they should be allowed to offer their consumers automobile leasing and insurance.

Not to be outdone, the CBA, in its submission to the Senate Standing Committee on Banking, Trade and Commerce on 29 September, formally endorsed the MacKay proposals and the general deregulatory spirit of the report. They supported the notion that all federally regulated financial institutions should be able to offer wider ranges of services through the creation or purchase of subsidiaries in a "holding company model." They also supported the task force's recommendation for more competition in the automobile leasing sector.

Not surprisingly, though, the CBA made little mention of mergers and the MacKay recommendation of an end to the "big shall not buy big" rule. Instead, it dryly noted that, "there is a divergence of views within our membership on how the financial services sector should evolve, and we trust that the Committee will hear from our members on the matter."[40] Raymond Protti, the head of the CBA, later joked about his position on the mergers:

> Harold MacKay ... said of the mergers that his report provides a flashing yellow light. Mathew Barrett, Chairman of the Bank of Montreal ... suggested that the MacKay report provides a green light for mergers. Peter Godsoe, CEO of Scotiabank ... said of the mergers that whatever the MacKay report says, the mergers deserve a red light. Well, I happen to work for both Messrs. Barrett and Godsoe ... I've told them and I'm telling you—I'm colour blind![41]

In a speech to the C.D. Howe Institute in early October, TD's Baillie outlined his views on the choice presented by the MacKay Task Force.

Arguing that the task force report presented a "balanced approach, with no clear winners or losers," he suggested that it laid out two possible trajectories for the Canadian financial services sector. The first was one in which Canada would be "at the table" as a major financial centre. The other suggested that Canada would not only be excluded from the table but would face the prospect of seeing its domestic financial services companies "dwindle" in the face of foreign competition. The path to the first option was simple: let the mergers go ahead. This would ensure that Canadian financial companies had the kind of customer base necessary to invest in the new technologies required to compete with the emerging US superbanks. It would also "cement Toronto as a thriving financial centre with banks that are sufficiently large not to be take-over targets." For Baillie, this was a crucial rebuttal to the concept that mergers would lead to massive job losses, as he argued that "Canadian ownership of global concerns means, ultimately, keeping more jobs in Canada." The alternative was to reject the mergers and embrace a "catastrophic" decline of the Canadian financial services industry.[42]

The arguments that Baillie and the other bank chairmen were making in support of the mergers received a second, more lukewarm endorsement in early October. The Senate Standing Committee on Banking, Trade and Commerce released its *Comparative Study of Financial Regulatory Regimes*, a much lower profile report than that of the Mackay Task Force. In summarizing what the committee had been told in its investigation of the regulation of financial services markets in the US, Australia, and New Zealand, the study attempted to directly assess whether "bigger was better" in the industry. The committee concluded that there was little evidence to support the claim that the global success of banks required that they be big domestically. However, it did emphasize that industry leaders in other countries had told them that "medium sized" firms were likely to face "difficult and growing problems in obtaining operational efficiencies" in the future. They also noted that a large domestic bank was essential to the success of a country's multinational corporations: "having a domestic bank that is a global player may ensure a reliable source of capital on a large scale for multinational companies based in Canada."[43] The Senate's study made little impact on the public's consciousness. However, it illustrated the fact that the parliamentary committees that would conduct hearings and release reports in response to the MacKay Task Force as the first step towards new legislation were relatively sympathetic to the banks' belief that bigger was better.

The Mergers Rejected?

"Round one" clearly went in the bank's favour. Indeed, following the release of the MacKay Report many felt that, despite the public's hostility to the mergers, Ottawa policy-makers might still approve them. However, in November the public glare was once again focused on the negative aspects of the mergers.

Tony Ianno, a backbench Liberal MP from Ontario who was particularly concerned with the problems small business faced in dealing with the banks released his own "Task Force" report on the mergers on November 4. The Ianno Report was drawn up after a series of ad hoc hearings into the issue with groups like the Canadian Federation of Independent Business and was signed by 50 Liberal MPs and four senators. Ianno bluntly recommended that the finance minister reject the mergers. He was careful to suggest that his recommendations were not simply "bank bashing": "There is persuasive evidence that the proposed mergers would be likely to have very adverse consequences for the Canadian public interests." He concluded that the mergers would lead to large-scale job losses and branch closures. This would in turn reduce consumer choice, increase banking costs, and make it difficult for small business to acquire financing. Finally, Ianno argued that the banks had, "never presented a clearly defined and persuasively documented a case as Canadians were reasonably entitled to expect" in support of their merger plans.[44]

Ianno did not simply stop there, however. His report also touched on a number of other bank regulatory concerns that had been put on the table by the MacKay Task Force. Jumping ahead of the formal legislative response to the MacKay recommendations, Ianno and his fellow MPs recommended that the finance minister should also:

- reject the idea of letting the banks sell insurance out of their branches;
- maintain the prohibition on allowing banks to provide auto leases;
- place limits on branch closures;
- encourage the banks to increase lending to small business; and
- encourage more foreign competition in the Canadian market.

The response from the banks was hostile. David Moorcroft, vice-president of the RBC, pointed out that, by saying "no" to mergers but "yes" to foreign banks setting up their own branches in Canada, "I would imagine today in Boston and Delaware and San Francisco there are smiling faces and parties being held. Because they will be able to expand and grow in our country. We're not being given the same right to grow and expand and take them on as competitors." CIBC president Holger Kluge was more measured. Saying that Ianno's report was only one of several government reports that Martin would have to take into consideration, he declared: "We've had one report which is the MacKay task force report indicating mergers is [sic] a legitimate banking strategy and we've had one report now saying no. So I believe it's one-one."[45]

The CBA, given the split in its ranks over the mergers, limited its analysis to those items in the Ianno Report that did not relate to the merger. It argued that, while the MacKay Report had suggested movement to more competition and choice in financial services (such as support for allowing the banks to get into the automobile leasing business), "This report seems to favor on-going protection of special interests."[46]

Others in the financial industry, such as insurance brokers and automobile dealers, applauded the Ianno Report. Richard Gauthier, president of the Canadian Automobile Dealers Association, labelled the report, "a victory for Main Street over Bay Street."[47] Indeed, the response by those opposed to the mergers was celebratory. The Council of Canadians argued that the banks had been given the opportunity in the Ianno hearings to justify why the mergers were necessary and that they had failed to do that. Executive Director Peter Bleyer argued that "The whole discussion about bank mergers is—or should be—a non-starter. The real discussion that needs to take place is about how to make banks more accountable to the public through better regulation. The banks hijacked that discussion earlier this year when they announced their proposed mergers."[48]

More importantly, the report emphasized the political problems posed by the mergers. For example, even the opposition Reform Party, aware of the public's anti-merger sentiments that Ianno had tapped into, began to suggest a "middle way" strategy (ironically, the one the government would eventually embrace). Reform critic Dick Harris, uncomfortable with the anti-business overtones of the report, suggested that the government should place a moratorium on the mergers until there was a policy process in place to deal with them. The immediate problem for the government was even more pronounced. Regardless of what happened in either parliamentary committee or at the OSFI and Competition Bureau, one-third of the government's sitting members had signed this report calling for a rejection of the mergers. The results could only increase Martin's discomfort over the issue. Lorne Nystrom, the NDP finance critic, concluded that "The mergers are dead."[49]

Indeed, the bank's public relations problems continued. Although stock prices continued to slump in late 1998, the banks continued to produce record profits. On 20 November, the RBC announced a 9 per cent increase in earnings over the previous year, with total profits reaching $1.8 billion for fiscal 1998. TD also announced another record year of profitability. Despite the inherent bad publicity of these numbers, the banks continued to argue that their mergers were necessary to stave off increased foreign competition. In response to the public's hostility, the banks launched a new public relations campaign. The RBC and BMO released a collection of "promises" to the public and to their customers if the merger were allowed to go ahead. They promised that the new bank would cut service charges by 10 per cent, loan $40 billion to small business—double the current level—have more staffed branches, and not close branches in small towns.[50] As part of this campaign, Barrett promised that the new RBC/BMO Bank would open a separate small business bank at some time in the future. However, a skeptical press corps noted that this seemed little more than a "flavour of the week" as Barrett never offered any serious proposal as to how this would be done. The effectiveness of this belated public relations campaign remains open to assessment. What is certain was that it was precisely these issues—the probable effect of branch closing and reduced competition in the market—that were being exhaustively analyzed by the Competition Bureau through the summer and fall of 1998.

In anticipation of the public release of the various reports that would, theoretically, determine the outcome of the banks' merger proposals, the Council of Canadians launched a "National Week of Action in Opposition to Bank Mergers" on 4 December. This was to end the almost year-long lobbying process in which business groups like the Canadian Federation of Independent Business, citizens' organizations like the Council of Canadians, and industry lobbies like the CBA (and the banks) had all dutifully reported before hearings to voice their position on the mergers. Throughout the fall the banks had been dealing with the Competition Bureau and the OSFI investigations of their proposed mergers. At the same time, both the Standing Senate Committee on Banking Trade and Commerce and the House of Commons Standing Committee on Finance had conducted hearings in response to the findings of the MacKay Commission. None of these inquiries (with the exception of the Ianno Report) was designed to directly address the specific merger proposals. They were, though, part of the larger on-going policy review triggered by the MacKay Task Force, and all served as ad hoc forums in which proponents and opponents of the mergers made their cases. As such, the two parliamentary committees

IV: Office of the Superintendent of Financial Institutions (OSFI)

Banking and financial services are crucial to the operation of the Canadian economy. Banks ensure not only that capital is available for investment in the economy, but that businesses and ordinary Canadians have a safe place to deposit their savings. Given the importance of this role and past experience of the difficulties generated by bank failures, the government and financial services industry have created a system of oversight and regulation to guarantee public confidence in their banks. The OSFI is one of the institutions that fulfills this role.

Established in 1987 by the Office of the Superintendent of Financial Institutions Act, the OSFI is responsible for the supervision of all "federally regulated financial institutions," including all banks, and all federally incorporated or registered insurance, trust, and loan companies and cooperative credit associations. The OSFI is also responsible for monitoring federally regulated pension plans.

The OSFI's primary function is to reduce the risk of "undue losses" for depositors and policy holders. While the Canadian Deposit Insurance Corporation helps ensure the stability of the industry by insuring some deposits against loss, the OSFI tries to prevent banks and financial services companies from collapsing or, in the event that they do, minimizes the risk of losses to depositors. To do so, it oversees the enforcement of many regulations stipulated by the Bank Act, ensuring that banks and other financial services companies are in ongoing compliance with industry regulation. The OSFI also monitors companies' activities to ensure that they do not engage in inappropriately risky behaviour that may lead to collapse.

Given this role of monitoring Canadian banks and the security of depositors' savings, the OSFI has been asked periodically to analyze large merger proposals in the financial services sector on behalf of the finance minister. The proposed 1998 mergers between Canada's largest banks resulted in just such an investigation. The OSFI was asked to analyze whether the mergers increased the risk of a bankruptcy or failure of one of the major banks and whether or not such a failure would be more difficult to manage in the post-merger environment.

The OSFI's report was one of the considerations that the government had to weigh in evaluating the merger proposals.

For more information on the OSFI and its activities, see http://www.osfi-bsif.gc.ca.

became venues in which the two sides tried to convince the members to recommend acceptance or rejection of the mergers in the hopes of pressuring Martin in his final decision.

During the Council of Canadians' "National Week of Action," both parliamentary committees released their reports.[51] In the end, both were careful to support the idea that mergers could be allowed in principle, supporting many of the claims the banks made in regards to how global changes in the industry required greater economies of scale within Canada.

However, they offered no definitive position on the specific mergers, but left the decision outstanding, pending the Competition Bureau and OSFI reports. The Commons Committee, in particular, argued that mergers should be allowed, but that there needed to be a clear process in place for evaluating their impact before government approval was granted. Everything now hinged on the reports of the Competition Bureau, the OSFI, and, ultimately, on Martin's final decision.

Within days of the committee reports, the OSFI report to the finance minister was publicly released (see Inset IV), with its conclusion that there were reasons to be concerned about the impact of the mergers for the Canadian financial market. It had been charged with resolving two questions on the mergers:

1. If the merger proposal were to be allowed, would there be circumstances or issues that would be likely to have a material, adverse impact on the financial viability of either merged bank, or would there be other material concerns as to the safety and soundness of either merged bank?
2. If the merger proposals were to be allowed and one of the merged banks was to experience serious financial problems, would the resolution of those problems be more difficult than would be the case if any one of the predecessor banks experienced such problems?

In order to assess the impact of the mergers, OSFI combined an analysis of the current financial situation and risk profiles of the banks with the existing literature on the likely effects of mergers. They also consulted with other regulators and federal agencies with merger experience,[52] although there was little evidence of past experiences with such a "merger of equals" either in Canada or internationally. The OSFI also took into consideration only the merger proposals as they were currently structured and did not consider possible modifications. Lastly, the OSFI argued that it was difficult to judge the level of risk engendered by the mergers until the process of merging actually began, as many of the risks would arise out of the process itself.

Despite these qualifications, the OSFI concluded that it was unable to find prudential reasons why the finance minister should not consider the mergers; what was unclear was whether the merged banks would be more or less "sound" than their predecessors. However, in regard to their second delegated task, the OSFI argued that, if one of the merged banks did run into trouble, it would pose a larger problem than would have been the case if they had not merged. The report noted that all the same mechanisms

V: The Competition Bureau

The Competition Bureau

The Competition Bureau is part of the federal department of Industry Canada and is headed by a Commissioner of Competition.

The bureau is guided by the assumption that competition is inherently good for both consumers and for the Canadian economy. As such, its mandate is to prevent business from combining or otherwise acting in a way that limits competition and thereby creates economic inefficiency. This involves both the ongoing oversight of business practices in some industries as well as detailed investigations into proposed mergers.

In carrying out its mandate, the bureau enforces the rules of the federal Competition Act. In the case of mergers, it is also guided by a set of *Merger Enforcement Guidelines* that lay out how, specifically, it should evaluate the likely effects of a large merger on levels of competition. Furthermore, it is guided by sector-specific legislation, like the Bank Act in the case of mergers or anti-competitive practices involving banks.

The current commissioner of the Competition Bureau, Konrad von Finckenstein, a veteran civil servant, has faced a number of difficult tasks since taking charge in 1997. Globalization and technological change have both fostered an environment of increasing economic concentration, and the Competition Bureau has been forced to make increasingly difficult decisions regarding mergers between firms in economically important and politically sensitive sectors like air transport and banking.

The Competition Bureau and Bank Mergers

Under the existing legislation, mergers are normally subject to a Competition Bureau review to assess their impact on competition levels. If the commissioner finds that there are problems with a proposed merger under the provisions of the Competition Act, he or she has the authority to demand remedies through a Competition Tribunal, essentially inhibiting the merger or demanding changes to the merger proposals to limit their effects on competition.

However, in the case of a merger between entities regulated by the Bank Act, the process is more immediately political. Such a merger requires the approval of the minister of finance, who has authority under section 94 of the Competition Act to set aside the normal process if he or she has ruled in favour of a merger between banks. Furthermore, neither the Bank Act nor the Competition Act spells out how the commissioner of the Competition Bureau and the minister of finance should interact in evaluating a bank merger. Thus, while the Competition Bureau is legislatively required to evaluate proposed mergers between Canada's banks, the role of its investigation in approving or disallowing such mergers is not straightforward.[53]

In the case of the proposed mergers between the big banks in the late 1990s, the Finance minister chose to view the Competition Bureau's investigation as a recommendation, which he had to weigh in making his final decision.

would exist for assisting a bank facing a collapse, "but, given the relative size of the institution in relation to potential buyers and investors ... a "least cost" resolution may be more difficult to achieve." Essentially, the OSFI said that the banks were not likely to run into more serious threats as a result of the mergers, but that if they did, it would be harder for the government to manage the process of rescue. Moreover, such rescues would inevitably involve further difficult public policy questions, as it was likely that only some sort of international partner would have the ability to buy out a troubled Canadian post-merger "super-bank."[54] The OSFI was careful to say that those kind of "downstream" concerns were for the minister to worry about, suggesting that, ultimately, the "prudential" concerns of the OSFI were secondary to the policy concerns of the minister.

The day following the OSFI report, the Competition Bureau's report to the finance minister was also released to the public (see Inset V). The bureau argued that the mergers would undermine competition. Under the *Merger Enforcement Guidelines as Applied to a Bank*, the bureau had no power to reject the mergers, but was responsible for evaluating the mergers' effect on competition and making recommendations to the minister, who had the ultimate authority to approve or reject them.

According to Konrad von Finckenstein, the Competition Bureau Commissioner, the review of the mergers had taken so long because of their complexity (they were the largest ever considered by the bureau) and because of the timing of the MacKay Task Force Report. The investigation was substantially different from the one conducted by the OSFI, since the bureau was not limited to considering the viability of the merged financial institutions or the risks that they might pose to the solvency of the Canadian financial services industry. Rather, the bureau's task was to evaluate whether or not the mergers would reduce competition for consumers of bank services. While this implies that the bureau posed a harder test for the mergers than the OSFI, the Competition Act, which governs the bureau's decisions, outlined that, in cases where the resulting efficiencies of a merger outweighed declines in competition, the bureau could allow a merger to proceed.[55]

The Competition Bureau's investigation was based on a well-established set of measures for industry competitiveness. It declared that if the two mergers went ahead at the same time (and it was impossible to judge the competitive impact of one without considering the impact of the other), a "substantial" reduction of competition would result. It concluded that this "would cause higher prices and lower levels of service and choice for several key banking services in Canada." In particular, the bureau argued that competition for basic banking services would be drastically affected. Securities dealing and the credit card business would also see reduced competition. While the report conceded that technological change did increase the possibility for further competition to the banks and more choices for consumers in the future, "these are unlikely to mitigate the anti-competitive impact of the merger in the next two years." In fact, one of the most important conclusions the bureau reached was that, in the wake of the mergers, it was not clear whether any effective competition to the two super-banks would remain. The bureau noted that many of the new entrants in the market were extremely small. Despite offering very favourable terms to customers, ING Direct, which was often cited as the principal threat to the big banks' competitiveness in a global market, had only managed to capture 0.2 per cent of total consumer deposits in the 15 months prior to the report.[56]

More ominously, the bureau questioned how the remaining smaller banks and credit unions could compete against the cost efficiencies of the new super-banks. Even the Bank of Nova Scotia, which was huge in relation to most smaller institutions, but would be less than half the size of either merged bank, would be "at a significant cost disadvantage and would not be able to compete effectively unless it also merged with another major bank."[57] In short, the bureau confirmed what analysts and pundits in the financial services industry had been saying about the CEOs of those financial institutions that opposed the mergers—that they were "dead men walking." It confirmed that rather than ending up with two super-banks and a host of smaller traditional and new competitors, Canada might end up with only two big banks.

The report challenged the findings of the MacKay Task Force. Von Finckenstein endorsed the task force's recommendations to increase competition in banking and to give a "yellow light" to the mergers. However, he suggested that the new competitors that MacKay assumed would challenge the domination of the big banks in Canada would not arrive soon enough to mitigate the effects of these mergers.[58] Essentially, the bureau agreed with MacKay, but argued that it was too soon to allow this kind of concentration. These findings, which Martin had known for some time, were a major defeat for the banks.

The Merger Decision: "No, But ... ?"

On 14 December, Paul Martin announced to the public that, given the reports he had received, it was not possible for the proposed mergers to go forward *at that time.* The banks had known that this would be the case for several weeks. While the public waited for the release of the various reports to emerge one by one, on 29 November RBC Chairman John Cleghorn was invited to a private breakfast at Martin's home in Montreal to discuss the mergers. At the meeting Cleghorn, feeling that Martin was not clear about his intentions, bluntly asked him if the mergers would be approved. Pressed, Martin said, "No." Cleghorn responded in the way the entire financial community did when the announcement was made public two weeks later. He asked, "No, but ...?" He had expected that, even if the government rejected the mergers there would be some sort of process left open by which they could alter the proposals for further considera-tion.[59] This was not the case. In the short term, the mergers between the RBC/BMO and CIBC/TD were rejected outright. Martin decided that they were unacceptable at that time and must await the lengthy legislative overhaul of Canada's banking regulations due in response to the MacKay Report. Martin promised that that overhaul would include new guidelines to govern the process for evaluating large mergers in the banking sector.

The press labelled the decision a "resounding defeat" for the banks, who made this clear in their reaction. One particular sore point was that the Competition Bureau had not allowed them to alter their proposed mergers for further consideration. Von Finckenstein had declared publicly that they would have to wait until the bureau's final ruling before discussing altera-tions to their proposals. However, when the bureau released its report, he suggested that the banks could have thought about altering the proposals, but that they never did so.[60] The banks viewed von Finckenstein's actions as a "clean kill," an attempt to ensure that Martin had the ammunition he needed to reject the merger. However, they were unwilling to dispute in public the way the merger proposals were handled by the bureau since they were likely to have new proposals before it again in the not-too-distant future.[61]

Based on a detailed geographic analysis of local branches, the bureau found that there would have to be a series of requirements for the banks to limit decreases in local competition. Hypothetically, had the Competition Bureau process allowed the banks to modify their proposals in response to anti-competitive concerns, they might have agreed to divest themselves of product lines or branches in areas where industry concentration would become too high. For example, they might agree to sell some branches to competitors in rural areas prior to their merging into a single institution in order to ensure that small-town Canadians still had a choice in basic banking services. However, such a compromise would undermine the efficiencies generated by the mergers, thereby eliminating the only exception to the bureau mandate to reject mergers that reduced competition—that if they increased efficiency they might be accepted. In any event, the banks were not given the choice to do so. There was no "but...."

Behind the scenes, Canada's big banks were outraged. Their CEOs complained privately to reporters that there had been too much parliamentary interference in reviewing the merger proposals. Some suggested doom for Canada's banks; others were even more strident. One senior banker told a reporter that the decision was like "living in Indonesia" and that, by rejecting the mergers, the government was "headed for dictatorship."[62]

Opponents of the mergers were quick to celebrate Martin's decision. Catherine Swift, president of the Canadian Federation of Independent Business, called his announcement a defeat for the banks but a victory for small business.[63] The Council of Canadians was also quick to call it a victory. However, Peter Bleyer, the Council's Executive Director, also worried that the rejection of the mergers provided the banks with a justification for a program of branch closings and service reductions. He argued that the banks, by hijacking the policy review process over bank regulation and turning it into a narrow debate over mergers, had laid the groundwork for them to blame service reductions on increased competition and their inability to respond to that challenge through mergers.[64] There seemed to be consensus on Bay Street that the banks would now aggressively pursue other strategies to increase competitiveness, through cost-cutting measures such as vastly reducing the number of existing branches. Bleyer also argued that Canadians needed to worry about the long term as well: "The Finance Minister's decision today leaves open the possibility that he intends to pursue further deregulation of the financial services sector."[65] Bleyer, like many of the other opponents of the mergers, was concerned that the decision was only a temporary setback in the government's steady progression towards allowing further industry concentration.

However, the government's stated intention was to increase the level of competition for banking services as soon as possible. Martin promised to table legislation as early as February 1999 that would make it easier for foreign banks to expand their branch banking operations in Canada: "under the proposed changes, a foreign bank could establish branches in Canada without establishing a Canadian subsidiary."[66] The government also considered giving credit unions the option of forming cooperative banks and making other regulatory changes that would make them more "dynamic" and "competitive."

Bleyer may have been correct; the government's response to the mergers was not entirely clear-cut. When Paul Martin informed the banks that their mergers could not go ahead as proposed *at that time*, he argued there was no policy to reject the principle that the banks could merge. Rather, the government intended to design a more transparent process for evaluating mergers pending the creation of a comprehensive package of reforms for the industry. Thus, the government did not so much say "no," as "maybe soon" to the mergers.[67] Despite the general celebration of Martin's decision by anti-merger groups, the Centre for Policy Alternatives, concluded that the decision was not really a "no" at all. "In effect," the CCPA maintained, "Martin has told the banks to regroup, re-grease their public relations machinery and then make him an offer he can't refuse."[68]

The Merger Aftermath: Approving Conglomeration?

The government's decision to reject the super-mergers of 1998 did not halt the process of industry concentration and government deregulation or even the consideration of mergers between big banks. In the wake of the MacKay Report, these trends accelerated. While mergers between Canada's biggest banks were temporarily off the table, the government attempted to facilitate increased competition in the sector through deregulation and also began the arduous process of creating a formal framework for evaluating bank mergers. While these legislative processes unfolded, the government was also challenged by a new merger proposal. While 1998 had been a year dominated by hearings, 1999 and 2000 promised a great deal of action by the government.

In the months immediately following the negative merger decision, the government made several deregulatory changes in the financial services industry. On 11 February 1999, it introduced new legislation to allow foreign banks to establish branches directly in Canada—The Foreign Bank Entry Bill. The MacKay Task Force had recommended that the government should allow foreign banks easier access to the Canadian market by offering them a "branch structure" or separately incorporated subsidiaries. The legislation, introduced by Jim Peterson, Secretary of State for International Financial Institutions, promised to "give foreign banks greater flexibility in structuring their Canadian operations and remove unnecessary regulatory obstacles to more effective competition from foreign banks."[69]

At that time foreign banks that wished to offer banking services in Canada were still required to establish separate subsidiaries subject to the full range of banking regulations. The government argued this was an "unnecessary regulatory requirement that adds to their cost of operations here," particularly for those banks that were not interested in offering retail deposits.[70] Under the legislation, foreign banks would have the option of establishing two kinds of branches. They could establish full-service lending branches, which were not subject to the same regulations as Canadian banks provided they were only allowed to accept deposits of more than $150,000. Or they could set up "lending branches," which could not accept any deposits except from other financial institutions. In either case, since they were not taking normal retail deposits, they were not subject to the same restrictive rules on new banks that would otherwise apply. Foreign banks still had the option to establish retail deposit-taking institutions, but they would be subject to the existing restrictions in the Bank Act. By offering foreign banks a wider range of options for establishing themselves in the Canadian market, the government argued that competition for banking services would be increased.[71]

Also, significantly, on 1 March Canada's obligations under the WTO GATS Agreement on Financial Services came into force, again increasing the potential for foreign competition in the industry. In addition, the federal government passed legislation to allow insurance companies to demutualize, which opened the possibility of more rapid ownership changes in the industry (including, eventually, possible bank takeovers of insurance companies). While these moves held the potential for increased competition for the banks, the big news in 1999 was the announcement of the massive policy overhaul in the financial services sector by the federal government and a proposed new TD-Canada Trust merger.

On 25 June, Finance Minister Martin announced the promised "New Policy Framework" for reforming the regulation of the financial services sector.[72] He argued that globalization and technological change in the financial services sector required a change in the basic principles that governed financial service sector regulation. Based on the two years of consultations with the industry by the MacKay Task Force and subsequent parliamentary inquiries, he argued that major reforms were needed to ensure an efficient, competitive, and profitable financial services sector.

Consistent with many of the MacKay Task Force's recommendations, Martin announced that the government intended to introduce legislation that would decrease the regulatory burden in the industry. Financial service sector companies would be allowed to adopt a "holding company" approach; for instance, banks could place some of their activities, such as their credit card services, outside of the regulatory regime of their core business activities. The government would also allow the emergence of "strategic alliances and joint ventures." Traditionally, banks had been precluded from forming alliances that would result in any one shareholder controlling more than 10 per cent of a bank's voting shares. To allow the banks the flexibility to find new partners, the government suggested that this threshold would be raised to 20 per cent for voting shares and 30 per cent for non-voting shares. The government was careful to note that it would still be vigilant to ensure that no individual shareholder could gain control of a bank.

Martin also said the government would examine the idea of reducing capital taxes to increase the international competitiveness of the industry, but noted this was made more complicated by the fact that jurisdiction over capital taxes was shared with the provinces.

More tangibly, the government promised to create a "Merger Review Process," designed to "increase transparency and public participation." Under this process, banks would be allowed to merge, but they would have to fulfill several additional reporting obligations. Large financial services companies would be required to prepare a "Public Interest Impact Assessment" for review by the House of Commons Standing Committee on Finance. This assessment was intended to head off the kind of unclear process that emerged when the Ianno Report created its ad hoc review of the bank mergers a year earlier. Potential merger participants would also continue to be required to go through reviews by the OSFI and Competition Bureau. The proposed framework suggested that the regulatory agencies' reports would be completed prior to the Finance Committee's review of the merger proposal.[73] Based on the committee's evaluation, the finance minister would still have the authority to approve or reject any merger, but, responding to the banks' complaints the previous December, banks would have the opportunity to make modifications to their proposals.

Recognizing that a "green light" on mergers threatened industry concentration, the government announced it would increase overall competition in the sector. Noting the MacKay Task Force's recommendations that barriers to entry and industrial consolidation were limiting competition, it announced regulatory changes designed to increase the size of a healthy second tier of deposit-taking institutions, which could compete with large banks in regional and local markets. This was to be accomplished by reducing the complex ownership restrictions for new banks, by allowing insurance companies to demutualize (which had actually already been approved by Parliament earlier in the year), and by approving the request from the credit unions that they be allowed to establish their own national cooperative banks.

To oversee customers' interests in such a rapidly changing environment, the government also planned to implement new measures aimed at consumer protection and designed to limit the ability of deposit-taking institutions to close branches without advance notice. A newly created Financial Consumer Agency and Canadian Financial Services Ombudsman would have oversight to ensure that the new consumer protection legislation was being adhered to within the industry.

Ray Protti, the head of the CBA, welcomed many of these recommendations. But he expressed the banks' disappointment that aspects of the MacKay Report that would have benefited the banks—such as the recommendation that banks be allowed access to the insurance and auto leasing businesses—were ignored by the government: "We find it hard to understand why the government has rejected the task force's recommendation."[74] Aside from the government's unwillingness to move on automobile leasing, there were also a number of other negative implications for the banks. The new oversight of their operations, for example, meant they would not be free to run their businesses as they saw fit. They would have to offer bank accounts to everyone, regardless of whether they were unemployed. They would not be allowed to engage in tied selling (they could not ask customers to buy one of their services or be denied another) in addition to continue being barred from selling insurance or offering auto leasing. While the banks complained that the government was dragging its feet on the MacKay Report recommendations, for the public and the media the important implication of Martin's proposed reforms was that it appeared to reopen the door to bank mergers. However, Protti pointed out that nothing could occur until the proposed framework became policy and the legislation itself could not be expected anytime soon.[75]

On 3 August, while the government began the work of preparing legislation to implement these principles, Charles Baillie, the head of TD Bank, publicly announced a proposed takeover bid of Canada Trust and the formation of "TD Canada Trust." He noted, "this transaction will vault two of Canada's smaller institutions to number three in asset size in Canada, and will put us in a better position to become a significant force in North America." Anticipating the media and public's likely linkage of this merger (which, if accepted, would be the largest merger in the Canadian industry's history) to the events of the preceding year, Baillie argued that it was fundamentally different from the previous proposals because:

1. The Mackay report had now been issued, and the government had responded.

2. There would still be five major banks if this merger was accepted, which should alleviate most of the concerns raised by the two regulatory agencies in December and which would reduce the anti-competitive impact of the merger. Thus, the Competition Bureau and the OSFI could not argue that this merger threatened the safety and soundness of the industry.

3. Anticipating the Competition Bureau's complex geographic review (with which he now had ample experience), Baillie noted that in every location where there were TD and Canada Trust branches there were also at least two other major competitors.

4. There were no rural communities where the two institutions were the sole providers of basic banking services.[76]

These points were intended to soothe the concerns of federal officials, but Baillie was also careful to try to head off any of the general anti-bank rhetoric that had hindered the earlier merger proposals. Indeed, he argued that, far from this being a process by which one of Canada's hated big banks closed down a more customer (and small business) friendly competitor, this merger offered TD the chance to learn from Canada Trust how to better service the needs of their own customers. He stated that TD would adopt Canada Trust's philosophy of expanded customer service, including longer business hours and its overall "retail service model." Baillie also argued that actual job losses from the merger would be limited to 2,900 employees of the 44,000 currently employed by both companies. He was extremely optimistic that the merger would be approved because it was with a trust company rather than another large bank and thus not subject to the same level of public review. When asked by the press, Baillie suggested that the government had in no way indicated the merger would be problematic.[77]

Baillie's merger partner, Canada Trust's CEO, Edmund Clark, also made an interesting ally. Before joining the financial services industry, Clark had gained notoriety in the business community and was nicknamed "Red Ed" for his role in designing the National Energy Policy for Pierre Trudeau. He was obviously "savvy" about how to handle the merger process in Ottawa. Of his relationship with the Ministry of Finance, he boasted, "I still have a lot of friends up there. The feeling is that this deal would not have been allowed to go on as far as it has if Mr. Martin didn't want it to go ahead. If Mr. Martin was generally opposed to it, that message would have been given."[78]

Although Clark had been a critic of the Bank of Nova Scotia's success-ful acquisition of National Trust several years earlier, in some ways his entire tenure at Canada Trust, the nation's largest trust company, had been directed at making it an ideal merger partner for one of the banks. When he become head of Canada Trust in 1994, he eschewed his large bank com-petitors' business strategy by pursuing a "less is more" approach. He took the company out of every business activity that did not involve their core customer services, including corporate lending, commercial mortgages, and wholesale car financing. Focusing on expanding the quality of serv-ice provided to retail clients, Clark fashioned Canada Trust into Canada's leading alternative to the "unfriendly" big banks.[79]

When the government turned down the banks' big merger proposals, industry insiders assumed it was only a matter of time until somebody found the "right price" for Canada Trust. For Clark that was the $6.8 bil-lion TD agreed to pay his shareholders. Clark personally stood to make a bonus of $7.8 million if the deal was approved. If Canada Trust's incentive to merge was money, TD's motivation was equally clear: the merger would vault TD from fifth to third biggest bank in Canada. Baillie argued that, even more importantly, it would solidify the bank's foundation for expan-sion into the US.[80]

Understandably, Canada Trust customers were skeptical of the merger. Many argued that the trust company had offered them better service than the banks; they did not believe that TD would offer them the same high quality personal service. The Consumers' Association of Canada, echoing the criticisms of the earlier merger proposals, stated: "We've got a situation where TD is paying for reducing the competition in the marketplace, all the other banks benefit, and the big loser is the customer."[81]

Aside from the spin that TD put on their merger for public consump-tion, the bank adopted a fundamentally different approach to the entire process of getting government approval:

> TD has gone to great lengths to make sure that Ottawa was kept in the loop, thereby, it hopes, heading-off political oppo-sition. Baillie and his executives met with Martin two weeks before the deal was announced to outline their plans, and also met in advance with liberal MPs from London Ont., to offer assurances that the city where Canada Trust was born would not lose any of its 2,000 jobs. One Martin advisor suggested that the meetings have been crucial; by getting MPs on side,

the TD hopes to avoid the sort of backlash that helped sink the 1998 bank mergers.[82]

TD and Canada Trust had also informed the government of their plans long before they were announced to the public. Some insiders suggested Ottawa knew of the deal a full six months before it was made public—which would mean that the deal was in the works immediately after the rejection of TD's merger with CIBC![83]

The government, prepared by the "heads up" they had been given about this merger, treated it as it had earlier, smaller mergers in the industry. Despite the fact that Canada Trust was a large company, it was not one of the "big banks," meaning that the merger did not violate the "big shall not buy big" principle and would not have to await the new merger evaluation framework. Rather, only the Competition Bureau would evaluate it. The finance minister would approve or reject the merger when he had that report in hand.

Thus, in marked contrast to the 1998 mergers, the TD/Canada Trust merger proceeded with little controversy. There was no ad hoc Ianno Task Force to serve as a springboard for groups opposed to the merger, even though many of the same groups that opposed the early mergers continued to oppose this one. Likewise, parliamentary business on reforming the financial service sector was not dominated by the merger. There were no public hearings conducted in regards to it; the Competition Bureau was left to evaluate it on its own merits. Furthermore, unlike 1998, the companies were given the opportunity to modify their proposal to satisfy anti-competitive concerns raised by the bureau.

Baillie and Clark remained confident of government approval. On 10 January 2000, six months after the merger was announced, Canada Trust's Board of Directors recommended shareholders accept TD's offer of $67.00 a share, for a total purchase price of $8 billion, even though the Competition Bureau had not approved the deal. There was some need for urgency as TD's offer was set to expire on 1 February. Three days before the deadline, the Competition Bureau informed Finance Minister Martin that, with some minor (already agreed to) changes to the proposal, the TD/Canada Trust merger was acceptable. The day before the expiry of the merger offer, Martin and Jim Peterson, the Secretary of State for Financial Institutions, announced that the government would accept the recommendations of the Competition Bureau that the merger be approved, provided TD remedy objections raised by the bureau.

The bureau employed the same methodology as it used to evaluate the 1998 proposals and concluded that while it remained true that there were significant obstacles to new entrants in the sector and that industry market shares were surprisingly stable, the merger posed only one basic problem. On the one hand, by expanding and adopting the Canada Trust service model to one of the big five banks, it could encourage further competition and innovation in the sector; on the other hand, it also represented the loss of a large competitor for financial services.[84] However, the bureau noted that Canada Trust was a "regional player" with operations concentrated in areas like southern Ontario and BC where there were generally higher numbers of competitors. Indeed, it found there was very little overlap in the products and services offered by the two companies other than basic branch banking and credit cards. The merger would reduce competition in only three of the 74 local markets in which the two companies competed but, unless Canada Trust was divested of its MasterCard portfolio, there would be significantly reduced competition in the sector. Thus, the major exception the bureau imposed was that TD was required to sell off Canada Trust's Mastercard business to another company. TD willingly agreed to this. Jim Peterson, drawing on Baillie's arguments in support of the merger the previous year, pointed out in his statement that this merger would "mean that TD customers will enjoy longer and more flexible bank branch service hours in keeping with Canada Trust practice."[85]

While the TD/Canada Trust merger had generally been under the radar of Canadian public opinion compared to the big merger proposals, the response to the government's endorsement was largely negative. Catherine Swift, president of the Canadian Federation of Independent Business, argued that the deal was a blow to small and medium business. The CFIB had fought virulently against the banks' merger proposals of the previous year and "those concerns are equally valid today. This deal marks the demise of the Trust industry, which was the best opportunity to develop a strong second tier of banking in Canada. This decision will have a negative impact on consumer choice." The CFIB was particularly upset that, unlike the earlier merger proposals, there had been no public consultation in the review process and that this might set the precedent for another round of big bank mergers which could be reviewed "behind closed doors."[86]

The "New Framework" for Financial Services

Such concerns have *so far* proven unfounded. On 13 June 2000, the government tabled Bill C-38, the legislation designed to implement Martin's

"New Framework" announced the previous year. While the legislation contained a number of provisions, including further efforts to increase competition in financial services, its most important aspect was the provision it set for how "bank mergers" would be managed in the future. The banks had been waiting for the legislative framework that would make it possible for them to once again propose big bank mergers. So, they welcomed the tabling of this new legislation and looked forward to working with the government in a "constructive manner" to ensure the legislation would make Canada's financial services industry globally competitive. However, once again, the banks were disappointed when Bill C-38 died on the order paper in November due to the calling of a general election.

In February 2001, the banks got a second chance when Bill C-8 was introduced. This bill was essentially a repeat of Bill C-38 and passed through Parliament with little controversy, receiving royal assent on 14 June. The bill created a merger review process which, while recognizing the legal right of banks to merge, required that any such proposal must be evaluated by the OSFI, the Competition Bureau, *and by Parliament*. Both the Commons Standing Committee on Finance and the Senate Standing Committee on Banking, Trade and Commerce would conduct reviews of the banks' proposals to judge whether they were in the "public's interest." While this was consistent with the spirit of the proposals that Martin had outlined in his "New Framework" in 1999, it fell somewhat short of streamlining the merger review process. Bill C-8 essentially left as an open political question how Parliament would interpret the "public interest" in mergers. For the banks, this raised the spectre of another Ianno process in which the banks' business strategies would be treated as a political football. Indeed, the banks' supporters made this point publicly. The Fraser Institute dismissed the framework as ignoring the "new realities" of the banking industry, instead imposing outdated and unfair parliamentary oversight over the business decisions of industry participants.[87]

Mergers Still Pending?

Despite the questions left unresolved by the long-awaited provisions of Bill C-8, in the wake of the TD/Canada Trust merger many insiders felt that a new round of mergers was inevitable. There were a number of reasons for this. For one, Canadians had had more time to get used to the idea that one of their banks might disappear. Also, as the Canada Trust acquisition showed, the banks had grown more sensitive to the need to carefully stroke public opinion. More importantly, the potential competition from new market participants had been legislatively expanded, and there were early indications that this was resulting in expanded market shares, particularly from foreign financial service providers.[88] The banks, through their cost-cutting, had paved the way for an easier merger review, and the preemptive closing or sale of branches altered the playing field for evaluating mergers.[89] Finally, the government was sending clear signals through their new legislation that, although mergers would be difficult, they were not out of the question.[90]

Throughout 2001, the heads of all the major banks continued to speak in favour of mergers and suggested they were simply awaiting the ground rules for how their proposals would be evaluated.[91] In April, even Peter Godsoe, head of Scotiabank and one of the strongest opponents of the 1998 mergers, changed his tune. TD's Baillie had argued that a further wave of proposed consolidations was inevitable and that Canada's six banks needed to be joined into three or "face extinction." Baillie suggested that formal merger proposals could be expected within a year or two. In response, in a speech to the Canadian Club in Montreal, Godsoe admitted that some form of consolidation was inevitable, either in the form of bank mergers or through bank acquisitions of other financial service companies, most notably the major insurance companies.[92] The following day, Gordon Nixon, the incoming head of the RBC, announced that his bank was anticipating another round of consolidation and that he was personally preparing for all eventualities.[93]

Indeed, once C-8 became law, all legal roadblocks to mergers were removed. However, many wondered if the "political roadblocks" remained. In 2002 the banks finally set about testing the water. While details have never been clear as neither proposal ever became public, two substantial mergers which would have required special government approval were put forward late that year. Manulife Financial, one of Canada's larger non-bank financial services companies, proposed to the government that it be allowed to take over CIBC in a deal that would have made the new company the largest bank in Canada by far, with assets of $433 billion. However, the new Finance Minister, John Manley, effectively "nixed" the deal by saying that he would not ignore rules that currently prohibited banks from merging with Canada's largest insurance companies.[94]

At the same time, Scotiabank proposed a takeover of the BMO. Again, however, the deal never became public; either John Manley rejected the merger behind closed doors, or, in the process of discussing the deal, the banks asked the minister to more clearly define what challenges the parliamentary review of merger proposals would entail. Whatever transpired, the result was that, at the banks' request, the finance minister asked both the Senate Standing Committee on Banking, Trade and Commerce and the Commons Finance Committee to hold hearings and prepare a report clarifying the merger policy. The banks anticipated that "what will come out of this Senate and House of Commons Review process, will be [a] much clearer road map as to whether mergers and consolidation can occur, and secondly, on what basis it can occur so that there is much greater transparency in the system."[95]

The banks felt that the process set out by Bill C-8 was still too vague and too political and that there needed to be a clearer sense of how Parliament would evaluate the banks' "public Interest Impact Assessments" and the "public interest" in the mergers generally. John Hunkin, the new chairman and CEO of CIBC, expressed the view of the other bank chairmen that mergers were necessary for the viability of Canada's banks. "A lot of us think about mergers a lot ... [but] I would have a great deal of difficulty under present circumstances recommending to my board that we move ahead with [one]."[96] However, the banks had new allies in the hearings. Joe Oliver, the head of the Investment Dealers Association, told the House of Commons Finance Committee hearings that, while his industry was increasingly dominated by the banks, allowing mergers would spur the growth of new smaller firms which would benefit small business.[97] The hearings put the issue to the government. While there was a growing resignation to the need or inevitability of mergers in a globalizing financial services sector, they would be too difficult under the current law. The banks wanted the evaluation of any merger proposals to be "depoliticized."

Nixon, the new RBC head, made the banks' arguments in a measured way in the March 2003 issue of *Policy Options*. He said that the lack of clarity and predictability in the merger review process was not in the public interest and that the uncertainty was standing in the way of merger proposals and was, therefore, "disruptive to employees, clients and investors." Remembering the events of 1998, he argued that, as the current situation stood, merger proposals "run the risk of being embroiled in a politically charged process. This would not be in anyone's interest, and is not conducive to the establishment of good public policy."[98]

Speaking to reporters in London, England, where he had recently become CEO of Barclays PLC after stepping down as head of BMO, Mathew Barrett was more direct. No longer requiring a cozy relationship with the Canadian government, he said of the squelched BMO-Scotiabank merger that Canadian politicians were "marginalizing" Canada's banks by "blocking consolidation" and that the government's opposition was "purely political and not about concentration."[99] The banks' position was clear: Parliament was interfering politically in the normal business decisions of the sector, and the banks would prefer to work with lower profile regulators who would produce more "predictable" decisions.

The Senate Committee's report was released in December 2002. Perhaps not surprising given its generally "warmer" relationship with the banks, the Senate report was a "ringing endorsement" of the banks' position. While it recommended the government further deregulate barriers to new competitors in the industry, the committee "urged the government to get out of the bank merger process as much as possible. The finance minister ... should only turn down a request if there are strong and unusual reasons."[100] The committee recommended there be no parliamentary review of merger proposals, that they should be left up to the Competition Bureau and the OSFI, and that legislation that would make this clearly the case should be passed before summer.[101]

At the end of March 2003, the Commons Finance Committee released its report on the bank merger policy.[102] Despite the Senate's endorsement of the banks' arguments, the Commons report was a major blow to any would-be mergers. First and foremost, the "Barnes Report" as the press labelled the document after Committee Chair Sue Barnes, said that there should be no major change in the existing principles of the merger review policy. Instead, there should still be a parliamentary committee review of any merger proposals of banks with over $5 billion in equity. The report was not simply "status quo," however. It went on to clarify the meaning of the Public Impact Assessment the merging banks would have to present to the parliamentary committees and thereby clarified how bank mergers would have to be in the "public interest." The report argued banks would have to provide evidence that the merger:

- would result in no less than the existing range of services to all Canadians;
- would increase access to capital for small and medium-sized businesses;
- would ensure services to rural and remote communities;
- would minimize job losses; and
- would benefit the domestic market and increase international competitiveness.

Furthermore, as the press noted in the days following the report's release, the government viewed this as the first step in yet another piece of legislation to clarify the rules for mergers. This suggested that it would be inappropriate to even consider a merger under the existing law until newer, clearer legislation had been created.[103]

Discussion

Given the current uncertainty of the merger review process, no merger announcements are expected soon, but they remain very much on the policy horizon. According to industry insiders, merger proposals between big banks are inevitable. Finance Minister John Manley (at the time, a candidate to replace Prime Minister Jean Chrétien) released an informal "time-line" for considering another round of mergers. He suggested that the government will accept proposals, pending the fine-tuning of the review process, after 30 September 2004. Manley told the banks that there will be no "first come first served" process; instead, banks will have a 60-day period in fall 2004 to put all their proposals on the table so they can be jointly considered.[104] While the banks celebrated this informal announcement, the outcome of the reviews of those merger proposals is uncertain. Will Parliament again "politicize the process" or will a more sympathetic prime minister and finance minister allow the Competition Bureau and the banks to work out the merger details among themselves?

When the banks announced their merger proposals in spring 1998, most seasoned political observers expected them to get government approval. They were simply too big and influential for the government to ignore. However, the future of such mergers remains unclear almost five years later. Most industry participants continue to assume mergers are necessary and inevitable given the globalization of the financial services industry, yet the process of consolidation between the banks has stalled. Why?

At the outset of this chapter, it was suggested that the mergers posed questions that the government was unprepared to confront. In winter 2004, some of those issues have been resolved, some have not.

First, the 1998 proposals were poorly timed, as the banks jumped the queue in the policy review of the sector and presented the government with arguments it could not evaluate effectively at the time. The merger proposals undermined the MacKay Task Force process and, if accepted, would have radically altered the financial services industry prior to the completion of the government's own investigation. Indeed, the mergers posed serious questions of public policy on which the government remains uncertain to this day. The mergers capped a decade of confusion between the government's desire to increase competition and the industry's desire to conglomerate and reduce domestic competition as a response to globalization. Likewise, the merger proposals highlighted the need (for some, particularly foreign, banks) to increase competition in Canadian banking.

Some of these concerns have been allayed. The government has engaged in a further deregulation of the industry and has moved to allow new competition in the industry. Furthermore, many officials have come to see bank mergers as a reasonable business strategy given the pressure of globalization.

Second, the mergers were politically unpopular, and the idea of "super-mergers" remains so. In 1998, public hostility to the mergers, combined with unclear rules for evaluating those mergers, placed the finance minister in an uncomfortable position. Paul Martin's desire to lead the Liberal Party, combined with the ad hoc political processes for reviewing mergers, made the mergers politically unfeasible *at that time*, despite their endorsement by the MacKay Task Force. Opposition from a wide array of organizations highlighted the public's general mistrust and hostility to the banks. This antipathy for spiralling profits and service charges in an industry that many Canadians already felt was uncompetitive formed a backdrop the government was loath to ignore. Opposition from business organizations, in particular groups like the Canadian Federation of Independent Business, seems to have been particularly difficult to disregard. The MPs that took part in the Ianno Task Force embraced their small business constituents' mistrust of the banks' proposals. Quite simply, the super-mergers of 1998 "touched a nerve" of discontent with the banks that Finance Minister Martin could not ignore. These political obstacles persisted through to Paul Martin's selection as Liberal leader. The merger review process will not be clarified legislatively for some time yet, and, given the content of the Barnes Report, it is unlikely that Parliament will abandon its right to investigate the "public interest" in any merger proposal between the big banks.

However, there are signs that the government's position may soon change. John Manley seemed to be less supportive of the banks' merger plans, but he withdrew as a leadership candidate. It is widely believed that Prime Minister Paul Martin is actually "merger friendly."[105] Many, including the banks, believe that Martin will be prepared to approve mergers when the window for considering them opens in September 2004—after the next general election. This would then see the following scenario. The banks would produce a shrewder, more carefully managed public relations campaign. The prime minister would rein in political opposition to the mergers. The process of reviewing the banks' proposals would be left in the hands of the Competition Bureau and the OSFI. As the TD/Canada

Trust merger illustrated, the government can make it relatively easy for big merger proposals to succeed provided the banks get the timing right.

Appendix A: Key Institutions

Government
    Department of Finance
    Competition Bureau
    Office of the Superintendent of Financial Institutions Canada (OSFI)
    Standing Committee on Finance
    Standing Senate Committee on Banking, Trade and Commerce
    Task Force on the Future of the Canadian Financial Services Sector
    Ianno Task Force

Banks
    Royal Bank
    Canadian Imperial Bank of Commerce (CIBC)
    Toronto Dominion
    Bank of Montreal
    Scotiabank
    Canada Trust

Associations and Institutes
    Canadian Bankers Association (CBA)
    Canadian Federation of Independent Businesses
    C.D. Howe Institute
    Fraser Institute
    Canadian Centre for Policy Alternatives (CCPA)
    Council of Canadians
    Credit Union Central

Chronology

1987: Bank Act Amended. Banks allowed to enter the securities trading sector for the first time.

1989: Canada/US Free Trade Agreement. Size restrictions on US bank operations in Canada were lifted.

1992: Bank Act amended. Banks could now own insurance companies. "Widely-held" non-bank financial service providers (trust companies, insurance companies, and credit unions) could now own schedule II banks without the required 10 year divestiture. All companies were now allowed to "network" different financial services offered by subsidiary or parent companies. Banks could now offer portfolio management and investment advice directly.

1994: The non-interest bearing reserve requirement for banks was eliminated as per the 1992 amendments to the Bank Act. Under the terms of the North American Free Trade Agreement (NAFTA), size restrictions on foreign bank operations were lifted for Mexican banks.

1996: MacKay Task Force on the Future of the Canadian Financial Services Sector appointed.

1997: Bank Act amended. It was proposed that foreign banks, which had been required to establish separately capitalized subsidiaries to operate in Canada, could now establish branches directly in Canada with only minor restrictions on their operations. This legislation was due in 1998, but was not tabled and passed until 1999. Under the terms of the WTO/ Uruguay Round Agreements, size restrictions on foreign bank operations in Canada were abolished.

12 DECEMBER: Final negotiations on GATS Agreement on Financial Services concluded.

1998

The legislation of new rules to allow foreign banks to directly operate branches in Canada (which was announced in the 1997 changes to the Bank Act) are finally tabled.

23 JANUARY: Royal Bank and Bank of Montreal announce their merger plans.

13 APRIL: Toronto Dominion and Canadian Imperial Bank of Commerce announce their merger plans.

14 SEPTEMBER: MacKay Task Force Report released.

OCTOBER: Standing Senate Committee on Banking, Trade and Commerce release report comparing financial regulatory regimes.

4 NOVEMBER: "Ianno Report" calling for a rejection of proposed merger released.

29 NOVEMBER: Finance Minister Paul Martin privately informs banks that the mergers will not receive approval.

DECEMBER: Standing Senate Committee on Banking, Trade and Commerce release their response to the MacKay Task Force. Commons Standing Committee on Finance releases its response to the task force.

10 DECEMBER: OSFI Report on the two mergers released.

11 DECEMBER: Competition Bureau Report on the two mergers released.

14 DECEMBER: Finance Minister Paul Martin announces that the proposed mergers could not go forward at that time. Instead, any mergers would have to await an overhaul of Canada's banking regulations, which was due in response to the MacKay Report. That overhaul would include new guidelines to govern the process for evaluating mergers in the banking sector.

1999

JANUARY: Legislation allowing insurance companies to demutualize passed.

21 JANUARY: Toronto Dominion and Canada Trust inform Department of Finance of their intention to merge.

1 MARCH: WTO GATS Agreement on Financial Services comes into force.

25 JUNE: Paul Martin announces a "New Policy Framework" which includes proposed guidelines for evaluating mergers.

3 AUGUST: Toronto Dominion/Canada Trust Merger announced.

2000

28 JANUARY: Competition Bureau informs Martin that the TD/CT merger was acceptable (with minor modification).

31 JANUARY: Martin announces that, with modifications, the TD/CT has received government approval.

13 JUNE: Government announces Bill C-38, which contains Martin's new Financial Services Legislation including the new merger rules.

NOVEMBER: Bill C-38 dies on the order paper as a general election is called.

2001

7 FEBRUARY: Bill C-8 introduced. The bill was a repeat of Bill C-38.

14 JUNE: Bill C-8 receives royal assent.

2002

28 MARCH: Commons Finance Committee releases the "Barnes Report" clarifying the bank merger review process.

25 JUNE: Finance Minister John Manley announces a 2004 timetable for considering new bank merger proposals.

12 DECEMBER: Senate study on *Competition in the Public Interest: Large Bank Mergers in Canada* is released.

Notes

1. The merger would make the new company the tenth largest bank in North America.

2. Charles Freedman and C. Goodlet, "The Financial Services Sector: Past Changes and Future Prospects," background paper, Ditchley Canada Conference, Toronto, 3-5 October 1997: 18.

3. See Charles Freedman, "The Canadian Banking System," Bank of Canada, March 1997, or Freedman and Goodlet 1997.

4. For a discussion of these issues see Freedman 9-10.

5. Freedman 14.

6. Freedman concludes that the impact of these changes, or the intended outcome, was to allow the emergence, for the first time, of true financial service conglomerates, offering a full range of financial services. See Freedman 15.

7. See Freedman 10.

8. Anne Kingston, "Stealth Banker," *Report On Business Magazine* (April 1998).

9. Price Waterhouse, *Canadian Banks: Analysis of 1997 Results*, Survey Report (1998): 8; available at <http://www.pwcglobal.com/extweb/ncsurvres.nsf/DocID/B4E85 1556D468BD485256759004CAB46> (downloaded 31 January 2003).

10. Freedman 17.

11. See Freedman 15.

12. Canadian Bankers Association, *Submission to the Task Force* (10 November 1997)<http://cba.ca/eng/CBA_on_the_Issues/Submissions/taskforce.htm>: 19.

13. CBA, *Submission to the Task Force* 19.

14. CBA, *Submission to the Task Force* 54-55.

15. Harvey Schachter, "The Great Debate," *Canadian Banker* 105,3 (May/June 1998): 18.

16. Schachter, "The Great Debate" 19, 20, 21.

17. Schachter, "The Great Debate" 21, 23.

18. Price Waterhouse 3.

19. Kingston.

20. Kingston.

21. Harvey Schachter, "Cleghorn and Creative Destruction," *McGill News Alumni Quarterly* (Summer 1997): 4; available at http://ww2.mcgill.ca/alumni/news/s97/cleghorn.htm>.

22. Kingston.

23. The new bank would have $453 billion in assets. In terms of size, this would make it the tenth largest bank in North America and the twenty-second largest in the world.

24. John Cleghorn and Mathew Barrett, "Remarks at the Announcement of the Agreement To a Merger of Equals With the Royal Bank of Canada," *Press Release* (28 January 1998), <http://www.bmo.com/company_info/speeches/barret/jan2398.html>.

25. Kingston.

26. Kingston.

27. Edward Greenspon, "St. Paul among the Philistines," *Report on Business Magazine* (March 1998).

28. Kingston.

29. Kingston.

30. Murray Dobbin, "Are the bank mergers good for the country?" <http://www.policyalternatives.ca/bc/opinion12.html> (downloaded 21 November 2001).

31. Dobbin.

32. CCRC, "Ending Power Without Accountability: Making Banks in Canada Better Before They Get Bigger," summary of CCRC Position Paper 6 (May 1998), <http://www.cancrc.org/english/Sumpp6.html> (downloaded 6 December 2002).

33. Canadian Federation of Independent Business, "Mega Banks: Issues for All Canadians to Consider on Bank Mergers," <http://www.cfib.ca/research/businfo/min0091.asp> (downloaded 11 June 2003).

34. Bob Jenness, "Current Issues in Canadian Banking," *Monthly Economic Review* 3 (26 October 1998).

35. Fraser Institute, "Bank Mergers Necessary: Investment Managers," press release (14 July 1988).

36. Trevor Cole, "Waiting for Godsoe," *Report on Business Magazine* (September 1998).

37. Cole.

38. CBA, "CBA's Preliminary Response to the MacKay Task Force Report, Submitted to the Standing Senate Committee on Banking Trade and Commerce," (1998) <http://www.cba.ca/eng/CBA_on_the_Issues/Submissions/980929-a.htm> (downloaded 10 December 2001).

39. TD, "TD Bank Applauds MacKay Task Force Recommendation on Mergers, Says Decision Needed Sooner Not Later," *Press Release* (16 September 1998) <http://www.td.com/communicate/199809161.html> (downloaded 11 December 2001).

40. CBA, "CBA's Preliminary Response to the MacKay Task Force Report."

41. CBA Speeches, "The MacKay Report and Beyond," <http://www.cba.ca/eng/media_Centre/Speeches/981119-a.htm>.

42. A. Charles Baillie, "Why Bank Mergers are in the National Interest," TD Financial Group Speeches, 14 October 1998 <http://www.td.com/communicate/speeches/14oct98.htm> (downloaded 10 December 2001).

43. Standing Senate Committee on Banking, Trade and Commerce, *Comparative Study of Financial Regulatory Regimes* (1998), <http://www.parl.gc.ca/36/1parlbus/com-mbus/senate/com-e/rep-e/report15-cov-e.htm>.

44. Les Whittington and Laura Eggerston, "Liberal Caucus Says No To Piggy Bank Mergers: Ball In Paul Martin's Court," *Toronto Star* Ottawa Bureau, <http://www.flipside.org/vol1/nov98/n98w1013.htm> (downloaded 11 December 2001).

45. "Merger Mania," CBC, <http://www.cbc.ca/national/pgminfo/banks2/update.html> (downloaded 11 December 2001).

46. Whittington and Eggerston.

47. Whittington and Eggerston.

48. Council of Canadians, 14 December 1998 <http://www.canadians.org/campaigns/campaigns-bankmedia06.html> (downloaded 11 December 2001).

49. Whittington and Eggerston.

50. "Merger Mania."

51. Standing Committee on Finance, *The Future Starts Now—A Study on the Financial Services Sector in Canada* (December 1998) <http://www.parl.gc.ca/Infocom-Doc/36/1/FINA/Studies/Reports/finarp12-e.htm>; and Standing Senate Committee on Banking Trade and Commerce, *A Blueprint for Change—Response to the Report of the Task Force on the Future of the Canadian Financial Services Sector* (December 1998), <http://www.parl.gc.ca/36/1/parlbus/commbus/senate/com-e/rep-e/report17dec98-e.htm>.

52. Office of the Superintendent of Financial Institutions (OSFI), *Proposed Mergers between the Royal Bank of Canada and the Bank of Montreal, and the Canadian Imperial Bank of Commerce and the Toronto-Dominion Bank: Report to the Minister of Finance* (10 December 1998), <http://www.fin.gc.ca/OSFI/osfirpt%5fe.html>.

53. See Competition Bureau, "The Merger Enforcement Guidelines as Applied to a Bank Merger," Competition Bureau (January 2003) 42-43.

54. OSFI.

55. Konrad von Finckenstein, Competition Bureau, 11 December 1998 <http://strategis.ic.gc.ca/ssg/ct01339e.html> (downloaded 5 December 2001).

56. von Finckenstein.

57. von Finckenstein.

58. von Finckenstein. In its analysis, the Competition Bureau was limited to examining the effects of mergers on market competitiveness over a two-year time frame. This short horizon meant that it could not consider the longer term impact of changing technology.

59. Kimberley Noble, "Bitterness on Bay Street," *Maclean's* 111, 52 (28 December 1998): 70-74.

60. Noble.

61. Noble. Many question the degree to which the minister responsible for the sector is able to determine the outcome of the Competition Bureau investigation. In the 1999 Air Canada acquisition of Canadian Airlines, von Finckenstein, despite his own public comments criticizing the lack of competitiveness in the airline industry, approved the merger of the two airlines under political pressure from Transport Minister David Collenette. Analysts noted that the difference in the two cases, despite the perceived independence of the Competition Bureau, really seemed to turn on the attitude of the minister: "In the bank case, Finance Minister Paul Martin showed no enthusiasm for the merger plans of four of the Big Five players. As if on cue, the Competition Bureau found the deals anticompetitive. While this may have been the case, the banks were given no opportunity to eliminate the anticompetitive elements. What Martin wanted, Martin got." Eric Reguly, "The Missing Invisible Hand," *Time Canada* 157, 20 (21 May 2001): 40.

62. Noble 70.

63. See <http://www.cfib.ca/nomerger/info/5039.asp> (downloaded 11 September 2001).

64. Council of Canadians, "Rejection of Bank Mergers A Victory, But Banks' Earlier Threats a Serious Worry," <http://www.canadians.org/campaigns/campaigns-bankmedia11.html> (downloaded 11 September 2001).

65. Council of Canadians, "Rejection of Bank Mergers."

66. Noble.

67. David Robinson, "No Mergers? Don't Bank on it," Canadian Centre for Policy Alternatives, press release (13 December 1998), <http://www.policyalternatives.ca> (downloaded 12 May 2001).

68. Robinson.

69. Department of Finance, Canada, news release 99-016, Ottawa (11 February 1999): 1.

70. Department of Finance 1.

71. Department of Finance 2.

72. Paul Martin, "Reforming Canada's Financial Services Sector: A Framework for the Future," Department of Finance (25 June 1999). References to Martin's announcements in the following paragraphs are from this source.

73. Martin 6.

74. CBA, "Banks Reviewing Martin's Financial Reform Paper," *News Release* (25 June 1999).

75. CBC, "Merger Mania: Paul Martin's Policy," <http://www.tv.cbc.ca/national/pgminfo/banks2/report.html> (downloaded 11 December 2001.

76. Charles Baillie, TD Bank Financial Group, *News Release* <http://www.td.com/communicate/speeches/04aug99.html> (downloaded 5 December 2001).

77. Kimberley Noble et al., "Going Green," *Maclean's* 112, 33 (16 August 1999): 40.

78. Noble et al.

79. Noble et al.

80. Noble et al.

81. Noble et al.

82. Noble et al. 40.

83. Canadian Press, "TD Bank, Canada Trust closer to completion after share purchase recommended by board" (10 January 2000).

84. Competition Bureau, <http://strategis.ic.gc.ca/ssg/ct01687e.html>, 6.

85. Department of Finance, "Federal Government Approves Acquisition of Canada Trust by The Toronto Dominion Bank," 31 January 2000 <http://www.fin.gc.ca/news00/00-006e.html> (downloaded 5 December 2001).

86. CFIB, "CFIB's Response to the Federal Government Approval of the Acquisition of Canada Trust by the Toronto-Dominion Bank," 31 January 2000 <http://www.newswire.ca/releases/January2000/31/c4451.html> (downloaded 11 December 2001).

87. Jason Clemons (Fraser Institute), "Financial Services Reform is Politicized and Dated," Canada News Wire, 16 July 2001 <http://www.newswire.ca/releases/july2001/16/c2287.html> (downloaded 10 December 2001).

88. Derek DeCloet, "Warm, cuddly bank mergers," *Canadian Business* 73 (29 May 2000): 29.

89. Despite record industry profits of $9.1 billion in 2000, the big banks were projecting combined job reductions of 17,000 over the next few years. See Canadian Press, "Cleghorn to giant-bank opponents: get over it" (25 January 2000).

90. DeCloet 28.

91. See for example, Canadian Press, "Bank mergers critical to Canadian economy's future: TD Chairman says" (26 February 2001); and Canadian Press, "Banks must do a better job of explaining merits of bank mergers: CIBC chief" (26 February 2001).

92. Canadian Press, "Scotiabank chairman says mergers coming among Canada's banks" (9 March 2001).

93. Canadian Press, "Royal's new CEO says bank is covering its options when it comes to mergers" (10 March 2001).

94. *Globe and Mail*, "Manulife tried to buy CIBC" (24 January 2003).

95. Keith Kalawsky, "Lift Veil on Bank Deals, Urges Nixon," *Financial Post* (20 November 2002): 1.

96. James Baxter, "No mergers in works, banker says," *Vancouver Sun* (26 November 2002): C3.

97. *Globe and Mail*, "Size matters in banking, IDA says" (4 February 2003).

98. Gordon Nixon, "Canada needs a clear and timely merger review process," *Policy Options* (March 2003): 19.

99. Paul Waldie, "Barrett blasts Ottawa on blocking banks," *Globe and Mail* (6 November 2002): B1. Barrett had left BMO two months after the failure of his initial merger proposal with the RBC. As the public face of the super-mergers, he left under a cloud of failure in which the BMO, far from being merged into one of North America's largest banks, instead slipped to fifth place in Canada. His career in London has also sparked controversy over his large compensation and introduction of service fees. Barrett is now planning a merger between Barclays and other major European banks.

100. *Globe and Mail*, "More Competition in Banking Urged" (13 December 2002).

101. Senate Standing Committee on Banking, Trade and Commerce, *Competition in the Public Interest: Large Bank Mergers in Canada* (Ottawa: Supply and Services Canada, December 2002).

102. Standing Committee on Finance, *Large Bank Mergers in Canada: Safeguarding the Public Interest for Canadians and Canadian Business* (Ottawa: Supply and Services Canada, March 2002).

103. Sean Pasternak and Sandra Cordon, "Commons report halts bank mergers," *Vancouver Sun* (28 March 2003): D3.

104. Sinclair Stewart, "Bank bidding wars expected," *Globe and Mail* (25 June 2003): B1.

105. Sinclair Stewart, "Martin seen as merger friendly," *Globe and Mail* (13 June 2003): B3.

CHAPTER FOUR

Speaking Loudly and Carrying a Very Large Stick: Hardball Politics and Softwood Lumber

ROBERT M. CAMPBELL, LESLIE A. PAL, AND ANDREA MIGONE

We have to stand our ground and fight US protectionism...We
demand free trade, we want free trade, we deserve free trade.
Pierre Pettigrew, Canadian Minister For International Trade[1]

We are going to expose Canada's dirty little secrets....
Canada's stubborn intransigence has left us with no choice.
The US lumber industry is in crisis. Mills are closing,
unemployment is rising and our companies are haemorrhaging.
Rusty Wood, Coalition for Fair Lumber Imports[2]

The case of softwood lumber highlights the mechanics of Canadian politics in the area of international trade and reflects the problems emerging from dealing with split provincial (timber harvesting) and federal (international trade) competencies. As a subplot we can glimpse the unequal distribution of costs deriving from trade disputes between the federal and provincial levels on the one hand, and the various provinces on the other.

The process we describe here also forces us to focus on the role of interest groups in influencing policy-making in international trade. It exemplifies a possible approach nation-states can take to counter these groups by adding to intra-national dispute resolution processes the ones that are embedded in the international trade regime created around the FTA, NAFTA, and WTO.

Introduction

One of the largest single export goods in Canada is so-called "softwood" lumber, that is, lumber—mainly spruce, pine, or fir—which is used almost exclusively in residential construction. Canada is one of the world's largest forest producers and, along with wood pulp and newsprint, the production and manufacture of softwood lumber is a multi-billion dollar industry employing tens of thousands of Canadians in all regions of the country except the far North. Well over one-half of Canadian softwood lumber is exported. Although Canadian governments have tried to diversify outside markets for Canadian products, almost all Canadian softwood lumber ends up in the United States, where it competes with US-produced lumber for the residential construction market. Much Canadian economic activity and employment, therefore, is directly linked to access for softwood lumber products to the US market. But as Canadian exports have grown, US lumber producers have launched a series of challenges to Canadian logging and forestry practices designed to penalize Canadian products and raise their price to make their own domestic lumber more competitive. These actions have thrust Canadian softwood lumber to the forefront of Canadian efforts to promote trade liberalization or "free trade" in North America and the world and have involved a series of arcane manoeuvres in dispute resolution bodies of international trade organizations such as the General Agreement on Tariffs and Trade (GATT), the World Trade Organization (WTO), and the North American Free Trade Agreement (NAFTA). This chapter discusses these manoeuvres and their outcome in this long-lasting dispute between Canada and the world's only remaining international superpower.

Within the dry language of global trade relations—in disputes over the meaning and imposition of terms such as "countervailing duties" and "anti-dumping practices"—lies the critical economic issue of the softwood lumber trade between the US and Canada and its place within the regional trade agreements to which both nations are parties. Powerful industry interest groups in both countries regularly try to gain the upper hand in what has become one of the longest running and certainly one of the most economically damaging trade disputes between the two countries. The core of the problem is deceptively simple: timber companies are allocated harvesting rights to standing trees differently in the two nations. In the US, lumber companies purchase these rights through an open auction, while in Canada, provinces set "stumpage fees." These latter are the equivalent of "royalties" paid for the use of Crown-owned resources and are charged to the companies by forest ministries using complex formulae which take into account a variety of factors such as market prices for final products and the employment goals of provincial governments. Most US lumber companies see this Canadian administrative process as flawed; stumpage fees, they argue, are set at arbitrarily low levels, resulting in a subsidy to Canadian firms, which then are able to flood the US market with cheap lumber, illegally undercutting US producers who must pay prevailing market rates for their timber supplies. The fact that the majority of softwood lumber harvesting, in both nations, is concentrated in very specific areas (the US southeast and northwest and British Columbia and Quebec in Canada) adds a regional element to the politics of softwood lumber that pops up over and over again.

Because it is difficult to establish who is right in this dispute and because enormous interests hang in the balance, a state of generalized trade conflict interspersed with weary periods of uneasy truce has come about in this sector. The weapon of choice of the US lumber industry has been heavy political lobbying in the US legislature, resulting in the implementation of various countervailing duties (CVD) and anti-dumping measures.[3] In Canada, the problem is exacerbated by the different jurisdictions—the provinces are responsible for costs and regulations concerning timber harvesting, while the federal government must deal with international trade. To keep the players and most important events straight, an appendix of organizations and agreements and a chronology can be found at the end of this chapter.

US trade actions against Canadian producers were a feature of the development of the pulp and paper industry at the turn of the century and even earlier in the lumber industry. However, in the modern era the first lumber disputes arose in the 1960s when American lumber production began to decline as easily available forests had been cut down and Canadian lumber exports began to fill a significant amount of increasing US demand for housing materials. The first countervail action by US lumber interests against what it considered the Canadian subsidy of its industry was launched in 1982 and, even though the US International Trade Administration (ITA) ruled against it, that action set the stage for further complaints. The second, in 1985, was a more sophisticated and successful process, but the third, beginning in 1991, dragged on until 1996 when a new five-year agreement was signed to end it. When that agreement expired in 2001, the dispute was renewed again, resulting in the imposition of punitive duties on Canadian softwood lumber headed to the US.

The softwood lumber dispute features a truly interesting set of characters and institutions, all focused on an issue which has changed remarkably little over the last 100 years: the market share that Canadian softwood is allowed to obtain in the US. The regularity with which this issue re-emerges is one theme we will explore. Another is its regional nature and impact. Since southern and western US states, British Columbia (BC), Quebec, Ontario, and New Brunswick all have high stakes in the industry, the interplay between regional and federal levels in both countries is of prime significance in understanding the unfolding of the softwood lumber saga. Finally, we will see that the US and Canada simply do not agree on the softwood lumber trade: not only are their systems for harvesting and managing the resource different, their outlooks on what should be done to solve the dispute are, too. This disagreement between two unequal partners in world trade organizations is instructive in understanding the strengths and limitations of current international trade agreements.

The softwood lumber dispute is a classic case of a very powerful industrial sector divided along a national dimension (US versus Canada) by legislative, structural, and economic realities that differ enough to bring about a sustained clash. However, even this picture is complex. At one level, the dispute can be seen as one in which one group of powerful and influential private US lumber companies seeks political and economic support from the US Congress to reduce the pressure brought on them by a cheaper, and often better, Canadian product. In doing so, they are pitted directly against the same type of companies operating in Canada. And these Canadian companies respond by seeking the protection of both Canadian provincial and federal authorities. Along the way, each group has picked up various, sometimes unexpected, allies such as environmental and consumer groups and trade unions. In modern times the reality of large, integrated multinational forest product companies is such that in many cases the companies on both sides of the borders share common ownership. Hence, on another level, the dispute is much less about business arrangements than it is about different philosophies of government and about the willingness or unwillingness of one country (Canada) to be dictated to by another, larger one (the US).

Certainly, truly free trade in softwood lumber (as in any other good or service) would have a positive impact: the industry on both sides of the border would be forced to rationalize its practices, prices would drop, and the consumers and sectors that depend on lumber supply for their businesses (like homebuilding) would benefit from increased competition. However, in the end, success for Canada in the dispute would mean jobs and profits lost in the US. The livelihood of tens of thousands of US workers and their families, dozens of companies, and a few resource towns would be directly affected. If cheaper (and better) Canadian softwood products were allowed a free market in the US, their Canadian counterparts would prosper to the same extent. The negotiation process invoked for resolving this dispute, then, itself presents both opportunities and risks for the politicians involved in it while testing the economic agreements that Canada and the US have established over the past two decades, especially the North American Free Trade Agreement and its precursor the Canadian-American Free Trade Agreement (CAFTA) first signed in 1989.

The Canadian And US Economies: Exports And Trade Regimes

Canada and the US have always enjoyed a very close economic relationship, dependent on geographical, economic, and political factors. The geography of Canada, extending from east to west across immense distances, favoured north-south economic exchange; for instance, it is more logical and economically efficient for Quebec's manufacturing products to go to Maine or New York than to travel across country to Alberta or BC.

Nonetheless, free trade was not always the *modus operandi* of this relationship. In the nineteenth century the goal of boosting Canadian manufacturing was left to tariff barriers. Both the Cayley-Galt tariffs of 1858-59 and the National Policy, which was devised in 1879 and kept in place until after World War II, were used not only to raise revenue but to protect the domestic manufacturing sector behind high tariff walls.[4] Many of the companies that grew in that sheltered environment (which were predominantly located in central Canada and often were subsidiaries of American firms and not local businesses) did not have any real incentive to become competitive with respect to foreign manufactures.

The development of the General Agreement on Tariffs and Trade (GATT) after World War II had an important impact on Canadian federal industrial policy, which shifted towards the creation of a market for Canadian products first by attracting foreign direct investment (FDI) and increasing the purchasing power of Canadians and then by expanding Canadian export markets. These policies began to show some strain in the 1960s when it became obvious that Canadian industries were not as advanced or efficient as those in the US and could not count on large economies of scale; were under pressure from low-tech, labour-intensive producers in the Third World; and were subject to strong regional disparities. The net effect of these problems almost wiped out the gains achieved by increased exports.

While it is difficult to even list with precision all of the industrial and economic policies that have been set in place by the federal government since the 1960s, it is fair to say that successive federal governments moved to address these concerns. The trend has been towards embracing the concept of free trade. Canada is party to both the World Trade Organization (WTO) and the North American Free Trade Agreement (NAFTA), both created in the late 1980s and early 1990s, and has signed bilateral free trade agreements with other nations like Chile and Israel. As a result, tariffs have fallen in most areas, and the domestic industry has had to contend with increased competition. This has not meant the end of industrial policy but, rather, its moulding within the framework of the new international regime that had its roots in the immediate post-World War II Bretton Woods accords, which emphasized free trade, financial and economic interdependence, and multilateralism. This important shift in Canadian policy had conflicting repercussions on the way the national economy functioned: opening new avenues of trade with other nations helped the Canadian resource industry but threatened the less competitive consumer product sector.[5] The general result has been increased dependence on the export market to finance the imports of manufactured goods for the domestic market. Thus, Canadian exporters and Canadian governments have generally tended in international forums towards the exploitation of what can be termed the Canadian comparative advantage: cuts in barriers to trade to favour exports of raw materials and semi-processed goods.

While international trade is crucial for Canada, its structure is heavily skewed because most of it (about 85 per cent of both exports and imports) is with the US.[6] The relative size and composition of trade flows (mainly, Canada imports manufactured goods and exports raw materials and semi-manufactured goods) also means that, while Canada is almost totally dependent on the US for the provision of most of the requisites for an advanced economy and lifestyle, the opposite is hardly true. The US has generally been interested in securing a reliable provision of raw materials for its economy, and Canada has historically been its logical, but not its only, source.

Given the US's favourable position not only in North America, but worldwide, it should come as no surprise, then, that US federal administrations, after World War II, began to put increasing pressure on Canadian and other governments to go along with free trade policies, which favoured the opening of domestic markets to US manufactured goods through the lowering or removal of tariffs on imports. In 1947, 23 countries signed the General Agreement on Tariffs And Trade (GATT).[7] It was supposed to represent the initial step towards a more structured organization that was to be called the International Trade Organization (ITO). As it turned out, the US Congress denied President Truman approval of the ITO treaty, and the GATT remained the core structure for world trade legislation and planning for the next 50 years. For a long time, the wording of the GATT remained relatively loose; new elements were added in an effort to clarify and strengthen the original rules, which remained largely unchanged. This arrangement meant that any emerging frictions could be dealt with in a flexible, practical manner so that they seldom escalated into fully fledged trade disputes or trade wars involving tit-for-tat retaliation on member countries' imports and exports. It also meant that the economically dominant members of the GATT could bend the rules to their advantage. It was not until 1994, when the Uruguay Round negotiations of the GATT ended, that a more formal institutional setting emerged with the creation of the World Trade Organization (WTO). The WTO incorporated the original GATT agreement covering tariffs, subsidies, and quotas but expanded its scope to include trade in the service industry and intellectual property. Furthermore, the WTO was ratified by all member states' legislatures, something that had not happened with the GATT, grounding it decisively in international law.[8] Among other things this made the final decisions of the WTO arbitration panels mandatory on members and thereby significantly strengthened the dispute resolution mechanisms available in the international sphere.

Although the GATT had been remarkably successful, a number of episodes during the 1980s and early 1990s appeared to threaten its results. For instance, the Uruguay Round, begun in 1986, was mired in endless controversy surrounding areas such as agricultural trade and trade in services; in addition, a ballooning US trade deficit prompted increasing calls for protectionism from US interests for the first time since the end of World War II. For Canada this presented the dual problem of potentially decreased access to the US market at the same time that it faced a slowdown in the ability to diversify its trading partners multilaterally. By the mid-1980s when the Royal Commission on the Economic Union and Development Prospects for Canada (the MacDonald Commission) delivered its report,[9] Canadian policy-makers decided that their best option was to lock in their economic and commercial integration with the US through a bilateral free trade agreement.

Prime Minister Brian Mulroney began negotiations for the Canada-US Free Trade Agreement (FTA) in 1984; it was finally signed three years later, becoming effective on 1 January 1989.[10] It met mixed responses in

Canada. The Mulroney government, left-wing critics argued, had sold out to US capital, leaving Canadian manufacturing workers open to wage cuts and layoffs as the true implications of free trade with an industrial giant like the US would come to bear. Many voices were also raised against what appeared to be a handy avenue for the Americanization of Canadian society through economic ties. The issue of free trade was at the core of the 1988 Canadian federal election, and, when Mulroney was returned as prime minister, he felt that the nation had given him a mandate to further implement his vision through the signing of the Canadian-American Free Trade Agreement (CAFTA). The US government then began bilateral talks for a similar arrangement with Mexico and the succeeding Canadian Liberal government under Prime Minister Jean Chrétien entered these negotiations in 1992, eventually resulting in the signing of the trilateral North American Free Trade Agreement with the US and Mexico, which replaced the CAFTA agreement in 1994.[11]

The reach of NAFTA, while not as comprehensive as other continental trade strategies such as those which created the European Union, is extensive and touches sectors as diverse as government procurement, energy, agriculture, and services, providing a set of dispute settlement and appeal processes that supplement those found in the GATT/WTO system and hinge on the results of binational panels set up to investigate trade problems. This means that NAFTA is not just about the creation of a common set of trade laws, but rather about providing an arena for dialogue.[12]

The NAFTA negotiation featured attempts by Canada to retain and extend the benefits of CAFTA and by Mexican President Carlos Salinas to institutionalize his own domestic market reforms by fixing them in the framework of an international agreement. Since US negotiators still hoped to reinvigorate the GATT Uruguay Round, they did not have to accept any conclusion for the regional agreement that fell short of their optimal expectations. This gave them a remarkable amount of bargaining power, which, coupled with the willingness of both the Mexican and Canadian sides to compromise, finally yielded an agreement that, while not harming any of the three parties, certainly was a masterpiece for the US administration.[13]

However, the impact of the regional agreement should not be overstated for either its negative or positive aspects. Far from creating a common economy, like the one the European Union is trying to craft, NAFTA is mainly a trade agreement aimed at securing and institutionalizing a degree of continental economic integration. Certainly, it has put pressure on Canadian manufacturing—but probably not as much as the competition from low-wage, labour-intensive countries has done—and it has benefited the export sector—but not as much as its supporters predicted. In the softwood lumber disputes, it has barely changed the situation: softwood lumber was initially excluded from the CAFTA but was brought into the NAFTA deal. However, there it is treated as any other commodity. NAFTA created an additional level at which contentions can be debated (the binational panels) but has not introduced any mandatory element. This means that anti-dumping and countervailing duty disputes still come up regularly since US producers feel that they are a viable means of putting pressure on Canadian provinces and companies to change their practices.

WTO and NAFTA are the basis for the development of neoliberal notions of free trade in Canada, but they cannot determine the behaviour of governments or large firms.[14] This is particularly clear in the softwood lumber dispute as various actors try to implement their own national and provincial policies in the sector. Although these policies were crafted against the backdrop of free trade, they always looked no further than the immediate patching-up of the most immediate problems without really addressing the grievances centred on relative market shares and different national regulatory styles. This is one of the reasons why the softwood lumber disputes appear locked in stubborn repetition of often-heard, often-seen demands and policies. In the next sections we shall look more closely at what exactly the US and Canada are fighting about and at the possibility that among the policy-implementation efforts, new policies may be emerging from the deadlock.

What Are They Fighting For?
The Means And Ends Of Softwood Lumber Disputes

The trade in softwood lumber products plays a very important part in the economies of both the US and Canada. In both nations forestry employs a substantial number of personnel, providing both direct jobs in its harvesting and milling operations and indirect jobs in both the transformation and sale of wood products and in the construction industry.

A large share of Canada's economy is related to the extraction and export of natural resources. In this context, lumber is particularly relevant, especially in the western and central provinces. Statistics Canada reports that in 2001 Canada produced over 17,000 MBF (million board feet) of lumber. Much of this lumber was exported to the US for a total value of CND $9.3 billion. The table below highlights some selected data on both the production of softwood products and their export value.

I: Volume of Canadian Softwood Exports to the US: Selected Years (MBF)

Region	2001	2002
Alberta	1,368,222,447	1,501,761,142
BC	9,036,251,838	9,644,524,860
Manitoba*	99,763,081	194,320,013
Ontario	1,846,418,566	2,044,362,976
Quebec	3,882,122,246	3,546,769,202
Saskatchewan*	222,060,838	263,246,074
Atlantic Provinces*	1,262,275,184	1,617,720,877
Yukon Territory, Northwest Territory, Nunavut*	31,237	0
Total	17,717,145,437	18,812,705,144

* Note: The Department of Foreign Affairs and International Trade (DFAIT) began monitoring exports from these provinces only on 1 April 2001. The 2001 data only represents exports from these provinces for the period April-December 2001 (prepared on 30 May 2003).

Source: DFAIT, *Lumber Sector Statistics*, 2001, http://www.dfait-maeci. gc.ca/~eicb/sofwood/Lumber_Sector_Statistics.html.

II: Selected Canadian Lumber Employment Statistics, 2001

Province	Number of employees
BC	35,000
Alberta	4,100
Ontario	7,400
Quebec	25,500
Canada	80,730

Source: Statistics Canada, *Labour Force Survey* (Ottawa: Statistics Canada, 2001).

In the US the forest and paper industry ranges from very advanced paper mills to small family-owned sawmills and some nine million individual woodlot owners. As a whole, this sector ranks among the top 10 manufacturing employers in 46 states, employs some 1.5 million people, and its products are valued at more than US $230 billion each year. America's forest products industry is also among the most competitive in the world exporting every year more than US $23 billion worth of goods.[15]

The many softwood lumber disputes that have arisen between the US and Canada have centred on alleged unfair advantages that the Canadian industry enjoys because of structural elements and political decisions affecting the forest sector in Canada. To assess the basis of the dispute we need to look at the way the harvesting of lumber resources is set up and regulated in the two nations. In the US timberland is divided among publicly owned and privately owned land, with the vast majority being under private ownership. Ownership is fragmented though, as only about 627,000 of the almost 10 million non-industrial owners own more than 100 acres of forested land.

III: Timberland Ownership in the US

	Thousands of Acres	Percentage
Publicly Owned	145,966	29 %
Federal	109,168	22 %
States & Counties	36,798	7 %
Privately Owned	357,698	71 %
Forest Industry	66,858	13 %
Non-industrial	290,840	58 %
Total US	503,664	100%

Source: Brad W. Smith, et al., *Forest Resources of the United States* (Washington, DC: USDA Forest Service, 2001).

The harvesting of timber takes place, by and large, on privately owned forests as well. Public lands yield only 11 per cent of the annual cut (5 per cent from national forests and 6 per cent from other public lands). The rest comes from either forestry industry lands (30 per cent) or non-industrial forests (59 per cent). In Canada, the ownership of timberland is almost exclusively in the hands of the Crown, which controls some 94 per cent of Canadian forests. It should be noted, though, that in the western US (California, Idaho, Oregon, and Washington State) the ratio of publicly owned to privately held timberland is in favour of the former. Even if the numbers are not quite as high as those in Canada, they still represent significant public ownership of timberland.

IV: Public Versus Private Ownership in the US Western States, Thousands of Acres

	Publicly owned	Privately held	Total	Percentage of publicly owned
California	10,516	7,437	17,953	58.6 %
Idaho	13,901	3,222	17,123	81.2 %
Oregon	15,123	8,625	23,748	63.7 %
Washington	8,514	8,904	17,418	48.9 %
Total	48,054	28,188	76,242	63.0 %

Source: American Forestry and Paper Association, *Paper And Forestry Industry At a Glance* (Washington, DC: AFPA, 2001).

Production in the US is concentrated in the south and west (respectively producing in 2001 16,048 MBF and 16,938 MBF), whereas in Canada, BC has the highest production followed by Quebec, Ontario, and Alberta. The US is a major user of softwood lumber. It produces a large amount and imports over one-third of its annual consumption.

V: US Softwood Lumber, Selected Statistics

	US Production	Imports in the US	Total Consumption
1985	31,077	14,608	44,169
1990	35,790	12,148	44,968
1995	31,910	17,347	47,269
2001	34,977	19,885	54,762

Various Sources. All figures in MBF and rounded to the nearest decimal.

The other substantial difference between the two systems is the way in which the right to cut timber is allocated. In the US timber-cutting fees are determined through a competitive bidding system. This means that companies desiring to harvest resources on both private and public lands must engage in an auction to ensure that they will be able to cut trees. This process can lead to high prices for timber cutting, especially when the demand for wood products increases as has been the case in the past few years.

With domestic demand on the rise, US producers have found it increasingly difficult to compete against Canadian softwood, partially because of structural reasons (i.e., the weaker Canadian dollar) and partially, they claim, because of the way in which timber is sold in Canada. As opposed to entering a competitive bidding process, forestry companies operating in Canada pay stumpage fees. These are, in fact, royalties set by the various provincial governments according to variable formulas. These formulas are designed to be profit sensitive: when lumber prices begin to slide, the stumpage fee is also reduced, and vice versa. This process allows for a higher degree of economic viability for lumber operations in Canada as compared to in the US, but is not as economically efficient for forest owners, generating billions less in royalties than the US model.

The easiest explanation as to why Canadian provinces should decide to forego such healthy profits is to be found in the traditional prioritization of employment stability in the Canadian resource sector. Governments are ready to exchange higher returns on their cutting rights for a viable, long-term forestry industry.[16] Many lumber companies in the US argue that these political and structural elements generate an unfair advantage for their Canadian counterparts and thus have sought protection through the imposition of countervailing duties (CVD) under US and international trade law.

We shall discuss these in detail below, but for now we shall briefly define CVDs and describe the process through which they are investigated and imposed. As we have seen, a crucial goal of post-World War II economic institutions was the creation of an open trading system in which high tariffs and barriers to the circulation of goods were to be eliminated altogether or greatly reduced. The philosophical underpinnings of this decision rested both on the neoliberal theory that unhindered markets offer the best possible efficiency returns and on the liberal notion that free economic exchange is an excellent tool to increase cooperation among nations and decrease the risk of conflict. Since then, all of the regional and multilateral economic and trade agreements that have been signed have incorporated and enhanced this vision. The result has been the creation of a very open international trade system even though both its rules and its direction are still, by and large, dictated by the needs and goals of the most industrialized nations. Within this system, though, embracing free trade also meant creating a set of tools that would ensure that it could be managed. These included responses to companies or states trying to flood foreign markets with below cost goods (*anti-dumping* policies) and responses to states that

VI: Countervailing Duty And Dumping

Countervailing Duty

A countervailing duty (CVD) is a duty that may be imposed against foreign goods to offset policies or practices that are deemed to give one side an unfair trade advantage. Countervailing duties neutralize the effect of foreign subsidy programs and prevent losses from accruing to domestic companies.

Dumping

Dumping occurs when a producer exports a product to a foreign market at a price that is lower than the selling price for the product on the domestic market. The difference between the two prices is called the dumping margin. An anti-dumping duty is imposed by the importing country to offset the amount of the price reduction.

VII: The US International Trade Commission

The ITC is an independent, quasi-judicial US government agency consisting of six commissioners. Each commissioner is nominated by the president and confirmed by the Senate and serves a single seven-year term. One commissioner is designated the chairman of the commission, and one is the vice-chairman.

In AD/CVD (anti-dumping/countervailing duty) cases, the ITC's function is to conduct the injury investigation. The ITC also conducts changed circumstances reviews and sunset reviews with respect to existing AD/CVD orders and suspension agreements. The ITC has no role in administrative reviews.

In addition to its AD/CVD responsibilities, the ITC conducts unfair competition investigations under Section 337 of the Trade Act of 1979, import relief proceedings under Section 201 of the Tariff Act of 1974, and other international trade-related investigations when officially requested. The ITC also publishes the Harmonized Tariff Schedule of the US Annotated, which is the document by which imports of merchandise are classified for customs purposes.

A team of staff personnel at the ITC, assigned to each AD/CVD proceeding, typically consists of one representative from each of the following offices: Investigations, Economics, Accounting, Industry, and General Counsel. The team's responsibility is to manage the proceeding, issue questionnaires to the parties, and prepare a staff report summarizing the information received in the proceeding to aid each commissioner's analysis. In addition, each commissioner has a staff to assist both in his or her analysis of the information and legal issues presented and in drafting determinations.

were still engaging in subsidies that had not been allowed within the framework of these treaties (*countervailing duties*).

CVDs, then, are fees that a certain government imposes on imported goods after it has determined that the goods to be taxed have received an

VIII: Countervailing Duty Petitions In The US

A US industry that perceives it is being injured by unfair competition from foreign imports has the right to file a petition with both the US International Trade Commission (ITC) and the International Trade Association (ITA). A preliminary CVD investigation is then conducted by the US Department of Commerce. If these agencies discover the existence of subsidies, they impose a preliminary CVD. This means that companies from the nation targeted who wish to continue exporting into the US market must post a bond or cash to cover the duty.

At this point, both the ITA and the ITC run a final investigation. If there is another finding of subsidies, the Department of Commerce instructs the US Customs Service to assess duties on the exports of the products deemed as subsidized. The assessed duties are equivalent to the subsidy. For example, if a 10 per cent subsidy margin is found, US Customs will assess a 10 per cent duty on the product upon importation into the US.

Every five years the Department of Commerce reviews the continued need for a CVD.

IX: Anti-Dumping Legislation in the US

Anti-dumping duties may be sought by US industries that believe they are being injured by unfair imports. They must file a petition with the International Trade Administration (ITA) and the US International Trade Commission (ITC). It is the ITA's role to determine if there has been a case of dumping and what is its extent. The ITC will determine whether the US industry is suffering injury as a result of the import of dumped products. These determinations are made following the three criteria contained in the Anti-Dumping Agreement of the WTO:

- Dumped imports exist.
- There has been material injury to a domestic industry.
- There is a causal link between the dumped imports and the material injury.

If the ITA and the ITC make a *preliminary* determination that dumping has occurred, an investigation may take place, and exporters from the investigated country must post a bond or cash to cover estimated duties that are evaded through dumping. If the ITC and ITA determine in their *final* investigation that dumping has occurred, the Department of Commerce instructs the US Customs Service to assess duties against the importers of the dumped product. Such duties are a percentage of the value of the imports and are equivalent to the dumping margins. A dumping penalty may also be assessed.

unfair subsidy in the nation where they have been produced. This procedure is codified in domestic and international trade law and aims at bringing the price of a certain good or service in line with its real market cost,

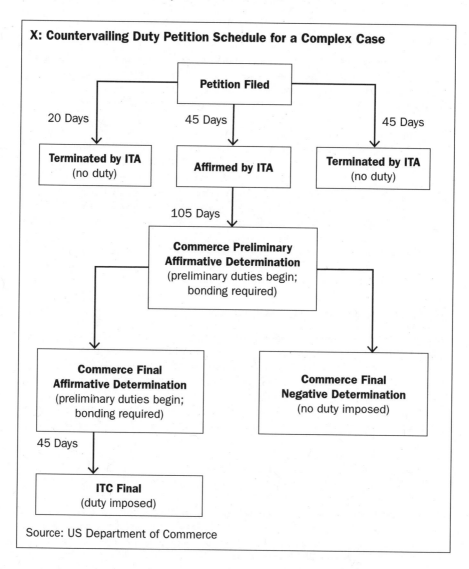

X: Countervailing Duty Petition Schedule for a Complex Case

Petition Filed

20 Days → Terminated by ITA (no duty)

45 Days → Affirmed by ITA

45 Days → Terminated by ITA (no duty)

105 Days → Commerce Preliminary Affirmative Determination (preliminary duties begin; bonding required)

Commerce Final Affirmative Determination (preliminary duties begin; bonding required)

Commerce Final Negative Determination (no duty imposed)

45 Days → ITC Final (duty imposed)

Source: US Department of Commerce

thereby shielding domestic industry from unfair competition. The administration of these measures rests with the US International Trade Administration and the US International Trade Commission.[17]

Two possible avenues are open to US authorities in the event of routine trade disputes: countervailing duties and anti-dumping actions. The former is taken against those producers who are unfairly subsidized by their government and can therefore out-compete American products, but only through illegal practices.

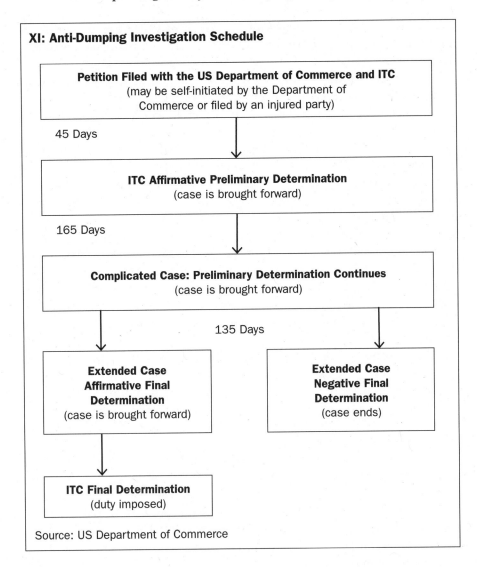

XI: Anti-Dumping Investigation Schedule

Petition Filed with the US Department of Commerce and ITC
(may be self-initiated by the Department of Commerce or filed by an injured party)

45 Days

ITC Affirmative Preliminary Determination
(case is brought forward)

165 Days

Complicated Case: Preliminary Determination Continues
(case is brought forward)

135 Days

Extended Case Affirmative Final Determination
(case is brought forward)

Extended Case Negative Final Determination
(case ends)

ITC Final Determination
(duty imposed)

Source: US Department of Commerce

The other possible recourse that companies have in the face of unfair trading practices materializes in the form of anti-dumping actions. Inset IX details the process followed by the US administration in this case.

The process of filing a CVD petition is both complicated and lengthy. Below are two examples of such processes. Inset X details the possible progress of a complex CVD petition schedule. In practice this occurs when the authorities that must make a decision on whether the duty is warranted or not have asked for a lengthier period during which to review the case because of the difficulty of the task at hand. As can be seen from the schedule, the parties could be waiting for some time for an answer to their problems.

Inset XI details the same process, but for an anti-dumping assessment. Because of the specific issues involved in assessing the existence of dumping practices, the length of the analysis is even longer in this case than for CVD.

Because the role of industry lobbies is so important in the process of beginning countervailing actions relating to softwood lumber, it is necessary to briefly illustrate how the US legislative process functions. The US Constitution was originally modelled after that of the ancient Roman Republic; its checks and balances prevent a strong executive from overcoming the will of the people; the states with larger populations are checked in the Senate from imposing their will over smaller polities, but allowed a measure of strength in Congress; and, finally, the powerful oversight functions of the Supreme Court cap it all.[18] The system works, arguably even better than the original one, but it has developed its own idiosyncratic mechanisms. In particular, the lobbying system, and its impact on policy-making, are relevant to our analysis.

Like most politicians in democratic countries around the world, elected representatives in the US must balance loyalty to their party with the need to keep the people in their electoral districts happy. Continued failure to at least maintain the economic and civil standards inherited at the moment of election is one of the surest ways to be relieved of the tension and workload associated with a congressional or senatorial seat.

While electors often communicate with their representatives in Washington, DC, it is the lobby system that ensures a continued flow of information and feedback between Congress and Senate on the one side and large industrial and economic interests on the other.[19] Working on the need for cooperation built into the system through its checks and balances, elected representatives can often squeeze important concessions out of the administration in return for legislative concessions they are willing to make. A case in point was the exchange, detailed below, that took place during President Ronald Reagan's term between the congressional approval of the CAFTA and a stronger stance regarding softwood products.

The US lumber industry has demonstrated a great aptitude for lobbying elected representatives and, until recently, has had little opposition from those groups that were penalized by duties imposed on Canadian softwood lumber, such as homebuilders and homebuyers who must pay higher prices for their materials and homes than would otherwise be the case. It is important to remember that the US presidency is often bound to listen very closely to the voices coming from the floors of its elected houses. Failure to do so can lead to crippling results with both the executive and the legislative being greatly impeded in their activity. It is enough to remember that, along with opposing the ratification of any international treaty, the legislature can, in a pinch and given the right timing, oppose the passage of the federal budget and block the ratification of federal judicial and other appointments.

The softwood lumber dispute has gained the place it has today not only because of its undeniable economic and social impact in both the US and Canada, but also through the skillful and consistent pressure exerted by the US lumber industry upon Congress and the Senate. With this understanding, we now examine the disputes in which the two nations have been engaged since the early 1980s.

The Softwood Lumber Disputes

There are four major flashpoints in the recent history of softwood lumber trade between the US and Canada.[20] As we saw above, all these actions were premised on the claim that Canadian wood was allegedly priced below its real market value. In 1982 the Coalition for Fair Canadian Lumber Imports, which is now called the Coalition for Fair Lumber Imports (CFLI), announced that it planned to seek the imposition of countervailing duties on Canadian softwood. In the mid-1980s the CFLI tried again to have a CVD imposed on shipments from Canada. This second action dragged on until both governments signed a five-year Memorandum of Understanding in December 1986.

In 1991, when the accord expired, the dispute was renewed, and new duties were again imposed on Canadian softwood lumber entering the US. The early 1990s saw a continuous back-and-forth of decisions from US, Canadian, and international bodies on the issue of whether the Canadian forest industry was unduly subsidized. In March 1996 the two nations signed a new five-year agreement that expired on 31 March 2001.[21] Since then, US trade authorities, under pressure from the US lumber industry and their political representatives, have imposed heavy duties on Canadian softwood lumber and, despite the reassurances of many politicians, a solution seems distant. Despite all these efforts on the part of the US government, Canadian softwood lumber exports to the US have continued to grow.

XII: The US-Canada Dispute in Softwood Lumber	
Period	**Activity**
1982	First Countervail
1985	Second Countervail
1986-1991	Memorandum of Understanding
1991-1996	Third Countervail
1997-2001	Softwood Lumber Agreement
2001-	Fourth Countervail

We will look in some detail at these specific actions in search of a common denominator that may help to explain the issue and to understand the players involved on both sides of the border. As noted above, the fundamental issue at the core of the softwood lumber dispute has been the apportioning of market shares for Canadian softwood lumber in the US market.

Because the Canadian product tends to directly substitute for the US one, US lumber companies have been extremely sensitive to the encroachment of Canadian companies on their markets. However, it is difficult to measure the relative impact that a weaker currency, relative efficiency, stumpage fees, and product quality each have on the continued growth of US imports of Canadian lumber.

The truth of the matter is that Canadian companies enjoy structural competitive advantages, like a weak dollar, and can offer an excellent product, while stumpage fees do not impose as heavy a burden on Canadian producers as the auction system does on US ones. The critical question, of course, is does this amount to *unfair* competition? Perhaps, but certainly not to the tune of a 27 per cent duty. The problem the US lumber industry faces is that the auction system works to enhance the effects of the business cycle: when the demand for lumber is buoyant, auction prices soar, and in an industry where mills must be kept running to turn a profit, one must have lumber to cut, and, therefore, one must buy. The reverse happens in times of downturns.

US lumber companies seem to perceive that a 30 per cent share of their national market is an absolute upper limit for Canadian imports. The goal of the many countervails is seldom stated in this manner, but it is, ultimately, the aim of US producers to bar enough Canadian softwood products from the US in order to maintain the economic viability of the US industry. These efforts, paradoxically, have worked to enhance the ability of Canadian producers to compete. That is, CVDs have had to be progressively increased as Canadian companies try to offset the duties by implementing ever better cost-cutting and efficiency enhancing measures, chief among them reducing labour costs. In BC alone, according to a recent Price-Waterhouse report, the lumber industry went from employing over 30,000 people in the early 1980s to less than 8,000 in 2003.[22] This, in turn, has undermined the reasons for the provinces retaining a low, administered, stumpage fee system as employment in the industry has declined so dramatically. Stumpage fees have gone up as a result of various agreements, and the provinces are now taking steps towards implementing a more market-oriented approach, with BC leading in this area. Still, this is not enough for the US lumber lobbies.

The complaint is recurrent: unfair advantage, unfair competition, massive in its scale.[23] The industry lobbyists have been able, over time, to fine-tune their skills and to develop well-honed strategies to bring congressmen and senators from lumber-producing states to their side. The fact that production of softwood lumber, as noted before, is regionally concentrated and that, therefore, losses are felt quite harshly in specific areas has given elected representatives a motivation that should not be underestimated. It was trial-and-error for the lobbyists in the beginning, but, since the 1990s, both the elected representatives and the US Trade Administration have come on side, again not surprisingly if one looks at the employment and income numbers that are at stake. The CFLI remains the strongest player in this game; no other group or association, either in Canada or in the US, has as good an organization or as large a resource pool, even if it has faced stiffer resistance of late from both US and Canadian consumer associations. Nonetheless, the biggest development has been the emergence and increasingly better organizational skills of these antagonistic groups.

From the point of view of governmental activity, the US side has seen a predominantly federal involvement. This is the obvious effect of the nature of the international trade-related policy instruments employed, like CVDs, which are designed to be handled within the federal sphere. On the Canadian side, intervention has been split between the federal and provincial levels.[24] Ottawa is required to deal with the international trade component of the dispute to provide some semblance of national guidance; the provinces enter the fray at perhaps the most important juncture, because it is their responsibility to manage forestry policy and to set stumpage rates. This cleavage in responsibilities is coupled with a stark differential in relative economic impact: it is the provinces that feel most directly the economic consequences of what happens to the lumber industry. To further complicate things, the relevance of lumber for the various provincial economies and the profits that can be extracted from it, also vary greatly. BC is the worst off, as it depends heavily on the industry but, at the same time, has already harvested the best and most accessible timber. Quebec and Ontario are the other two provinces with a large lumber industry, but their economies are both more diversified and stronger than BC's, and their timber resources are, after some decades of transition, returning to a peak with large stocks of prime timber just about ready to be harvested.

These cleavages mean that, while Canadian federal authorities have had a generally more pugnacious attitude towards CVDs, the provinces have been more open to meet US demands. Even this generalization, though, requires some further analysis as BC, both because of its larger exposure and, after the election of a provincial Liberal government in 2001, for ideological reasons, has moved to implement large market-oriented changes in its forest code.

The other trend that emerges from the analysis of the softwood lumber CVDs dispute is that, over time, positions seem to have radicalized and international adjudication processes appear to have more effect than negotiation. This is likely dependent on the nature of the issues that are on the table and on the fact that US authorities, pressured by the CFLI, stubbornly continue to impose crushing duties on softwood lumber, even when a string of FTA, NAFTA, and WTO rulings has suggested that these duties should be substantially reduced.

The Early US-Canada Trade Disputes, 1982-1991

The US and Canada signed two five-year agreements regarding trade in softwood lumber: the 1986 Memorandum of Agreement and the 1996 Softwood Lumber Agreement. Both documents temporarily addressed the issue of Canadian market share in the US softwood lumber markets but did not, and could not, go to the core of the problem: the structural differences between the two industries.

The ten years of relative trade peace they encompassed will be treated only cursorily here; the best thing that can be said to have emerged from those times is a bit of respite from the hardship of trade confrontation. Both agreements provided only a temporary stopgap.

Two issues can serve as guiding threads in the dispute: the first is the charge, coming through US business interests and filtered and taken up by US elected representatives and the administration, that stumpage fees amount to *de facto* subsidies for the Canadian lumber industry. The second is the progressive organization of the US lumber industry in its quest to limit the access of Canadian lumber to their markets.

The first claim of unfair practices was fielded in 1982, when the US Congress, responding to complaints from American lumber producers, ordered a "fact-finding" investigation by the US International Trade Commission (ITC). In April the ITC reported that lower timber costs explained much of the inroads that Canadian lumber had made in the US market. While not making any specific recommendation, the report focused attention on a US lumber sector struggling against Canadian imports. Republican Representative Bob Packwood (Oregon) suggested that the US government take legal action against this state of affairs.

At the time, the reaction of many US groups, with the possible exception of the Northwest Independent Forest Manufacturers (NIFM), which noted that it would consider requesting the imposition of a duty on Canadian products, appeared moderate. Nevertheless, there were signs that the industry was beginning to organize. The Coalition for Fair Canadian Lumber Imports (CFCLI) was created in July. It included lumber companies from the softwood producing regions of the US where the increased market share garnered by Canadian lumber had hit the hardest and producers were most sensitive to the issue. The newly minted organization announced that it would seek CVDs on imports from Canada to counterbalance the alleged subsidies that the forestry sector enjoyed there; it did so shortly after.[25]

The results were not what the CFCLI had expected. The ITC ruled that a "reasonable indication" did exist that the US industry was being injured, but its preliminary and final decisions both showed that there was no unfair subsidy on Canadian softwood lumber and allowed Canadian exports to continue their duty-free status.[26]

No appeal was presented to the trade authorities. Instead, US lumber manufacturers aimed at stepping up political pressure. Between 1984 and 1985 the Southeastern Lumber Manufacturers Association (SLMA) began lobbying members of Congress to introduce legislation that would effectively change tariff regulations,[27] while US companies pressured Congress to seek some kind of action leading to a restriction of duty-free softwood imports. This lobbying culminated in the December hearings held by the House Interior Subcommittee, which painted a gloomy picture of the US lumber industry and linked it directly to the issue of unfairly priced Canadian lumber. A Democratic representative for Oregon, Jim Weaver, went as far as promising to introduce legislation to limit this influx, and, when Congress reconvened in early 1985, this is exactly what happened.

This was not the only voice raised on the issue. While Congress was under strong pressure from industry lobbyists, the US executive believed that free trade should be the central pillar of its regional economic strategy, and US President Ronald Reagan was very reluctant to give in to calls limiting trade with Canada or imposing tariffs. The North American Wholesale Lumber Association, the Manufactured Housing Institute (MHI), and the National Lumber and Building Material Dealers Association (NLBMDA) noted that it was in the best interest of the economy, and of the public, to have free trade in lumber products and opposed any legislative tool that would disrupt such flows.

The same mantra was repeated by Canadian industry and political representatives, and BC Premier Bill Bennett actually travelled to Washington, DC, in an effort to present stumpage fees as a legitimate and fair means to allocate harvesting rights. The visit was reciprocated later in 1985 when Representative Sam Gibbons, a Democrat from Florida, met with Canadian officials in Vancouver.

This did not deter the build-up of the political offensive. In September 1985, the US Congress had to deal with five bills introduced in the previous months all aimed at reducing Canadian lumber exports to the US or at raising the cost of these imports. The supporters of the US lumber industry decided that the bill introduced by Gibbons stood the best chance of being approved. This was, in fact, a middle ground between more severe restrictions and minor changes in the tariff system and became a rallying point for the industry. If it were to pass, it would impose CVDs on some Canadian goods that were produced using natural resources extracted with the aid of a subsidy. However, before the bill could become an issue itself, the situation rapidly deteriorated.

An ITC report commissioned by President Reagan and released in October found that lumber costs were lower in Canada than in the US, but did not identify any injury for US producers arising directly from this state of affairs. It provided ammunition for both camps to either demonstrate the fairness of the stumpage system or to hail it as proof of US concerns. The next year, though, the ITC found that Canadian exports of shake and shingles had injured US firms and advised that a 35 per cent duty should be imposed on these products.

Of course, there had been contacts between the US and the Canadian administrations to try and fend off the possibility of a disruptive set of trade confrontations, but the results had been very disappointing. No real progress was forthcoming, and, if anything, the two parties were now convinced that their counterparts were stubbornly holding on to a partisan view of lumber trading.

In the face of mounting pressures from both Congress and the Senate, confronted by the findings of the ITC and by the apparent failure of lumber negotiations, eager to obtain fast-track authority for the US-Canada Free Trade Agreement (FTA), the Reagan administration decided that it was worthwhile to change its stance on lumber duties to appease powerful domestic pressure groups. Duties were imposed on shake and shingles.

The newly renamed Coalition for Fair Lumber Imports (CFLI) pressed its political advantage to the maximum, filing a CVD petition seeking a 27 per cent duty on lumber imported from Canada.

Responses from Canada were mixed. Some observers noted that, in the face of the US domestic situation, the Canadian industry and the provincial governments would be well advised to enact voluntary restraints. These would ensure that the extra money paid by Canadian companies would find its way to Canadian rather than US coffers. Others refused this approach because it would mean recognizing the validity of the US claim that Canadian lumber producers were unfairly subsidized.

Further pressure was applied on the Canadian provinces and the lumber industry in the form of a preliminary ITA decision rendered on 16 October 1985, which found that the stumpage fee system amounted to a subsidy and imposing a temporary duty of 15 per cent on Canadian softwood exports to the US.[28] A final decision was expected by the end of the year.

Canada was rapidly running out of options, the looming economic damage appeared staggering, and, while initially the Canadian federal government seemed intent on seeking legal and diplomatic redress for the CVD, the ten provinces (with Ontario the lone dissenter) indicated their willingness to negotiate.

In November Canada offered to impose a 15 per cent export duty on its lumber shipments (to be replaced over time with increased stumpage fees) in exchange for the withdrawal of the CFLI's CVD petition. Soon afterwards, the representatives of the two countries met in a tense environment. Little progress was made, and on Christmas Eve both left the table. The US representatives made it clear, however, that they would listen to any proposal presented to them before the end of the year. Six days later, just minutes ahead of the final ITA ruling, the two parties signed a Memorandum of Understanding (MOU). It contained the basic elements of the earlier proposal: in exchange for the CFLI dropping its CVD petition, Canada would impose a 15 per cent tax on softwood lumber exports directed to the US market, the interim duty collected by US Customs since mid-October was cancelled, and all bonds posted were to be returned. The MOU was to become effective on 8 January 1987; in the meantime US authorities would collect a 15 per cent "surcharge" on lumber shipments.

Four months later, the Canadian Parliament approved the 15 per cent tax on lumber shipments, and provincial governments looked at replacing the export tax with an increased stumpage fee rate. BC and Quebec were the most interested in seeing this solution implemented even though it meant going through a legislative process both in Canada and the US; Ontario was more reluctant to follow suit. BC unilaterally increased its stumpage fees at the beginning of October and began a program to rebate the increased stumpage fee for as long as the 15 per cent export tax remained in place.

Ottawa also brought to the attention of the US administration its proposal to replace the export tax with a mix of increased stumpage fees and/or provincial taxes. As the CFLI did not oppose this course of action, things began to move, so that by December BC producers no longer had to pay the export tax.

While Canada and the US signed the FTA protocol in 1987, the agreement had remarkably little to say about the immediate worries of the lumber industry. Both administrations allowed for a higher degree of friction regarding the lumber issue not only because of domestic pressures in the US and a need on both sides to conclude the negotiations for the FTA quickly, but, because of the real complexities and very entrenched beliefs surrounding the lumber issues, only slow progress was achieved.

The early CVD actions highlighted two themes. The first was the concern with which the US lumber industry viewed the penetration of Canadian products into their market, and the second was the capacity of the US lumber lobby to capture the attention of the US administration and stir it into action. Neither other US business interests, nor the Canadian lumber industry, nor the two levels of Canadian government (federal and provincial) were able to summon enough political firepower to prevent the imposition of duties.

The years of the MOU were quiet ones. Both nations worked to fine-tune the agreement's elements, and duties were dropped across the board once its contents were implemented. Things were set to change, though, as the 1986 MOU turned five and was, therefore, set to expire.

Later Countervailing Actions, 1991-2003

That no effective resistance could be mustered in the mid-1980s to the demands of the CFLI did not mean that everyone was happy with the way things were going. Canadian lumber producers were particularly irked by the situation, and, in 1991, they began to pressure the federal and provincial governments to renegotiate the 1986 MOU so that the export tax could be cancelled. This was the opening shot in a new round of trade wars and the first signal of a more pugnacious attitude from north of the border. It was, of course, met with strong negative reactions by the Bush administration, Congress, and the US lumber industry.

Giving a month's notice, Canada announced that it would terminate the 1986 agreement on 4 October and reiterated that there was no subsidy in place for Canadian softwood lumber producers.[29] Although representatives met in Washington to try to work out a solution, no progress was achieved. When the MOU terminated, the US administration imposed tariffs on Canadian imports. These ranged from 0 per cent for BC lumber in view of the higher stumpage fees imposed there, to 6.2 per cent assessed on Quebec softwood, and 15 per cent for products entering the US from Alberta, Saskatchewan, Manitoba, and Ontario. And, once again, the ITC began a CVD investigation to determine if Canadian procedures resulted in injury to the US industry. Its decision that they did triggered a subsidy investigation by the ITA. The ultimate result was a provisional duty of 14.48 per cent on all Canadian softwood lumber entering the US with the exception of wood coming from the Maritimes and from a few specific companies.[30]

Reactions to this decision were overwhelmingly negative in both countries. Only the US lumber companies favoured the protection of their industry, while representatives of other sectors were strongly opposed to the increased cost of lumber. Overall, a relatively small minority stood to benefit from the tariff, while many could expect hardship. Later in the year, the provisional duty was first reduced to 6.51 per cent by the ITA and then made permanent by the ITC.

At this point, Canada decided to seek redress at the international level, another new development, and filed three separate appeals against the duty imposed on its exports. One was to be heard by the GATT, while two separate appeals were filed under the terms of the dispute resolution mechanisms embedded in the 1989 FTA to address both the issue of injury and that of subsidies. The complexities involved made for split decisions from both organizations, with panels reasoning consistently that claims from both parties had some merit. Nonetheless, the international arena seemed to lend credence to the Canadian argument that the US administration had been hasty in assessing duties and not particularly fair in setting the amounts.

The GATT panel never did reach a formal conclusion, however a press release noted that the US acted within its rights in imposing a CVD on Canadian softwood lumber but that it should not have imposed interim import bonds on Canadian shipments. The FTA binational panel that reviewed the ITA subsidy decision stated that the latter had failed to present sufficient supporting evidence, and, although it did not cancel the duty, it asked the ITA to review its decision. The same ruling came from the second binational panel, the one dealing with the ITC's finding of injury.

Canadian federal authorities were overjoyed. In a press release on 6 May, the International Trade Minister Michael Wilson said, "this is a very positive result for the Canadian lumber industry and demonstrates that the FTA dispute settlement mechanism is working. We have used the FTA successfully to defend the Canadian lumber industry's access to the United States market.... The federal government, the provincial governments and the industry mounted a strong defence before the panel, all parties concerned have worked together closely over the past two years. I have been very pleased with this cooperative effort."[31] Not everyone, though, shared this note of optimism; the industry felt its problems ran deeper, especially with regard to labour costs, as noted by Noranda Forest Products Chairman Adam Zimmerman: "I have believed for a long time jobs aren't worth what they are being paid in this country. We're not as rich as we think we are."[32] At the same time, the Canadian timber industry had already shown that it understood that the issue was one of political rather than economic grievance; early in 1992 industry spokesperson Mike Apsey declared that "in 1986 [the Canadian timber industry] learned a very hard lesson. Decisions are not made purely on the facts of the case."[33]

Another decision rendered by an FTA binational panel regarding the dutability of predrilled studs also went well for Canada.[34] International Trade Minister Wilson called it "a very positive decision. It is the best result we could have had, it shows how the free trade agreement can benefit Canadian industry."[35] Tom Buell, Chairman of the Canadian Forest Industries Council, was even more sanguine: "The bi-national panel today flunked the [US] Commerce Department in Economics 101 ... we are confident that the Commerce Department [will correct] its mistakes, the claim of subsidy will disappear and the duty will be dropped."[36]

The CFLI was not impressed at all by these decisions. Lawyer John Ragosta, who represented the US timber lobby, went on record saying that the FTA panel had overstepped its bounds: "these people are way off in terms of what they are supposed to do."[37] As a result of these reviews both findings were confirmed, and the Commerce Department actually raised the 6.51 per cent duty to 11.54 per cent, even though it would wait for a binational panel review in December before imposing them.[38]

After a series of reviews and appeals, the Extraordinary Challenge Committee (ECC) ruled that the US did not have a CVD case against Canadian exports and that deposits collected by US Customs on or before 17 March 1994 had to be returned.[39] The decision was final, as the ECC was the last possible appeal under the FTA provisions, but US representatives made no mystery of their disappointment at what they saw as national voting not only within the binational panels but also within the ECC decision. Many advocates of duties remained convinced that Canadian stumpage fees were too low and often quoted the decision made by the BC government to increase these fees to finance its forest renewal program as evidence of artificially low prices in Canada. As a result of the ECC ruling, the US and Canada entered an agreement according to which the US returned all bonds collected on Canadian softwood lumber regardless of when they were imposed, and the two nations agreed to set up a consultative structure to try to resolve through negotiation the still outstanding elements of lumber trade.

Canada had stood up to the US in the international arena and had been delivered, if not an outright victory, something that looked much better than a new set of duties. Events between 1991 and 1994 had shown that there was an alternative to bowing to US pressure.[40] Appealing to international trade tribunals clearly reduced the power of the US lumber lobby; however, it did not discourage it. In the following years, the US administration showed that it was ready to impose duties and live through the seemingly interminable series of international appeals and counter-appeals while the Canadian lumber industry slowly bled to death.

In the short term the climate remained heated with fears of a surge of Canadian softwood lumber flooding the US (after all, in 1994 Canada had exported a record 16.4 billion board feet of softwood). The CFLI used its political muscle to threaten a new countervail. Between the end of 1995 and the beginning of 1996 the two sides finally engaged in constructive dialogue, and representatives from the two governments signed an Agreement-In-Principle on 16 February. This agreement reflected both the US lumber industry's concerns and the new strategy implemented by the Canadian federal government. It set up a quota for Canadian softwood lumber exports into the US, but this quota was made more flexible and generous than what the CFLI demanded.

The Softwood Lumber Agreement was to frame, however imperfectly, softwood lumber trade between the US and Canada for the next five years. It raised the amount of duty-free exports from 9 to 14.7 billion board feet per year. Exports over that amount would incur a two-tier duty: for the first 650 million board feet a $50 charge per thousand board feet would be assessed, with $100 per thousand board feet duty charged for exports exceeding that amount. A clause allowed for "bonuses" in the amount of non-dutiable softwood if a trigger price was met in the US market and assured that no CVD action would be launched during the life of the agreement (1 April 1996 to 31 March 2001).[41] The Maritimes, Saskatch-ewan, and Manitoba were exempted from these rules.

In September, Canada made public the final set of provincial quotas for lumber exports. The lion's share went to BC where companies were allowed to export 8.67 billion board feet (BBF) to the US; this was the equivalent of 59 per cent of all Canadian exports. Next came Quebec with a comparatively small quota set at 3.38 BBF, equivalent to 23 per cent of the yearly Canadian quota. Ontario was assigned 1.51 BBF, and Alberta 1.13 BBF, respectively, representing 10.3 per cent and 7.7 per cent of the agreed-upon limit. The response in Canada was mixed, with companies on the west coast being particularly pleased with the allocation of export quotas while eastern producers were generally less impressed by what they perceived as a skewed allotment.

Reaching a final agreement on the quantity and modality of Canadian softwood lumber imports into the US was a crucial step in reducing the level of conflict in this sector. Nonetheless, US domestic demand for con-struction and industrial-use lumber still remained high, and prices began to increase. While this was certainly good news for US producers, it impacted negatively on homebuilders, lumber retailers, and the like, who now saw their costs increase and their profits drop. Any calls by other groups, such as the National Lumber and Building Material Dealers Association (NLBMDA), for a renegotiation or a revision of the Softwood Lumber Agreement generated a hail of negative responses from the CFLI and its members.

Another familiar concern emerging from the US at regular intervals was the claim that "a wall" of Canadian lumber was about to flood the US market. Some observers believed that, given that quotas were assessed on a quarterly basis, Canadian companies would hold on to large quantities of lumber at the end of any given quarter to stay within their non-dutiable allowances and would then engage in mass exports at the beginning of the next quarter. This spurred fears of negative effects on the price of lumber in the US. As a matter of fact, Canadian companies consistently remained within their allotments, taking advantage of the bonus clause built into the agreement that allowed for increased exports when lumber prices in the US soared but otherwise never engaging in the behaviour described above.

This attitude and the attendant concerns of the US producers should, in hindsight, have been interpreted as a signal that the 1996 agreement, while temporarily quelling the worst of the problems, did not fully address the main issue; namely, the anachronistic attempt to reverse the trend towards a higher market share for Canadian lumber in the US. Given how bad things had started to look, however, Canadian International Trade Minister Art Eggleton counted his blessings and said that he would "monitor the system closely over the next few months to ensure that these assurances are being kept and that the system is working to the benefit of all segments of the softwood lumber industry."[42] Apart from that, he could take some solace in the fact that both the FTA and NAFTA panels did not share the US administration's opinion that stumpage fees constituted a large subsidy to the Canadian forestry industry.

The CFLI began almost immediately to lobby against the new *status quo*. As a result, the years of the agreement were rife with uneasy policy decisions, lobbying, and international appeals. The latter had become the norm now, on the one hand because they offered more latitude to the Canadian government, on the other because of the complexity of the political atmosphere in which the issue was couched.

For instance, in 1997, US Customs exempted spruce-pine-fir studs which were 8 to 10 feet long and had pre-drilled holes for wiring, from the category covered by the Softwood Lumber Agreement. This ruling created a colossal loophole for Canadian producers to exploit. Given that, in 1996, Canada produced about 3 billion board feet (BBF) of such studs, the CFLI was very concerned and quickly appealed the Customs' decision Between the launch of the appeal in April and the following December, Customs collected an estimated 6,000 comments regarding its decision. These included 4,000 hole-punched postcards sent in by lumber workers that read: "This card may have a hole in it but it still is a postcard."

In the meantime, lobbying efforts by the NLBMDA and the National Associations of Home Builders (NAHB) aimed at revising the Softwood Lumber Agreement generated a first practical result. Representative Jack Quinn of New York introduced a bill in Congress that would effectively change US trade legislation so that Canadian trade practices could not be subject to CVDs. The initiative drew bitter criticism from the CFLI, as expected, but was just the beginning of a political offensive launched by sectors that had been hurt by increased lumber costs. While, in the end, these attempts would not be very successful, they represented the first serious domestic opposition to the CFLI in the US.

The following year, 1998, was noticeable for two events. On the Canadian side, BC decided to lower its stumpage fees. On the US side, there was a push towards including as many softwood imports as possible into the dutiable quota provided for in the Softwood Lumber Agreement of two years earlier. This process began with the decision in September that pre-drilled studs should, in fact, be included in the Softwood Lumber Agreement and, therefore, should count towards the Canadian quota of non-dutiable lumber. It continued with various attempts at reclassification of wood products, such as notched studs and rougher-headed lumber, as falling within the scope of the agreement. Both issues were important challenges to the legislative superstructure imposed by the agreement on the lumber sector and dragged on well into the next year, thus exerting considerable pressure on the system. A quote from Montana Senator Max Baucus gives an idea of the climate: "A few months back [US Customs] decided that a board with a small hole drilled in one end is not a board anymore, so Canadian mills are drilling a lot of holes." CFLI's John Ragosta played the same tune: "They [Canadian lumber mills] are shipping so much through this category that if this problem is not solved, there is no lumber agreement." Canadians saw the whole thing as a domestic American issue; Jake Kerr, CEO of Lignum Ltd., one of the Canadian companies that had taken advantage of the earlier pre-drilled decision, noted: "It is a US issue ... we support the lumber agreement. We don't look on this as a loophole issue. This is a product that the US Customs says is not part of the deal. I don't know what could be expected of us."[43]

As a result, a decision was reached through the courts that classified pre-drilled studs as counting towards the non-dutiable quota of softwood lumber. As could be expected, the US administration's decisions were not met with any favour by the Canadian industry and government. They were labelled as an attempt to change the rules set out in the Softwood Lumber Agreement in an unfair manner, and protection was sought by appealing them in front of the World Customs Organization (WCO) and the US Court of Appeal.

With a 21-1 vote (the US representative, unsurprisingly, voted against), the WCO subcommittee charged with the analysis of the issue found that pre-drilled studs should be classified as joinery and carpentry and, therefore, were exempt from the Softwood Lumber Provisions. The final decision, delayed until October, was in favour of the Canadian side, but, this being a non-binding ruling, the US was free to ignore it and proceed with its quotas. The last outstanding issue, the trade in rougher-headed lumber, was not settled until October 2000 when Canada was allowed to export up to 72.5 BBF to the US free of duty.

Just as the issue of exactly what types of softwood products should count towards the calculation of the Softwood Lumber Agreement non-dutiable quota was heating up, the provincial government in BC was reviewing its forestry policies. The New Democratic Party (NDP), worried by economic conditions in the sector, had begun in 1998 to assess the relative impact of stumpage fees on companies operating in different parts of the province. The general message was that stumpage fees were too high and should be reduced, but that this reduction would come within the parameters dictated by the agreement.

When the new fees were announced, mills in the interior could expect average savings of C$3.50 per cubic metre, while mills operating in the coastal area would enjoy an average reduction of C$8.10 per cubic metre.[44] The CFLI immediately labeled this as an attack on the Softwood Lumber Agreement and a new subsidy to Canadian lumber producers directed at undermining the US industry. The CFLI engaged in a sustained lobbying effort, contacting officials in both the Commerce Department and the US Trade Representative Office and putting increased pressure on the members of Congress who were most sensitive to the issue of lumber imports. As a result, a set of informal contacts between the trade representatives of the two countries took place that June. In the end, though, it was clear that the two sides could not agree at the negotiating table, and, therefore, the decision was made to seek arbitration by a three-person panel.

Since the three members of the panel were not chosen until December, and with substantial briefs to be heard from both Canada and the US, the arbitration panel decision kept sliding forward. It was made irrelevant when US and Canadian representatives managed to reach a negotiated solution in August 1999.[45] This called for a change in both the upper and lower fee shipments of wood from BC so that they would be set at the averages for the first and second years of the Softwood Lumber Agreement. In other words, BC would see its share of lower fee timber reduced by almost 90 MBF each year and its upper fee export limited to 110 MBF. Anything exceeding these figures would be hit with a fee of C$146.25 per thousand board feet in the fourth year and a C$148.47 fee in the fifth.

The future of the Softwood Lumber Agreement looked gloomy. Both sides had increasingly lost faith in it and felt that the other party was not committed to respecting its terms but, rather, was trying to find loopholes in the system. In October 1999, Trade Minister Pettigrew received a letter from Peter Scher, the US trade ambassador in Canada, who stated that government regulation of the lumber trade should be abandoned both in the US and Canada (although this remark was directed towards the stumpage fee system) and that the US was not inclined to renew the agreement once it expired in March 2001.[46]

Even those who were being hurt by the US-imposed duties had no love for the system. Tom Ross, NLBMDA Chair, went on record stating that:

> The quota agreement was presented as managed trade. What it really is is mis-managed trade. It was a bad agreement at inception, and it became worse from there. It has created tremendous financial hardships—no matter the size of the operation. While in the past the market was driven by demand, now it is driven by access. The timing of inventory purchases are not driven by product need, but by fear of product price escalation. When you couple the loss of access to US wood fiber production with the restriction on imports from Canada, you create chaos, uncertainty, and the possibility for financial disaster within our industry. Free trade is the only answer.[47]

The pressure on provincial economies was now starting to tell, but it was distributed unevenly with BC suffering quite a bit more than Ontario and Quebec, not only because BC depended more on lumber than the two eastern provinces put together, but also because its best and more easily harvestable timber had been cut in the previous decades. Quebec and Ontario, on the other hand, were now beginning to see the long-term results of reforestation and could more easily access larger reserves of softwood and were, therefore, better positioned to weather the crisis.

After 1999 things rolled on in a climate of tense expectations towards what appeared to be a pre-scripted end. Heightened political pressure, bad feelings, and reciprocal accusations spilled over the previous years made the two sides apparently deaf to each other's demands and sensitivities. Voices from the BC lumber sector sounded the alarm. Bob Plecas, President of the BC Lumber Council, stated: "This is the number one economic issue facing not only the forest industry but the entire Province in the year 2001. The impact on this Province of a double-digit countervailing duty rate would be absolutely catastrophic."[48]

In the US, 32 congressional representatives met in February and introduced a motion not to renew the Softwood Lumber Agreement when it expired in March. In Canada the four provinces affected by the agreement and the federal government all called for an end to it as well. Whether they supported more regulation or unfettered free trade, Canadians almost unanimously supported the notion that the 1996 Softwood Lumber Agreement had been a bad piece of legislation and should not be renewed. There was, at the same time, the awareness that this type of agreement would lead inevitably to another trade conflict with the US since the issues that had been broached by the previous negotiated solution had festered rather then improved.

The latest round of disputes fed on the mistrust and frictions accumulated over the previous years. This situation also helped to reshape the frame within which the dispute existed. On the one hand, it focused interest groups in both nations, which opposed the CFLI's demands, to organize a credible opposition; on the other, it made negotiations even less of an option that they had been before. Ottawa consistently referred to international dispute resolution mechanisms, although each side held preconceived negative images of the other. Caught in the middle were lumber workers on both sides of the border and Canadian provincial authorities who found themselves one degree too many removed from international trade negotiation and one degree too close to economic fallout.

In 2000, as the situation worsened, the various sides began to organize for what everyone predicted would be a major trade dispute between the US and Canada.[49] For the first time, there were Canadian organizations like the Free Trade Lumber Council (FTLC) ready to fight the CFLI on its own terms; namely, by pressuring the domestic political sector and by reaching out to those US interest groups that would be hurt by a possible countervail on Canadian softwood imports into the US. Lumber companies in Ontario, Alberta, BC, and Quebec joined to form the Canadian Lumber Trade Alliance (CLTA), an organization that would present a united front to the demands of both the CFLI and the US government and that might be able to function as a credible interlocutor during the forthcoming CVD.

On the other side of the border, the CFLI maintained its traditional position, by now seemingly shared by the US Trade Administration, that the provincial allocation of timber harvesting rights through payment of stumpage fees was an outright subsidy to Canadian producers. From the Free Trade Lumber Council (FTLC) came a call for "unfettered free trade" of lumber, a rhetorical argument which was very dear to the US public and which was supported by think tanks like the Cato Institute,[50] which published a study titled *Nailing The Homeowner: The Economic Impact of Trade Protection of the Softwood Lumber Industry*.

What is interesting to note is that, since the Softwood Lumber Agreement was implemented in 1996, the level of Canadian softwood being exported to the US continued to increase; by 1999 it was already above 18 billion board feet. Over the five years of the agreement, the trigger price that allowed Canadian companies to export extra quantities of non-dutiable lumber into the US was reached consistently, and that led to increased quantities of softwood products entering the US market. So the quantity of lumber the US bought from Canada was increasing instead of decreasing.[51] This, in and of itself, from the US perspective, was a sign that something was wrong with the nature of the agreement, which was supposed to make it easier for US mills to operate by stopping the flood of cheap Canadian wood. A 2000 study by the Industrial, Wood and Allied Workers of Canada highlighted this apparent contradiction by noting that between 1996 and 1999 Canada exported an extra 6.6 BBF of softwood into the US. It also pointed out that depressed markets accounted for the redirection of 2.6 billion feet of logs and lumber, which would have traditionally gone abroad, to the same US market. Not only was the Softwood Lumber Agreement not preventing increased imports of softwood lumber, it was also distorting raw log markets. This process naturally fed the fears and suspicions of the US producers by presenting them with an even more difficult situation than the one they had tackled in 1996.

Meanwhile, contacts between the two federal governments regarding the renewal of the agreement began in July 2000 and ended up going nowhere quickly. At early meetings the two sides held on to their respective positions and separated with no better achievement than the commitment to meet again in the fall. This second meeting never took place. Elections were imminent in both nations, and, if a new US administration appointed a new US trade representative, the whole process could be delayed for months. The CFLI announced that its members were ready to file a CVD petition on 2 April 2001 unless some "meaningful progress" was achieved by the negotiators. The governors of 18 southern states came out in support of this hard line by calling on the administration and Congress to enforce the Softwood Lumber Agreement to its fullest.

Newly elected President George W. Bush and Canadian Prime Minister Jean Chrétien met in Washington after the 2001 presidential election to discuss the relationship between the two countries; the issue of the softwood lumber trade came up again. While little if any concrete achievement was reported from either these high-level talks or the meetings among the trade administrations, both countries agreed that the current quota system should be eliminated. In effect, the US Trade Administration was fully committed to push the envelope; US Trade Representative Robert Zoellick noted that his government not only was not inclined to seek a settlement before the deadline of 31 March, but that it was also in favour of filing a CVD.[52] As the situation heated up in the final weeks of March, the US lumber industry leaned very hard on the Bush administration to secure the support it needed in the forthcoming CVD case. In Canada, Trade Minister Pierre Pettigrew denied that Canadian softwood lumber producers were subsidized and showed particular optimism when he said that he was confident that a CVD case would end with a decision favourable to Canada. The Canadian industry seemed less homogeneous in its response than either the federal government or their US counterparts. Ontario and Quebec were certainly ready to challenge the US CVD action, while some BC producers announced that they might not be completely opposed to the imposition of an export tax on Canadian softwood. The very suggestion that this procedure be implemented drew a hail of negative reactions from the industry and the federal authorities. Producers in the east were dead set against it, and Minister Pettigrew noted, not without reason, that this would amount to admitting that some level of subsidy existed in the industry.[53]

The CFLI submitted its CVD petition to the US trade authority on 2 April 2001,[54] opening the way to the by now familiar dual process of assessing injury and/or subsidy as related to the exports of Canadian softwood into the US. Ultimately, this led to the federal and provincial governments of Canada, the BC Lumber Trade Council, the Ontario Forest Industries Association, and the Ontario and Quebec Lumber Manufacturers Associations filing a Chapter 19 request with NAFTA to interpret the legality of the countervail in the light of US law.

This time the CVD contained particularly harsh terms. The CFLI demanded a 40 per cent duty on Canadian softwood and an additional 28 to 38 per cent anti-dumping tariff for all Canadian producers.[55] The US International Trade Commission found that Canadian imports injured the US industry.[56] This unanimous vote allowed the CVD case to proceed. In the meantime, the price of lumber rose sharply in the US. In the end the new duty amounted to a staggering 27.2 per cent on the price of softwood lumber entering the US from Canada.[57]

The size of these duties boosted negotiation efforts, and over the following months officials from both countries tried to bring about a solution to the problem.[58] At the same time the election of a Liberal government in BC bode well, on paper at least, for a resolution of the issue, as Forestry Minister Mike de Jong's first goal was to quickly overhaul the timber-pricing mechanism by bringing it in line with market practices. His progress would not, in the end, be as quick as he had hoped, but it still was a step in the market direction.[59] This did not mean that the province would just roll over and do as the CFLI wanted; Premier Gordon Campbell made that clear during a speech to the annual truck loggers convention held in Vancouver in January 2002:

It is time for the US lumber industry and their government to come forward and to demonstrate a genuine commitment to long-lasting open markets, a genuine commitment to their consumers, to their builders, to their home buyers, and to the principles they espouse.... We have yet to discover whether the American industry that brought this case forward is really interested in free and open access to the American market and for competition or are they really trying to skew the competition because they can't compete.[60]

The WTO ruled in September 2002 on the validity of the CVD.[61] Both contenders claimed victory: Canada, because the WTO noted that the US used improper methods in determining the countervailability of provincial stumpage programs, and the US, because the WTO found that the sale of timber from public lands can constitute a subsidy under the WTO subsidies agreement. As this case showed, the US and Canadian administrations have, to date, made very little progress in their attempts to resolve the softwood lumber issue through negotiation, but neither has either side achieved its aims through international arbitration and dispute adjudication. From Ottawa and Washington there has been more rattling of sabres than coordinated efforts towards a deal.

The US strategy changed somewhat in 2003. US trade representatives have been less interested in meeting with Canadian federal representatives and keener on talking with provincial officials. This makes sense because the responsibility for setting stumpage fees falls with the provinces and because, having been put through the economic wringer, the provinces may now be keener to cut a deal with the US administration than is Ottawa. In September 2002 the US Undersecretary for International Trade, Grant Aldonas, went to Quebec City to meet with provincial officials to discuss such a possibility, and similar meetings were held in Vancouver. The Toronto *Globe and Mail*[62] reported that the US-owned timber giant Weyerhaeuser planned to allow 25 per cent of its timberlands, recently aquired in its takeover of long-time Canadian industry leader Mac-millan-Bloedel, in the coast region of BC to be allocated by competitive bidding, a move that would both stimulate the industry and partially meet US demands that 50 per cent of the annual provincial timber harvest be allocated in this way.

The Canadian federal government approved a $246.5 million aid package to assist displaced workers, support community economic development, and aid research.[63] Reactions in British Columbia, where the forestry sector has lost thousands of jobs since 1998, were not overly positive. BC Forestry

Minister de Jong labelled the program inadequate and called for additional aid.[64] At the same time, in the US, the National Association of Home Builders and the NLBMDA filed a brief with NAFTA asking that the 27 per cent duties on Canadian softwood lumber be rejected on the grounds that Canadian exports and US native species are very different and that the Canadian softwood, therefore, does not warrant the imposition of duties.

On the economic side, the reality is that the surviving Canadian mills have found ways to further reduce their production costs and to remain competitive even when saddled with very large tariffs, while American mills can still not match Canadian prices and continue to see reduced sales and loss of jobs.

The province with the most to lose in Canada from a protracted trade war with the US is certainly BC. In December 2002, provincial authorities tabled a proposal according to which the current tariff on Canadian softwood lumber crossing to the US should be replaced by a border tax. The most obvious advantage of this measure is to keep the high duty imposed on Canadian softwood in Canadian coffers; it is also an "olive branch" extended to the US Department of Commerce. International Trade Minister Pettigrew, however, insisted that Canada should continue to approach the current trade dispute with the US in a dual manner: on the one hand, Canada should negotiate, but on the other, it should continue to press its point in all available legal dispute resolution mechanisms, such as those offered by the WTO and NAFTA.

Late in 2002, the US Department of Commerce released a draft copy of its *Proposed Analytical Framework: Softwood Lumber From Canada*,[65] a detailed set of proposals aimed at finding a solution for the current impasse. Its contents are not new. It recognizes that the provinces are a necessary part in the process of negotiation because they hold the keys to timber harvests and economic development of forestry resources in Canada. It points out that a variety of local approaches could be accepted by the Department of Commerce if they lead to the ultimate result of eliminating the unfair advantage that Canadian softwood producers are perceived to hold over their US counterparts.

The 30-page draft report effectively provides Canadian provinces with a set of benchmark elements that expresses the policy goals of the US government. The core demand is still that the provinces abandon their current timber allocation practices in favour of what the document defines as a market-based system of timber sales, which in fact translates into the auction sale of standing timber. While the document assures readers that the US Department of Commerce is offering only "policy guidance" and is not interested in impeding provincial legislative and regulative activity in the forestry sector in any way, the message is very clear. Unless major changes are introduced to address the alleged unfair competitive advantage Canadian softwood enjoys, the US is not prepared to remove CVDs on softwood.

This approach, of which the *Proposed Analytical Framework* is simply the latest element, seems to be focused on allowing individual provinces, especially BC, which relies heavily on the forestry sector for its economic welfare, to move closer to the position currently held by the US Department of Commerce. The first results were achieved in December 2002, when the BC government proposed to move towards an export tax and to go back to the negotiating table. A series of talks followed, and, in March, the BC Ministry of Forests tabled its *Forestry Revitalization Plan*,[66] which allowed for the auctioning of 20 per cent of Crown timber and, in general, for a marked move towards the positions advocated by the draft report.

This should not be a complete surprise. Even discounting the fact that the BC Liberal Party has a neoconservative economic agenda, the pressure under which the provincial forestry sector has been put in the past six years would, alone, have produced changes. The plan itself reminds readers that since 1997 BC saw its tax revenues from the forestry sector decline—by $600 million in 2003. In the process thousands of workers have lost their jobs, 27 mills have closed (and this does not take into account temporary shutdowns), and many resource communities have been dramatically affected.

Still, while there may be signs of compromise in BC, much of the Canadian lumber industry supports the approach followed by Ottawa. On 10 February 2003 Frank Dottori, CEO of Tembec and co-chair of the Free Trade Lumber Council, appeared before the Senate Standing Committee on Foreign Affairs and asked that the appeals before the WTO and NAFTA be renewed to prevent the US from using what he deemed unfair methods to assess subsidies. At the same time, he communicated the urgency of the softwood lumber industry's position:

> If you want to know the real reason why Canada is back at the negotiating table, it is not because the US is any more flexible than it was last March, when we walked away from the table, when it was plain that US authorities would not rein in their protectionist industry and its unreasonable demands. It's because we are running out of money, and they know it.[67]

Later that year the CFLI proposed that a quota system be instituted covering the whole of Canada. This approach was opposed vociferously by industry representatives in the Maritimes where 75 per cent of the harvested timber comes from private lands, which are not under a stumpage agreement, and has weak support elsewhere. Diana Blenkhorn, President of the Maritime Lumber Bureau (MLB) noted that: "We understand that the proposal attempts to envelop the entire country into the terms of an agreement which will restrict the flow of lumber to the United States ... This proposal is a bad deal for Atlantic Canada and is unacceptable."[68]

It is likely instead that the focus will remain on more market-inspired solutions. This is how we should interpret the new Forest and Range Practices Act that will form the backbone of the BC Liberals' forestry policy and that aims at reducing administrative costs and complexities while retaining high environmental standards and opening access possibilities to new entrants in the sector—a tall order indeed! We shall see if it will be enough to satisfy the US administration. The *Proposed Analytical Framework* makes it very clear that, while the US Department of Commerce will deal with each provincial case individually, minor changes will not be sufficient to have CVDs rescinded, as non-market practices must be eliminated from tenure practices.

A WTO decision of 27 May 2003 on the validity of the US-imposed 18.79 per cent CVD on Canadian softwood did very little to clear the air. It noted that, while provincial timber sales constitute a "financial contribution" that may eventually become a subsidy, the US Department of Commerce did not prove that this constitutes a greater benefit for Canadian lumber producers than the one that may be extracted by purchasing lumber from a private wood lot. However, the ruling opens the door for the US administration to compare provincial and private wood lot prices in Canada to prove that there is a subsidy.[69]

Reactions from the two sides were diametrically opposed. A US trade official is quoted as saying that "[T]his is a victory for both the US lumber industry and the environment ... [T]here is no longer any question that the United States can impose countervailing duties on softwood lumber imports from Canada. The only question now is the amounts." Canadian Trade Minister Pierre Pettigrew replied that "[Y]et again, it appears that the [United States] is being told that its attempts to prove that our softwood industry is subsidized are flawed," and noted that more of the same results were expected from NAFTA and WTO rulings over the summer of 2003.[70]

According to CFLI lawyer John Ragosta, Minister Pettigrew may have counted his chicks before they hatched: "That's ridiculous," he said of Pettigrew's comments, "[t]he panel said the method the United States used to measure the benefit [of the subsidies] is impermissible. Fine, we'll fix it."

The same pattern holds true for the latest NAFTA panel ruling, given on 13 August 2003.[71] The panel held to the same decision that we have seen so many times before: the stumpage fee favours the Canadian industry, but the duties should be reviewed. BC Forestry Minister de Jong noted that he was "looking forward to the US doing the right thing and recalculating these duties."[72] Both sides claimed victory over the latest decision, while attempts at negotiation have gone nowhere.

To go back to the BC proposal, it appears unlikely that putting up 20 per cent of timber for open auction will satisfy the US requirements. At the same time it certainly sends a very clear message to Ottawa that BC cannot wait much longer for the two-pronged strategy of negotiation and litigation to yield some concrete result. However, BC may be alone in this fight: Ontario and Quebec seem much closer to Minister Pettigrew's position, and the rest of Canada does not depend as much on forestry. As far as the US is concerned, the new forestry policy sends the signal that the BC government is keen on finding a solution to the trade dispute, but that some kind of mutually acceptable agreement must be found.

The issue of capping the Canadian share of the US lumber market was plainly stated in the most recent proposal hammered out on December 6, 2003 in Washington by trade negotiators: in return for limiting their exports south of the border to 31.5 per cent of that market, Canadian companies would see about half of the punishing duties they paid up to now returned to them. The rest would go to the CFLI.[73] The deal was rejected by all Eastern lumber companies and by many Western ones. The only exceptions were some large BC operators that would benefit from the quota allocation mechanism embedded in the proposal. This is a very bad deal for most Canadian companies and not very logical in light of the recent WTO and NAFTA decisions. Of course, it looks like a winner if you are CFLI's point man John Ragosta, who hailed it as an opportunity to build stable relations. On the other side of the border, espcially in BC, the situation is perhaps better summed up by the words of Duncan Davies, President of Interfor: "The two-and-a-half years of fighting and the billion dollars we are going to forego in deposits may just simply be the price of getting a deal that has a policy reform package and the long-term durable solution. I add it all up, take a deept breath and say it's time to move on."[74]

Discussion

The issue of fair trade in softwood lumber between the US and Canada has been a recurrent problem in the trade regimes of the two countries.[75] Its solution is, at best, problematic. The US lumber producers continue to demand that softwood imports from Canada be artificially capped since structural differences between the two economies cyclically bring Canadian market share to a level where it directly threatens them.[76] Over the past two decades this issue has played out in a series of trade disputes. Progressively, the US lumber industry has become more capable of capturing the support of admittedly interested political actors in the Senate, Congress, and the US Trade Administration.

At the same time, as economic pain is felt on both sides of the border, positions have crystallized around reciprocal distrust. Ottawa has resorted ever more frequently to international arbitration venues (FTA, NAFTA, WTO) where the relative weight of US business lobbies could be effectively countered.[77] As a result of this more confrontational attitude, the space for negotiated settlements has progressively shrunk, and interest groups in both countries have begun to organize against the CFLI.

In the end, this means that trade disputes are likely to continue, creating increased hardship for those who depend on this industry for their livelihood. Canadian provinces, especially BC, are going to experience particularly difficult times as jobs are lost, tax revenues must be foregone, and political pressure to aid affected communities is increasing. The US administration, well aware that financial hardship is disproportionately borne by the provinces, has increasingly tried to bypass the Canadian federal government by attempting to negotiate changes in the stumpage fees system directly with provincial authorities.

It is hard to say how successful this approach will be in the long run. The systems on which the two countries rely to extract and market this natural resource are quite different and account for some of the problems that have emerged at regular intervals. It is not possible, though, to reduce the whole process to this one fact. For instance, oil extraction in Canada is structured upon the same type of system, and trade in it between Canada and the US has been quite smooth. Surely an irritant for the US timber industry is the gains made by Canadian products in what they seem to still consider "their market."

The US companies that are hurting the most from the consistent inflow of cheap, high quality Canadian softwood are concentrated in the south and west of the country, and many of the almost 255 companies that signed on to the CFLI claim are also located there. These companies have become increasingly able to shift US congressional and senatorial support in favour of their demands for duties on Canadian softwood by increasing pressure on the legislative bodies that have traditionally been more responsive to similar pleas. They have had the support of a deteriorating economic situation in the US lumber sector and have the grim determination to see their demands through, even if that means economic hardship for other groups like homebuilders and perspective homeowners.

The situation has not been helped by the differences between the two timber harvesting regimens that have been exploited with such success by the CFLI in its demands, nor by the fact that within Canada itself there is a split between groups who are in favour of the allocation of timber rights through a process of competitive bidding and those who are determined to continue the existing system. The recurrent nature of the dispute and the apparent unwillingness of US officials and interests to come to any agreement not involving reduced shipments of Canadian lumber have strengthened the resolve of most Canadian players to fight the duties rather than seek accommodation.[78] At the same time, the US is irked by the Canadian unwillingness to make any significant changes to its timber allocation process.

A crucial aspect of the softwood issue in Canada is the regional structure of the industry and the intersecting elements of federal-provincial responsibility that the negotiation of international trade agreements and economic policy involve. Formally, it is up to the federal authorities in Ottawa to negotiate trade with foreign states, but the importance of softwood lumber to the economy of many of the largest provinces is such that it is impossible to simply discount their input and their needs in the negotiation process. Well aware of this, and finding the current Canadian federal government much less malleable than its predecessors, the US administration has recently looked more closely at interacting directly with provincial governments, especially BC and Quebec, who are in the economic frontline of the dispute.

Although federal-provincial relations are well-developed in Canada, the softwood lumber issue has always created rifts. The structural distribution of the industry is very strongly skewed, with BC (followed at a distance by Quebec and Ontario) accounting for over half of all softwood exports to the US and, therefore, being hit very hard by US duties. The stance taken by Canadian International Trade Minister Pierre Pettigrew that Canada is not subsidizing softwood lumber producers and that Ottawa will appeal all US-imposed duties in the proper international arenas is courageous and based on more than simple nationalistic pride; nonetheless, it is a strategy that imposes high costs on the provinces. While BC adds the crushing duties imposed on softwood to the crisis in its salmon fishery and general economic malaise, the provinces of Ontario, Quebec, and Alberta, which are less exposed to US retaliation and are doing better from an economic point of view, seem more likely to endure a prolonged trade conflict.

In the end, though, a chain is only as strong as its weakest link. In the first half of 2003, the BC government has shown itself keen to reach some kind of an agreement with the US. These contacts may not have replaced the negotiations between Ottawa and Washington, but are certainly a sign that the latter have reached a situation of impasse that the provincial government cannot tolerate.

It should be said, though, that from the Canadian perspective US action often looks like the act of a schoolyard bully. Over and over again US administrations have endorsed and pushed the ideals and practices of free trade in other areas, but here it continues to force ever-increasing duties on Canadian softwood. The US will buy oil from Canada, because it does not want to deplete its own strategic reserves, even though oil extraction in this country is allocated in much the same way as softwood timber harvesting rights. The US will not allow more competitive softwood products to cross the border without heavy duties being imposed, but it will press for the export of raw logs, which represent a certain economic loss for Canadian sawmills. And yet, the issue is still not as simple as this. Even within Canada dissonant voices regarding the viability of stumpage rates and their overall fairness have gained force as increasing pressure is being exerted on provinces, companies, and local communities.

In December 2002, much of the US lumber sector was in dire straits as the duties failed to reduce Canadian softwood exports to a degree that had any positive impact on the US industry. As mill closures increased on both sides of the border, Dick Bennet, western region vice-chairman for CFLI, noted that the coalition would likely seek an agreement that would, in fact, impose quotas on Canadian lumber exports to the US, as the 1996 Softwood Lumber Agreement had done. This may be difficult to achieve, especially considering that Canadian producers have reduced costs dramatically to cope with the increased duties and that provincial and federal governments alike do not appear very interested in this type of solution. That same month, BC Forestry Minister de Jong offered CFLI the option of replacing CVDs with a border tax until the parties involved could agree upon a market pricing system. The proposal was greeted warmly by Steven Rogel, Chairman and CEO of Weyerhaeuser, who had himself proposed a similar solution to the trade war a couple of weeks earlier. According to his idea, Canada and the US should negotiate a long-term agreement for the problem, substitute an export tax for the duties, and suspend legal action during the negotiation period.[79]

Increased political activity may signal that the situation is taking its toll on both sides. The status quo is unsustainable for the US industry and for provinces that rely heavily on softwood exports to the US for their economic well-being. In the current dispute, the Canadian federal government seems to have quite a bit of stamina in its attempt to stick by the policies set by previous trade regimes. It remains to be seen if the provinces can match that stamina or if new policies will emerge from the recent contacts between Quebec, BC, and the US trade authorities.

Meanwhile, on 18 June 2003, the Bush administration announced its commitment to seek a long-term solution to the "decade long" confrontation with Canada. Undersecretary of Commerce for International Trade, Grant Aldonas, noted:

> on a range of issues, President Bush and Secretary Evans have consistently said that they are committed to resolving the root causes of disputes, and this policy bulletin on softwood lumber demonstrates that commitment in a big way. By confronting the underlying problems in one of the longest running and most difficult trade problems, we hope to encourage an integrated North American lumber market and put an end to the softwood lumber dispute once and for all.

The policy bulletin, however, only once again outlines the standards for a market-based timber sales system. In it, Canadian provinces are encouraged to make changes to meet such standards and then to apply to the US Department of Commerce for a "changed circumstance review" which may lead to a revocation of the CVD order. The content of the policy bulletin is remarkably similar to the demands made before for open auction of timber.[80]

Once again, the US administration has targeted the provinces as the weakest link in Canada. This may be a winning strategy, especially as ready-made neoconservative polices are offered to provincial governments that may not be all that distant in ideological terms from the Bush administration. Nonetheless, large problems and obstacles still must be overcome. One thing is sure: as the situation stands, the US and Canadian public at large are hurt by this trade dispute, but the CFLI has managed to foster a leaner, more competitive forestry sector in Canada that has been able to continue its competitive exports into the US in spite of the imposition of brutal duties.

Appendix A

Select Organizations and Agreements

USA

CFLI	Coalition for Fair Lumber Imports
NAHB	National Association of Home Builders

| NLBMDA | National Lumber and Building Material Dealers Association |

Canada

BCLC	British Columbia Lumber Council
BCTC	British Columbia Trade Council
CLTA	Canadian Lumber Trade Alliance
FTLC	Free Trade Lumber Council

International

FTA	US-Canada Free Trade Agreement
GATT	General Agreement On Tariffs And Trade
NAFTA	North American Free Trade Agreement
WCO	World Customs Organization
WTO	World Trade Organization

Chronology

7 OCTOBER 1982: The Coalition for Fair Lumber Imports (CFLI) files a countervailing duty petition (CVD) against softwood lumber from Canada, alleging that softwood lumber production is subsidized by artificially low prices set by provincial governments.

31 MAY 1983: The US Department of Commerce (DOC) terminates the case by determining that the stumpage fees do not confer a subsidy because the industry is not specifically given lower than average rates.

1986

19 MAY: The CFLI files a second CVD petition using new evidence and a legislative change to prove that subsidies exist.

OCTOBER: The US Department of Commerce issues a preliminary decision according to which stumpage fees are sold at preferential rates and benefit a specific industry. A preliminary CVD is assessed at 15 per cent.

30 DECEMBER: Canada and the US sign a Memorandum of Understanding (MOU) imposing a temporary tariff of 15 per cent on the sales value of imports of Canadian softwood lumber, in exchange for a termination of the investigation.

1991

8 SEPTEMBER: Canada advises the US government that it will terminate the MOU effective 4 October 1991 as it believes that the subsidy has ceased to exist.

4 OCTOBER: The US Department of Commerce self-initiates a new CVD investigation of alleged subsidies derived from stumpage fees and provincial log export restrictions; the US Trade Representative initiates a Section 301 investigation requiring the posting of bonds on imported Canadian softwood lumber.

1 NOVEMBER: Canada invokes the panel review process of the General Agreement on Tariffs and Trade (GATT) to challenge the initiative.

1992

28 MAY: The US Department of Commerce finds that both Canadian stumpage fees and log export bans confer subsidies on Canadian softwood.

JUNE-JULY: Canadian actors challenge the DOC and International Trade Commission (ITC) final determinations before US-Canada Free Trade Agreement (FTA) dispute-settlement panels.

1993

19 FEBRUARY: The GATT panel issues a final report that states that the US Department of Commerce has sufficient evidence for its investigation, but that the Section 301 bond requirements are invalid.

6 MAY: The FTA panel reviewing the DOC decision determines it to be invalid.

3 AUGUST 1994: An FTA Extraordinary Challenge Committee dismisses a US challenge of the 6 May 1993 ruling.

29 MAY 1996: The US administration drags its feet on the issue, and, under considerable economic pressure, Canada agrees to enter into a US-Canada Softwood Lumber Agreement (SLA). The SLA is to be in effect from 1 April 1996 to 31 March 2001; under it Canada agrees to impose an export tax of $50 per 1,000 board feet on softwood lumber exports in excess of 14.7 billion board feet and $100 per 1,000 board feet on exports in excess of 15.25 billion board feet.

2001

31 MARCH: The Softwood Lumber Agreement expires.

2 APRIL: The US Department of Commerce begins a fourth countervailing duty action.

9 AUGUST: The US Department of Commerce imposes 19.3-per-cent provisional duty on Canadian softwood imports. The ruling is challenged in front of the World Trade Organization.

2002

22 MARCH: The US Department of Commerce reaches a final decision on tariffs to be imposed on Canadian softwood; they equal 29 per cent of the value of lumber.

3 MAY: Canada begins a WTO challenge of the duty.

18 JUNE: WTO consultations between Canada and the US fail to resolve the dispute.

27 SEPTEMBER: WTO rules against US findings that Canada is providing subsidies.

1 OCTOBER: The WTO, on a request by Canada, establishes a panel to resolve the dispute.

2003

27 MAY: The WTO panel's interim decision finds that provincial stumpage programs are not subsidies.

13 AUGUST: The binational NAFTA panel finds that stumpage fees favour the Canadian industry but the US duties should be recalculated.

Notes

1. *The Boston Globe* 9 April 2001.
2. *The Boston Globe* 9 April 2001.
3. We are going to deal with both countervailing duties (CVDs) and anti-dumping practices in more detail later (see Inset VI, 228). For now, let it suffice to say that CVDs are fees imposed on imported goods that have been determined to have received an unfair subsidy in the nation of origin. Anti-dumping practices can involve a more varied set of policies aimed at preventing imports priced below what they fetch in the producing nation from entering a country unhindered. The tactic of offering goods below the domestic retail price is sometimes employed by the exporter to undercut manufacturers in the country to which the goods are imported or to gain a larger than otherwise achievable market share.

4. Michael Howlett, Alex Netherton, and M. Ramesh, *The Political Economy of Canada* (Oxford: Oxford University Press, 1999) 298.

5. See Sylvia Ostry, "The NAFTA: Its International Background," *North America Without Borders? Integrating Canada, the United States, and Mexico*, ed. Stephen J. Randall, et al. (Calgary, AB: University of Calgary Press, 1992) 21-31; and John Young, *Canadian Commercial Policy* (Ottawa: Royal Commission on Canada's Economic Prospects, 1957).

6. Michael Howlett, Alex Netherton, and M. Ramesh, *The Political Economy of Canada* (Oxford: Oxford University Press, 1999).

7. Theodore H. Cohn, *Global Political Economy: Theory and Practice* (New York: Longman, 2000).

8. Bernard Hoekman, and Michel Kostecki, *The Political Economy Of The World Trading System: From GATT To WTO* (Oxford: Oxford University Press, 1995).

9. Royal Commission On The Economic Union And Development Prospects For Canada (MacDonald Commission), *Report Of The Royal Commission On The Economic Union And Development Prospects For Canada*, 3 vols (Ottawa: Ministry of Supply and Services, 1985).

10. Murray G. Smith, and Frank Stone, eds. *Assessing the Canada-US Free Trade Agreement* (Halifax: Institute for Research on Public Policy, 1987).

11. Leonard Waverman, "A Canadian Vision Of North American Economic Integration," *Continental Accord: North American Economic Integration*, ed. Steven Globerman (Vancouver, BC: Fraser Institute, 1999).

12. General disputes—those that do not involve either CVDs or anti-dumping duties—can be referred to the Free Trade Commission (FTC) if a mutual agreement cannot be reached among the parties. If the FTC itself cannot resolve the problem, any NAFTA party may ask it to create a dispute resolution panel that will render a ruling to which the aggrieving party must comply or face retaliation. An innovative element of the NAFTA dispute resolution mechanism is that private investors can now bring grievances against the governments of the three member states if they feel they have been discriminated against.

13. M. Cameron and Brian W. Tomlin, *The Making of NAFTA: How the Deal Was Done* (Ithaca, NY: Cornell University Press, 2000).

14. David Leyton-Brown, "The Political Economy of North American Free Trade," *Political Economy and the Changing Global Order*, ed. Richard Stubbs and Geoffrey R.D. Underhill (Toronto: McClelland and Stewart Inc., 1994) 352-65.

15. Brad W. Smith, et al., *Forest Resources of the United States* (Washington, DC: USDA Forest Service, 2001).

16. The list of costs that must be borne by forestry companies operating in Canada is somehow more complicated than what is often purported by US companies. For example, many infrastructure services like logging roads, reforestation expenses, and firefighting are usually paid for by the US government while companies operating in Canada must pay for them out of their own pockets.

17. For the organization of the USITA see <http://www.ita.doc.gov/ooms/ITAChart.htm>; for the structure of the ITA Import Administration, the unit charged with the administration of countervailing duties, see <http://www.ita.doc.gov/ooms/wrc5.jpg>. The structure of the USITC can be found in the USITC *Strategic Plan*, available online at <http://www.usitc.gov/STRATPLN.PDF>.

18. Alan Grant, ed., *Contemporary American Politics* (Aldershot: Dartmouth, 1995).

19. Ronald J. Hrebenar, *Interest Group Politics In America* (Armonk: M.E. Sharpe, 1997).

20. FLC Reed and Associates, *Two Centuries of Softwood Lumber War Between Canada and the United States—A Chronicle of Trade Barriers Viewed in the Context of Saw Timber Depletion* (Montreal: FLC Reed and Associates, May 2001).

21. Ben Cashore, "Flights of the Phoenix: Explaining the Durability of the Canada-US Softwood Lumber Dispute," *Canadian-American Public Policy* 32 (December 1998).

22. Quoted in the *Vancouver Sun* 3 September 2003.

23. Cashore, "Flights of the Phoenix."

24. Ben Cashore, "What Should Canada Do When the Softwood Lumber Agreement Expires?" <http://www.policy.ca/PDF/slft.pdf>.

25. Michael B. Percy and Christian Yoder, *The Softwood Lumber Dispute And Canada-US Trade in Natural Resources* (Halifax: Institute for Research on Public Policy, 1987).

26. US Department of Commerce, International Trade Administration, "Final negative countervailing duty determination: Certain softwood lumber products from Canada," *Federal Register*, 48/105, 31 May 1983.

27. Gilbert Gagné, "The Canada-US Softwood Lumber Dispute: An Assessment after Fifteen Years," *Journal of World Trade* 33 (1999).

28. US Department of Commerce, International Trade Administration, "Preliminary affirmative countervailing duty determination: Certain softwood lumber products from Canada," *Federal Register*, 51/204, 22 October 1986.

29. Government of Canada, *News Release 232*, 4 September 1991.

30. US Department of Commerce, International Trade Administration, *Certain Softwood Lumber Products from Canada Redetermination Pursuant to Binational Panel Remand*, 17 September 1993; US Department of Commerce, International Trade Commission, *Softwood Lumber from Canada*, First remand, 2689, October 1993.

31. Government of Canada, Press Release, 6 May 1993.

32. *Financial Post* 15 July 1992.

33. *Vancouver Sun* 16 January 1992.

34. CAFTA, Article 1904 Binational Panel Review USA-92-1904-01, *Certain Softwood Lumber Products from Canada*, Decision of the panel, 6 May 1993.

35. *Globe and Mail* 7 May 1993.

36. *Globe and Mail* 7 May 1993.

37. *Financial Post* 27 July 1993

38. George Hoberg and Paul Howe, "Law, Knowledge, And National Interests In Trade Disputes: The Case Of Softwood Lumber," *Journal of World Trade* 34 (2000): 109-30.

39. ECC USA-94-1904-01, *Certain Softwood Lumber Products from Canada*, Committee Opinions Of 3 August 1994.

40. Charles F. Doran, "Trade Dispute Resolution 'on trial': Softwood lumber," *International Journal* 51 (1996).

41. *Softwood Lumber Agreement between the Government of Canada and the Government of the United States of America* (Canada, Treaty series 1996/16).

42. DFAIT, *Press Release*, 10 September 1996.

43. *Globe and Mail* 5 March 1998.

44. Government of British Columbia, *Budget For The Fiscal Year 1998/1999* (Victoria, April 1998).

45. Government of Canada, *News Release 191*, 30 August 1999.

46. *Globe and Mail* 2 October 1998.

47. Tom Ross, NLBMDA Chair, Gilcrest-Jewett Lumber Co., Des Moines, Iowa.

48. *Vancouver Sun* 29 December 2000.

49. Cashore, "What Should Canada Do."

50. The Cato Institute is a non-profit neoliberal think tank based in Washington, DC. Its mandate is to expand public policy discussion within the scope of the traditional US values of limited government, individual liberty, free markets, and peace. The Cato Institute's web address is <http: www.cato.org>.

51. CINTRAFOR "A Study of the Effects of the Canada-US Softwood Lumber Agreement" <http://www.cintrafor.org/RESEARCH_TAB/Regions/N.America/sla_fs_can_us.htm>.

52. *Vancouver Sun* 29 March 2001.

53. *Vancouver Sun* 29 March 2001.

54. *Globe and Mail* 3 April 2001.

55. *Inside US Trade* 6 April 2001: 1.

56. US Department of Commerce, International Trade Commission, *Softwood Lumber from Canada*, 3426, May 2001.

57. Government of Canada, *News Release 46*, 2 May 2002; Government of Canada, *News Release 53*, 17 May 2002.

58. Gilbert Gagné, "The NAFTA And The Softwood Lumber Dispute: What Kind Of Canada-US Partnership?" *Cahier de Recherché* (12 February 2002): 22-23 <http://www.unites.uqam.ca/gric/pdf/Cahier_Gagne.pdf>

59. *Vancouver Sun* 5 December 2001.

60. *Vancouver Province* 20 January 2002.

61. World Trade Organization, United States—Preliminary Determinations With Respect To Certain Softwood Lumber From Canada, WT/DS236/R, 27 September 2002.

62. *Globe and Mail* 13 September 2002.

63. *Vancouver Sun* 11 October 2002.

64. *Vancouver Sun* 11 October 2002.

65. *Vancouver Sun* 6 January 2003.

66. A detailed analysis of the plan can be found at <http://www.for.gov.bc.ca/mof/plan>.

67. Free Trade Lumber Council, Press Release, Montreal 12 February 2003 <http://www.ftlc.org/index.cfm?Section=7&Detail=70>.

68. *Globe and Mail* 30 May 2003.

69. *Globe and Mail* 28 May 2003.

70. *Globe and Mail* 28 May 2003.

71. World Trade Organization Catalogue United States—Final Countervailing Duty Determination with Respect to Certain Softwood Lumber from Canada—Report of the Panel WT/DS257/R, 29 August 2003.

72. *Vancouver Sun* 14 August 2003.

73. *Vancouver Sun* 8 December 2003.

74. *Vancouver Sun* 8 December 2003.

75. FLC Reed and Associates.

76. Gagné.

77. On the role of international venues for softwood arbitration, see Billy Garton and James Duvall, "The Canada-US Softwood Lumber Dispute: Is Canada Stumped Again?," *Canadian Business Law Journal* 36 (2002).

78. Lawrence L. Herman, *Softwood Lumber: The Next Phase*, C.D. Howe Institute (6 December 2001) suggests that Canada seek all avenues of legal redress for the softwood lumber dispute.

79. *Globe and Mail* 5 December 2002.

80. US Department of Commerce, *Bush Administration Issues Policy Bulletin on Softwood Lumber*, Press Release, 18 June 2003.

CHAPTER FIVE

Whose Land is it Anyway?: The Long Road to the Nisga'a Treaty

KAREN E. LOCHEAD

[The Nisga'a Treaty] marks a new beginning.... It helps to resolve an injustice that has gone on for too long.
Glen Clark, Premier of British Columbia[1]

The Nisga'a Treaty signifies our willingness as a society to reconcile major historical and cultural differences through negotiation and compromise.
Robert Nault, Minister of Indian Affairs and Northern Development[2]

[The Nisga'a Treaty] proves to the world that reasonable people can sit down and settle historical wrongs. It proves that a modern society can correct the mistakes of the past.
Joseph Gosnell, Chief of the Nisga'a Nation[3]

In January 1887, chiefs of the Nisga'a Nation canoed more than 1,100 kilometres down the Pacific Coast to assert their Nation's continuing rights to its traditional territories and demand that the government of British Columbia negotiate an honourable treaty with them in respect of those rights. When they reached the legislature's doors, however, they were turned away. There is no need for a treaty, the province asserted, because the rights you claim do not exist. The Nisga'a Chiefs were forced to return home, but the Nisga'a Nation could not be forced to abandon its cause.

It took more than a century of determined effort but on 13 April 2000 the landmark Nisga'a Treaty finally received royal assent.

What transpired between January 1887 and April 2000 maps out the complex history of Aboriginal land claims policy in Canada and brings at least three perennial features of this dynamic policy sector into sharp relief. First, it demonstrates Aboriginal peoples' unrelenting and strategic pursuit of rights recognition and respect in the face of changing opportunity structures. Second, it highlights the courts' influential role in the development of Aboriginal land claims policy over time. And third, it draws attention to the difficulties involved in resolving outstanding Aboriginal land claims in a federal system of government where legislative responsibility for "Indians and land reserved for the Indians" and legislative control over "lands and resources" is divided between the federal and provincial levels of government.

Who owns Canada? The Aboriginal peoples who have inhabited the northern half of North America for somewhere between 15,000 and 25,000 years or the colonial newcomers who "discovered" this land and declared sovereignty over it only 500 years ago? Although the British Crown (now embodied in the federal and provincial governments of Canada) arguably acquired title to vast regions of the Canadian land mass through the conclusion of historic "land surrender" treaties in the eighteenth and nineteenth centuries, this practice was not consistently applied by political authorities in Canada during the early years of colonial settlement. As a result, equally vast regions of the Canadian land mass remained the subject of outstanding Aboriginal land claims throughout the twentieth century, especially in Quebec and the Northwest Territories. This situation is still the case in British Columbia (BC) today, where only 15 treaties were ever concluded in the mid-nineteenth century. Because these treaties cover a mere 5 per cent of the province's total land mass, the Aboriginal peoples of BC continue to maintain that nearly all of the province's 950,000 square kilometres are rightfully theirs. Can their land claims succeed?

Aboriginal land claims are not new. The Aboriginal peoples of Canada have been seeking an equitable resolution to the so-called land question since European newcomers first began encroaching on their traditional territories during the earliest years of colonial settlement. The possibility of an early and comprehensive resolution, however, was foiled when Canadian governments began denying the legal merits of outstanding Aboriginal land claims during the mid-1800s and early 1900s. For more than a century, the Aboriginal peoples of Canada fought vigorously to have their rights to land recognized and respected. It was not until 1973, however, that a Canadian government began to take the land claims issue seriously. In that year, six members of the Supreme Court of Canada unanimously agreed that the Aboriginal peoples of Canada continued to hold legally defensible title to their traditional territories where this title had not been extinguished through conquest, treaties, or other lawful means.

This landmark legal decision in the *Calder* case propelled Aboriginal land claims into the political spotlight and served as a catalyst for a series of important policy developments. First, it compelled the federal government to introduce a comprehensive claims policy designed to facilitate the resolution of outstanding Aboriginal land claims through treaty negotiations. Second, it facilitated the recognition of "existing aboriginal and treaty rights" in section 35(1) of the *Constitution Act, 1982*. And third, it eventually led to the political recognition of Aboriginal peoples' inherent right to self-government. As a result of these important policy developments, 16 new Aboriginal land claims settlements—or modern treaties—have been successfully concluded in Canada in the 30 years since the *Calder* decision. One of the most remarkable of these is the Nisga'a Treaty.

The Nisga'a Treaty is the fourteenth modern treaty to be successfully concluded in Canada. Covering the area of the Nass River Valley of northwestern BC, it is the first to be signed by a BC government since 1854, the first to be signed by any provincial government since 1978, and the first treaty in Canadian history to include constitutionally protected Aboriginal self-government rights. According to the terms of this landmark agreement, some 6,000 Nisga'a citizens are now entitled to a wide range of constitutionally protected rights and interests, including:

- a cash settlement of $196.1 million;
- transition, training, and one-time funding of $40.6 million;
- fee simple title to 2,019 square kilometres of land;
- ownership of all mineral and forestry resources on 1,992 square kilometres of land;
- guaranteed domestic and commercial fishing rights within the Nisga'a Settlement Area;
- guaranteed domestic wildlife harvesting rights within the Nisga'a Settlement Area;
- the authority to operate their own government;
- the authority to make and enforce certain laws;

- the authority to control certain aspects of the administration of justice; and,
- dedicated funding to help the new Nisga'a government deliver health, education, and social services to Nisga'a citizens and other area residents.[4]

Pursued for more than a century and negotiated over the course of 24 long years, the Nisga'a Treaty spans the history of Aboriginal land claims policy in Canada and draws attention to several interesting aspects of the real worlds of Canadian politics. First, it reveals the evolving dynamics of Aboriginal peoples' unique relationship with the Canadian state. Second, it exposes the particular challenges involved in redressing historic injustices within the context of contemporary socio-economic realities. Third, it highlights the notable impact public opinion can exert on the policy agenda. Fourth, it illustrates the difficult task policy actors face when trying to create, amend, and/or execute policies in areas of shared jurisdictional competence. Fifth, it demonstrates the potentially pivotal role that each of the three branches of government—executive, legislative, and judicial—can play in the public policy process. And sixth, it shows how Aboriginal rights issues have come to assume an increasingly prominent presence in mainstream political discourses.

In order to make sense of the long road to the Nisga'a Treaty, this chapter begins with a brief overview of Canada's early treaty-making history. It then goes on to explain why BC decided to abandon the treaty-making enterprise in the mid-1800s and how both the Aboriginal peoples of BC and the government of Canada responded to this decision. Subsequent sections of the chapter will chronicle the political, legal, and constitutional developments that precipitated the conclusion of the landmark Nisga'a Treaty and discuss some of the major controversies that surrounded this conclusion. To help in tracking the Nisga'a Treaty's long and complex policy history, a chronology of major events has been appended to this chapter.

Background to the Nisga'a Treaty: Canada's Early Treaty-Making History

During the earliest years of colonial settlement in Canada, the issue of who "owned" the land was not a major concern. Predominantly interested in prospering from the fur trade, the early colonial newcomers to present-day Canada actively solicited the assistance, skills, and knowledge of Abo-

I: The Two-Row Wampum

The nature and scope of Canada's earliest treaties (the "peace and friendship" treaties) is symbolized by the Iroquois (*Hadenosaunee*) Confederacy's Two-Row Wampum (*Gus-Wen-Tah*). The Two-Row Wampum (which signified "One River, Two Vessels") "reflects a diplomatic convention that recognizes interaction and separation of settler and First Nation societies."[*] As leading Aboriginal legal academic Robert A. Williams Jr. explains:

> When the Haudenosaunee first came into contact with the European nations, treaties of peace and friendship were made. Each was symbolized by the Gus-Wen-Tah, or Two Row Wampum. There is a bed of white wampum which symbolizes the purity of the agreement. There are two rows of purple, and those two rows have the spirit of your ancestors and mine. There are three beads of wampum separating the two rows and they symbolize peace, friendship and respect. These two rows will symbolize two paths or two vessels, travelling down the same river together. One, a birch bark canoe, will be for the Indian people, their laws, their customs and their ways. The other, a ship, will be for the white people and their laws, their customs, and their ways. We shall each travel the river together, side by side, but in our own boat. Neither of us will try to steer the other's vessel.[†]

According to contemporary Aboriginal political leaders Ovide Mercredi and Mary Ellen Turpell, "[t]he two-row wampum captures the original values that governed [the Aboriginal-colonial newcomer] relationship—equality, respect, dignity and a sharing of the river we travel on."[‡]

Notes

[*] John Burrows, "Wampum at Niagara: The Royal Proclamation, Canadian Legal History, and Self-Government," *Aboriginal and Treaty Rights in Canada: Essays on Law, Equality and Respect for Difference*, ed. Michael Asch (Vancouver, BC: University of British Columbia Press, 1997) 164.

[†] Robert A. Williams, Jr., "The Algebra of Federal Indian Law: The Hard Trail of Decolonizing and Americanizing the White Man's Indian Jurisprudence," *Wisconsin Law Review* (1986): 219.

[‡] Ovide Mercredi and Mary Ellen Turpell, *In the Rapids: Navigating the Future of First Nations* (Toronto: Viking Press, 1993) 35.

riginal peoples in order to do so. The two dominant groups of colonial newcomers—the English and the French—also sought the friendship and military allegiance of Aboriginal peoples in order to facilitate their respective nations' dominance over the resource-rich North American continent. Inspired by their own strategic interests (which included obtaining useful

European tools, materials, food stocks, and medicines and augmenting their military strength in the face of rival Aboriginal Nations) the Aboriginal peoples of Canada willingly reciprocated. To secure continuation of these mutually beneficial relationships, Aboriginal peoples and colonial newcomers concluded a disparate series of "peace and friendship" treaties between 1701 and 1779. These earliest Canadian treaties, which predominate in the southeastern regions of the country, generally did not include provisions for the purchase or surrender of traditional Aboriginal territories but instead served to solidify mutually beneficial cooperative alliances.

The European concept of treaties—formal, binding agreements between independent nations—was not new to the Aboriginal peoples. Many used treaties before the arrival of colonial newcomers to secure inter-nation agreement on a wide range of important matters (for example, establishing reciprocal trade relationships; securing strategic military alliances; and regulating the use of hunting, fishing, and trapping areas). This made the early "peace and friendship" treaty process a more or less mutually understood and respected means of concluding cooperative arrangements (see Inset I for an Aboriginal understanding of these treaties).[5]

After the defeat of the French and with increasing European settlement, however, European treaty priorities shifted from securing the friendship and allegiance of Aboriginal peoples to securing lawful title to their traditional territories. To facilitate this change Canada's first Aboriginal land claims policy was instituted and outlined in the *Royal Proclamation of* 1763, issued by King George III of Britain on 7 October of that year (see Inset II).[6]

The Royal Proclamation of 1763

Through the terms of the *Royal Proclamation of 1763*, the British Crown formally recognized Aboriginal peoples' continuing rights to their traditional territories and endeavoured to protect those rights from land hungry colonial settlers. It did so by:

1. reserving all lands not ceded to or purchased by the Crown to the "Indians" as "their Hunting Grounds";
2. ordering all British subjects settled on unceded Aboriginal territories to remove themselves from these lands immediately; and,
3. prohibiting colonial authorities from granting Warrants of Survey (i.e., allowing new settlement lands to be staked out) or passing Patents for Land (i.e., issuing land title to settlers or corporations) in the absence of specific instructions from the Crown.

II: Excerpt from the *Royal Proclamation of 1763* (RSC 1985, App. II, No. 1)

And whereas it is just and reasonable, and essential to our Interest, and the Security of our Colonies, that the several Nations or Tribes of Indians with whom We are connected, and who live under our Protection, should not be molested or disturbed in the Possession of such Parts of Our Dominions and Territories as, not having been ceded to or purchased by Us, are reserved to them or any of them, as their Hunting Grounds—We do therefore, with the advice of our Privy Council, declare it to be our Royal Will and Pleasure that no Governor or Commander in Chief in any of our Colonies of Quebec, East Florida or West Florida, do presume, upon any Pretence whatever, to grant Warrants of Survey, or pass any Patents for Lands beyond the Bounds of their respective Governments as described in their Commissions: as also that no Governor or Commander in Chief in any of our other Colonies or Plantations in America do presume for the present, and until our further Pleasure be known, to grant Warrants of Survey, or pass Patents for any Lands beyond the Heads or Sources of any of the Rivers which fall into the Atlantic Ocean from the West and North West, or upon any Lands whatever, which, not having been ceded to or purchased by Us as aforesaid, are reserved to the said Indians, or any of them.

And We do further declare it to be Our Royal Will and Pleasure, for the present as aforesaid, to reserve under our Sovereignty, Protection, and Dominion, for the use of said Indians, all the Lands and Territories not included within the Limits of Our said Three new Governments, or within the Limits of the Territory granted to the Hudson's Bay Company, as also all the Lands and Territories lying to the Westward of the Sources of the Rivers which fall into the Sea from the West and North West as aforesaid.

And We do hereby strictly forbid, on Pain of our Displeasure, all our loving Subjects from making any Purchases or Settlements whatever, or taking Possession of any of the Lands above reserved without our especial leave and Licence for that Purpose first obtained.

And We do further strictly enjoin and require all Persons whatever who have either wilfully or inadvertently seated themselves upon any Lands within the Countries above described or upon any other Lands, which, not having been ceded to or purchased by Us, are still reserved to the said Indians as aforesaid, forthwith to remove themselves from such Settlements.

And whereas great Frauds and Abuses have been committed in purchasing Lands of the Indians, to the great Prejudice of our Interests and to the great Dissatisfaction of the said Indians: In order, therefore, to prevent such Irregularities for the future, and to the end that the Indians may be convinced of our Justice and determined Resolution to remove all reasonable Cause of Discontent, We do with the Advice of our Privy Council strictly enjoin and require that no private Person do presume to make any purchase from the said Indians of any Lands reserved to the said Indians, within those parts of our Colonies where We have thought proper to allow Settlement: but that if at any Time any of the Said Indians should be inclined to dispose of the said Lands, the same shall be Purchased only for Us, in our Name, at some public Meeting or Assembly of the said Indians, to be held for that Purpose by the Governor or Commander in Chief of our Colony respectively within which they shall lie: and in case they shall lie within the limits of any Proprietary Government they shall be purchased only for the Use and in the name of such Proprietaries, conformable to such Directions and Instructions as We or they shall think proper to give for that Purpose ...

Given at our Court at St. James's the 7th Day of October 1763 in the Third Year of our Reign.

Note: A full text of the Royal Proclamation of 1763 is available at: http://www.solon.org/Constitutions/Canada/English/PreConfederation/rp_1763.html

In addition, however, the terms of the proclamation also set out a formal policy for the lawful extinguishment of Aboriginal peoples' continuing rights to land.

The overarching purpose of this colonial land acquisition policy was to preserve the honour of the Crown in colonial-Aboriginal relations by preventing land-related frauds and abuses. Towards this end, the proclamation explicitly prohibited all private land dealings with Aboriginal peoples, asserting that only the Crown, or individuals acting on explicit behalf of the Crown, could lawfully purchase or accept the surrender of land from them. It also entrenched substantive Aboriginal consent as a prerequisite for all acts of lawful colonial land acquisition by requiring a "public Meeting or Assembly" of the Aboriginal peoples involved to precede all acts of colonial land acquisition.

It is these terms of the proclamation that compelled colonial authorities (and later, the Dominion Government of Canada) to conclude formal "land surrender" treaties with the Aboriginal peoples in advance of colonial settlement.

The "Land Surrender" Treaties

Following the terms of the *Royal Proclamation of 1763*, between 1764 and 1867 colonial representatives of the Crown negotiated the first series of "land surrender" treaties in present-day southern Ontario. Although the terms of these pre-confederation or lettered treaties varied greatly, they generally included the surrender of relatively small areas of land in exchange for an initial gift or small one-time cash payment. They also occasionally included the guarantee of small reserve grants of land; preferential access to colonial trading posts; and exclusive hunting, trapping, and fishing rights in designated areas.

As settlement increased, however, so too did the colonial demand for land. As a result, the nature and scope of "land surrender" treaties began to expand dramatically. The beginning of this trend is witnessed in the Robinson-Superior and Robinson-Huron treaties of 1850, which set the precedent for the surrender of increasingly large areas of land in exchange for a more comprehensive range of so-called treaty rights, benefits, and entitlements.

In 1867 the British Colonies of Canada West (Ontario), Canada East (Quebec), Nova Scotia, and New Brunswick united to form the Dominion of Canada. Determined to facilitate westward expansion, the new government used its constitutionally accorded authority over "Indians and the lands reserved for the Indians" (section 91[24] of the British North America Act, 1867 [BNA Act]) to continue the "land surrender" treaty practice of the earlier treaties and negotiated a series of so-called numbered treaties (Treaties 1 to 11) with First Nations in Ontario and the West. The terms of these numbered treaties included the surrender of increasingly vast areas of land in exchange for reserve grants of land, one-time cash payments and/or gifts, and small monetary annuities, as well, generally, as guaranteed hunting, fishing, and trapping rights over unoccupied Crown land and promises for the provision of such treaty entitlements as schools, medicines, cattle, agricultural implements, and ammunition (see Inset III for a map of historic treaty areas).[7]

Aboriginal Perspectives on the "Land Surrender" Treaties

Although the terms of the post-1763 "land surrender" treaties clearly reflected a change in priorities on the part of colonial and Dominion authorities, the treaty priorities of Aboriginal peoples remained unaltered. Provided with copies of the *Royal Proclamation of 1763*, they believed that their understanding of treaties was mutually understood and accepted.[8] They were later appalled to discover that their European friends presumed to have extinguished their territorial rights and sovereign authority through the post-1763 treaty process. As Allan McMillan explains:

> Native people whose ancestors signed treaties tend to view these documents as recognition of their sovereign status and affirmation of their aboriginal rights. The treaties provide for a continuing relationship between Canada and First Nations. Governments and non-aboriginals, however, tend to see the treaties as historic agreements which extinguished aboriginal rights to the land and established federal control over the lives of Native people.[9]

To support their position, Canadian authorities point to the written terms of the treaties, which closely resemble deeds of sale. Aboriginal peoples, however, dispute the validity of these terms, arguing that there are great differences between the treaty agreements their ancestors negotiated and consented to (as recorded in oral history) and the formal documents themselves (as recorded in written form by colonial authorities, frequently some time *after* their formal conclusion).[10] Aboriginal peoples also argue that the legal validity of the "land surrender" treaties is decidedly put into question by the fact that many of the terms of these historic agreements have not been honourably upheld by the Crown (now embodied in the federal and provincial governments of Canada).

Although not inconsequential disagreement about the nature and intent of the post-1763 "land surrender" treaties continues, the simple and undisputed fact of their existence is important for at least two reasons. First, they provide documented evidence that colonial and Dominion authorities adhered to the terms of the proclamation during the early years of colonial settlement. And second, by logical extension, they provide persuasive evidence that these same political authorities accepted and respected the royal prerogative's recognition of continuing Aboriginal rights to land.

The terms of the proclamation, however, were not consistently applied throughout Canada (see Inset III for a map of historic treaty areas). As a result, large areas of the Canadian land mass were never formally surrendered or purchased by the Crown during the early colonial settlement period. These areas included most of what became BC, the Yukon, Nunavut, and the Northwest Territories, as well as Labrador and Northern Quebec. While remote location and harsh environmental conditions preventing or limiting settlement largely explain the absence of historic treaties in some of these regions, the absence of treaties in BC is the direct result of political circumstances.

BC: A SPECIAL CASE

When Vancouver Island was officially made a British colony in 1849, the British Crown gave exclusive trading rights to the Hudson's Bay Company and left it in charge of immigration and settlement. Toward these ends, the Hudson's Bay Company instructed its Chief Factor for Fort Victoria—James Douglas—to purchase land from the Aboriginal peoples of Vancouver Island in order to facilitate economic development and colonial settlement. Douglas, when appointed governor of the new colony in 1851, was given similar instructions by his imperial superiors in Britain and so

III: Historical Indian Treaties in Canada

HISTORICAL INDIAN TREATIES IN CANADA
Boundary lines are approximate

Source: Thomas Isaac, *Aboriginal Law: Commentary, Cases, and Materials*, 3rd ed. (Saskatoon, SK: Purich Publishing, 2004). Reproduced with permission of the author and publisher.

According to the Department of Indian Affairs and Northern Development, there are approximately 68 known historic treaties between Aboriginal Nations and the Crown. National Archives estimates, however, place the number of known historic treaties at nearly 600. (Assembly of First Nations, "Treaties With the Crown," *Fact Sheet* [May 2000] 2.)

Note: Treaty 8 is a federal treaty, meaning that provincial governments took no part in either its negotiation or conclusion. To extend Treaty 8 in the northeastern corner of BC, the federal government took advantage of the relatively small Crown land holdings it retained in the region following BC's entry into Confederation. As a result, the province (which did not recognize continuing Aboriginal rights and title within its jurisdiction) made no formal objection to the conclusion of Treaty 8.

negotiated a series of 14 "land surrender" treaties on Vancouver Island between 1850 and 1854.[11]

When a mainland colony was established in 1858, Douglas was appointed governor there as well (the twin colonies were subsequently united in 1866 into what is now British Columbia). Although imperial authorities instructed him to purchase all remaining Aboriginal lands in the twin colonies, the funds they reserved for this purpose were grossly insufficient to the task. Unable to continue the "land surrender" treaty practice, Douglas attempted to respect Aboriginal peoples' continuing rights to their traditional territories in two ways. First, he extended pre-emption (homesteading) rights to Aboriginal peoples, and second, he ordered that "Indian reserves ... be defined as they may be severally pointed out by the Natives themselves."[12] These conciliatory policy measures, however, did not endure for long.

When Douglas retired in 1864 his successor, Governor A.E. Kennedy, appointed Joseph Trutch as Chief Commissioner of Lands and Works, thus placing him in charge of all Aboriginal land dealings in the colony. In contrast to Douglas, Trutch viewed Aboriginal peoples as inferior savages incapable of understanding, let alone holding, legal property rights. In one of his first acts as commissioner, he revoked their pre-emption rights and reduced the size of their allocated reserves to a mere 10 acres per family. He then went on to convince the colonial authorities that the conclusion of further "land surrender" treaties was not only unnecessary but also unconscionable. The essence of his position was outlined in an 1867 memorandum to the colonial authorities in which he stated:

> [t]he Indians really have no rights to the lands they claim, nor are they of any actual value or utility to them and I cannot see why they should either retain these lands to the prejudice of the general interests of the Colony, or be allowed to make a market of them either to the Government or to Individuals.[13]

Faced with a continuing shortfall in treaty funds and a massive influx of eager settlers, the colonial authorities were quick to embrace the practical merits of Trutch's position.

To support their new policy of denying Aboriginal rights, the colonial authorities developed a unique interpretation of the *Royal Proclamation of 1763*—that it was never intended to apply within their jurisdiction. This interpretation rested on two premises:

1. Vancouver Island and mainland BC did not appear on most maps drawn by British cartographers (who had not yet travelled to the west coast) when the proclamation was issued; and
2. the use of the present tense in the phrase "the Indians with whom we are *now* connected" (emphasis added) exempted the colonies created after the date of the proclamation from its provisions.

In sum, the colonial authorities argued that their colony had been considered a legal *terra nullius* (land belonging to no one) by the British Crown when it asserted its sovereignty over the land mass in 1846.

This rather convoluted argument went on to assert that because the first Douglas Treaty was concluded in 1850 and no further treaties were concluded after 1854, Douglas had been acting as Chief Factor of the Hudson's Bay Company (a position he held until 1858) and not as a colonial representative when he concluded the Vancouver Island land purchases (he was governor of the Island colony from 1851-64 and governor of the mainland colony from 1858-64). Thus, according to the BC government position, the so-called Douglas Treaties were not true treaties (negotiated according to the terms of the *Royal Proclamation of 1763*) but rather Crown-sanctioned land dealings conducted by a private company (the Hudson's Bay Company). This, it was asserted, provided additional convincing evidence that BC had been considered a legal *terra nullius* by the British Crown and beyond the intended scope of the *Royal Proclamation of 1763*.[14]

When BC joined the Dominion of Canada in 1871, no mention was made of this unique interpretation of the *Royal Proclamation of 1763* and the unlawful acquisition of Aboriginal territories that it was propagating. Instead, the new provincial government was accorded exclusive legislative authority over Crown lands and resources and was instructed to pursue a reserve policy "as liberal as that hitherto pursued." These exceptional Terms of Union suggest that the Dominion government was largely unaware of BC's unique Aboriginal affairs policy.

Although all provincial governments were accorded exclusive legislative authority over the management and sale of public lands and resources by virtue of section 92(5) of the BNA Act,[15] when other new provinces were created (Manitoba, Saskatchewan, and Alberta, for example) the Dominion government reserved Crown lands and resources for itself. In other words, it retained the exclusive right to conclude "land surrender" treaties in these provinces. By transferring Crown lands and resources to BC, however, the Dominion Government in effect made the "land surrender" treaty practice an issue of shared jurisdiction.[16]

The other exceptional aspect of BC's Terms of Union related to its endorsement of existing reserve allocation practices (i.e., Trutch's 10-acres-per-family formula). As Daniel Raunet explains, although reserve size varied greatly across time and space, "[i]n the rest of the Dominion, the practice at that time was to carve out reserves on the basis of 80 acres per family [and] in the Prairies, the first treaties signed between 1871 and 1873 made provision for tracts of land ranging from 160 to 640 acres [per family]."[17] In sum, BC's reserve allocation practices can hardly be described as conventional, let alone liberal.

Whether the Dominion government was truly ignorant of BC's position on the Aboriginal land question in 1871 or simply chose to disregard this position in favour of its own westward expansion priorities remains unclear. What is clear, however, is that the Aboriginal peoples of the province were both abundantly aware and abundantly dissatisfied with BC's refusal to negotiate treaties in accord with the terms of the *Royal Proclamation of* 1763, as the long road to the Nisga'a Treaty illustrates.

The Long Road to the Nisga'a Treaty Begins[18]

The traditional territories of the Nisga'a Nation lie in the Nass River Valley of north-western BC about 600 miles up the coast from Vancouver, just below the tip of what became known in 1867 as the Alaska panhandle. Although the Nisga'a had had sporadic contact with colonial newcomers since British sea captain George Vancouver sailed into Observatory Inlet (*Ts'im Gits'oohl*) in 1773, it was not until the mid-1880s that government surveyors began to seriously threaten their traditional land holdings. The Nisga'a attempted to resist these encroachments both physically, by frustrating their surveying efforts, and politically, by issuing written notices of protest to the surveyors, such as the following:

> Whereas, we, the Indian people of the Aiyansh Valley, Nass River, British Columbia, being the lawful and original inhabitants and possessors of all the lands contained therein from time immemorial; and being assured In our possession of the same by the Proclamation of His Majesty, King George III, under date of October 7th, 1763 which Proclamation we hold as our Charter of Rights under the British Crown;
>
> And whereas, it Is provided In the said Proclamation that no private person do presume to make any purchase from us of any lands so reserved to us, until we have ceded the same to

the representatives of the Crown in public meeting between us and them;

And whereas, up to the present time our lands have not been ceded by us to the Crown, nor in any way alienated from us by any agreement or settlement between the representatives of the Crown and ourselves; ...

We do therefore, standing well within our constitutional rights, forbid you to stake off land In this valley, and do hereby protest against your proceeding further Into our country with that end in view—until such time as a satisfactory settlement be made between the representatives of the Crown and ourselves.[19]

When written notices failed to stop the incursions of surveyors and settlers, the Nisga'a decided to take their grievances directly to the provincial government.

In January 1887, Chiefs of the Nisga'a Nation canoed more than 1,100 kilometres down the Pacific Coast to Victoria to demand that the new provincial government respect their Nation's rights to its traditional territories and negotiate an honourable treaty with their Nation in respect of those rights. When they reached the legislature's doors, however, they were turned away. There is no need for a treaty, Premier William Smithe informed them on 3 February 1887, because the rights you claim do not exist. The Nisga'a Chiefs were forced to return home, but the Nisga'a Nation could not be forced to abandon its cause.

In 1890 the Nisga'a established the Nisga'a Land Committee to formally pursue colonial recognition of, and respect for, their continuing rights to land. They later joined forces with other north coast Aboriginal peoples to form a more broadly based Aboriginal land claims coalition—the Native Tribes of British Columbia, which in March 1909 dispatched a delegation representing 20 Aboriginal Nations to London, England to present their land-related grievances directly to the imperial government. In the end, however, imperial sympathies to Aboriginal land grievances resulted in no formal governmental action.

Frustrated with the political authorities' refusal to deal with their outstanding Aboriginal land claim, the Nisga'a hired the London law firm of Fox and Preece to help it prepare a legal defence. As a result of this strategic move, a formal petition was brought before the Judicial Committee of the Privy Council (the JCPC, then Canada's highest legal authority) on 21 May 1913.[20] "A Petition to His Majesty's Privy Council in the Matter of the Territory of the Nisga'a Nation or Tribe of Nations"[21] outlined the geographic extent of the Nisga'a Nation's traditional territories and described the BC government's refusal to comply with the terms of the *Royal Proclamation of 1763*. It also requested that the JCPC determine two critical issues: 1) the nature and extent of the Nisga'a Nation's continuing rights to its traditional territories; and 2) the legality of BC's Land Act, a statute which "purport[ed] to deal with lands thereby assumed [as] the absolute property of the said Province ... and [conferred] title in such lands free from the right, title or interest of the Indian Tribes, notwithstanding the fact that such right, title or interest has not been in any way extinguished."[22] The JCPC, however, refused to receive the Nisga'a petition without a formal referral from either a Canadian government or a Canadian court and sent the matter back to Canada for domestic resolution.

In response, in 1914 the federal government offered to sponsor the Nisga'a petition in Court provided, however, that the Nation consent to two non-negotiable conditions. First, it would have to permit the federal Department of Indian Affairs to select and instruct legal council for the case on its behalf; and second, it would have to agree that "if the Court, or, on appeal, the Privy Council, decides that [it has] a title to lands of the Province, [it will] surrender such title...."[23] Although the federal government knew that neither the Nisga'a Nation nor any other Aboriginal Nation would consent to such conditions, it nonetheless used their refusal to comply with its conditions as a formal reason for blocking the requested referral.

In February 1915, the Allied Tribes of British Columbia (Canada's first province-wide Aboriginal representative body) was formed to support the Nisga'a land claim and the settlement of the Aboriginal land question more generally. Under the leadership of Squamish Chief Andrew Paull and Haida Methodist minister Peter Kelly, the Allied Tribes of British Columbia compiled a detailed enumeration of all outstanding Aboriginal land claims in the province and, in 1919, petitioned both the federal and BC governments to equitably resolve these claims by: 1) guaranteeing reserves based on 160 acres per family; 2) fairly compensating Aboriginal peoples for the loss of all non-reserve territories (with the main part of this compensation to be provided in the form of modern medical and educational services); and, 3) respecting Aboriginal peoples' continuing rights to fish, hunt, and trap as formerly throughout their unceded traditional territories. Although the Allied Tribes' petition was precise, federal Interior Minister Charles Stewart refused to deal with the petition on the grounds that it was too vague and ambitious.[24]

An important legal development in another part of the British Empire, however, soon forced Canadian governments to take the Allied Tribes' petition (and the 1913 Nisga'a petition) more seriously.

Amodu Tijani v. Southern Nigeria[25]

In 1921, the JCPC was asked to provide its legal opinion on the nature and extent of Aboriginal rights to land in the British colony of Southern Nigeria. The case at issue—*Amodu Tijani v. Southern Nigeria* [1921]—was initiated following the expropriation of traditional lands by the British Colonial Secretary of Southern Nigeria. As a representative of his people, Tijani asserted a full ownership right (i.e., Aboriginal title) to the lands in question and demanded that appropriate compensation be paid in the wake of colonial expropriation of traditional territories.

In its 1921 ruling in favour of Tijani, the JCPC determined that the simple assertion of British sovereignty did not, and could not, serve to extinguish the legal rights of Aboriginal peoples to their traditional territories. It went on to assert that although Aboriginal rights to land could be extinguished by the sovereign Crown, any such extinguishment would normally require some degree of Aboriginal involvement to be lawful and effective. As a result, the Colonial Secretary was ordered to provide compensation.

Written in such a generic way as to be equally applicable throughout the British Empire, the *Amodu Tijani v. Southern Nigeria* decision served to dramatically bolster the legal merits of outstanding Aboriginal land claims in BC, as well as elsewhere in Canada. Well aware of this fact, Canadian political authorities took several actions aimed at preventing such claims from reaching the judicial arena.

Closing the Door on Aboriginal Land Claims Litigation

In 1925, the Allied Tribes once again dispatched a petition to Ottawa demanding either a settlement of all outstanding Aboriginal land claims in BC or a referral of those claims to the JCPC. In response, the federal government appointed a Special Joint Committee of the Senate and House of Commons in 1927 to determine the legal merits of these land claims. After five days of hearings in the spring of 1927, the committee ruled that the claim had no merit and castigated outside "agitators" for unreasonably raising the expectations of Canada's Aboriginal populace.[26]

Upon accepting the committee's final report, the federal government approved an annual grant of $100,000 to the Department of Indian Affairs to match in BC "the yearly payments made to Natives in other provinces who had signed treaties ... and to be used for improving education, health and living conditions on the reserves."[27] This annual grant, incidentally, is still being paid today and amounts to approximately $2 for every registered "Indian" in BC.

At roughly the same time (1926), Chief William Pierrish of Neskonlith, BC, with two other Aboriginal chiefs, travelled to London, England, armed with a petition requesting formal imperial action on the outstanding land claims of BC's Aboriginal peoples. There, however, the chiefs were intercepted by the Canadian High Commissioner who promised to deliver the petition on their behalf and convinced them to go home. The High Commissioner, however, did not follow through on his promise, and the petition entrusted to him was never delivered.

To prevent any further Aboriginal land claims activities, the federal government introduced a carefully tailored Indian Act[28] amendment in the fall of 1927, which made it an offence punishable by law to "receive, obtain, solicit or request from any Indian any payment for the purpose of raising a fund or providing money for the prosecution of any claim." Unable any more to obtain legal counsel, the Allied Tribes of British Columbia collapsed, and the Nisga'a Land Council was rendered mute. Thinking the Aboriginal land question had been put to rest once and for all, the governments of Canada and BC turned their attentions to other matters, namely assimilating Aboriginal peoples into the mainstream of Canadian society.

BC's Aboriginal peoples, however, could not be so easily dissuaded from pursuing their long-outstanding claims; in 1931 they established the Native Brotherhood of British Columbia

> as a vehicle for continuing the ideals of the Allied Tribes while avoiding any explicit pursuit of the now prohibited land claim. The founding meeting approved a petition for better schooling, for increased recognition of aboriginal rights in hunting, fishing, trapping and timber-harvesting in off-reserve traditional lands and for a meeting with Ottawa officials.[29]

Nudging the Nisga'a Land Claim Back into the Political Spotlight: Postwar Developments

From the late 1920s to the mid-1940s, the Aboriginal land question remained taboo. In the postwar period, however, heightened attention to the rights of minority populations in general slowly nudged it into the political spotlight once again. As Ken Coates explains:

Canada, like other liberal democracies, found it difficult to sustain a critique of the racist policies of other countries, such as South Africa, when it neglected so systematically the needs and aspirations of its own First Nations. In fairly quick order, the protests that had long emanated from Aboriginal communities found a more receptive ear.[30]

A slow process of policy readjustment was begun in 1946, when the federal government established a special Joint Committee of the Senate and House of Commons to review the federal Indian Act as well as the administrative and operational structure of the Department of Indian Affairs, including its administration of so-called Indian claims and grievances.

Aboriginal peoples saw a gross conflict of interest in the federal government's Department of Indian Affairs' exclusive authority over the classification, assessment, and adjudication of their claims and had been lobbying Ottawa for years to revise this inherently biased system.[31] In response and in accordance with its mandate, the Special Joint Committee conducted a thorough assessment of the US Indian Claims Commission and weighed its potential applicability to the Canadian case. In its final report, it recommended the creation of a special government body similar in nature to the US commission, but much more limited in its scope and authority. This recommendation, however, was rejected by the federal government, which opted to retain the existing system of Indian claims.

Other committee recommendations, however, were accepted and in June 1951 the federal parliament passed some significant amendments to the Indian Act, including the removal of provisions that prohibited Aboriginal land claims activities.

Almost immediately, the Nisga'a Nation began discussing how best to proceed with its long-outstanding land claim. These discussions resulted in the revival of the Nisga'a Land Committee in 1952, the establishment of the more formally structured Nisga'a Tribal Council in 1955, and the approval of a "new" Nisga'a land claims petition in 1959. An excerpt from this petition (essentially a revised version of the 1913 Nisga'a petition to the JCPC) reads as follows:

> We claim to be the aboriginal inhabitants of the territory defined, and that under the terminology of the proclamation, we are the tribal owners of said territory, and that no part of it be taken from the Nishga nation or tribe of Indians, or the land and natural resources, such as timber resources, be sold and disposed of until the same has been purchased by the Crown.

We claim that our aboriginal rights have been guaranteed by the proclamation of King George the Third and recognized by acts of parliament of Great Britain, and by our aboriginal rights, we claim tribal ownership of all fisheries, minerals, timber and other natural resources within the realm of the territory outlined.[32]

The *Nisga'a Tribal Council* circulated this petition widely and tried to get it endorsed by other Aboriginal organizations such as the Native Brotherhood of British Columbia. Its unshakable conviction that its land claim would eventually have to be tried in a court of law, however, seemed too dangerous for other Aboriginal organizations to contemplate. As Raunet explains: "[o]ther Native leaders feared that such a challenge, if it failed, would forever jeopardize Native land claims in the country."[33] As a result, the Nisga'a Nation was forced to go it alone.

In 1963, facing both a substantial backlog of Indian claims and increasing Aboriginal opposition to the existing system, the federal government introduced legislation for the creation of an Indian Claims Commission. Due to a "change in the government, internal departmental conflict, the need to consult with the Indians, and the Indians' desire to see how this legislation would deal with their claims against the provincial governments,"[34] however, this piece of legislation was never passed into law.

The idea of establishing an Indian Claims Commission was again taken up by the federal government following the Supreme Court of Canada's final decision in *R. v. Bob and White* [1965].[35] This case involved two members of the Nanaimo Indian band (Vancouver Island)—Clifford White and David Bob—who were arrested in 1963 for killing six deer out of season and without a permit. Lawyer Thomas Berger obtained an acquittal by successfully arguing that an 1854 treaty signed by Governor James Douglas recognized the Nanaimo Indian band's continuing rights to hunt on unoccupied Crown land. In his 1963 decision on this case, "Justice Swencisy of the County Court ruled that [the 1854 document in question] was indeed a treaty and that 'the aboriginal right of the Nanaimo Indian tribes to hunt on unoccupied land, which was confirmed to them by the royal proclamation of 1763, [had] never been abrogated or extinguished and [was] still in full force and effect.'"[36] This decision was later upheld by both the BC Court of Appeal (1964) and the Supreme Court of Canada (1965). The *Bob and White* case not only invested the Douglas Treaties with a newfound authority but also affirmed the contemporary relevance of both the *Royal Proclamation of 1763* and pre-existing Aboriginal rights.

In response to this legal decision, the federal government presented a revised version of the 1963 proposal for an Indian Claims Commission to the House of Commons in June 1965. As James S. Frideres explains:

> [t]he terms of the bill provided for a five-person Indian claims commission, at least one member of which was to be a status Indian, with a chairman who had been a judge or lawyer for at least ten years. The jurisdiction of the commission would have been limited to acts or admissions of the Crown in right of Canada or of the United Kingdom, but not in right of a province. Because of this and because of stipulations about evidence, there was substantial doubt that the commission would have been able to decide the merits of the Aboriginal title issue in British Columbia, a claim that was one of the main reasons for the creation of the body.[37]

Upon second reading in the House of Commons, the Indian Claims Commission bill was referred to another Joint Committee of the Senate and House of Commons for review and revision. However, it was ultimately allowed to die on the order paper following the dissolution of Parliament later that same year. Although nothing further was done to establish an Indian Claims Commission in Canada, the federal government's intention to do so appears to have remained. In September 1968, the Minister of Indian Affairs again reaffirmed his intention to introduce a bill creating a commission the following December.

By this time, however, the Nisga'a had already hired lawyer Thomas Berger of *R. v. Bob and White* fame and were preparing to take their land claim to court.

The Long Road to the Nisga'a Treaty Finally Passes Through the Courts

On 27 September 1967, Chief Frank Calder, acting on behalf of the Nisga'a Tribal Council, and his lawyer, Thomas Berger, filed a lawsuit in BC's Supreme Court[38] asking for a declaration confirming that:

1. the Nisga'a had held title to their traditional territories prior to the assertion sovereignty by the British Crown;
2. this title had never been lawfully extinguished; and
3. this title was a legal right.

This Aboriginal title claim (which bears remarkable resemblance to the Nisga'a Nation's 1913 petition to the JCPC) was heard by BC's Supreme Court in 1969, the BC Court of Appeal in 1970, and the Supreme Court of Canada in 1972. In 1973 it ultimately resulted in one of the most influential, if divided and complex, legal decisions in Canadian history.

The Legal Arguments

In presenting their case to the court, the Nisga'a argued that, prior to the declaration of Crown sovereignty (1864 in BC's case), they had existed as a self-governing nation and had exercised effective territorial control over all lands within their government's sovereign jurisdiction (i.e., their traditional territories). In other words, they argued that in terms of the "ladder of social evolution" used to adjudge indigenous inhabitants during the early colonial settlement period they could not have been plausibly considered as either "uncivilized" or incapable of holding judicially recognizable property rights. They furthermore argued that the specific legal terminology used in the *Royal Proclamation of 1763* clearly demonstrated the fact that the British Crown had recognized both:

1. their status as a nation: "... *the several* Nations *or Tribes with whom we are now connected* ..." (emphasis added); and,
2. their legal rights to their traditional territories: "... *should not be molested or disturbed in the* Possession *of such Parts of Our Dominions and Territories as, not having been ceded to or purchased by Us are reserved to them* ..." (emphasis added).

This imperial recognition, the Nisga'a's argument continued, was formally accepted by the colonial and dominion authorities of Canada, who willingly participated in the land acquisition policy set forth in the royal proclamation through the conclusion of "land surrender" treaties. Since their traditional territories had never been ceded, sold, surrendered, or lost in war, the Nisga'a concluded, they must continue to hold lawful title to their traditional territories, and, therefore, the general land legislation enacted by the colonial authorities to control and regulate their territories must be considered unlawful.

The BC government countered with the argument, explained earlier in this chapter, that the royal proclamation had not been intended to apply to the land mass now known as the province of British Columbia. As a result, they argued, the Nisga'a Nation's claims of continuing rights and title were entirely devoid of legal merit. Even *if* the Nisga'a had at one time held legal rights to their traditional territories, these rights had been lawfully extinguished before BC entered Confederation through either the declaration of Crown sovereignty itself or general "land legislation" (i.e., statutory Land Acts), which appropriated the lands in question for public purposes.

The Decisions

The *Calder* case was initially heard by the Supreme Court of British Columbia,[39] where the Nisga'a suffered a crushing defeat at the hands of a single trial judge. In his October 1968 decision, Justice Gould accepted the province's arguments that the *Royal Proclamation of 1763* did not apply to BC and, therefore, determined that the pre-existing land rights (i.e., Aboriginal title) claimed by the Nisga'a either did not exist or had never been recognized in the colony. Thus, he ruled that the Nisga'a's claim to lawful ownership of their traditional territories was without legal merit. He went on to argue that even if the Nisga'a had at one time held some kind of legal rights to their traditional territories, these rights had been "implicitly extinguished" by general land legislation competently enacted by colonial authorities before BC joined Confederation in 1871.

Chief Calder appealed the Gould decision to the BC Court of Appeal,[40] but in May 1970 a three-member panel of this court unanimously upheld the lower court ruling and dismissed the appeal. According to its ruling, the Nisga'a had been too "primitive" in the nineteenth century to have held concepts of property ownership that could be considered on an evolutionary par with the concept of property ownership upheld by the common law. If any form of Aboriginal title had at one time existed, the court reasoned, it had been "explicitly extinguished" by the assertion of British sovereignty and/or "implicitly extinguished" by general land legislation enacted prior to 1871.

The only legal avenue that now remained open to Chief Calder was to appeal both lower court decisions to the Supreme Court of Canada. This move, however, was risky. Two courts had already rejected the Nisga'a Nation's Aboriginal title claim and supporting legal arguments. A similar rejection by the Supreme Court of Canada would not only adversely affect the outstanding Aboriginal land claim of the Nisga'a Nation but likely all outstanding Aboriginal land claims in Canada. Recognizing this fact, some Nisga'a citizens and numerous Aboriginal organizations from across the country appealed to Calder not to proceed with his legal battle. Calder, however, could not be dissuaded, and in November 1971 he presented his Nation's case before a panel of seven Supreme Court justices.[41]

Reserved for 14 long months, the highly anticipated *Calder* decision was finally delivered in January 1973. Three justices held that the Nisga'a possessed Aboriginal title to their traditional territories, and three justices held that they did not. All six justices, however, agreed that Aboriginal title existed, and continued to exist, until consensually surrendered to, or validly extinguished by, the Crown. The issue that divided the court was whether or not the specific Aboriginal title claimed by the Nisga'a Nation continued to exist.

The majority decision, written by Justice Judson (with Justices Ritchie and Martland concurring), accepted BC's argument that the *Royal Proclamation of 1763* had not been intended to apply to the pre-confederation colonies of British Columbia. At the same time, however, they confirmed that Aboriginal title did in fact exist by virtue of Aboriginal peoples' occupation and use of their traditional territories *prior to* the declaration of Crown sovereignty. As Justice Judson's often quoted statement on the matter makes clear: "... Indian title in British Columbia cannot owe its origins to the *Proclamation of 1763*, the fact is that when the settlers came, the Indians were there, organized in societies and occupying the land as their forefathers had done for centuries. This is what Indian title means...."

Justice Judson, however, went on to describe Aboriginal title as "a mere burden" on the Crown's underlying title to all lands within sovereign jurisdiction and as a right "dependent on the goodwill of the sovereign." Therefore, he reasoned, the Crown had the exclusive right to extinguish Aboriginal title, and it had clearly exercised that right in respect of the Nisga'a Nation's traditional territories.

In the end, Justices Judson, Ritchie, and Martland concluded that whatever Aboriginal title rights the Nisga'a might have had prior to the declaration of Crown sovereignty in 1864, the absence of any Crown recognition and/or protection of those rights (i.e., through the *Royal Proclamation of 1763*) meant that such rights had already been lawfully extinguished before BC entered Confederation in 1871. According to Judson's reasoning, this extinguishment had been effected through either the declaration of Crown sovereignty itself (explicit extinguishment), or the competent enactment of Crown-sanctioned general land legislation (implicit extinguishment).

The minority or dissenting decision, written by Justice Hall (with Justices Laskin and Spence concurring) concluded that the *Royal Proclamation of 1763* had in fact been intended to apply to the pre-confederation colonies of British Columbia. In the same breath, however, it concluded that the terms of the royal proclamation had no bearing whatsoever on the continuing existence of Aboriginal title. As Justice Hall explained: "[the proposition asserting that] after conquest or discovery the native peoples have no rights at all except those subsequently granted or recognized by the conqueror or discoverer ... is wholly wrong...." In other words, Justices Hall, Laskin, and Spence concluded that Aboriginal title existed whether it was formally recognized by an imperial sovereign or not.

Although the minority decision went on to confirm the Crown's exclusive authority to extinguish Aboriginal title, it did not accept the majority justices' legal opinion on the validity of implicit extinguishment. According to Justice Hall's reasoning, the lawful extinguishment of Aboriginal title could only be accomplished by specific legislation directly sanctioned by the Crown or through an otherwise "clear and plain" expression of the Crown's intention to extinguish Aboriginal title. Having been presented with no proof of explicit Crown intentions or instructions to extinguish the Nisga'a Nation's Aboriginal title and having determined that implicit extinguishment (i.e., general land legislation) was unlawful, the minority decision concluded that the Nisga'a did in fact continue to hold Aboriginal title to their traditional territories.

The seventh justice on the Supreme Court panel—Justice Pigeon—rejected the Nisga'a appeal for procedural reasons related to how the case had first been brought to the courts[42] and made no comment on the Aboriginal title question. As a result, the Nisga'a lost their case on a technicality when their appeal was dismissed by a four-to-one majority.

Land Claims Policy in the Post-Calder Era

The peculiar split decision of the seven-member panel in *Calder* served to increase dramatically the legal viability of outstanding Aboriginal land claims in Canada. As Douglas Sanders explains:

> [Following the release of the *Calder* decision,] Prime Minister Trudeau met with Frank Calder and representatives of the Nishga Tribal Council and, separately, on the same afternoon, with representatives of the Union of BC Indian Chiefs and the National Indian Brotherhood. The Prime Minister described the Supreme Court judgement as meaning that "perhaps" the Indians had more "legal rights" than he had thought ... He still refused to use the term "Aboriginal title" or "Aboriginal rights." He advised the Indians to speak of "legal rights."[43]

Although the exact content of these legal rights remained largely undefined in 1973, their acknowledged existence by the *Calder* justices was enough to cast serious doubt on the merits of the federal government's, and especially BC's, existing Indian claims policy.

In a landmark statement issued on 8 August 1973, the federal government announced that it was prepared to settle the outstanding land claims of Canada's Aboriginal peoples in all parts of the country where Aboriginal title had not been dealt with previously through treaties or other lawful means. Under the auspices of the federal government's new comprehensive claims policy, Aboriginal peoples were encouraged to forgo costly and uncertain litigated settlements of their outstanding land claims in favour of equitably negotiated final settlement agreements or modern treaties.

To facilitate implementation of this new policy, an Office of Native Claims was established within the Department of Indian Affairs in July 1974. This office was subsequently flooded with an overwhelming number of outstanding Aboriginal land claims, which, until then, had not been accepted as legitimate or credible. Not surprisingly, a large number of these claims came from BC. As a result, the federal government announced in 1976 that it would negotiate only six comprehensive claims at any one time and only one comprehensive claim per province. This announcement came on the heels of Canada's first comprehensive claims settlement agreement, which demonstrated just how detailed modern treaties needed to be in order to effectively resolve the issue of outstanding Aboriginal title.

The James Bay and Northern Quebec Agreement, 1975

The first land claim settlement, or modern treaty, to be concluded in Canada was precipitated by the construction of a huge hydroelectric project in Northern Quebec. It involved blocking several rivers in the James Bay/Ungava region resulting in the flooding of vast wilderness areas where Cree and Inuit peoples had engaged in hunting and trapping since time immemorial. Concerned about the destruction of their traditional territories and the Quebec government's blatant disregard for their continuing Aboriginal title rights, the Cree and Inuit peoples of Northern Quebec asked the Superior Court of Quebec for an injunction to stop all work on the hydroelectric project until a resolution of their outstanding Aboriginal land claims could be concluded.

Although the *Calder* decision had confirmed Aboriginal title as a judicially enforceable property right, the Superior Court of Quebec was the first Canadian court to apply this doctrine to an outstanding Aboriginal land claim. The November 1973 ruling in favour of the Cree and Inuit was thus the first Canadian legal decision to:

1. confirm the practical existence of Aboriginal title to a specific tract of land;
2. offer a legal opinion on the content of this right; and,
3. affirm that Aboriginal title can take precedence over other legal rights (namely, a provincial government's right to manage and control Crown lands).

The Superior Court of Quebec confirmed that the Cree and Inuit peoples of Northern Quebec did in fact hold Aboriginal title to the region in question. It also confirmed that they had unique Aboriginal rights to the natural resources attached to their traditional territories. And finally, it determined that the government of Quebec had an unfulfilled legal obligation under the Quebec Boundaries Extension Act (which transferred the region at issue to the province in 1912) to resolve outstanding Aboriginal land claims before undertaking either development or settlement in the vast unceded regions of the province.

This decision was immediately appealed by the government of Quebec and subsequently overturned by the Quebec Court of Appeal several days later. A further appeal by the Cree and Inuit to the Supreme Court of Canada was pre-empted, when the governments of Canada and Quebec agreed to enter into comprehensive land claim negotiations with them rather than gamble on the uncertain outcome of a court imposed settlement.

The subsequent James Bay and Northern Quebec Agreement was formally concluded on 11 November 1975 and came into effect in 1977 after enabling legislation was passed by the legislatures of Canada and Quebec. This comprehensive land claims settlement (or modern treaty) provided the Cree and Inuit with over 13,600 square kilometres of land; $225 million in cash compensation (to be paid over 20 years), exclusive hunting and trapping rights over 150,000 square kilometres of community lands, participation in an environmental and social protection regime, and an income security program for hunters and trappers. It also made provisions for the Cree and Inuit to establish new systems of local government on lands set aside for their use and to establish Aboriginal-controlled education and health authorities for the benefit of their peoples. Other terms of the agreement included a series of special measures related to policing and the administration of justice on Cree- and Inuit-owned lands, provisions for continuing federal and provincial benefits to Cree and Inuit people living in the settlement area, and the creation of special social and economic development strategies to help meet the long-term needs and aspiration of the Cree and Inuit peoples. In exchange for this final settlement package, the Cree and Inuit agreed to surrender, finally and forever, "all of their native claims, rights, titles and interests, whatever they may be."

Understanding the Federal Government's Comprehensive Claims Policy

In 1981 the federal government launched a review of the comprehensive claims policy it had initiated in 1973. This review resulted in the publication on 16 December 1981 of *In All Fairness: A Native Claims Policy, Comprehensive Claims*. This federal policy guide represents the first formal and public articulation of the overarching objectives and general operating principles of the federal government's comprehensive claims policy and thus serves as a useful vehicle for understanding this groundbreaking policy initiative. As it explains:

> When a land claim is accepted for negotiation, the government requires that the negotiation process and settlement formula be thorough so that the claim cannot arise again in the future. In other words, any land claims settlement will be final. The negotiations are designed to deal with non-political matters arising from the notion of aboriginal land rights such as land, cash compensation, wildlife rights, and may include self-government on a local basis. The thrust of this policy is to exchange undefined aboriginal land rights for concrete rights and benefits. The settlement legislation will guarantee these rights and benefits.[44]

In order to effect the full and final settlement of outstanding Aboriginal land claims, then, final settlement agreements were envisioned to include a comprehensive range of legislated rights, benefits, and other treaty entitlements, such as:

- full ownership of (i.e., fee simple title to) defined tracts of land;
- guaranteed wildlife harvesting rights in designated areas;
- guaranteed participation in land, water, wildlife, and environmental management initiatives;
- financial compensation (for lost lands and resources);
- resources revenue-sharing provisions;

- specific measures to stimulate economic and social development;
- defined roles in the management of heritage resources and parks; and
- local or municipal-styled administrative rights (where appropriate).[45]

Comprehensive claims negotiations begin once an Aboriginal group's formal Statement of Claim is favourably assessed by the federal Office of Native Claims as meeting the criteria of being based on continuing Aboriginal title to specific tracts of land and "sufficiently developed" to initiate "productive" negotiations geared towards achieving a final settlement. To pass the first hurdle, Aboriginal land claimants are required to establish that the Aboriginal title they claim meets the four-part test first outlined by the Federal Court (Trial Division) in *Hamlet of Baker Lake v. Minister of Indian Affairs and Northern Development* [1979] and subsequently adopted by the Supreme Court of Canada. This requires Aboriginal land claimants to prove:

1. that they were, and are, an "organized society";
2. that their traditional use and occupancy of the territories in question was sufficiently established at the time sovereignty was asserted by European nations to be considered a fact;
3. that their occupation of the territories in question was largely to the exclusion of other organized societies; and,
4. that they continue to use and occupy the territories in question for traditional purposes.[46]

It also requires Aboriginal land claimants to prove that no lawful act of government (i.e., the conclusion of a treaty) has effectively extinguished the title they claim. To pass the second hurdle, Aboriginal land claimants are required to establish that they are both willing and ready to participate in productive treaty negotiations. This requires proof of substantive community support for treaty negotiations, a demonstrated institutional capacity to proceed with treaty negotiations, and the identification of reasonable treaty goals.

In areas of exclusive federal jurisdiction (i.e., the Northwest Territories and the Yukon), the negotiation of comprehensive claims proceeds between the Aboriginal claimant groups and the federal government, with provisions for territorial governments' involvement in these negotiations. In areas where outstanding Aboriginal land claims are located within provincial, rather than territorial, boundaries, the negotiation of comprehensive claims settlements proceeds between the Aboriginal claimant groups, the federal government, and the relevant provincial government.

As explained in *In All Fairness*: "potential claimant groups requiring assistance in the preparation of a claim will be given straightforward indications of the many aspects of settlement that may need to be considered and upon which the government is prepared to concede."[47] Further provisions of the policy assert that "[c]laimant groups should have enough money to develop and negotiate their claims,"[48] with the qualification that spending restraints and limits on the federal government be "kept in mind" with respect to government-funded land claims research and negotiation. In practice, most federal government funding of comprehensive land claims activities is provided to Aboriginal land claimants in the form of government loans. These are interest free until an agreement-in-principle is initialled by all relevant parties and must be repaid after a final settlement agreement has been successfully concluded. If an Aboriginal group withdraws from comprehensive claims negotiations, its outstanding loans must be repaid immediately and with interest. It was hoped that the resulting final agreements, or modern treaties, would not only effect the resolution of outstanding Aboriginal land claims, but also facilitate the economic growth and self-sufficiency of Aboriginal land claimants in the future.

By 1981, however, only two comprehensive claims agreements had been concluded in Canada—the James Bay and Northern Quebec Agreement of 1975 discussed above, and the supplementary Northeastern Quebec Agreement of 1978, which amended the James Bay and Northern Quebec Agreement to integrate the Naskapi people of the same region. BC's continuing refusal to recognize and respect continuing Aboriginal right and title was a major stumbling block to the timely resolution of outstanding Aboriginal land claims in the immediate post-*Calder* era.

Understanding Post-Calder British Columbia

Contrary to popular opinion, the legal merits of Aboriginal title remained tenuous following the 1973 Supreme Court decision in *Calder*. Although six justices had confirmed Aboriginal title as a common law right in their written opinions on the case, the ultimate rejection of the Nisga'a Nation's appeal by a four-to-three majority meant that this landmark legal precedent was not binding on future courts. As a result, the BC government held fast to its historic denial of Aboriginal rights and title in the immediate post-*Calder* era and staunchly refused to participate in the federal government's comprehensive land claims policy. As a 10 January 1978 position paper on the issue explained, the position of the province continued to be that if any Aboriginal title or interest may once have existed, that title or interest had been extinguished prior to the union of BC with Canada in 1871.[49]

Not surprisingly, however, British Columbia's continuing refusal to recognize their long-outstanding Aboriginal land claim did not deter the Nisga'a Nation from taking advantage of the federal government's comprehensive claims policy.

The Long Road to the Nisga'a Treaty Continues

In 1974 the Nisga'a Nation submitted its outstanding Aboriginal land claim to the federal Office of Native Claims. Despite BC's refusal to participate in the comprehensive claims policy, the federal government accepted the Nisga'a Nation's Statement of Claim and began formal bilateral treaty negotiations on 12 January 1976. In 1989 these negotiations produced the Nisga'a Framework Agreement, which set out the scope of the substantive bilateral negotiations which would follow and the processes (including extensive public consultations and information campaigns) that would govern those negotiations. Soon, a series of important constitutional, political, and legal developments inspired by the 1973 *Calder* decision compelled a major shift in the province's policy course.

Constitutional Developments

After more than a decade of intense constitutional negotiations, the Constitution Act, 1982 was formally adopted. Originally intended to repatriate Canada's constitution and amend it to include an entrenched Charter of Rights and Freedoms, the negotiations leading up to the new constitution's enactment rapidly became an important vehicle for the recognition of Aboriginal rights.

Since Aboriginal peoples were not given a formal seat at the constitutional negotiating table, their demands for Aboriginal rights recognition were pursued through concerted lobbying campaigns and extensive public demonstrations. The most widely publicized of these was the Constitutional Express, "a train which left Vancouver in November 1980 and picked up more than a thousand people before arriving in Ottawa for a demonstration on Parliament Hill."[50] Aboriginal peoples also travelled to London, England, where they pounded drums outside the British Houses of Parliament to protest the repatriation of Canada's constitution without their participation or consent. When the Constitution Act, 1982 was finally concluded, Aboriginal peoples' determined lobbying efforts had gained them three important constitutional concessions.

First, to meet Aboriginal peoples' concerns that the individual rights bias of the Charter of Rights and Freedoms might be employed to deny or diminish the generally collective rights asserted by Aboriginal peoples, a new section 25 was adopted, which read:

> 25. The guarantee in the Charter of certain rights and freedoms shall not be construed so as to abrogate or derogate from any aboriginal, treaty or other rights of freedoms that pertain to the aboriginal peoples of Canada including
> *(a)* any rights or freedoms that have been recognized by the Royal Proclamation of October 7, 1763; and
> *(b)* any rights or freedoms that may be acquired by the aboriginal peoples of Canada by way of land claims settlements.

Second, to meet their demands for formal constitutional recognition of their unique rights as Canada's original inhabitants, section 35 was added:

> 35. (1) The existing aboriginal and treaty rights of the aboriginal peoples of Canada are hereby recognized and affirmed;
> (2) In this Act, "aboriginal peoples of Canada" includes the Indian, Inuit and Métis peoples of Canada.

And finally, a forward-looking section 37 committed the prime minister of Canada to convene a constitutional conference of first ministers on "matters that directly affect the aboriginal peoples of Canada, including the identification and definition of the rights of those peoples to be included in the Constitution of Canada" and to invite Aboriginal representatives "to participate in the discussions on that item."

This conference was convened in March 1983, the first time in Canadian history that Aboriginal leaders formally participated in constitutional debate. They presented two major proposals at this meeting: 1) that the word "existing" be removed from section 35(1); and 2) that Aboriginal self-government rights be formally recognized in Canada's constitution.

Although Prime Minister Trudeau was relatively supportive of these two proposals, a majority of provincial premiers (including BC's premier, Bill Vander Zalm) were not. Concerned about the practical implications of both a broader definition of "aboriginal and treaty rights" and the constitutional recognition of Aboriginal self-government rights, provincial premiers attempted to narrow the scope of formal discussions in the hopes of securing a limited constitutional definition of the phrase. As a result, the 1983 first minister's conference accomplished relatively little. Although section 35 was amended to specify that treaty rights included "rights that now exist by way of land claims agreements or may be so acquired" (new subsection 3) and that the "aboriginal and treaty rights" recognized and affirmed in section 35 "are guaranteed equally to male and female persons" (new subsection 4),[51] no substantive progress was made on the broader issue of Aboriginal self-government. Optimistic that progress could be made, however, Prime Minister Trudeau made provisions for additional first ministers' conferences to be held in the future and created a parliamentary task force to look into the subject.

Political Developments

In 1983, the federal government received the final report of its Task Force on Indian Self-Government (referred to as the Penner Report after its chairman, Keith Penner). As Allan McMillan explains:

> This all party committee [established in 1982] made several far-reaching recommendations. Particularly important was the call for the federal government to establish a new relationship with Indian First Nations, that an essential element of this relationship be recognition of Indian self-government, and that the right to self-government be entrenched in the Constitution.[52]

These recommendations were embraced by the Trudeau government who used them to advance the Aboriginal self-government agenda on the national stage. As Prime Minster Trudeau stated at the 1984 First Ministers Conference on Aboriginal Issues: "we are not here to consider whether there should be institutions of self-government but how these institutions should be brought into being."[53] The provincial premiers, however, were not similarly inspired by the Penner Report:

> At the following meetings, [held] in 1985 and 1987, the government of Prime Minister Brian Mulroney attempted to make the [self-government] proposal acceptable to the provincial premiers. In the end, however, the talks collapsed in rancour and squabbling between the federal government, the provinces and leaders of the four major national aboriginal organizations.

The federal proposal for recognition of an aboriginal right to self-government, without full definition of terms and costs, was unacceptable to the governments of British Columbia, Alberta, Saskatchewan and Newfoundland.[54]

Outside of the constitutional conference arena, however, Aboriginal self-government was already being recognized in political practice. In 1984 and 1986 respectively, the Cree-Naskapi (of Quebec) Act and the Sechelt Band Self-Government Act were passed by the federal legislature, creating municipal-styled local governments for the Cree, Naskapi, and Sechelt peoples and transferring powers previously exercised by the minister of Indian Affairs to them.[55]

At roughly the same time, ongoing federal consultations with Aboriginal peoples resulted in some significant amendments to the comprehensive claims policy. First, in December 1986, the federal government announced that it was prepared to recognize continuing Aboriginal rights and title following the conclusion of final settlement agreements provided, however, that such rights and title were not "inconsistent" with the terms of these agreements themselves (i.e., Aboriginal rights and title would be fully and finally defined in the terms of the final settlement agreements). At the same time, the federal government also announced that it was prepared to include "commitments to negotiate" *parallel* Aboriginal self-government agreements in the terms of modern treaty agreements (i.e., the "commitment to negotiate" an Aboriginal self-government agreement could be constitutionally protected as a formal treaty entitlement, but any actual self-government agreement would have to be achieved outside the modern treaty process and thus would be devoid of constitutional protection). And finally, in 1990, the federal government announced that it would no longer limit treaty negotiations to either one claim per province or six claims at any one time. These changes, the federal government hoped, would not only accelerate the resolution of outstanding Aboriginal land claims but also deter Aboriginal peoples' from continuing to pursue rights recognition and respect through the courts.

Legal Developments

Following the *Calder* decision of 1973 and the subsequent recognition of "existing aboriginal and treaty rights" in section 35(1) of the Constitution Act, 1982, the litigation of Aboriginal rights issues increased dramatically. With each new legal decision, the reality of continuing Aboriginal rights and title became more firmly entrenched and the character of continuing Aboriginal rights and title became more precisely defined. Although a full history of Aboriginal rights litigation in Canada is beyond the scope of this chapter, the following three case summaries provide a useful illustration of the significant legal developments that marked this period.

GUERIN V. THE QUEEN (1984)[56]

In 1955, at the instigation of federal officials, the Vancouver Musqueam band approved a conditional surrender (or surrender "in trust") of 162 acres of reserve land so that they could be leased to the Shaughnessy Heights Golf Club.[57] In 1970, however, the band discovered that the leasing transaction that had been described to it in detail by federal officials in 1955 was significantly different from the final leasing agreement concluded with the Shaughnessy Golf Club in 1958. In sum, federal officials (who had presumably been acting on behalf of the Musqueam band) had provided the golf club with a long-term, below market value leasing agreement that did not reflect Musqueam interests. As a result of this discovery, the Musqueam band filed suit against the federal government in 1975 for breach of trust.

In its 1984 judgment and reasoning on this case, the Supreme Court of Canada found it necessary to address the nature of Aboriginal title in order to determine whether or not the federal government had been required to act in the best interest of the Musqueam band when it negotiated the Shaughnessy Gold Club lease. This led them to confirm Aboriginal title as an existing common law right and to elaborate on its nature and scope. As explained by Chief Justice Brian Dickson:

> [The Indians'] interest in their lands is a pre-existing legal right not created by the Royal Proclamation, by ... the Indian Act, or by any other executive order or legislative provision. It does not matter ... that the present case is concerned with the interest of an Indian band in a reserve [rather] than with unrecognized title in traditional tribal lands. The Indian interest in the land is the same in both cases.

The Supreme Court then went on to opine that the general "inalienability" of Aboriginal title (i.e., the fact that Aboriginal title cannot be transferred, sold, or surrendered to anyone other than the Crown) made Aboriginal peoples vulnerable to federal discretionary decisions. As a result, it determined that the federal government had a fiduciary obligation to act in the best interests of Aboriginal peoples when dealing with their lands. Returning to the case at hand, the Supreme Court ruled that the federal government had clearly breached its fiduciary obligation to the Musqueam band when it "promised ... to lease the land in question on certain specified terms and then, after surrender, obtained a lease on different [and much less valuable] terms" and ordered it to pay $10 million in damages to the Musqueam band.

PACIFIC FISHERMEN'S DEFENCE ALLIANCE V. THE QUEEN (1987)[58]

As part of its opposition to the Nisga'a treaty negotiations, the Pacific Fisherman's Alliance (PFDA)[59] commenced a legal action against the federal government in the mid-1980s. The PFDA sought declarations from the court confirming that the federal government was constitutionally unable to reach a land claims agreement with the Nisga'a and that its membership was entitled to participate in the Nisga'a Treaty negotiations. It also applied for an injunction preventing the federal government from concluding a comprehensive claims agreement with the Nisga'a Tribal Council.

In rejecting the PFDA's case on 12 February 1987, Justice Dubé of the Federal Court (Trial Division) had this to say:

> In short, the plaintiffs cannot in principle oppose the settlement of aboriginal rights which are recognized by the courts and enshrined in the constitution. Obviously, settlement and negotiations are the better way to proceed and there is no room for all interested groups to be present.
>
> In these negotiations, only the national government can speak for all interested third parties. In British Columbia there are 26 tribes and only the Nisga'a aboriginal rights are being negotiated. Others are flooding the Courts. Because of their socio-economic and political nature, it is indeed much preferable to settle aboriginal rights by way of negotiations than through the Courts.[60]

This decision was quickly appealed by the PFDA, but "[i]n December 1987, the Federal Court of Appeal dismissed the action altogether on the basis that it disclosed no cause of action and that it was plain and obvious that the case could not possibly succeed."[61]

IV: The BC Treaty Process

The BC Treaty Process is a voluntary process involving the government of BC, the government of Canada, and BC First Nations. It is based on the principle that tripartite negotiations, rather than litigation, are the best means of determining the rights, jurisdictions, and responsibilities of all parties on issues such as land, resources, and self-government.

The BC Treaty Process encompasses six stages, which roughly correspond to the six stages of the federal government's comprehensive claims policy (of which the BC Treaty Process is a part):

1. Submission of Statement of Intent: a First Nation indicates that it wants to enter the treaty process.
2. Readiness to negotiate: the parties assemble negotiating teams and prepare for negotiation.
3. Negotiation of Framework Agreement: an agenda is negotiated which identifies what is to be negotiated in Stage 4 and outlines any special procedural arrangements.
4. Negotiation of Agreement-in-Principle: the parties reach the major agreements which will form the basis of a treaty.
5. Negotiation to finalize treaty: the parties formalize the agreements reached in the previous state and agree on a implementation plan.
6. Implementation of treaty: the parties work together to implement the treaty according to their agreed plan.

Once concluded, treaties negotiated under the auspices of the BC Treaty Process are protected under section 35 of the Constitution Act, 1982. This means final treaty settlements cannot be unilaterally amended or revoked.

Additional information on the BC Treaty Process and the BC Treaty Commission can be found at www.bctreaty.net.

R. V. SPARROW[62]

In the mid-1980s, Ronald Sparrow of the Musqueam Nation was caught fishing in the lower Fraser River with a driftnet that exceeded the length specification for "Aboriginal food fishing" as defined in the federal Fisheries Act. He was subsequently charged and convicted of violating the act. Sparrow appealed his conviction on the grounds that the federal regulations on net length were an unconstitutional infringement of his Aboriginal right to fish, a right recognized and protected by section 35(1) of the Constitution Act, 1982.

In its 1986 decision on the *Sparrow* case, the BC Court of Appeal found in favour of Sparrow. In its reasoning and judgment, "[t]he British Columbia Court of Appeal stated that, contrary to submissions made by the prov-

---

V: The BC Treaty Commission

The BC Treaty Commission (BCTC), comprising five appointed commissioners and 14 full-time staff, is the independent, neutral body responsible for facilitating modern treaty negotiations between the federal government, the provincial government, and First Nations in BC. The BCTC does not negotiate treaties itself—that is done by the three parties at each negotiating table—but oversees the treaty negotiation process to make sure the parties are being effective and making progress in negotiations.

The BCTC is responsible for accepting First Nations into the treaty process and for assessing when the parties are ready to start negotiations. It also develops policies and procedures applicable to the six-stage treaty process, monitors and reports on the progress of treaty negotiations, identifies problems, offers advice, and sometimes assists the parties in resolving disputes. The BCTC allocates support funding, primarily in the form of loans, to First Nations in the treaty process and also has a major role to play in public information and education on modern treaties and their negotiation.

Additional information on the BC Treaty Commission is available at www. bctreaty.net.

---

ince of British Columbia, it was bound by the Supreme Court of Canada's decision in the *Calder* case to find that there is an existing aboriginal right to fish held by the Musqueam Indians (and by implication by other Indian nations in British Columbia). Moreover, the Court agreed that the aboriginal right to fish is protected by s. 35(1) of the Constitution Act, 1982."[63]

The BC government appealed this decision, but in 1990 the Supreme Court of Canada upheld the lower court decision and found in favour of Sparrow. Ruling that any government regulations that infringed on the exercise of an Aboriginal right must be constitutionally justified, the Supreme Court directed that fishery regulations must provide for a "priority allocation" to the Aboriginal fishery to be constitutionally valid.

The Dawning of a New Policy Era in BC

By the late 1980s, the costs of BC's refusal to participate in modern treaty negotiations were beginning to tell. Resource development projects were being stalled pending court decisions on Aboriginal rights and title, economic activity was being frustrated by the direct action campaigns of Aboriginal land claimants, and new investment in the province was being lost due to the uncertain ownership of both lands and resources.[64] In fact, a 1990 Price Waterhouse study estimated that unresolved land claims in BC were costing "15,000 jobs a year and $1 billion in lost investment in mining and forestry alone."[65] Once supportive of the government's denial of Aboriginal rights, public opinion was beginning to turn. As a result, the provincial government was compelled to take action.

In August 1990, Premier Vander Zalm finally announced that his government would join Aboriginal peoples and the government of Canada in modern treaty negotiations. To facilitate the initiation of such negotiations, a tripartite task force on the future of treaty negotiations in BC was established. Reporting in the summer of 1991, it recommended that the provincial government establish a six-stage treaty process (see Inset IV) to parallel the federal government's comprehensive claims process and create an impartial treaty commission (see Inset V) to oversee the process at the provincial level. These and 17 other recommendations were subsequently accepted by the provincial government, the federal government, and the First Nations Summit (an Aboriginal representative organization).[66] On 15 December 1993 the newly appointed BC Treaty Commission began receiving Statements of Intent from Aboriginal land claimants.

Concluding the Nisga'a Treaty

In October 1990, the BC government formally entered into treaty negotiations with the Nisga'a Nation and the federal government. Because treaty negotiations with the Nisga'a Nation had been ongoing since 1976, however, it was determined that they should proceed outside of the BC Treaty Process. This meant that the Nisga'a Nation would not have to represent a Statement of Intent to the BC Treaty Commission and that provincial negotiators already involved in treaty negotiations with the Nisga'a Nation would not have to follow any negotiation or settlement guidelines that might subsequently be established by the Treaty Commission. As a result, the original bipartite Framework Agreement concluded between the Nisga'a Nation and the federal government in 1989 was replaced with a new tripartite agreement in 1991, and substantive tripartite treaty negotiations began in earnest.

Five years later, on 12 February 1996, negotiators representing the Nisga'a Tribal Council, the government of Canada, and the BC government announced that they had concluded an Agreement-in-Principle (AIP) on the full range of topics to be included in the terms of the Nisga'a Final Agreement. The Nisga'a Nation voted to proceed on the basis of the AIP on 25 February 1996, and on 22 March 1996 the Nisga'a AIP was formally adopted by all parties at a signing ceremony in New Aiyansh (the capital city of the Nisga'a Nation).

The Political Recognition of Aboriginal Peoples' Inherent Right of Self-Government

It is important, at this point, to make note of an important policy development that preceded the conclusion of the Nisga'a AIP and significantly influenced both its content and the harsh criticisms that it would soon attract: the political recognition of Aboriginal peoples' inherent right of self-government. This was first articulated formally in the 1992 Charlottetown Accord which, among many other things, proposed amending the Constitution Act, 1982 to recognize and affirm Aboriginal peoples' inherent right of self-government and recognize and affirm Aboriginal governments as one of three orders of government in Canada.[67] Although the Charlottetown Accord was ultimately defeated in a national referendum held on 26 October 1992, surveys conducted immediately afterwards "indicated that some 60 per cent of Canadians supported the constitutional changes that had been proposed to deal with Aboriginal issues. Moreover, half of those questioned, notwithstanding the failure of the accord, were in favour of the government giving a high priority to Aboriginal self-government."[68] As a result, the Aboriginal self-government issue remained a firmly entrenched agenda item for Canadian governments.

In the October 1993 federal election, the Liberal Party of Canada won a majority of seats in the federal legislature and quickly began implementing the agenda it had set for itself in the election manifesto *Creating Opportunity: The Liberal Plan for Canada*, better known as the Liberal Red Book. This agenda, among many other things, committed the Liberal government to "act on the premise that the inherent right of self-government is an existing Aboriginal and treaty right."[69]

Rather than attempting to define Aboriginal self-government in abstract terms, the government announced in May 1994 that it would prefer to negotiate practical and workable Aboriginal self-government agreements "through processes at the provincial, treaty, or regional level."[70] One year later (August 1995), after conducting extensive consultations with Aboriginal leaders, provincial/territorial governments, and interested third parties, the government released a groundbreaking federal policy guide entitled *The Government of Canada's Approach to Implementation of the Inherent Right and the Negotiation of Aboriginal Self-Government*. It identified five foundational principles as the cornerstones of the federal government's new Aboriginal self-government policy:

1. Aboriginal Peoples have the right to govern themselves, to decide on matters that affect their communities, and to exercise the responsibility that

is required to achieve true self-government. As a result, direct law-making control over such vital fields as health care, child welfare, education, housing, and economic development is open to negotiation.

2. The right to self-government is inherent as an existing Aboriginal right under subsection 35(1) of the Constitution. Although the federal government believes that this right is currently enforceable through the courts it has a strong preference for having the content and parameters of this right resolved through negotiated agreements rather than through litigation.

3. Aboriginal governments will not all be the same. They will naturally possess varying degrees of authority in areas of federal and provincial jurisdiction, reflecting the presence of separate negotiations and the impact of differing local circumstances and community objectives. The federal view is that self-government agreements, once negotiated, will acknowledge that Aboriginal peoples have the right to decide matters "internal to their communities, integral to their unique cultures, identities, traditions, languages and institutions, and with respect to their special relationship to their lands and resources."

4. The costs of Aboriginal self-government will be shared among federal, provincial, territorial, and Aboriginal governments and institutions. Special financial transfer agreements will need to be negotiated between the governments and Aboriginal groups concerned, similar in nature to the financial transfers that are now provided by the federal government to all provinces and territories.

5. The self-government process should be triggered by the Aboriginal peoples; that is, it will be up to Aboriginal peoples to commence self-government negotiations with Canadian governments.[71]

Because the federal government's new policy allowed existing comprehensive claims negotiations to be used as a vehicle for concluding Aboriginal self-government agreements (when all parties agree), the Nisga'a Nation was able to bring the Aboriginal self-government issue into the purview of its ongoing treaty negotiations. As a result, the 1996 Nisga'a AIP included provisions for the creation of a central Nisga'a "Lisims" government and four Nisga'a village governments, the law-making authority of which were to be detailed in the terms of the Nisga'a Final Agreement itself. Furthermore, because section 35(3) of the Constitution Act, 1982 defines constitutionally protected treaty rights as including "rights that now exist by way of land claims agreements or may be so acquired," these self-government arrangements were to become constitutionally protected upon the successful conclusion of the Nisga'a Final Agreement.[72]

Concluding the Nisga'a Final Agreement

Between 1996 and 1998, negotiations to draft the Nisga'a Final Agreement were undertaken on the basis of provisions detailed in the AIP. These negotiations concluded on 15 July 1998, and on 4 August negotiators representing the three parties gave their consent to the Nisga'a Final Agreement at an initialling ceremony in New Aiyansh. Before being implemented, however, the Nisga'a Treaty had to be formally ratified by all three principal actors. This required a positive referendum result for the Nisga'a Nation and formal legislative approval for Canada and BC.[73]

On 6 and 7 November 1998, the Nisga'a Nation held their required referendum. In the final tally, 1,451 (61 per cent) of eligible Nisga'a voters approved of the Final Agreement and 558 (23 per cent) did not (with 356 eligible Nisga'a voters, or 15 per cent, not taking part). "Among Nisga'a opponents of the Final Agreement, the primary concern appeared to be that too much territory had been conceded, as Nisga'a negotiators settled for a fraction [less than 10 per cent] of the traditional lands initially claimed."[74] In the end, however, the minimum approval requirement of 50 per cent plus one of eligible voters was exceeded, and representatives of the Nisga'a Nation formally ratified the terms of the Nisga'a Final Agreement on 9 November 1998.

Three weeks later, on 30 November 1998, Nisga'a tribal elders paddled a red cedar canoe into Victoria's inner harbour and climbed the steps of the BC Legislature. "We know that 111 years ago the Nisga'a tried to negotiate treaties and visited parliament and the door was closed," said BC Aboriginal Affairs Minister, Dale Lovick, to a crowd of several hundred spectators, "But today the doors will be open."[75] Following a brief ceremony commemorating the Nisga'a Nation's long journey toward rights recognition and respect, some 100 Nisga'a citizens filled the public galleries to watch history being made as Bill 51—the Nisga'a Final Agreement Act (BC)—was formally tabled by the BC government.

Following a detailed study of the act in the committee of the whole and the longest legislative debate in BC's history (120 hours over 30 long days), the Legislative Assembly finally voted in favour of the landmark treaty on 22 April 1999—39 "yeas" to 32 "nays."[76] What should have been an historic day, however, was overshadowed by a government motion of closure that cut short the clause-by-clause legislative debate of the bill and gave it third reading in a single day. According to Premier Glen Clark, further debate would have been pointless given that the BC Liberals were unalterably opposed to the bill: "They're filibustering this because they are opposed to the Nisga'a treaty, everybody knows that. We're not going to have the legislature held hostage to those kinds of tactics, we're going to pass it." For BC Liberal Leader Gordon Campbell, however, although "it was wrong for the provincial government to slam the door on the Nisga'a when they came to Victoria [in 1887] seeking justice, ... it [was] just as wrong to slam the door on the people of BC before the debate [was] complete."[77] Although many key issues had been exhaustively debated over the preceding 30 days, the BC Liberals claimed that they had only completed two-thirds of their questions by 22 April and were, in fact, in need of at least six more weeks to finish their work.[78] As a frustrated Campbell told the media on 22 April, "This is the largest single piece of legislation we have ever had before us in the province of British Columbia. This is the first treaty that has been brought forward [and] it is going to be a template for future treaties. Surely we should know exactly what is taking place before this is imposed and pushed on the people of British Columbia." According to Aboriginal Affairs Minister Gordon Wilson, however, "In the early stages of debate, virtually all of the substantive, philosophical issues with respect to self-government, fiscal arrangements, and land questions ... were quite thoroughly canvassed."[79] As a sort of consolation, Mr. Wilson reminded the BC Liberals that issues not discussed in the BC legislature could still be debated in Ottawa: "I'm sure the federal Reform party, who have members from British Columbia, are going to be there to make sure whatever the Liberals didn't ask here will be asked there."[80]

On 21 October 1999, Bill C-9—the Nisga'a Final Agreement Act (CA)—was introduced in the Canadian House of Commons, and the federal Reform Party picked up where the BC Liberal Party was forced to leave off. Critical of almost every aspect of the Nisga'a Final Agreement, the Reform Party aired its concerns both formally, during House of Commons debates and parliamentary committee hearings, and informally, during daily media scrums. Its most creative attack, however, came on 8 December 1999 when it tabled a staggering 471 amendments to the proposed legislation. What followed was a voting marathon lasting 42 hours and 34 minutes that cost Canadian taxpayers more than $1 million in overtime pay for Commons clerks, guards, and translators.[81] In the end, all 471 Reform amendments were decisively defeated by the Liberal, NDP, and Bloc Québécois MPs whose frustration level grew with every passing hour of voting. "Have you read the front page of the *National Post*?" a Liberal MP yelled at a Reform counterpart after some 30 hours of voting; "It says you're stupid."[82] Typical Reform amendments included changing the word "Canadians" to "all Canadians," replacing the word "significant" with "meaningful," changing commas to semi-colons, and changing semi-colons to periods. Rejecting complaints about his party's so-called shenanigans, Reform leader Preston Manning asserted, "We do not accept the argument that this somehow tied up the business of the House. This is the business of the House. If dealing with a bill like this is not the business of the House of Commons, I don't know what is."[83] In the end, however, Chief Joseph Gosnell gloated over the defeat of the Reform's proposed amendments: "Let me just repeat the score here: Nisga'a, 471, Reform, zero. That makes me feel good."[84] The Reform Party's filibuster finally over, federal MPs voted 217 to 48 in favour of the Nisga'a Final Agreement Act (CA) on 13 December 1999, and the proposed legislation was introduced in the Senate the following day.[85]

After a lengthy round of Senate committee hearings (16 February to 28 March), extensive third-reading debates (30 March to 13 April), a motion forcing an end to debate, and the defeat of two amendments—one that would have permitted the federal government to unilaterally alter the Nisga'a Final Agreement in the future and a second that would have suspended approval of Bill C-9 until the Supreme Court of Canada could rule on the constitutionality of its self-government provisions—the Nisga'a Final Agreement Act was finally approved by a Senate vote of 52 to 15 (with 13 abstentions) on 13 April 2000. That same evening, Adrienne Clarkson, Governor General of Canada, gave it royal assent, completing the year-and-a-half ratification process and marking the end of the Nisga'a Nation's 113-year journey towards rights recognition and respect.

On this momentous occasion, an emotional Chief Joseph Gosnell proclaimed the significance of BC's first modern treaty agreement:

> The Royal Assent of our treaty signifies the end of the colonial era for the Nisga'a People. It is a great and historic day for all Canadians, and this achievement is a beacon of hope for colonized people in our own country and throughout the world. Today, the Nisga'a people became full-fledged Canadians ... Finally, after a struggle of more than 130 years, the government of this country clearly recognizes that the Nisga'a were a self-governing people since well before European contact. We remain self-governing today, and we are proud to say that this inherent right is now clearly recognized and protected in the Constitution of Canada ... The dreams of our ancestors are made real today.[86]

Discussion

Modern treaty-making offers the possibility of a comprehensive, honourable, and durable resolution of the Aboriginal land question. The challenge, however, is to find a way to reconcile historic injustices with contemporary realities. Canadian courts have offered some guidance on this issue by affirming that:

- Aboriginal rights are judicially enforceable rights;
- Aboriginal rights include Aboriginal title, which is a unique communally held property right;
- Aboriginal rights are distinct and different from the rights of other Canadians (i.e., they derive from Aboriginal peoples' use and occupancy of their traditional territories prior to the assertion of sovereignty by the Crown);
- Aboriginal rights take priority over the rights of others, subject only to the needs of conservation;
- Aboriginal rights are capable of evolving over time and must be interpreted in a generous and liberal manner; and,
- Aboriginal rights cannot be extinguished by legislative acts of government because they are protected by the Constitution Act, 1982.

Without a treaty, however, there is uncertainty about how and where those rights apply. To resolve this situation, Canadian governments and Aboriginal peoples have two options:

1. they can negotiate land, resource, governance, and jurisdiction issues through a modern treaty process; or
2. they can go to court and have Aboriginal rights and title decided on a case-by-case, right-by-right basis.

Heralded by many as proof that the first (negotiation) option can facilitate an equitable resolution of the Aboriginal land question, the Nisga'a Treaty has also been the subject of substantial criticism both within and outside the Aboriginal community. Central to this criticism are the issues of cost, constitutionality, overlapping claims, and process.

The Cost Issue

According to the federal Department of Indian Affairs, "[t]he total estimated one time cost of the [Nisga'a] Final Agreement to Canada and

British Columbia is $487.1 million, including capital transfers, estimates of land values and lost forestry revenues, and implementation."[87] In addition to these one-time costs a series of ongoing costs are also attached to the Nisga'a Treaty. These include:

- $15 million over five years to facilitate implementation of the Nisga'a Final Agreement;
- $15 million over five years to upgrade physical infrastructure in Nisga'a communities;
- $10.6 million to fund certain activities necessary to implement the Nisga'a Final Agreement (conducting fisheries studies, implementing forestry transition training programs, creating Nisga'a eligibility and enrolment processes, and facilitating the preparation of Nisga'a laws, etc.); and,
- $327 million (in the first five years) to support the Nisga'a government's provision of agreed-upon programs and services in the areas of health, social development, education, local services, land and resource management, and capital infrastructure (with additional funding of these programs to be negotiated every five years thereafter).[88]

With more than 100 outstanding Aboriginal land claims currently lodged with the federal Office of Native Claims (44 in BC alone), many Canadians have been led to question the economic viability of settling outstanding Aboriginal land claims through modern treaty agreements.

According to a 1999 report commissioned by the BC government, however, the economic impact of the Nisga'a Treaty and other modern treaty settlements is not nearly as devastating as many Canadians have been led to believe:

> The benefits accruing to the Nisga'a Nation resulting from these transfers will likely include greater self-reliance and increased employment, together with positive economic effects. Applied to British Columbia as a whole, this greater self-reliance and increased employment is expected to improve economic conditions for First Nations. Reduced uncertainty from obtaining treaty settlements may improve the investment climate, although many factors apart from unsettled treaties affect investment. Also following treaty settlements there may be opportunities for governments to achieve savings in program expenditures.

Taking into account the Nisga'a experience, once completed, the total financial benefit of all treaty settlements to British Columbia's First Nations is estimated at between $6.3 and $6.8 billion. After British Columbia's share of the costs, including cash, pre-treaty and negotiation costs, as well as BC taxpayer's share of federal costs, the net financial benefit to British Columbia as a whole is estimated to be between $3.8 billion and $4.7 billion.[89]

In sum, although modern treaties are certainly expensive, they do hold the potential for economic spin-offs both within and outside the Aboriginal community. When this fact is juxtaposed with the high costs and uncertain outcomes of litigated land claims settlements (which, it must be remembered, can include imposed land and resource transfers as well as cash compensation), the economic viability of modern treaties is cast in a much more favourable light.

The Constitutional Issue

Another major attack concerns the Final Agreement's unprecedented Aboriginal self-government provisions, which have been the subject of at least two major court challenges. The first was launched on 17 October 1998 by a group of plaintiffs with interests in the BC fisheries,[90] and the second was launched two days later by Gordon Campbell, leader of the BC Liberal Party.

The first action alleged that the Nisga'a Final Agreement was unconstitutional because it purported to establish a distinct "third level" of government, failed to ensure that the Nisga'a government was sufficiently "responsible," and established a commercial fishery based on "race." The second action made similar allegations and asked the court for a declaration confirming that:

1. the Nisga'a Final Agreement was unconstitutional because it would establish a Nisga'a government with authority to make laws which, in certain areas, would prevail over federal and provincial laws to the extent of any inconsistency or conflict;
2. the Nisga'a Final Agreement would constitute an unauthorized and unconstitutional derogation of the powers and authority of the BC Legislative Assembly and of the federal Parliament; and,

3. The Nisga'a Final Agreement would breach the Charter guarantee of democratic rights by denying non-Nisga'a citizens any right to vote for, or participate as members in, the Nisga'a Lisims government.[91]

On 5 February 1999, a BC Supreme Court judge concluded that these two cases ought not to proceed until legislation ratifying the Nisga'a Final Agreement had been formally adopted by both the provincial and federal legislatures. Although the BC fisheries group subsequently dropped its case, Campbell re-presented his case to the BC Supreme Court just days after the Nisga'a Final Agreement received royal assent. On 24 July 2000, however, Justice Paul Williamson upheld the Nisga'a Final Agreement on the grounds that:

> Section 35(1) [of the Constitution Act, 1982] ... provides the solid constitutional framework within which aboriginal rights in British Columbia may be defined by the negotiation of treaties in a manner compatible with the sovereignty of the Canadian state. I conclude that what Canada, British Columbia, the Nisga'a have achieved in the Nisga'a Final Agreement is consistent both with what the Supreme Court of Canada has encouraged, and consistent with the purpose of s. 35 of the Constitution Act, 1982.[92]

An anticipated appeal of this decision to the Supreme Court of Canada was dropped by Campbell when his party, after winning 77 of 79 seats in the May 2001 provincial election, resolved to hold a province-wide referendum on the future of treaty negotiations in BC (see Insert VI).

The Overlap Issue

A third line of criticism comes from within the Aboriginal community itself and involves the issue of overlapping Aboriginal title claims. According to the neighbouring Gitanyow Nation, more than 80 per cent of their traditional territory sits within the Nisga'a wildlife management area mapped out in the Nisga'a Final Agreement. In March 1998, this Nation asked the BC Supreme Court for declarations confirming:

1. that in undertaking to negotiate a treaty with the Gitanyow under the BC treaty process, and in proceeding with those treaty negotiations,

the federal and provincial Crowns are obliged to negotiate in good faith and to make every reasonable effort to conclude and sign a treaty with the Gitanyow; and,

2. that for the federal and provincial Crowns to conclude a treaty with the Nisga'a "or to allow designation for any purpose related to the Nisga'a Treaty over lands and resources in respect of which Gitanyow, Canada and British Columbia are involved in a treaty process until treaty negotiations with the Gitanyow are concluded" would be contrary to the Crown's duty to negotiate in good faith, significantly undermine the Gitanyow claim to "overlapping" territory in the Nass Valley and nullify the Gitanyow treaty process.[93]

In November 1998, Justice Williamson ruled that the Gitanyow case could proceed on the first issue but that proceedings on the second issue would have to wait until a ruling on the first was delivered. On 23 March 1999, he declared in his ruling on the first issue "that while the federal and provincial Crowns were not under an obligation to enter into treaty negotiations with the Gitanyow, having done so their fiduciary obligations toward Aboriginal peoples resulted in 'a duty to negotiate in good faith' that was binding on all Crowns."[94]

In April 1999, Canada and BC appealed this ruling on the grounds that subjecting the treaty process to court supervision could turn negotiations into an avenue for litigation.[95] The entire Gitanyow case was subsequently placed in abeyance, however, when an agreement was reached in early July 1999 to resume active Gitanyow treaty negotiations on an accelerated basis.

At least two other Aboriginal Nations, the Gitxsan and the Tahltan, also claim that their territories overlap with those of the Nisga'a Nation. According to these, and other Aboriginal nations in Canada, neither the federal government's comprehensive claims policy nor the BC Treaty Process respects the fact that multiple Aboriginal Nations frequently controlled use and access within overlapping sovereign territories. According to many non-Aboriginal peoples, however, on-going disputes related to the scope and extent of traditional Aboriginal territories only serves to reinforce the notion that outstanding Aboriginal land claims are little more than historical relics of a pre-colonial age incapable of modern remedy.

The Process Issue

Since its genesis in 1973, the modern treaty process which produced the landmark Nisga'a Treaty has been criticized by virtually all Aboriginal peo-

VII: The 2002 BC Referendum

Since Canada began negotiating the settlement of outstanding Aboriginal land claims through modern treaty processes only 16 settlements have been achieved. This fact has led to serious concerns among Aboriginal peoples that the modern treaty process is designed to do little more than pay lip service to judicially enforceable Aboriginal rights and title while postponing (if not stonewalling) their practical recognition and respect.

These concerns are particularly prominent in BC where a controversial province-wide referendum was conducted between 2 April and 15 May 2002. The mail-in referendum ballot contained an opening question and eight separate statements to which voters were required to indicate whether they agreed or disagreed by marking either the "yes" or "no" box beside each statement. Criticized by Aboriginal and non-Aboriginal people alike for subjecting minority rights to majority approval, each referendum question subsequently was approved by a margin of between 84 per cent to 94 per cent. Although only 35 per cent of registered voters returned unspoiled referendum ballots, the BC government now maintains that the following eight principles will be upheld in all modern treaty negotiations in the province:

1. Private property should not be expropriated for treaty settlements.
2. The terms and conditions of leases and licences should be respected; fair compensation for unavoidable disruption of commercial interest should be ensured.
3. Hunting, fishing, and recreational opportunities on Crown land should be ensured for all British Columbians.
4. Parks and protected areas should be maintained for the use and benefit of all British Columbians.
5. Province-wide standards of resource management and environmental protection should continue to apply.
6. Aboriginal self-government should have the characteristics of local government, with powers delegated from Canada and BC.
7. Treaties should include mechanisms for harmonizing land use planning between Aboriginal governments and neighbouring local governments.
8. The existing tax exemptions for Aboriginal people should be phased out.[96]

In response, numerous Aboriginal peoples have threatened to return to the courts and force what they are certain will be a more equitable resolution of their outstanding land claims than they can hope to achieve by remaining parties to the BC Treaty Process. In sum, it appears as though the final word in the long history of Aboriginal land claims policy in Canada has yet to be written.

ples in Canada. Central to this criticism is the issue of blanket extinguishment. According to the federal government's 1973 comprehensive claims policy, the resolution of outstanding Aboriginal land claims required the cession, surrender, and release (i.e., extinguishment) of all present *and* future Aboriginal title and Aboriginal rights claims in exchange for "ordinary" common law title to land in settlement areas and "legislated" treaty benefits. In other words, the 1973 comprehensive claims policy gave political recognition to judicially enforceable Aboriginal title and Aboriginal rights only to precipitate their legal extinguishment upon the conclusion of a land claim settlement agreement. This aspect of the policy was completely unacceptable to large numbers of Aboriginal peoples who balked at the idea that the legal rights they had held since time immemorial could be negotiated out of existence to satisfy the self-serving interests of Canadian governments and/or non-Aboriginal people.

Although the federal government's comprehensive claims policy was slightly amended in 1986 to allow for the retention of Aboriginal rights on lands which Aboriginal peoples hold following the conclusion of land claims settlements, these rights are only available in delineated settlement areas and only to the extent that they are not inconsistent with the terms of the settlement agreements themselves. According to Aboriginal peoples, however, this modified rights approach effects little real change to the modern treaty process. Rather than relying on the judicial recognition and confirmation of their legal rights to lands and resources, Aboriginal peoples must still accept that Canadian governments will only respect their legal rights once these are fully and finally limited to the terms of a legislated treaty agreement.

Aboriginal peoples also argue that the modern treaty negotiation process established by Canadian governments denies Aboriginal land claimants equal bargaining status and places Canadian governments in a clear conflict of interest. In sum, although Canadian governments are parties to all modern treaty negotiations, the terms of the comprehensive claims policy (and the terms of parallel provincial policies) afford them unimpeded unilateral control over:

1. the assessment of outstanding aboriginal land claims;
2. the allocation of treaty research and negotiation funding (both for themselves and for Aboriginal land claimants);
3. the range of issues open to discussion and negotiation; and,
4. the final outcome of negotiations (since no final agreement can be concluded without express federal and provincial consent).

VIII: Comprehensive Claims Settlements, 1973-2003

As of January 2004, 16 comprehensive claims settlements, or modern treaties, had been concluded in Canada. These are:

- The James Bay and Northern Quebec Agreement (1975)
- The Northeastern Quebec Agreement (1978)
- The Inuvialuit Final Agreement (1984)
- The Gwich'in Agreement (1993)
- The Nunavut Land Claims Agreement (1993)
- The Sahtu Dene and Métis Agreement (1994);
- The Nisga'a Agreement (2000)
- The Tli Cho Agreement (2003)
- Eight Yukon First Nations Final Agreements based on the Council for Yukon Indians Umbrella Final Agreement (1993). These involve:
- The Vuntut Gwich'in First Nation (1995)
- The First Nation of Nacho Nyak Dun (1995)
- The Teslin Tlingit Council (1995)
- The Champagne and Aishihik First Nation (1995)
- The Little Salmon/Carmacks First Nation (1997)
- The Selkirk First Nation (1997)
- The Tr'ondëk Hwëch'in First Nation (1998)
- The Ta'an Kwach'an Council (2002)

Only the James Bay and Northern Quebec Agreement (1975), the Northeastern Quebec Agreement (1978), and the Nisga'a Agreement (2000) have been negotiated with provincial governments. All other agreements were negotiated with the federal government, owing to the fact that the land claims in question fell within federally administered territories (i.e., the Northwest Territories and the Yukon Territory).

Without an impartial and authoritative treaty mediator, it is argued, Aboriginal land claimants really have no means of pursuing fair and equitable settlements of their outstanding land claims within the parameters of the existing modern treaty process.

A further objection is that it forces Aboriginal land claimants to abandon their sovereign status as distinct nations with inherent rights to self-government in order to secure a limited degree of legislated governing authority defined in modern treaty settlements. Although the federal government formally recognized Aboriginal peoples' inherent right to self-government in the early 1990s and claims to respect this right in current modern treaty negotiations, the fact remains that Aboriginal self-government is considered a topic for negotiation by Canadian governments and not a legal right. Canadian governments require that the nature and scope of Aboriginal governments be definitively defined by, and limited to, the terms of the final settlement agreements.

In sum, although the modern treaty process represents a notable improvement on the previous administration of outstanding Aboriginal land claims by Canadian governments, it is still considered a grossly colonial-minded policy by many Aboriginal peoples. These sentiments have been particularly strong in the wake of the Supreme Court of Canada's 1997 decision in *Delgamuukw v. British Columbia*,[97] a decision which offered the most comprehensive statement to date on the nature and content of Aboriginal peoples' unique rights to land.

Delgamuukw v. British Columbia [1997]

The *Delgamuukw* case was initiated in 1984 by the Gitksan and Wet'suwet'en Peoples in an attempt to secure judicial confirmation of their continuing rights and title to over 58,000 square kilometres of land in northwestern BC. Although the Supreme Court ultimately determined that errors made in the findings of fact by lower court justices "were so fundamental as to be beyond the scope of an appeal court to repair"[98] and declared a mistrial, it proceeded to define the exact content of Aboriginal title that the law would legitimate. According to Chief Justice Lamer this was both warranted and necessary given that "all of the parties [in this case] have characterized the content of aboriginal title incorrectly."

Although the Supreme Court's characterization of *sui generis* Aboriginal title in the *Delgamuukw* case is riddled with legal complexities, its general contours can be summarized as follows:[99]

1. *Source*: Aboriginal title owes it origins to the occupation by Aboriginal peoples of their territories prior to the assertion of Crown sovereignty (primary source), Aboriginal peoples' pre-existing legal systems, and recognition (not creation) of Aboriginal title by the *Royal Proclamation of 1763*.

2. *Nature*: Aboriginal title is a right to the land itself (not a "personal and usufructory" right); it is a communally held right; it is inalienable except to the Crown; it is a burden on the Crown's underlying title to all lands within her sovereign jurisdiction; and it is protected by section 35(1) of the Constitution Act, 1982.

3. *Content*: Aboriginal title confers a right of exclusive use and occupancy and a choice of land uses (not restricted to pre-contact practices

but not irreconcilable with the continued use and enjoyment of Aboriginal title); Aboriginal title includes mineral rights.

4. *Proof:* To prove continuing Aboriginal title, Aboriginal land claimants must establish that they occupied the lands in question at the time sovereignty was asserted by the Crown; demonstrate some degree of continuity between present and pre-sovereignty occupation (although a broken chain of continuity and/or a change in the nature of occupation will not normally preclude an Aboriginal title claim); prove exclusive occupation at the time sovereignty was asserted (although joint title can arise from shared exclusivity); and identify, with some precision, the specific area which has been continuously used and occupied since the declaration of sovereignty.

Aboriginal title demands a unique approach to the treatment of evidence, and, therefore, Aboriginal perspectives (including oral history) must be accorded due weight in the assessment of Aboriginal title claims.

5. *Extinguishment:* Prior to 1982, Aboriginal title could be extinguished by either voluntary surrender to the Crown or ordinary legislation evincing a "clear and plain" intention to extinguish aboriginal title.

According to the Constitution Act, 1982, Aboriginal title can now only be extinguished by voluntary surrender.

6. *Jurisdiction to Extinguish:* Section 91(24) of the BNA Act, 1867 (now section 91(24) of the Constitution Act, 1982) gives the federal government the exclusive right to extinguish Aboriginal title.

7. *Right to Consultation/Consent:* Aboriginal title holders' right to choose land uses leads to a right of consultation in good faith and possibly to a right of involvement and/or consent when decisions taken by governments infringe on Aboriginal title.

8. *Right to Compensation:* Compensation *may* be required when Aboriginal title is extinguished (both pre- and post-1982). Fair compensation will ordinarily be required when Aboriginal title is infringed (post-1982). The amount of compensation payable will vary in accordance with the nature of the particular Aboriginal title affected, the nature and severity of the infringement, and the extent to which Aboriginal interests were accommodated.

Although the Supreme Court ultimately concluded that the Gitksan and Wet'suwet'en were entitled to a new trial of their case, it also reiterated the recommendation made by almost every Supreme Court panel to hear an Aboriginal land claims case since 1973: disputes concerning the title, rights, and jurisdiction of Aboriginal peoples, non-Aboriginal peoples, and Canadian governments are best settled through negotiation rather than through litigation. Given Aboriginal peoples' dissatisfaction with the modern treaty process (described above) and the fact that this process has only produced 11 final settlement agreements since it was inaugurated in 1973, however, litigation is likely to continue to be an increasingly favourable option for Aboriginal peoples in the post-*Delgamuukw* era.

Chronology

1701-1799: "Peace and Friendship" Treaties.

7 OCT 1763: *Royal Proclamation of 1763.*

1763-1849: "Pre-Confederation"/ "Lettered" treaties.

1850-1854: "Douglas" Treaties.

LATE 1860S: BC denies the existence of Aboriginal rights.

1867: Confederation.

1867-1923: "Post-Confederation"/ "Numbered" Treaties.

1871: BC joins Confederation.

1876: The first Indian Act is adopted by the federal government.

1885: The Nisga'a Nation resists surveyors' incursions into their traditional territories and begins an organized pursuit of their land claim.

1887: Nisga'a chiefs travel to Victoria, BC; they demand rights recognition and a treaty settlement but Premier William Smithe refuses their requests.

1890: The Nisga'a Nation establishes its first formal land claims organization, the Nisga'a Land Committee.

1909: A delegation representing 20 Aboriginal Nations (including the Nisga'a Nation) travels to London, England to make a presentation to the Crown on the Land Question in British Columbia.

21 MAY 1913: The Nisga'a Land Committee submits a land claims petition to the JCPC; the petition is referred back to Canada for domestic resolution.

1914: The federal government offers to sponsor the Nisga'a Nation's petition in court but only if the Nisga'a consent to two non-negotiable conditions; the Nisga'a refuse.

1919: The Allied Tribes of British Columbia presents the governments of Canada and BC with a comprehensive enumeration of all outstanding aboriginal land claims in BC.

1925: The Allied Tribes of British Columbia dispatches a second petition to Ottawa demanding that a federal inquiry be held on the nature and extent of Aboriginal rights to land and the legality of BC's refusal to recognize those rights.

1927: A special Joint Committee of the Senate and House of Commons unanimously concludes that the land claims of BC's Aboriginal peoples are without merit.

The federal government amends the Indian Act to make it an offence punishable by law to raise funds for the purpose of pursuing Aboriginal land claims.

1948: A special Joint Committee of the Senate and House of Commons on Indian Affairs recommends the establishment of an Indian Claims Commission; this recommendation is ignored by the federal government.

1951: The federal government rescinds the anti-Aboriginal land claims provision of the 1927 Indian Act.

1961: A second special Joint Committee of the Senate and House of Commons on Indian Affairs recommends establishing an Indian Claims Commission.

1963: Enabling legislation for an Indian Claims Commission receives first reading in the House of Commons but is never passed into law.

1965: The Supreme Court of Canada upholds two lower court decisions confirming: (1) that the "Douglas Treaties" are true treaties; (2) the *Royal Proclamation of 1763* recognized Aboriginal peoples pre-existing rights to hunt throughout their traditional territories; and, (3) these rights were confirmed (not extinguished) by the treaty in question (*R. v. Bob and White*).

An amended version of the 1963 proposal for an Indian Claims Commission is introduced in the House of Commons; on second reading it is referred to a Joint Committee of the Senate and House of Commons but is ultimately allowed to die on the order paper following the dissolution of Parliament later in the year.

1967: Chief Frank Calder presents the Nisga'a Nation's "Aboriginal title" claim to the Supreme Court of BC (*Calder v. Attorney General of British Columbia*).

OCTOBER 1968: Justice Gould of the Supreme Court of British Columbia dismisses the Nisga'a Nation's "Aboriginal title" claim; Chief Calder decides to appeal this decision to the BC Court of Appeal.

MAY 1970: A three-member panel of the BC Court of Appeal unanimously upholds the Supreme Court of British Columbia's dismissal of the Nisga'a Nation's "Aboriginal title" claim; Chief Calder decides to appeal this decision to the Supreme Court of Canada.

1973

JANUARY: Three Supreme Court Justices find that the Nisga'a Nation holds "Aboriginal title" to its traditional territories and three Justices find it does not; all six Justices, however, find that "Aboriginal title" is a legally defensible common law; the Nisga'a Nation ultimately loses its case, however, when the seventh deciding Justice dismisses the appeal for procedural reasons.

8 AUGUST: The federal government announces that it is prepared to settle the outstanding land claims of Aboriginal peoples and introduces a comprehensive claims process to guide modern treaty negotiations.

NOVEMBER: The Superior Court of Quebec confirms that the Cree and Inuit Peoples of Northern Quebec continue to hold "Aboriginal title" to the James Bay/Ungava region of Northern Quebec; this decision is quickly overturned by the Quebec Court of Appeal, but an appeal to the Supreme Court of Canada is pre-empted when the governments of Canada and Quebec agree to commence modern treaty negotiations with the Cree and Inuit Peoples.

1974: The federal government establishes an Office of Native Claims within the Department of Indian Affairs; the Office is subsequently flooded with outstanding Aboriginal land claims.

The Nisga'a Nation submits its land claim to the federal Office of Native Claims; despite BC's refusal to participate in modern treaty negotiations, the federal government accepts the claim for negotiation.

1976: The federal government announces that it will negotiate only six Aboriginal land claims at any one time and only one Aboriginal land claim per province.

12 JANUARY 1976: Negotiators representing the government of Canada and the Nisga'a Nation begin modern treaty negotiations.

19 APRIL 1982: The Constitution Act, 1982 is formally adopted; section 35(1) recognizes and affirms "existing Aboriginal and treaty rights."

FALL 1982: The federal government establishes a Parliamentary Task Force on Indian Self-Government.

1983: Section 35(1) of the Constitution Act, 1982 is amended to specify that "treaty rights" include "rights that now exist by way of land claims agreements or may be so acquired" (new ss. 3).

The Parliamentary Task Force on Indian Self-Government, established in 1982, releases its report *Indian Self-Government in Canada* (termed the Penner Report after its chairman); among other things, this report recommends that Aboriginal peoples' right to self-government be entrenched in the Constitution.

Ruling on *Guerin v. R.*, the Supreme Court of Canada reaffirms that "Aboriginal title" is a pre-existing right and confirms that it continues to exist in the province of British Columbia.

Canada's first Aboriginal self-government legislation—the Cree-Naskapi (of Quebec) Act—is unanimously passed by both Houses of Parliament.

9 OCTOBER 1986: Canada's second aboriginal self-government legislation—the Sechelt Band Self-Government Act—is passed by the federal legislature.

DECEMBER 1986: The federal government amends its comprehensive claims policy to allow for the retention of "Aboriginal rights" on lands which Aboriginal peoples hold following the conclusion of land claims settlements.

1989: Negotiators representing the Nisga'a Nation and the government of Canada sign a framework agreement setting out the scope and process of bilateral treaty negotiations to follow.

1990

JANUARY-DECEMBER: Deciding on *R. v. Sparrow*, the Supreme Court of Canada rules that any government regulations that infringe on the exercise of an Aboriginal right must be constitutionally justified; it also rules that Aboriginal and treaty rights are capable of evolving over time and must be interpreted in a generous and liberal manner.

Price Waterhouse estimates that unresolved Aboriginal land claims are costing BC 15,000 jobs a year and $1 billion in lost investment in mining and forestry alone.

AUGUST: The BC government agrees to join the federal government and the Nisga'a Nation in modern treaty negotiations.

25 SEPTEMBER: The federal government revokes existing limits on the number of Aboriginal land claims that can be negotiated at any one time.

OCTOBER: The BC government formally enters into modern treaty negotiations with the Nisga'a Nation and government of Canada.

3 DECEMBER: The BC Claims Task Force is established to make recommendations on modern treaty negotiations in the province.

1990-98: The governments of Canada and BC hold approximately 500 public consultations and information meetings on issues related to Nisga'a treaty negotiations.

1990: Negotiators representing the government of Canada, the government of BC, and the Nisga'a Nation sign a new framework agreement to govern tripartite treaty negotiations.

SUMMER 1991: The report of the BC Claims Task Force is released; its 19 recommendations include establishing a six-stage BC Treaty Process and an impartial BC Treaty Commission; all 19 recommendations are accepted.

1992: The BC government officially recognizes the inherent rights of Aboriginal peoples to Aboriginal title and self-government; it also pledges to negotiate fair and honourable treaties with Aboriginal peoples in respect of those rights.

1993

15 APRIL: The first BC Treaty Commission is appointed.

DECEMBER: The new federal Liberal government publicly announces that it will act on the assumption that section 35 of the Constitution Act, 1982 includes the Aboriginal right to self-government.

15 DECEMBER: The BC Treaty Commission begins receiving Statements of Intent from Aboriginal Nations interested in negotiating modern treaty settlements with the governments of BC and Canada; some 40 Aboriginal groups give notice of their intent to enter into modern treaty negotiations.

AUGUST 1995: The federal government releases *The Government of Canada's Approach to Implementation of the Inherent Right and the Negotiation of*

Aboriginal Self-Government; the terms of this policy included a statement confirming that the federal government is prepared to constitutionally protect rights set out in negotiated self-government agreements as "treaty rights" within the meaning of section 35 of the Constitution Act, 1982 (where other parties agree); such protection, it is asserted, can result from either new treaties, negotiated self-government agreements, or the amendment of existing treaties.

1996

12 FEBRUARY: Negotiators representing the government of Canada, the government of BC, and the Nisga'a Nation announce that they have concluded an Agreement-in-Principle (AIP).

15 FEBRUARY: The Nisga'a AIP is initialled by federal Minister of Indian and Northern Affairs Ronald A. Irwin; BC Aboriginal Affairs Minister John A. Cashore; and Nisga'a Tribal Council President Joseph Gosnell, Sr.

25 FEBRUARY: The Nisga'a People vote to proceed on the basis of the AIP negotiated by their representatives.

22 MARCH: The Nisga'a AIP is formally adopted at a signing ceremony in New Aiyansh.

11 DECEMBER 1997: The Supreme Court of Canada rules on the Gitksan and Wet'suwet'en Land Claim (*Delgamuukw v. British Columbia*). Although it declares a mistrial of the case, it goes on to offer the most comprehensive reasoning to date on the precise legal nature of Aboriginal title.

1998

MARCH: Hereditary chiefs of the Gitanyow initiate legal proceedings in the Supreme Court of British Columbia; they claim that more than 80 per cent of their traditional territory sits within the Nisga'a wildlife management area mapped out in the Nisga'a AIP and seek to halt negotiations with the Nisga'a until their overlapping claim is equitably dealt with (*Luuxhon et al v. Her Majesty The Queen in Right of Canada et al.*).

15 JULY: Negotiation of the Nisga'a Final Agreement is completed.

4 AUGUST: Negotiators representing the Nisga'a Nation, the government of Canada, and the government of BC initial the Nisga'a Final Agreement in New Aiyansh.

17 OCTOBER: A group of plaintiffs with interests in the BC fisheries file a Statement of Claim in the BC Supreme Court asking that the Nisga'a

Final Agreement be either struck down or submitted to a province-wide referendum; a BC Supreme Court judge rules that the case ought not to proceed until legislation ratifying the Nisga'a Final Agreement is adopted by both the provincial and federal legislatures.

19 OCTOBER: The BC Liberal Party (led by party leader Gordon Campbell) initiates proceedings in the BC Supreme Court against the federal and BC governments and the Nisga'a Tribal Council; the BC Liberal Party alleges that the self-government provisions of the Nisga'a Final Agreement are unconstitutional

6-7 NOVEMBER: The Nisga'a Nation holds a referendum on the Nisga'a Final Agreement; 1,451 (61 per cent) of eligible Nisga'a voters give it their support.

9 NOVEMBER: Representatives of the Nisga'a Nation formally ratify the Nisga'a Final Agreement.

30 NOVEMBER: Bill 51—the Nisga'a Final Agreement Act (BC)—is introduced in BC's Legislative Assembly.

4 DECEMBER: A group of plaintiffs led by the BC Citizens First Coalition launches a class action suit alleging the Nisga'a Lisims Government created by the Nisga'a Final Agreement is unconstitutional and that neither the Parliament of Canada nor the Legislative Assembly of British Columbia has the authority to transfer land and resources to the Nisga'a Nation.

1999

13 JANUARY: Bill 51 receives second reading in BC's Legislative Assembly.

14 JANUARY: A detailed study of Bill 51 begins in the Committee of the Whole (BC).

5 FEBRUARY: A BC Supreme Court judge concludes that the BC Liberal Party's case against the Nisga'a Final Agreement ought not to proceed until legislation ratifying this agreement is adopted by the provincial and federal legislatures.

16 FEBRUARY-28 MARCH 1999: Senate Committee Hearings on Bill C-9 are held.

MARCH: Justice Williamson of the BC Supreme Court rules that, while the federal and provincial Crowns are not under any obligation to enter into treaty negotiations with the Gitanyow, having done so their fiduciary obligations toward Aboriginal peoples results in "a duty to negotiate in good faith"; the decision is appealed by the governments of Canada and BC but is later placed in abeyance when the three parties agree to accelerated treaty negotiations (*Luuxhon et al v. Her Majesty The Queen in Right of Canada et al.*).

30 MARCH-13 APRIL 1999: Senate debates on Bill C-9 proceed.

22 APRIL: Bill 51 is passed by BC's Legislative Assembly.

26 APRIL: The Nisga'a Final Agreement Act (BC) is given royal assent.

27 APRIL: The *Nisga'a Final Agreement* (BC) is signed by representatives of the Nisga'a Nation and BC government.

21 OCTOBER: Bill C-9—the Nisga'a Final Agreement Act (CA)—is introduced in the House of Commons.

13 DECEMBER: Bill C-9 is passed in the House of Commons by a vote of 217 to 48.

14 DECEMBER: Bill C-9 is introduced in the Senate.

2000

13 APRIL: Two Senate amendments to Bill C-9 are defeated—one would have made the Nisga'a Final Agreement changeable in the future and the second would have held Bill C-9 to the side until the Supreme Court of Canada could rule the constitutionality of the Nisga'a Final Agreement. Bill C-9 is approved in the Senate by a vote of 52 to 15 (with 13 abstentions). The Nisga'a Final Agreement Act (CA) is given royal assent.

11 MAY: The Nisga'a Final Agreement comes into effect in accordance with the terms of the settlement legislation passed by BC's Legislative Assembly and the Parliament of Canada. Just days after the Nisga'a Final Agreement is brought into effect, the BC Liberal Party re-presents its October 1998 case against the Nisga'a Final Agreement to the BC Supreme Court.

24 JULY: Justice Paul Williamson of the BC Supreme Court upholds the constitutionality of the Nisga'a Final Agreement and dismisses the BC Liberal Party's case.

14 SEPTEMBER: The new Nisga'a Lisims Government building opens in New Aiyansh.

8 NOVEMBER: The first Nisga'a election is held.

2001

16 MAY: The BC Liberal Party wins 77 of 79 seats in the provincial election; it promises to hold a province-wide referendum on treaty negotiations.

AUGUST: The BC Liberal Party announces that it will not appeal the July 2000 decision of the BC Supreme Court on the constitutionality of the Nisga'a Treaty.

2 APRIL-15 MAY 2002: The BC government conducts a province-wide referendum on the principles that should guide modern treaty negotiations; although only 34 per cent of registered voters return unspoiled ballots, the government accepts the high approval rating of its eight treaty negotiating principles and directs its treaty negotiators to put them into practice.

Notes

1. As quoted in Michael Smyth, "Glen Clark hands 'new beginning' to Nisga'a: Gordon Campbell pledges to pursue case against treaty," *The Province* (Vancouver) 28 April 1999: A6.

2. As quoted in Canada, Federal Treaty Negotiation Office, "Nisga'a legislation introduced in the House of Commons," *Treaty News* October 1999 <http://www.ainc-inac.gc.ca/nr/nwltr/trty/1999/treatynews_october_1999_e.pdf>.

3. As quoted in: "Treaty with the Nisga'a, People of the Nass River: Chief Joseph Gosnell's Historical Speech to the BC Legislature," *Common Ground* January 1999: 6.

4. Canada, Indian and Northern Affairs Canada (2002), "The Nisga'a Treaty," *Fact Sheet*, <www.ainc-inac.gc.ca/pr/info/nit_e.html>. A full text of the Nisga'a Final Agreement (or "Nisga'a Treaty") can be found at <http://www.ainc-inac.gc.ca/pr/agr/nsga/nisdex_e.html>.

5. For an insight into Aboriginal perspectives on treaties see, "Treaty 7 Elders and Tribal Council," *The True Spirit and Original Intent of Treaty 7* (Montreal and Kingston: McGill-Queen's University Press, 1996) esp. ch. 3.

6. The primary purpose of the *Royal Proclamation of 1763* was to establish British sovereignty throughout the British territories of North America following the Seven Years War and the signing of the Treaty of Paris. In addition to creating four new British territories and establishing a government in each, however, the *Royal Proclamation of 1763* also endeavoured to facilitate the peaceful colonial settlement of British North America by establishing a formal policy for colonial land dealings with Aboriginal peoples (then termed "Indians").

7. For a concise overview of Canada's historic treaties, see James S. Frideres and René T. Gadacz, *Aboriginal Peoples in Canada: Contemporary Conflicts*, 6th ed. (Toronto: Prentice Hall, 2001) Ch. 7. For a detailed discussion of the historic treaties, see Alexander Morris, *The Treaties of Canada with the Indians of the Manitoba and the North-West Territories Including the Negotiations on Which They Were Based* (1880; Toronto: Coles

Publishing, 1991); and Robert Mainville, *An Overview of Aboriginal and Treaty Rights and Compensation for their Breach* (Saskatoon, SK: Purich Publishing, 2001).

8. See John Burrows, "Wampum at Niagara: The Royal Proclamation, Canadian Legal History, and Self-Government," *Aboriginal and Treaty Rights in Canada: Essays on Law, Equality and Respect for Difference*, ed. Michael Asch (Vancouver: University of British Columbia Press, 1997) 155-172.

9. Allan McMillan, *Native Peoples and Cultures of Canada*, 2nd ed. (Vancouver/Toronto: Douglas and McIntyre, 1995) 316.

10. For an excellent account of Aboriginal perspectives on treaty negotiations see Treaty 7 Elders and Tribal Council.

11. The so-called "Douglas Treaties" cover approximately 358 square kilometres of land around present-day Victoria, Saanich, Sooke, Nanaimo, and Port Hardy. Their Aboriginal signatories were paid 30 shillings per family (for lands in the Victoria region) or three blankets per square mile (for lands in the Saanich, Sooke, Nanaimo, and Port Hardy regions). They were also promised the right to hunt on unsettled lands and to carry on their fisheries "as formerly."

12. BC, Treaty Negotiations Office, "References." <http://www.gov.bc.ca/tno/history>.

13. As quoted in Thomas R. Berger, "The Importance of the Nisga'a Treaty to Canadians," Corry Lecture, Queen's University, Kingston, ON (2 October 1999).

14. This argument was formally presented by the province in both *R. v Bob and White* (1965) and *Calder v Attorney-General of British Columbia* (1969)—SCBC, 1970; BCCA, and SCC, 1973—and was unremittingly adhered to until legal and political developments finally compelled its rejection in 1990.

15. This section reads: "In each Province the Legislature may exclusively make Laws in relation to ... 5. The Management and Sale of the Public Lands belonging to the Province and of the Timber and Wood thereon."

16. The four original provinces of Canada—Quebec, Ontario, Nova Scotia, and New Brunswick—were accorded Crown interests in "All Lands, Mines, Minerals and Royalties [derived therefrom]" by virtue of section 109 of the BNA Act. The provinces of Manitoba, Saskatchewan, and Alberta, however, were not placed in the same constitutional position until the terms of the *British North America Act, 1930* officially transferred these interests to them. Including the transfer of Crown interest in land to British Columbia in 1871, therefore, was more than somewhat exceptional.

17. Daniel Raunet, *Without Surrender, Without Consent: A History of the Nisga'a Land Claims* (Vancouver/Toronto: Douglas and McIntyre, 1996) 77.

18. The Nisga'a Nation began actively defending its traditional territories against colonial encroachments during the mid-eighteenth century. Although this was neither the first, nor the only, Aboriginal Nation to pro-actively confront BC's denial of Aboriginal rights and refusal to enter into treaty negotiations, its actions are notable for both their intensity and duration. For this reason, the following discussion of Aboriginal resistance in BC will focus on their activities.

19. Referenced in *Petition to His Majesty's Privy Council in the Matter of the Territory of the Nisga'a Nation or Tribe of Nations*, lodged with the Privy Council on 21 May 1913; <http:www.schoolnet.ca/aboriginal/nisga1/petit-e.html>.

20. The Supreme Court of Canada became Canada's highest judicial authority in 1949.

21. A text of this petition is available at <http//:www.schoolnet.ca/aboriginal/nisga1/pet-e.html>.

22. Raunet 136.

23. As quoted in Raunet 139.

24. As quoted in Raunet 140.

25. *Amodu Tijani v. Southern Nigeria* (1921) 2 AC 399 (PC).

26. As quoted in Raunet 140-41.

27. Raunet 141.

28. The Indian Act is a federal statute designed to facilitate the administration of Aboriginal affairs in respect of "status Indians."

29. Paul Tennant, *Aboriginal Peoples and Politics: The Indian Land Question in British Columbia, 1849-1989* (Vancouver: University of British Columbia Press, 1990) 116.

30. Kenneth Coates, *The Marshall Decision and Native Rights* (Montreal and Kingston: McGill-Queen's University Press, 2000) 73.

31. For discussions of the handling of land claims during this early period see R. Daniel, *A History of Native Claims Processes in Canada, 1867-1979* (Ottawa: Research Branch, Department of Indian Affairs and Northern Development, 1980).

32. Joint Committee of the Senate and the House of Commons on Indian Affairs (Joint Committee), *Minutes of Proceedings and Evidence* (Ottawa: Supply and Services Canada, 1960) 582, as quoted in Raunet 146.

33. Raunet 146.

34. Frideres and Gadacz 192.

35. *R. v. Bob and White* [1965] 6 CNLC 684.

36. Raunet 149.

37. James S. Frideres, *Aboriginal Peoples in Canada: Contemporary Conflicts*, 5th ed. (Scarborough, ON: Prentice Hall/Allyn and Bacon Canada, 1998) 89.

38. According to Daniel Raunet, the Nisga'a decided to take the government of British Columbia (rather than the Government of Canada) to court owing to the fact that their traditional territories and all resources except for fisheries were within provincial jurisdiction (see Raunet (1996), p. 150).

39. *Calder v. Attorney General of British Columbia* [1969] 8 DLR (3d), 59-83 (SCBC). The quotes that follow concerning this judgment are from this source.

40. *Calder v. Attorney General of British Columbia* [1970] 7 CNLC 43 (BCCA). The quotes that follow concerning this judgment are from this source.

41. *Calder v. Attorney General of British Columbia* [1973] 7 CNLC 91 (SCC). The quotes that follow concerning this judgment are from this source.

42. Justice Pigeon determined that the Supreme Court of Canada had no jurisdiction to hear or determine a claim of title against the Crown in right of BC in the absence of a fiat (or sanction) from the lieutenant-governor of the province. This is because the doctrine of immunity (which shields the Crown from lawsuits against it) continues to apply in BC (this doctrine has been legislatively revoked at the federal level and in most other provinces).

43. Douglas Sanders, "The Nishga Case," *The Recognition of Aboriginal Rights: Case Studies 1, 1996*, ed. Samuel W. Corrigan and Joe Sawchuk (Brandon, MB: Bearpaw Publishing, 1996) 94.

44. Canada, Indian Affairs and Northern Affairs Canada, *In All Fairness: A Native Claims Policy, Comprehensive Claims* (Ottawa: Supply and Services Canada, 1981) 1.

45. Canada, Indian and Northern Affairs Canada, "Comprehensive Claims."

46. Canada, Indian and Northern Affairs Canada, "Comprehensive Claims (Modern Treaties) in Canada," *Information Sheet* (March 1996), available at www.ainc-inac.gc.ca/pr/info/trty_e.html.

47. Canada, Indian and Northern Affairs Canada, "Procedures—Process," 1981.

48. Canada, Indian and Northern Affairs Canada, "Procedures—Process."

49. As quoted in Raunet 164.

50. McMillan 332.

51. The national Aboriginal Women's Association of Canada was denied formal participation in this (and subsequent) first ministers' conferences by the federal government, which asserted that the four national Aboriginal associations given a seat at the negotiation table served as adequate representatives for both male and female Aboriginal peoples. Aboriginal women's concerns over equality issues related to the recognition of "existing Aboriginal and treaty" rights however, were concertedly vocalized through protests, petitions, and media reports. It is largely as a result of their (informal) efforts that subsection 4 was added to section 35 of the Charter of Rights and Freedoms; see Lilianne Ernestine Krsenbrink-Gelissen, "The Native Women's Association of Canada," Frideres, Ch 9.

52. McMillan 333.

53. McMillan 333.

54. McMillan 333.

55. A full text of the Cree-Naskapi (of Quebec) Act (1984) is available at <http://laws.justice.gc.ca/en/C-45.7/>. A full text of the Sechelt Band Self-Government Act (1986) is available at <http://laws.justice.gc.ca/en/S-6.6/>. See also, Canada, Indian and Northern Affairs Canada, "The Cree-Naskapi (of Quebec) Act," *Information Sheet* (May 1999) <http://www.ainc-inac.gc.ca/pr/info/info11_e.html>; and Canada, Indian and Northern Affairs Canada, "Self Government Sechelt Style." *Information Sheet* (October 1995),<http://www.ainc-inac.gc.ca/pr/info/info20_e.html>.

56. *Guerin v. The Queen* [1984] 2 SCR 335. Quotations that follow are from this source. A useful summary and analysis of this decision is available at <http://www.bloorstreet.com/200block/rguerin.htm>.

57. The federal Indian Act asserts that lands in a reserve shall not be sold, alienated, leased, or otherwise disposed of until they have been surrendered (conditionally or unconditionally) to Her Majesty by the band for whose use and benefit in common the reserve was set apart (see sections 37 and 38). This surrender provision is based on the terms of the *Royal Proclamation of 1763* which prohibit private land dealings with Aboriginal peoples.

58. *Pacific Fishermen's Defence Alliance v. The Queen* [1987] File no. 119871, 3 FC 272. A full text of this decision is available at <http://www.landclaimsdocs.com/court/w-pfdavr.htm>.

59. The PFDA was composed mainly of associations of licensed commercial fishermen who feared that a portion of the tidal fisheries on which they operated would be granted to the Nisga'a Tribal Council as part of a land claim settlement.

60. "Legal Background to Nisga'a Land Claims Negotiations" (14 March 1988) <http://www.schoolnet.ca/aboriginal/nisga1/back-e.htm>.

61. "Legal Background to Nisga'a Land Claims Negotiations."

62. *R. v. Sparrow* [1990] 3 CNLR 160 (SCC).

63. "Legal Background to Nisga'a Land Claims Negotiations."

64. BC Treaty Commission, "Why are We Negotiating Treaties?," *Treaty Handbook* (Vancouver: British Columbia Treaty Commission, 2001).

65. BC Treaty Commission.

66. First established in 1988 as the BC First Nations Congress, the First Nations Summit represents the interests of the great majority of Aboriginal communities and nations in BC on modern treaty-related matters.

67. Canada, *Consensus Report on the Constitution* (Charlottetown), Final Text 28 August 1992. For a detailed discussion of the Charlottetown Accord, see Robert M.

Campbell and Leslie A. Pal, "Ch. 3: The Rise and Fall of the Charlottetown Accord," *The Real Worlds of Canadian Politics: Cases in Process and Policy*, 3rd ed. (Peterborough, ON: Broadview Press, 1994) 142-210.

68. John H. Hylton, "Future Prospects for Aboriginal Self-Government in Canada," *Aboriginal Self-Government in Canada: Current Trends and Issues*, ed. John H. Hylton (Saskatoon, SK: Purich Publishing) 439.

69. Liberal Party of Canada, *Creating Opportunities: The Liberal Plan for Canada* (Ottawa: Liberal Party of Canada, 1993) 98.

70. Ron Irwin, "Speech presented to the federal, provincial/territorial meeting with ministers and Aboriginal leaders" (May 1994).

71. For a more detailed analysis of the federal government's 1995 policy, see Bradford W. Morse, "The Inherent Right of Aboriginal Governance," Hylton 27-35.

72. Previous practice, as followed from 1986 onwards, had forced self-government provisions to be included in parallel political accords, which were devoid of constitutional protection.

73. Although the historic treaties became effective upon approval by the Crown, modern practice requires the passage of federal and provincial land claims settlement legislation. This practice began with the James Bay and Northern Quebec Agreement, 1975, which was brought into force by the James Bay and Northern Quebec Native Claims Settlement Act.

74. Canada, "The Nisga'a Final Agreement," a report prepared by Mary C. Hurley, Law and Government Division (9 February 1999; revised 27 July 1999) <http://dsp-psd.pwgsc.gc.ca/Collection-R/LoPBdP/EB/prb992-e.htm>. The Nisga'a Nation's original claim covered just over 24,000 square kilometres of land. The terms of the Nisga'a Final Agreement left them with title to exactly 2,019 square kilometres of land.

75. As quoted in Jim Beatty, "Royal welcome set for Nisga'a visit to Victoria: After the ceremony, MLAs will debate the treaty deal," *Vancouver Sun* 30 November 1998: A1.

76. Debates on Bill 51 may be consulted on the BC Legislative Assembly's website at <http://www.legis.gov.bc.ca/hansard>.

77. Craig McInnes and Jim Beatty, "Liberals, NDP prepare for vote on treaty," *Vancouver Sun*, 22 April 1999: A1.

78. Jim Beatty, "Death knell for the great debate," *Vancouver Sun*, 23 April 1999: A15.

79. McInnes and Beatty.

80. As quoted in Beatty, "Death knell for the great debate."

81. Sheldon Alberts, "Electronic balloting more alluring after Nisga'a marathon," *National Post* 10 December 1999: A6.

82. Colin Grey, "Corn chips, quips and a sleepy Ironman: The Reform party's filibuster brought out the best and worst of Hill politics," *Ottawa Citizen* 10 December 1999: A4.

83. As quoted in Alberts.

84. As quoted in Alberts.

85. Only Reform Party members voted against the Nisga'a Final Agreement Act. Members of the Liberal Party, Bloc Québécois, Progressive Conservative Party, and New Democratic Party all voted in favour of the proposed legislation.

86. "Historic Nisga'a Treaty Ratified; Receives Royal Assent," *Press Release*, Ottawa (13 April 2000); <http://www.ntc.bc.ca/speeches/gosnell7.html> .

87. Canada, Indian and Northern Affairs Canada, "Nisga'a Final Agreement," *Issue Papers* (Ottawa: Indian and Northern Affairs Canada, 2002) 23.1.

88. Canada, Indian and Northern Affairs Canada, "Nisga'a Final Agreement."

89. Grant Thornton Management Consultants, *Financial and Economic Analysis of Treaty Settlements in British Columbia* (March 1999), <http://www.gov.bc.ca/tno/rpts/thornton.htm>.

90. This group included the BC Fisheries Survival Coalition, individual commercial fishers, the Area C Salmon Gillnet Association, and Reform Member of Parliament, John Cummins.

91. BC Liberal Party, "Press Statement on Nisga'a Court Proceedings," Victoria, BC (19 October 1998) as cited in Canada, "The Nisga'a Final Agreement."

92. Canada News Wire, "Nisga'a Lisims Government—New Aiyansh, BC." Press Release (24 July 2000), <http://www.newswire.ca/release/July2000/24/c5907.html>.

93. *Gitanyow First Nation v. Canada* [1999] 1 CNLR 66, par. 1 (BCSC).

94. *Luuxhon et al v. Her Majesty The Queen in Right of Canada et al*, File No. C981165 [23 March 1999] par. 70-75.

95. Canada, Department of Indian Affairs and Northern Development, "Federal Government Concerned Decision Undermines Treaty Negotiation Process—Appeals *Luuxhon* Ruling," News Release, Vancouver, BC (21 April 1999), <http://www.aaf.gov.bc.ca/aaf/news/gitanyowappeal.htm>.

96. BC, Treaty Negotiations Office (2002), "Treaty Principles," <http://www.gov.bc.ca/tno/news/2002/eight_new_treaty_principles.htm>.

97. *Delgamuukw v. British Columbia* [1998] 1CNLR 14 (SCC).

98. Dara Culhane, *The Pleasure of the Crown: Anthropology, Law and First Nations* (Burnaby, BC: Talon Books, 1998) 369.

99. For a more detailed explanation of the *Delgamuukw* decision see Culhane 363-68.

Index